The Classic Skinner Method to
SPEECH ON THE STAGE

♦

SPEAK
with
DISTINCTION

by Edith Skinner

♦

Revised with new material added
by
Timothy Monich and Lilene Mansell

Edited by Lilene Mansell

♦

♥APPLAUSE♥
THEATRE BOOK PUBLISHERS

An Applause Original

SPEAK WITH DISTINCTION
by Edith Skinner
Revised with New Material Added by Timothy Monich and Lilene Mansell
Edited by Lilene Mansell

Book Team:
   In-House Editor: Alexis Greene
   Production and Design Editor: Sue Knopf

For information:

APPLAUSE THEATRE BOOK PUBLISHERS
USA   UK
211 W. 71st Street   406 Vale Road
New York, NY 10023   Tonbridge, KENT TN9 1XR
(212) 595-4735   0732 357755

Library of Congress Cataloging-In-Publication Data:

Skinner, Edith.
    Speak with distinction / by Edith Skinner ; revised with new material added by Timothy Monich and Lilene Mansell ; edited by Lilene Mansell.
        p.   cm. -- (Applause acting series)
    Includes bibliographical references (p.   ) and index.
    ISBN 1-55783-047-9 : $32.95. -- ISBN 1-55783-052-5 (Audio cassette/booklet) : $17.95. -- ISBN 1-55783-053-3 (Textbook & cassette) : $44.95.
    1. Acting. 2. Voice culture. 3. Speech. 4. English language--pronunciation. I. Monich, Timothy. II. Mansell, Lilene. III. Title. IV. Series.
    PN2071.S65S55   1990
    792'.028--dc20   90-1039
                                                                    CIP

Through voice and speech, more than any other qualities, the actor lays bare before an audience the soul of the character impersonated. Since the words express the meaning of what the actor says, and the tone of voice reveals feelings about what is said, the actor's vehicle for carrying words—the voice—must be flexible. It must communicate the nuances of the most hidden emotions being portrayed in the most effective and convincing way that is possible.

The speech of a character must bring to life the character itself.

If the role calls for refined utterance, the audience must receive that impression, or else the actor's tool has not been trained sufficiently and gets in the way of the performer's art. If the character speaks a dialect, then the actor must create the illusion by changes in sounds and melody. However, the actor must not create so much dialect that it interferes with understanding the lines being spoken.

Distinct utterance is the prime requisite of an actor. In fact, the audience should be able to take for granted that they can hear and understand everything the actor says, without straining to do so.

Obviously, training in voice and speech is imperative and fundamental. In search of the best, we look to the stage; for the theater has a responsibility too often neglected: to foster the finest sound of Spoken English.

Edith Skinner
From the Preface to the First Edition

◆ REMEMBERING EDITH SKINNER ◆

It was in the late 1960s, as a fledgling production assistant in Ellis Rabb's famed APA Repertory Company, that I first came under the spell of Edith Skinner. Ellis, the organization's founder and artistic director, brought Edith to us periodically as we worked on texts of Shaw and Shakespeare, Giraudoux and Pirandello, Ionesco and Messieurs Kaufman and Hart. She would appear among us like a sly matron at a garden party, impeccably dressed, her spiral notebook and pencil juxtaposed precariously with an elegant purse, and pursue us all—from those playing the leads to the stage management—with fervor, purpose and the ever-present "Ask-List." Of course, her ear was extraordinary, and soon everyone began to "hear themselves" through her tenacious objectivity. The clarity of a remarkable vowel might be praised in the midst of her request for coffee, and yet, the thrill of pleasing Edith remains with me today, as one of the ineffable treasures of initiation by a truly great teacher.

What is known now as Good Speech, certainly for the stage, is to me unquestionably the sole province of this remarkable woman. The generations of students she guided at Carnegie Mellon University, The Juilliard School, American Conservatory Theatre (ACT), and elsewhere are legion and legendary. Her influence extends from coast to coast and even abroad, and the standard of excellence she both identified and represented remains as fixed today as anything in our theatrical cosmos.

This welcome edition of Edith Skinner's *Speak with Distinction* is more than simply the preferred text of theater directors and actors the country over; it represents an essential link of our craft with something at once indigenously North American and essential to our respect for skill and technique. Only with the fullest expression of skill and technique is an actor truly free, truly able to communicate the actual depth and range of his or her talent. In a world in which respect for craft tends to shrink daily, this volume represents a light sustained and held aloft, an emblem of pride as sure and unmistakable as the eloquent speech it protects.

Jack O'Brien
Artistic Director, The Old Globe Theatre
San Diego, California

◆ CONTENTS ◆

◆ INTRODUCTION ◆

The original version of Edith Skinner's *Speak with Distinction,* first published in 1942 and last revised by her in 1966, was initially meant to be used by Mrs. Skinner and her students at the Carnegie Institute of Technology (now called Carnegie Mellon University). As her students entered the professional theater and some of them found careers themselves as "Edith-trained" teachers in drama schools, or as coaches for professional productions, the book became widely recognized as the most complete and rigorous text of its kind and was pressed into wider and wider service.

Mrs. Skinner was beginning plans for a new edition of *Speak with Distinction* in 1981, the year of her death. She wanted the new edition to retain its comprehensive format in a more simply organized and readable way, to make it accessible to teachers and students of any training and background. The current popularity of classics and plays with intricate language on all English-speaking stages, which beg for accurate portrayals of many varieties of English, demands thorough and intensive speech training of today's artists and those of the future. To that end, *Speak with Distinction* is now available to a wide readership.

While continuing to present a comprehensive study of the sounds of Spoken English in their most important phonetic environments, we have also added much material for comparisons of speech sounds; suggestions for accurate, efficient and conversational ways of combining the sounds into connected utterance; indications that foster a working knowledge of two dialects of speech (General American and what Mrs. Skinner called Good Speech for classic and elevated texts); and beginning material to show application of the principles of Good Speech to well-written texts.

Some important additions to the book are the extensive Glossary and Index, abundant guides to pronunciations, new sections featuring such details as the complete "Ask-List" of words, a program for the elimination of glottal attacks of vowel and diphthong sounds, greatly expanded practice material of phrases and sentences, and an updated Chart showing several levels of phonetic transcription and spelling equivalents in current usage.

The new edition can be used in several ways: as a primary educational textbook for both the beginning and advanced actor; as a supplementary textbook for teachers and students who have their own methods and agenda for study; and as a reference book for teachers, speech coaches and directors.

All work has been set forth with our best understanding of Mrs. Skinner's philosophy, teaching methods and high standards.

Numerous friends and colleagues have cheerfully given of their expertise during the course of this project. We extend gratitude for the editorial assistance of Theresa Ceruti, Alexis Greene and Glenn Young. We deeply appreciate the valuable contributions of David Baker, Brooks Baldwin, James Browne, Robert Browning, Kathleen F. Conlin, Thomas Crawley, Noel S. Dowling, Tom Dunlop, Bonnie Johns-Fisher, Paula Fritz, Elizabeth Himelstein, Cindia Huppeler, Lyle Karlin, Bes Kimberly, Sue Knopf, Jane Kosminsky, Robert McBroom, Ingrid MacCartney, Carla Meyer, Elizabeth Smith, Susan Sweeney, Daniel Pardo, Robert Parks, Tom Peacocke, Janet Reed, and Jim Willard. Thanks are extended to Jessie Walker for the drawings, to Barry Heins for the sentences on page 72, and to Pierre Lefevre for the dialogues on pages 329-332.

And finally, we wish to acknowledge the many students whose curiosity and intelligent questioning have pointed the way to some of the clarifications in this revision.

This project has been a labor of love, and our efforts express our gratitude to Edith—our muse of fire.

Timothy Monich and Lilene Mansell
New York City
August, 1989

From the moment we are born, the sounds and voices of the world around us influence our speech. The language we speak, the way we make the sounds of that language, the melody of the words, even the speed at which we talk are directly related to forces we encounter when we first start listening and responding to the world about us. As children, we learn to speak by imitating others. We often grow up "sounding like" our mother or father, an aunt or uncle. We may talk quickly if they talked quickly. Surrounded by many brothers and sisters, we may have learned to raise our voice to be heard, or talk softly to get a point across. The region of the country in which we were brought up has also left its mark on our speech, be it the aggressive sound of Northeastern cities, the tight-jawed delivery of the Ottawa Valley, the South's warm drawl, or the matter-of-factness of Northwest Canada and the American West. And radio, television, films, and music have left their traces on our speech patterns as well.

In addition to "what" we hear, our self-image, personality and overall emotional make-up contribute to the "way" we hear, and how we respond. And our physical well-being, even such factors as the physiology of our particular vocal mechanism, has affected the way we sound.

Yet the speech we have developed while growing up is not necessarily the best speech for an actor. The challenge to the actor is to imitate new sounds; to retrain the way the actor hears in order to acquire the best speech habits possible. Good habits of speech will enable the actor to make informed choices that are appropriate to whatever character, style of play or production concept the performer comes across during a career. The actor who is well trained in the best modes of Spoken English will feel equally at home in a kitchen sink drama and the Forest of Arden, at ease with both Shepard and Sheridan. The command of Spoken English will ensure that an actor is easily heard and immediately understood in any theater, and will allow the actor to work with accuracy and confidence no matter what accent, dialect or variety of English a script calls for.

To help the actor achieve these goals, *Speak with Distinction* provides the details of what is known as Spoken English. Two varieties of Spoken English are examined in this book: General American and what is known as Good Speech. General American is that dialect of North American English most frequently found in the ordinary speech of people who live in the western United States. It does not sound like the speech of any particular region, yet it sounds distinctly contemporary and distinctively American; an equivalent term currently in use is "Western Standard." General American is acceptable to all American listeners.

Good Speech is hard to define but easy to recognize when we hear it. Good Speech is a dialect of North American English that is free from regional characteristics; recognizably North American, yet suitable for classic texts; effortlessly articulated and easily understood in the last rows of a theater. Good Speech is sometimes known as "Eastern Standard" or "Theater Standard."

Speak with Distinction is divided into five chapters.

Chapter One—"An Introduction to Speech and Phonetics," is an overview of the concepts that are emphasized throughout the book and is presented in the recommended order of study. The chapter begins with an introduction to the Process of Voice and Speech; moves to the Sounds of Spoken English; presents an introduction to the International Phonetic Alphabet (IPA), which is used in the body of the textbook; continues with overviews of the sounds of Spoken English, from vowel and consonant sounds to combinations of sounds in connected speech; and concludes with guidelines and exercises for daily speech practice.

Chapters Two, Three and **Four**—"The Vowel Sounds of Spoken English"; "The Diphthong and Triphthong Sounds of Spoken English"; and "The Consonant Sounds of Spoken English"—contain practice material presented in the traditional phonetic order.

Chapter Five—"The Application of Well-Spoken English," presents what are called in this textbook the "Challengers for the Actor with Good Speech" and applies the principles of well-spoken English to lines from Shakespeare's comedy *Twelfth Night, or, What you Will*. This chapter also contains "Creating A Score," an approach that helps the actor develop an ear for the music in a piece of writing, in this case two poems: "Tarantella," by the early-twentieth century English writer Hilaire Belloc; and Shakespeare's Sonnet LXXI, "No Longer Mourn for Me." This chapter also includes selections from the work of a variety of renowned writers, to stimulate the actor's creative use of the spoken word. While the complex and personal process of interpretation is beyond the scope of this book, it is valuable for the actor to begin to apply the knowledge of Spoken English to many other forms of literature that can nourish artistic sensibilities.

Speak with Distinction concludes with appendices that will further help the student. **Appendix A** provides additional information regarding the Levels of Phonetic Transcription and **Appendix B** is a Chart of IPA and Non-IPA Signs, as used in this textbook. There is also a **Glossary of Terms** (the student should feel free to consult this Glossary from the first day of study), and **Suggestions for Further Study**.

To speak with distinction requires many hours of disciplined and dedicated practice. The student may wish to listen to the audio tape that is available with this textbook and will probably also wish to collaborate with a qualified speech teacher.

Yet despite the scope of the work, the student should not feel obligated to grasp the material at once, but should rather be patient and study any section of the book as often as necessary. For the eventual mastery of the best habits of Spoken English will free an actor to pursue the goal of this art, which is to communicate thought and feeling to an audience. The ability to speak with distinction, along with other essential tools such as a flexible voice and an expressive body, will produce a tuned instrument capable of playing on any English-speaking stage in the world.

CHAPTER ONE

AN INTRODUCTION TO
SPEECH AND PHONETICS

ARTICULATORY AGILITY

Articulatory agility
is developing the ability
to effortlessly and believably
    utter clearly
        the most conceivably
            convoluted consonant combos
            in the world.

Flexible lips and strengthened tongue-tips
are needed to toss off Cowardian quips.

And who can dispute a relaxed lower jaw
for spewing forth a torrent of Shaw?

It takes superlative diction
    to theatrically mumble
        and clearly be misunderstood in the jumble.

Be it couplets or prose—be it "dese," "dem" or "dose"
    from Shakespeare to Simon
    from Molière to Mamet
        it simply won't do
            if they don't understand it!

Lilene Mansell

◆ THE PROCESS OF VOICE AND SPEECH ◆

The production of voice involves the coordination of breathing, vibration and resonation. In other words, a good voice is one that is firmly supported by the breathing mechanism in the body, specifically the interplay of the diaphragmatic and intercostal muscles. A good voice issues from a relaxed throat and resonates freely through the pharynx, mouth and nasal passages, producing an appropriate balance of resonance. A good voice is flexible; it can vary in pitch, timbre, volume, and tempo. Speech, the final step in the process, is articulated breath, or breath that is shaped by the articulators into the sounds of language.

THE FOUR ESSENTIAL COMPONENTS OF VOICE AND SPEECH

The Excitor is the force that triggers the production of voice. The respiratory muscles, mainly the diaphragm and the intercostal muscles, regulate and control the supply of air necessary to produce voice. An efficient inhalation of breath is both inaudible and invisible throughout all areas of the face, neck and throat. An economic use of exhalation gives rhythmical endurance and support of tone.

The Vibrator, or vocal folds (also known as vocal cords), produce sound waves or sound vibrations when breath travels across them; this action is an involuntary one that relies on concentration and mental images. For this reason, it is essential that the breath and the vocal folds function with relaxation, so that the speaker can achieve a smooth initiation of tone and avoid a tightening of the throat, which results in what is known as glottal attacks of vowel and diphthong sounds.

The Resonators, or cavities of the chest, throat, mouth, and nose, serve to reinforce and amplify sound waves. The production of tone is dependent on internal and external physical conditions, as well as on mental attitude and emotional response.

The Articulators shape the breath as it passes out through the mouth and the nose. What are known as the movable articulators (lips, lower jaw, tongue, and soft palate) work with the immovable articulators (teeth, upper gums, hard palate, and throat) to give definite shape to each separate speech sound. COMPLETE COOPERATION IS NECESSARY BETWEEN THE EXCITOR AND THE ARTICULATORS, the only two parts of the voice and speech process that the speaker can control directly.

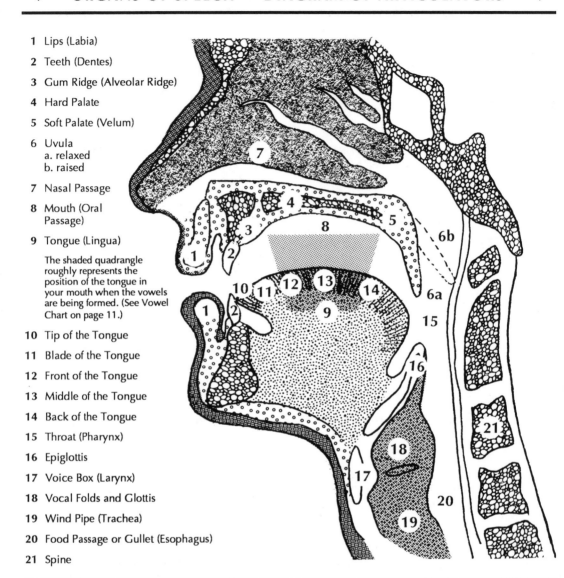

1 Lips (Labia)

2 Teeth (Dentes)

3 Gum Ridge (Alveolar Ridge)

4 Hard Palate

5 Soft Palate (Velum)

6 Uvula
   a. relaxed
   b. raised

7 Nasal Passage

8 Mouth (Oral Passage)

9 Tongue (Lingua)

The shaded quadrangle roughly represents the position of the tongue in your mouth when the vowels are being formed. (See Vowel Chart on page 11.)

10 Tip of the Tongue

11 Blade of the Tongue

12 Front of the Tongue

13 Middle of the Tongue

14 Back of the Tongue

15 Throat (Pharynx)

16 Epiglottis

17 Voice Box (Larynx)

18 Vocal Folds and Glottis

19 Wind Pipe (Trachea)

20 Food Passage or Gullet (Esophagus)

21 Spine

EIGHT ESSENTIAL ARTICULATORS give definite shape to each separate speech sound as the AIR passes out through the mouth or through the nose.

Four Movable Articulators

- Tongue
- Lips — ɪ: Slightly spread "L**ee**"
  ʌ relaxed "c**u**p"
  u: rounded "wh**o**"
- Lower Jaw
- Soft Palate*

Four Immovable Articulators

- Teeth
- Gum Ridge
- Hard Palate
- Throat or Glottis

* The Soft Palate closes the passageway between the mouth and the nose. In spoken English it is **relaxed** and **lowered** (6a) for "m," "n" and "ng," allowing the air to be directed through the nose. It is **raised** and **closed** (6b) for ALL other sounds in English, so that the air is directed through the mouth.

◆ THE SOUNDS OF SPOKEN ENGLISH ◆

WRITTEN LANGUAGE AND SPOKEN LANGUAGE

WRITTEN LANGUAGE is organized by punctuation and the visual arrangement of words on a page. SPOKEN LANGUAGE is governed by time (rhythm, phrasing and pauses) and by melody (pitch, intonation and inflection).

ELEMENTS OF **WRITTEN** ENGLISH ARE **SEEN**
- ◆ letters of the alphabet
- ◆ words
- ◆ sentences

ELEMENTS OF **SPOKEN** ENGLISH ARE **HEARD**
- ◆ vowel, diphthong and consonant sounds
- ◆ syllables
- ◆ phrases or rhythmic thought groups

The individual speech sounds of any language are defined by how the breath, whether voiced or voiceless, is used in making the sound. A voiced sound is produced with vibration of the vocal folds; a voiceless sound is produced without vibration. In Spoken English,

A Vowel Sound

- ◆ Is made with an open, uninterrupted flow of air, the breath flowing through the mouth only: an *oral* sound. French, by contrast, contains four vowel sounds made with the breath flowing through the mouth and the nose simultaneously: nasalized vowels;
- ◆ Is a single sound, involving no movement or change of the articulators during the creation of the sound. Therefore, vowels are PURE sounds;
- ◆ In most languages, including English, is always a *voiced* sound.

Every Vowel Sound

- ◆ Is made with the tip of the tongue resting behind and touching the back of the lower front teeth. The front, middle or back of the tongue arches to various heights, from high to low in the mouth, to create distinct, pure vowel sounds;
- ◆ Is made with a RELAXED LOWER JAW;
- ◆ Is made with the soft palate raised. This prevents the vibrated breath from escaping into the nasal passage, assuring that it flows through the oral cavity, or mouth, only.

The following words each contain a single vowel sound:

we   bit   death   plaid   flood   do   should   law   dog   calm

The same vowel sound can be represented by several different spellings:

see=sea   seize   deceive   key=quay   machine   Caesar   phoenix

There are fifteen pure vowel sounds in well-spoken English.

A Diphthong Sound

◆ Is made by movement of the articulators that can be seen, heard and felt by the speaker;
◆ Is a blend of two vowel sounds into a single phonetic unit;
◆ Is perceived as *one* sound.

Some words that contain a single diphthong sound:

day date gr*eat*=gr*ate* *I*=*eye* t*ie*=Th*ai* n*o*=kn*ow*=N*oh* n*ow*

The same spoken diphthong sound can be represented by several spellings:

B*o*=b*ow*=b*eau* d*oe*=d*ough*

There are ten diphthong sounds in well-spoken English.

A Triphthong Sound

◆ Is a blending of three vowel sounds to form one sound comprising one syllable.

Some words that may contain a triphthong and may be pronounced as one syllable:

h*ire* fl*ower*=fl*ow'r*=fl*our*

The same spoken triphthong sound is represented by several spellings:

l*iar*=l*yre* *our*=*hour*

There are two triphthong sounds in well-spoken English.

A Consonant Sound

◆ Is made with a stopped, impeded or interrupted breath, either through the mouth (oral) or through the nose (nasal);
◆ May be *voiced* (vibration through the vocal folds) or *voiceless* (no vibration through the vocal folds). These are also known as breathed or whispered consonants;
◆ May have stationary articulators during the formation of the sound itself or moving articulators forming the sound.

Some words that contain a single consonant sound:

| *b*e | a*bb*ey | i*s* | o*f* | o*ff* | *w*eigh=*w*ay | *wh*ey | n*o*w |
| *sh*ow | *th*igh | *th*ine | e*gg* | *ch*ew | I'*ll*=ais*le* | *wh*o | i*ss*ue |

The same spoken consonant sound can be represented by several spellings:

*n*o=*kn*ow *pn*eumonia *gn*ome *mn*emonic

There are 26 consonant sounds in well-spoken English.

An Affricate Sound

◆ Is comprised of a stop-plosive and a fricative consonant blended together so closely as to seem like a single sound;

◆ Is considered part of the plosive family of consonant sounds.

Some words that contain a single affricate sound:

*ch*eese   *J*une

The same affricate consonant sound can be represented by several different spellings:

*c*ello   ki*tch*en   na*t*ure   *g*ent   sol*d*ier   *j*u*dg*e   reli*g*ion   exa*gg*erate

There are two affricate consonant sounds in well-spoken English.

◆ THE INTERNATIONAL PHONETIC ALPHABET ◆

The sounds of Spoken English will be studied in this book through the use of the International Phonetic Alphabet (IPA). The IPA, first published in 1888, notates the SOUNDS of the world's languages, so that anyone can be taught to speak a language accurately, regardless of the alphabets or characters of a language's written form. The guiding principle of the IPA is that one sound is represented by one particular phonetic letter only; and conversely, each letter represents one, and only one, sound.

In the beginning, the IPA used two kinds of phonetic transcription: VERY NARROW TRANSCRIPTION, which is the detailed notation of speech sounds and employs DIACRITICAL MARKS; and BROAD TRANSCRIPTION, or simplified notation of speech sounds, which employs a minimum of diacritical marks. However, over the years, the IPA has undergone modification, and what was intended originally to be one standard method of writing out sounds has now become a range of slightly different methods, even in the most established pronouncing dictionaries. So for the student who may at some point look into all the available texts, Appendix A of *Speak with Distinction* offers easily understood Levels of Phonetic Transcription. (See pages 376-379.)

Diacritical marks modify the phonetic letters in various ways. They denote details of spoken language such as lengths of sounds, stressed syllables, intonation, and minute features of placement and articulation that distinguish shades of sound within the same speech sound. *Speak with Distinction* also uses a number of signs unrelated to the IPA, to suggest further details of utterance; and a Chart of IPA and Non-IPA Signs used in this textbook is found in Appendix B. (See pages 380-383.)

The IPA used in this textbook is shown in very narrow transcription, meaning that the notation of the sound is very detailed. The letters are in their script form. The spelling is different in each of the following words, but the words share the same vowel sound *i:* as in "Lee."

A VOWEL SOUND, since it is one pure sound, is represented by a single phonetic letter:

she	′ʃi:	we	′wi:	queen	′k,wi:n
field	′fi:l:d	ease	′i:z	people	′pʰi·pˌl̩
quay=key	′kʰi:	seize	′si:z	Aesop	′i·sɒpʰ
Phoenix	′fi:nɪk,s	thieve	′θi:v	thee	′ði:
physique	fɪ′zi·kʰ	ceased	′si·st̚		

A DIPHTHONG SOUND, though it counts as a single sound, is a blending of two vowel sounds and therefore is represented by two letters, which are written closely together and form a single unit. The spelling is different in the following words, but each word shares the same diphthong sound *a·i·* as in "my":

my	′ma·i·	time=thyme	′tʰa·i·m	I'll=aisle	′a·i·l
sigh	′sa·i·	buy	′ba·i·	guide	′ga·i·d
tie=Thai	′tʰa·i·	I=eye=ay (yes)	′a·i·		

A TRIPHTHONG SOUND is a blending of three sounds and is represented by three letters written closely together but spoken as one syllable to maintain rhythm in verse and poetry. The spelling is different in the following words, but each word may share the same triphthong sound:

higher=hire *aĭə*   flower=flow'r=flour *aŭə*

A CONSONANT SOUND, no matter what the spelling and no matter what the language, will be represented by a single phonetic letter. In English, the consonant *f* occurs in the following words:

fist *'fɪstʰ*   off *'ɒf*   tough *'tʌf*

phone *'fo·ŭ·n*   diphthong *'dɪfθɒŋ*

An AFFRICATE CONSONANT SOUND is a blending of a stop-plosive and a fricative and is therefore represented by two letters that are spoken as a single sound. The spelling differs, but "Chelsea," "cello" and "fortune" are spoken with *tʃ* and "graduate," "Jordan" and "George" are spoken with *dʒ* :

Chelsea *'tʃelsɪ*   cello *'tʃeloŭ*   fortune *'fɔətʃn̩*

graduate *'grædʒueɪtʰ* Jordan *'dʒɔədn̩*   George *'dʒɔədʒ*

A vowel sound is produced as the breath is freely emitted through a single shape or position of the mouth. In Spoken English the breath is always voiced and exits through the mouth only.

The Shape of the Tongue

For ALL vowel sounds the tip of the tongue is relaxed behind the lower front teeth. The body of the tongue arches in various heights toward the roof of the mouth.

FRONT VOWELS: The front of the tongue arches toward the hard palate:

i:	I	e	æ	a
Lee	will	let	Pat	pass.

MID VOWELS: The middle of the tongue arches toward the middle of the palate:

3:	ə	ʌ
Stir	the surprise	cup.

BACK VOWELS: The back of the tongue arches toward the soft palate:

u:	ʊ	o	ɔ:	ɒ	ɑ:
Who	would	obey	all	honest	fathers?

The Height of the Arch of the Tongue and the Degree of Opening of the Lower Jaw

HIGH CLOSED VOWELS: The tongue is arched high, and the lower jaw is relaxed high.

$$i: \quad I \quad u: \quad \upsilon$$

LOW OPEN VOWELS: The tongue is arched low, and the lower jaw is relaxed open.

$$æ \quad ə \quad ʌ \quad ɒ \quad ɑ:$$

The Position of the Lips

FRONT VOWEL SOUNDS: The lips are slightly smiling.

MID VOWEL SOUNDS: The lips are relaxed or neutral.

BACK VOWEL SOUND ɑ: : Again, the lips are relaxed or neutral.

BACK VOWEL SOUNDS: The lips are rounded.

The Potential Length or Duration of the Sound in Spoken English

LONG VOWELS: There are five vowels found in various lengths, but conveniently classified in three lengths: long, half-long and short.

SHORT VOWELS: There are nine vowels found only short in length in Spoken English.

The VOWEL CHART on page 11 summarizes in visual form the information on this page and introduces the diphthong and triphthong sounds of Spoken English.

✓ *Reminder*——————————————————————————————————————

IN THE CORRECT FORMATION OF ALL ENGLISH VOWELS:

1 The tip of the tongue is relaxed behind the lower front teeth.
2 The vocal folds are vibrating, producing a voiced sound.
3 The air is emitted through the mouth ONLY.

◆ THE VOWEL CHART ◆

This chart is a simplified visualization of the tongue-arch, jaw and lip placement, noted on the preceding page, of the FIFTEEN vowel sounds of Spoken English. Remember that for all vowel, diphthong and triphthong sounds of Spoken English:

◆ The tip of the tongue is relaxed behind the lower front teeth;

◆ The soft palate is raised, making vowels oral sounds;

◆ The sounds are voiced.

The vowel sounds are classified according to the part of the tongue that is arched:

FRONT VOWELS: The FRONT of the tongue is arched toward the hard palate;

MID VOWELS: The MIDDLE of the tongue is arched toward a place between the hard and soft palates;

BACK VOWELS: The BACK of the tongue is arched toward the soft palate.

The quadrangle below roughly represents the inside of the mouth. Imagine that the head is in profile, facing left. Refer also to the chart on page 4.

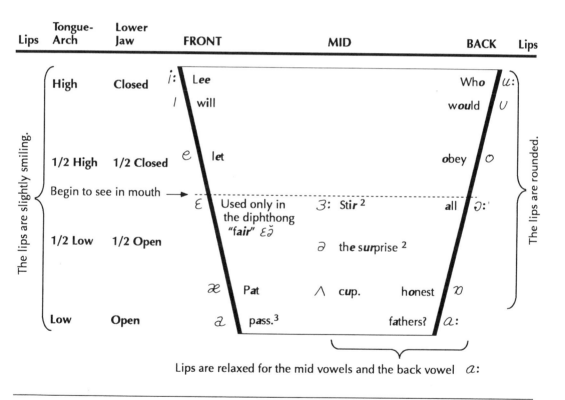

THE FIVE SO-CALLED "LONG" DIPHTHONG SOUNDS:

e·ĭ· a·ĭ· ɔ·ĭ· o·ŭ· a·ŭ·
Pay   my   boy.   Go   now.

THE TWO TRIPHTHONG SOUNDS:

ɑĭə̆
hire[2]

ɑŭə̆
flower[2]

THE FIVE ALWAYS-SHORT DIPHTHONG SOUNDS OF "R":

ɪə̆   ɛə̆   ʊə̆   ɔə̆   ɑə̆
Here's their   poor   ore   car.

Throughout this textbook a [2] or [3] at the upper right corner of a word indicates that the word has two or three variants or standards of pronunciation.

The fundamental difference between the vowel and consonant sounds of Spoken English lies in the manner of their articulation. A vowel sound employs an uninterrupted flow of air, while a consonant uses an interrupted flow of breath; the mouth passage for consonants is either completely stopped for a moment or is narrowed to create friction.

Consonant sounds are classified according to:

1   Vibration;

2   Where the sound is made in the mouth;

3   How the sound is made.

VIBRATION

Is the consonant sound voiced or voiceless? In other words, is the consonant produced with vibration of the vocal folds, resulting in tone, or is the consonant produced without vibration of the folds? You can readily feel and identify a voiced or voiceless sound by placing the tips of your fingers on your Adam's apple while producing a consonant sound. You will feel vibration during the production of all voiced sounds, but the area will remain still, and you will not feel vibration during the production of any voiceless sound.

There are 16 voiced consonant sounds in well-spoken English:

b	d	g	m	n	η
bay	Dan	gone	my	no=know	sing
l	v	$\eth$	z	$\math3$	r
law	vine	thine	zoo	genre	red
h	w	j	$d\math3$		
behind	witch	you	gin		

There are 10 voiceless consonant sounds in well-spoken English:

p	t	k	f	θ
pay	tan	con	fish	thigh
s	$\int$	h	$\textrm{м}$	$t\int$
so=sew	shin	he	which	chin

Cognates are pairs of different consonant sounds that are related by being produced in the *same place* of articulation, in the *same manner* of articulation, with one of the pair voiced and the other voiceless.

There are 10 pairs of cognates in Spoken English:

p & b t & d k & g f & v θ & $\eth$

s & z $\int$ & $\math3$ h & h $\textrm{м}$ & w $t\int$ & $d\math3$

WHERE IS THE SOUND MADE IN YOUR MOUTH?

What articulators are used to stop, or hinder, the voiced or voiceless breath during production of the sound?

PLACE I	Both Lips	p b m ʍ w
PLACE II	Lower lip and upper teeth	f v
PLACE III	Tip of tongue and upper teeth	θ ð
PLACE IV-A	Tip of tongue TOUCHING gum ridge	t d n l
	Affricates tʃ dʒ	a blending of place IV-A to IV-B*
PLACE IV-B	Tip of tongue pointing toward gum ridge, NOT TOUCHING	s z ʃ ʒ r
PLACE V	Front of tongue and hard palate	j
PLACE VI	Back of tongue and soft palate	k g ŋ
PLACE VII	Throat or glottis	h ɦ

* Affricates: Part of the stop-plosive family, an affricate is a combination of a stop-plosive and a fricative, blended so closely as to seem like a single sound.

HOW IS THE SOUND MADE, OR WHAT IS THE MANNER OF ARTICULATION?

In what way do the articulators influence the breath stream to create the sound?

Stop-Plosives

The air is stopped and then exploded.

$$p \quad b \quad t \quad d \quad k \quad g$$

When a voiceless stop-plosive is followed by a vowel or diphthong sound or by silence, the breath is quickly released. It is said to be aspirated.

$$p^h \qquad t^h \qquad k^h$$

When a voiceless stop-plosive is followed by another consonant sound, either within the same word or in the next word of a phrase, the plosive is unreleased, or held. It is said to be unaspirated.

$$p, \qquad t, \qquad k$$

Affricates

Part of the stop-plosive family, an affricate is a combination of a stop-plosive and a fricative, blended so closely as to seem like a single sound.

$$t\int \qquad dʒ$$

Nasals

The air is sent through the nose.

$$m \qquad n \qquad ŋ$$

Lateral

The only sound in Spoken English in which the air is emitted over the sides of the tongue.

$$l$$

Fricatives

The air is forced through a very narrow opening formed by the articulators, resulting in a kind of audible friction.

$$f \quad v \quad θ \quad ð \quad s \quad z \quad \int \quad ʒ \quad \underline{r} \quad h \quad ɦ$$

Glides

The articulators begin in a particular shape and then "glide," or swiftly move, from this position to the position of the vowel or diphthong sound that follows.

$$ʍ \quad w \quad j$$

PLACE OF ARTICULATION		SOUND AND PHONETIC LETTER			INITIAL POSITION	MEDIAL POSITION	FINAL POSITION
			Printed	Script			
PLACE I	BILABIAL: Both lips	1	p	p^h asp.	pay	caper	cape
				$p_,$ unasp.	play	lapse	leap frog
		2	b	b	bay	maybe	Abe
		3	m	m	my	swimming	hymn
		4	ʍ	$ʍ$	which	anywhere	-----
		5	w	w	witch	quit	-----
PLACE II	LABIO-DENTAL: Lower lip and upper teeth	6	f	f	fish	office	calf
		7	v	v	vine	lives	love
PLACE III	DENTAL: Tip of tongue and upper teeth	8	θ	$θ$	thigh	ether	teeth
		9	ð	$ð$	thy	either	teethe
PLACE IV-A	ALVEOLAR: Tip of tongue TOUCHING gum ridge	10	t	t^h asp.	tan	ratty *	hat
				$t_,$ unasp.	tray	hits	hot dog
		11	d	d	Dan	caddy	had
		12	n	n	know=no	final	bone
		13	l	l	law	silly	tall
PLACE IV-B	ALVEOLAR: Tip of tongue pointing toward gum ridge, NOT TOUCHING	14	s	s	so=sew	raced	tax
		15	z	z	zoo	dissolved	loves
		16	ʃ	$ʃ$	shin	ocean	bash
		17	ʒ	$ʒ$	genre	lesion	beige
		18	r *	r	red pray	so-rry	ginger ale
PLACE V	PALATAL: Front of tongue and hard palate	19	j	j	you=ewe Jugoslavia	muse, tune Bjorn, Sonja	-----
PLACE VI	VELAR: Back of tongue and soft palate	20	k	k^h asp.	con	locking	hock
				$k_,$ unasp.	clay	backs	rock pile
		21	g	g	gone	logger	hog
		22	ŋ	$ŋ$	-----	sink	sing
PLACE VII	GLOTTAL: Articulated in throat	23	h	h	he	mishap	-----
		24	ɦ	$ɦ$	-----	behind	-----
	AFFRICATES: A blending of PLACE IV-A to PLACE IV-B, or two consonants blended to form one sound	25	tʃ	$tʃ$	chin	leeches	batch
		26	ʤ	$dʒ$	gin	legion	badge

-----These sounds do not occur in these positions in Spoken English.

* Beginning with this page and continuing throughout the text, any "r" in the spelling of a practice or example word that is pronounced as a consonant r is underlined.

Descriptive chart of Consonant Sounds of Spoken English
PLACE = Where the sound is made in the mouth

Horizontal rows indicate MANNER OF ARTICULATION or How the sound is made in the mouth	PLACE I BILABIAL — Two lips articulating against one another		PLACE II LABIO-DENTAL — Lower lip articulating against upper front teeth		PLACE III DENTAL — Tip of tongue articulating against edge of upper front teeth		PLACE IV-A ALVEOLAR — Tip of tongue TOUCHING upper gum ridge directly behind upper front teeth		PLACE IV-B ALVEOLAR: 1 Post-dental — Extreme front of upper gum ridge, or upper teeth		2 Palato-alveolar — Middle of upper gum ridge		3 Post-alveolar — Extreme back of upper gum ridge		PLACE V PALATAL — Front of tongue articulating against hard palate		PLACE VI VELAR — Back of tongue articulating against soft palate (velum)		PLACE VII GLOTTAL — In the larynx	
VOICELESS = VS / VOICED = VD	VS	VD	VS	VD	VS	VD	VS	VD	VS	VD	VS	VD	VS	VD	VS	VD	VS	VD	VS	VD
STOP-PLOSIVES	p	b					t	d									k	g		
NASALS		m						n										ŋ		
LATERAL								l												
FRICATIVES			f	v	θ	ð			s	z	ʃ	ʒ		r̠		j			h	ɦ
GLIDES	ʍ	w																		
AFFRICATES (combination of consonant sounds)							tʃ	dʒ												

◆ COMBINING THE SOUNDS OF SPOKEN ENGLISH ◆

To combine the sounds of Spoken English in a way that appears to be conversational and unstudied is central to effective communication and must be mastered at the most elementary level of study. In any language, the words in a spoken phrase consist of unbroken streams of sounds, although some of the sounds are more prominent than others. For instance, vowels tend to be more sonorous than consonants, and open vowels are more resonant than closed vowels. Voiced nasal consonants and the lateral consonant have more musicality than other voiced consonants, and all voiced consonants have more carrying power than voiceless consonants. In addition, syllable stress, the lengths of sounds and the rhythmical contribution of operative ideas or words juxtaposed with unimportant words ensure that some sounds become more prominent than others.

SYLLABICATION

Definite SYLLABICATION makes for beauty and clarity of speech, and accurate articulation of syllables that begin with a consonant is essential for understandability. For instance, the word "criminal" is pronounced CRI-mi-nal, each syllable beginning with a consonant sound, rather than CRIM-in-al. To pronounce distinctly a word such as "merry," which contains an intervocalic r, use the consonant r to begin a syllable rather than to end the previous syllable: pronounce the word "merry" as ME-rry and not MARE-ee, which mars the vowel sound with r-coloring. Pronounce "starry" as STA-rry and not STAR-ee.

Stressed Syllables

A STRESSED SYLLABLE is one that has a stronger degree of prominence in relation to other syllables in the same word. With the exception of weak forms of words, all words when considered separately have a stressed syllable. In phonetic transcription, a stress mark is placed above and before a stressed syllable:

cup ˈkʰʌpʰ   speak ˈspʰiːkʰ   break ˈbreɪkʰ

Unstressed Syllables

UNSTRESSED SYLLABLES are left completely unmarked in phonetic transcription:

cupboard ˈkʰʌbəd	unspeakable ʌnˈspʰiːkʰəbl̩	breakfast ˈbrekˌfəstʰ
model ˈmɒdl̩	motel moˈtʰel:	
apple ˈæpl̩	applause əˈpʰlɔːz	
cou-rage ˈkʰʌrɪdʒ	cou-rageous kʰəˈreɪdʒəs	
eunuch ˈjuːnəkʰ	unique juˈniːkʰ	
PERfect (adj) ˈpʰɜːfɪkˌtʰ	perFECT (verb) pʰəˈfekˌtʰ	
OBject (noun) ˈɒbdʒɪkˌtʰ	obJECT (verb) əbˈdʒekˌtʰ	

Secondary Stress

SECONDARY STRESS applies to a weak degree of stress given a syllable that is spoken with less stress than the syllable receiving a strong stress. In phonetic transcription, a secondary stress is placed below and before the syllable:

CA-li-FORN-ia ˌkʰæləˈfɔːnjə   COS-mo-PO-li-tan ˌkʰɒzməˈpʰɒlətʰən

re-SPEC-ta-BI-li-ty rɪˌspʰekˌtʰəˈbɪlətʰɪ

LENGTHS

LENGTH refers to the duration of a speech sound achieved without change in its phonetic quality. Since vowel sounds and continuant consonant sounds (nasals, the lateral consonant sound and fricatives) involve a single articulatory position, they could conceivably last as long as a breath can last. The same is true of the glide from one vowel element to another in the creation of a diphthong sound.

The lengths of speech sounds are governed by phonetic laws of which most people are unaware; however, an understanding of these laws is essential to the student who wants to speak without a regional dialect or to the person learning to speak English as a second language. Since the lengths of the sounds in a language are the very essence of its rhythms, knowing about them is invaluable for both the student of oral interpretation and for the actor endeavoring to enter the rhythmic life of a character. In this book, and in any general discussion of Spoken English, length refers to the duration of sounds in proportion to one another, rather than to their length in real time. No one is actually going to time the length of a sound with a stop watch. Bear in mind also that even in persons whose speech conforms to one standard of pronunciation, there is a good deal of individual and contextual variation in sound-length and rhythm.

In Spoken English, the rules for the length of a sound are many and complex, depending on *stress* and on what sounds *follow* within a word. In general, all sounds tend to be:

- ◆ longer in stressed syllables
- ◆ shorter in unstressed syllables
- ◆ longer before voiced consonants
- ◆ shorter before voiceless consonants

The following lists of words show how the stress and phonetic environment of a given sound change its length. The designated sound in each line is longest in the word at the left and gradually becomes shorter in the words toward the right:

i: beams   beads   bees   bead   bee   beaming   beady   being   beast   beat   Biafra   *i*

3: burls   burns   burned   birds   bird   burr   burning   birdy   burst   Burt   Berlin   *3*

ei: pales   pained   pain   pays   pay   painless   paint   paying   pace   pate   peyote   *ei*

l: builds   billed   bill   building   built   able   billing   ability   pa-rabola   *l*

Considering that each of these lists includes only a few words for comparison, it is a relief to know that the IPA has simplified the study and notation of lengths by referring to:

THREE lengths of VOWELS	LONG	HALF-LONG	SHORT
TWO lengths of DIPHTHONGS	LONG		SHORT
TWO lengths of CONTINUANTS	LONG		SHORT

In very narrow transcription of the IPA:

3: Two dots to the right of a phonetic letter mean LONG;

3· One dot to the right of a phonetic letter means HALF-LONG;

3 SHORT sounds are left unmarked;

ei Each element of a diphthong is marked half-long to note when the sound is LONG.

Rules for Lengths of the Vowel Sounds

NINE pure vowels are always SHORT in Spoken English. These nine SHORT VOWELS are always transcribed without dots to the right:

$ı$	e	$æ$	a	$ə$	$ʌ$	$ʊ$	o	$ɒ$
wıll	let	Pat	pass	the	cup	would	obey	honest

FIVE pure vowel sounds are pronounced in different lengths. They are known as the LONG VOWELS:

$i:$	$3:$	$u:$	$ɔ:$	$a:$
Lee	stir	who	all	fathers

In reality these FIVE LONG VOWELS can have an infinite number of lengths, but they are generally described in THREE LENGTHS:

	$i:$	$3:$	$u:$	$ɔ:$	$a:$
LONG in a stressed syllable of a word:					
◆ As the last sound of the word	free	burr	rue	saw	spa
◆ Before one or more voiced consonants	reeds	burns	rooms	Saul's	palms
	freeze	burl	rouge	sawed	massage

	$i·$	$3·$	$u·$	$ɔ·$	$a·$
HALF-LONG in a stressed syllable of a word:					
◆ Before one or more voiceless consonants	freaks	burst	roost	exhaust	-----
	reap	birth	roof	sought	Masha
◆ Before another vowel sound	freeing	-----	ruin	sawing	-----
◆ Before a voiced consonant that is in turn followed by a voiceless consonant	-----	burnt	-----	salt	Dante

	i	3	u	$ɔ$	a
SHORT:					
◆ In an unstressed syllable	meander	urbane	routine	Esau	blasé
◆ In WEAK FORMS (wf) of words	me	her	to	or	are
	he	were	do	for	
	she	sir	you	nor	
	we		into		
	be		onto		
			unto		

✓ Reminder ——————————————————————————————————

ALL SOUNDS (vowels, diphthongs, continuants) ARE SHORT IN UNSTRESSED SYLLABLES.

Rules for Lengths of the Diphthong Sounds

The FIVE diphthong sounds of "r" and the TWO triphthong sounds of "r" are always SHORT:

ı̯ə̆	ɛə̆	ʊə̆	ɔə̆	aə̆	aı̆ə̆	aʊə̆
here's	their	poor	ore	car	hire	flower

FIVE diphthong sounds are pronounced in many lengths; they are known as the LONG DIPHTHONGS:

e·ı̆·	a·ı̆·	ɔ·ı̆·	o·ʊ̆·	a·ʊ̆·
pay	my	boy	go	now

In reality these FIVE LONG DIPHTHONGS have an infinite number of lengths, but they are generally described in TWO LENGTHS:

LONG in a stressed syllable that is the last syllable of a word:	e·ı̆·	a·ı̆·	ɔ·ı̆·	o·ʊ̆·	a·ʊ̆·
◆ As the last sound of the word	pay	apply	employ	go	endow
◆ Before one or more voiced consonants	pained	blind	boiled	coves	drowned
	pays	applied	poise	cone	down

SHORT in all other cases:	eı̆	aı̆	ɔı̆	oʊ̆	aʊ̆
◆ In a stressed and final syllable before a voiced consonant that is in turn followed by a voiceless consonant	paint	pints	point	colt	counts
◆ In a stressed and final syllable before one or more voiceless consonants	paste	pikes	voiced	coasts	jousts
	pace	plight	Detroit	coat	doubt
◆ In any syllable but the last	painful	pliant	poison	coded	dowdy
◆ In an unstressed syllable	peyote	Diana	Royale	echo	landau

Rules for Lengths of Continuant Consonant Sounds

All of the continuant consonants are subject to the rules of lengths, but because of their particular tone and resonance, only the nasals and the lateral consonant sound need to be studied.

m n ŋ and l   are LONG when they are in a stressed syllable that is the last one of the word:

	ˈkͅraı̆·mːz	ˈfrenːdz	bɪˈlɔŋːz	dɪˈfaı̆·lːd
◆ Before one or more voiced consonants	crimes	friends	belongs	defiled

	ˈhım̆ː	ˈmæn̆ː	bɪˈlɔŋ̆ː	ˈfʊlː
◆ As the last sound of a word when preceded by one of the short vowels	hymn	man	belong	full

STRONG AND WEAK FORMS OF WORDS

A sensitive use of STRONG AND WEAK FORMS OF WORDS ensures communication of thought and feeling in a conversational manner. In speech, words that express main ideas tend to have prominence (especially nouns and verbs). These are called "operative," or "key-idea," words. Unimportant words tend to be weakened: prepositions; conjunctions; personal pronouns; articles; and auxiliary verbs are usually weak, except where the context calls for contrasting emphasis. The speaker achieves this weakening either by giving such words less force, a faster tempo, a slightly lower pitch, or by making changes in the actual sounds uttered. In phonetic transcription, weak forms of words in a sentence are not given stress marks, because in speech these forms are unstressed syllables. Speak the following phrases in a conversational manner and note that you instinctively pronounce the unimportant words in the weakened form:

Tell them that I want to go.

Don't tell me, tell them!

We need some help in here.

Some people just don't care.

The STRONG FORM (sf) is the one usually listed in dictionaries and is useful when the word is stressed or in a strong position:

Yes, he **can**.   "can" is spoken as

WEAK FORMS (wf) are used when the word is unstressed, that is, unimportant to the main thought being conveyed:

You can say **that again**.   "can" is spoken as

Weak forms tend to subordinate the unessential and preserve the sentence rhythm and flow of Spoken English:

Tell them that they can go.

A weak form of a word may evolve from the strong form by one or all of the following:
◆ Taking away the stress
◆ Making the sounds in the weak form SHORT
◆ Changing to a weaker vowel
◆ Omitting a sound completely

There is a difference between the legitimate weakening of unimportant sounds to preserve the sentence rhythm and the omission of sounds through carelessness or inertia. Appropriate usage of strong and weak forms promotes meaning and enhances understandability.

COMMONLY USED WORDS HAVING WEAK FORMS IN SPOKEN ENGLISH

		Strong Form (sf)	Weak Form(s) (wf)			

Articles

1	a	ˈeɪ·	ə			
2	an	ˈæn:	ən			
3	the	ˈðiː	ði	or ðɪ	before a vowel	
			ðə		before a consonant	

Auxiliary Verbs

4	am	ˈæm:	əm			
5	are	ˈɑ̆	ɑ	ə		
6	can	ˈkʰæn:	kʰən			
7	could	ˈkʰʊd	kʰəd			
8	do	ˈduː	du	dʊ	də	
9	does	ˈdʌz	dəz			
10	had	ˈhæd	həd	əd		
11	has	ˈhæz	həz	əz		
12	have	ˈhæv	həv	əv		
13	must	ˈmʌst	məst	məs		
14	shall	ˈʃæl:	ʃəl	ʃl		
15	should	ˈʃʊd	ʃəd	ʃd		
16	was	ˈwɒz	wəz	(NEVER wʌz)		
17	were	ˈwɜː	wɜ	wə		
18	would	ˈwʊd	wəd			
19	be	ˈbiː	bi			

Personal Pronouns

20	he	ˈhiː	hi	i		
21	her	ˈhɜː	hɜ	ɜ	hə	ə
22	his	ˈhɪz	ɪz			
23	me	ˈmiː	mi			

PERSONAL PRONOUNS, Cont.

		Strong Form (sf)	Weak Form(s) (wf)	
1	she	ˈʃiː	ʃi	
2	some	ˈsʌm	səm	sm̩
3	them	ˈðem	ðəm	ðm̩
4	their=they're	ˈðɛə	ðɛ	
5	us	ˈʌs	əs	
6	you	ˈjuː	ju	jʊ
7	your	ˈjʊə	jʊ	
8	we	ˈwiː	wi	

Prepositions

9	at	ˈætʰ	ətʰ		
10	for	ˈfɔə	fɔ	fə	
11	from	ˈfrɒm	frəm	(NEVER frʌm)
12	into	ˈɪntʰu	ɪntʰʊ		

    ɪnˈtʰuː   (especially in poetry)

13	of	ˈɒv	əv	(NEVER ʌv)
14	to	ˈtʰuː	tʰʊ	before a vowel
			tʰə	before a consonant

Connectives and Conjunctions

15	and	ˈænd	ənd	before a vowel
			ən	before a consonant
16	as	ˈæz	əz	
17	but	ˈbʌtʰ	bətʰ	
18	for	ˈfɔə	fɔ	fə
19	or	ˈɔə	ɔ	ə
20	nor	ˈnɔə	nɔ	nə
21	that	ˈðætʰ	ðətʰ	
22	than	ˈðæn	ðən	ðn̩

Some words that may be weakened by being unstressed and by having short sounds, but that do not ever change the vowel or consonant sounds:

'ɪn:	'ɒn:	'ʍen:	'ðen:	'ʍɒtʰ	'dʒʌstʰ
in	on	when	then	what	just

'wɒzntʰ	't‿wɒz	bɪ'kɔ:z	'getʰ	'enɪ	'kʰænɒtʰ
wasn't	'twas	because	get	any	CAnnot

EXAMPLES OF THE USE OF STRONG AND WEAK FORMS OF WORDS

		Strong Form (sf)	**Weak Form (wf)**
		'ði:	ðɪ ðə
1	the	This is **the** place to eat sushi.	Show me the end of the film.
		'æm:	əm
2	am	You know that I am.	I am a seagull.
		'aǎ	ə
3	are	Whe<u>re</u> are they?	Bob and Pam are here. ("pammer")
		'kʰæn:	kʰən
4	can	Yes, you can.	You can be su<u>re</u> of that.
		'kʰʊd	kʰəd
5	could	We could if we wanted to.	I knew we could do it.
		'dʌz	dəz
6	does	Do you know what she does?	What does it matter?
		'hæd	əd
7	had	They had two tickets.	The t<u>r</u>ain had al<u>r</u>eady left the station.
		'mʌstʰ	məs
8	must	Yes, I must.	I must go now.
		'ʃæl:	ʃl
9	shall	We shall, my lord.	We shall t<u>r</u>y, my lord.
		'ʃʊd	ʃd
10	should	Should we do it?	We should do it sometime.
		'wɒz	wəz
11	was	What was it?	It was a lie.
		'hɜ:	ɜ
12	her	It's her fault, not mine.	Take her to dinner.
		'hɪm:	ɪm
13	him	It's not up to him.	Give him his book.
		'sʌm:	sm
14	some	Some people have all the luck.	Let's have some people over for dinner.
		'ðem:	ðm
15	them	Don't tell me, tell them!	Tell them to wait.
		ætʰ	ət
16	at	What are you looking at?	Look at that!

USE OF STRONG AND WEAK FORMS OF WORDS, Cont.

		Strong Form (sf)	**Weak Form (wf)**
1	for	*ˈfɔə̆* Who's it for?	*fə* It's for you.
2	from	*ˈfrɒm:* Where are you from?	*frəm* I'm from California.
3	of	*ˈɒv* I don't know him, but I know of him.	*əv* I've heard of that.
4	to	*ˈtʰu:* I'm driving to work, but not from work.	*tʰə* *tʰʊ* I'm going to work and then to eat lunch.
5	and	*ˈæn:d* And? And? And then?	*ənd* *ən* Knock and enter, and then sit down.
6	as	*ˈæz* What are you going as?	*əz* It's as if I were dreaming.
7	but	*ˈbʌt,ʌ* No if's, and's or but's!	*bət,* I'm tired but happy.
8	nor	*ˈnɔə̆* Nor shall death brag thou wand'rest ...	*nə* It's neither this nor that.
9	that	*ˈðætʰ* Please don't tell me that. (pronoun)	*ðət,* Don't tell me that you're leaving. (connective)

At the end of a phrase or sentence, the VOWEL SOUND of the strong form, NOT the strong form itself, is used when the word is unimportant to the sense. See example 16 on page 24 and example 6 on this page as well as the following:

10	to	*tʰu* What are you up to?	*tʰə* It's up to you.
11	to	*tʰu* Do you want to?	*tʰə* I want to go.
12	do	*du* Yes, I know they do.	*də* Where do they live?
13	at	*ætʰ* What are you sta-ring at?	*ət,* The dance is at nine.
14	from	*frɒm* Where do you come from?	*frəm* I'm from Alberta.
15	was	*wɒz* Are you sure it was?	*wəz* Yes, it was green.
16	was	*wɒz* What a night that was!	*wəz* It was a hoot!
17	of	*ɒv* What are you thinking of?	*əv* We've thought of that.

CONNECTING THE SOUNDS OF SPOKEN ENGLISH

The meaning of a phrase and the physical necessity of breathing determine where to pause when speaking; yet within a breath group, all sounds are connected, or linked, in some fashion. The end sound of one word is linked to the beginning sound of the next word to maintain the flow of breath and sustain the meaning. Any linking that changes meaning or jars the listener should be avoided.

Guidelines for linking in connected utterance

1   Linking a consonant to a vowel is accomplished by LIGHTLY connecting the ending consonant to the vowel that follows it:

   SAY: a _red_ apple   NOT: a _reh_ dapple

   SAY: a _ripe_ olive   NOT: a _rye_ pollive

2   Linking a vowel to a vowel is accomplished by completing the ending vowel and initiating the beginning vowel of the next word with a fresh impulse of breath and WITHOUT a pause or a glottal attack:

   SAY: She asked for no ice.   NOT: She yasked for no wice.

3   A linking consonant _r_ is used to connect words in a phrase such as "a pair of shoes." Care must be exercised to use a clearly articulated consonant _r_ and avoid a carelessly spoken "hard r," as in "a paira shoes":

   SAY: a pai-_r_ of shoes   NOT: a pairrr of shoes

4   Same-consonant blends connect a particular consonant at the end of a word to the same consonant at the beginning of the next word. The articulators maintain their positions, and the second sound in the sequence is achieved through a fresh impulse of breath:

   Beth thought   wash shelves   tell lies

5   Cognate blends connect a voiceless sound to its voiced partner or vice-versa. Again, the articulators maintain their positions, and the second sound in the sequence is achieved through an impulse of breath and the addition or omission of vibration:

   'Tis so   Bob paid   smooth things

6   The voiceless stop-plosives _p_ , _t_ and _k_ are held, or unaspirated, when they are followed by another consonant sound in the next word. Inappropriate aspiration sounds self-conscious and pedantic:

   lip service   drop dead   roast beef   kick things

An interpretative choice could alter this guideline. For instance, "**Drop dead!**"

CONNECTING THE SOUNDS OF SPOKEN ENGLISH, Cont.

7 The pronunciation of the word "the" is determined by the sound that follows it. When followed by a vowel sound, "the" should be spoken as "thi" or thee," and when followed by a consonant, "the" should be spoken as "thuh":

ðiː
the apple

ðɪ
the eager boy

ðɪ
the energy

ðə
the pear

ðə
the boy

ðə
the den

8 "And" in its weak form (wf) should be spoken as ənd when followed by a vowel or diphthong sound, and as ən when followed by a consonant sound:

ənd
apples and o-ranges

ən
apples and pears

◆ HOW TO PRACTICE ◆

Since each student of speech has distinctive speech requirements, and each student's rate of development is different, it would be inappropriate for this book to provide one outline of what a student should practice on a daily basis. Still, a few general guides may help you to proceed at the outset.

Improved speech habits and skills can only be acquired through a commitment to consistent practice. The ideal amount of practice would be five 45-minute sessions each week; however, finding the time to study can occasionally be daunting, so remember that QUALITY of practice is more important than QUANTITY. It is more valuable to practice for 30 minutes several days a week than to do a marathon on the weekend, and it is always more beneficial to practice when you are alert than when you are tired. Find a time when you can devote the whole of your attention to the work. Locate a space that gives you privacy and also has lively acoustics that can bounce sounds back to you, to help educate your ear. In general, include some stretching, relaxation, easy-breathing, and vocalization exercises in each session, followed by some articulation warm-ups to ready yourself for specific speech exercises that address your particular needs (a sample warm-up is provided on pages 30-35).

Above all, remember that the subtle work of training your ear requires patience, judgement, taste, and sensitivity. Do not pressure yourself as you begin to become familiar with new sounds and concepts.

To embark on long, arduous drill sessions during your first weeks of study would be self-defeating. Instead, study the material in Chapter One of this textbook (you will probably find that you want to review this chapter many times). Listen to the *Speak with Distinction* audio cassette, which will acquaint you with the fundamentals of Good Speech and provide accurate examples of the sounds of well-spoken English in isolation, in comparison and in connected utterance. Do the ear-training exercises selected by your teacher and practice the articulation warm-up exercises, numbers 1-9, on pages 30-32. For the moment, do not attempt the rest of the exercises and tongue-twisters on those pages until you can make the individual speech sounds accurately. If you try too much too soon, you may just end up speaking your inaccurate sounds with greater speed and misplaced confidence.

At first you may feel overwhelmed by the amount and scope of the work before you; it may even seem that every sound out of your mouth needs some improvement. But don't panic! Your teacher will tell you what to address first, so that the confusion can disappear and your private work can bring steady, efficient improvement. Five 45-minute sessions are the ideal, but do not devote each session just to one sound, because then your ear will simply tire of hearing the same sound and lose its keenness. Thirty minutes on your "s" sound, for instance, and halfway through you may not be able to hear the difference between a poor "s" and a better one (in fact, it is likely that all your "s" sounds, even the improved ones, will drive you crazy). So before your ear loses the ability to discriminate, move on to a different sound—perhaps a vowel or diphthong.

By the fourth or fifth month of study, you will probably have a good sense of which sounds need your attention most, and your ear-training, understanding of this textbook and sheer imitative ability may enable you to produce a fair approximation of the correct sounds. It is at this point that your discipline and patience must be at their peak, so that your new speech sounds will live in YOUR mouth.

Up to this stage, most students' practice will focus on the exercises in *Speak with Distinction*. Eventually, however, you will also want and need to practice by using works of literature, which will both stimulate your appreciation of the spoken word and help you to explore the dramatic values of speech sounds. There are many good sources for suitable material, both dramatic and non-dramatic (poems, fiction and non-fiction). (Some suggested material is found in Chapter Five, on pages 363-374.) You should select pieces that are meant to be spoken and heard and that contain language that has texture, sense and rhythm. As you will discover, the combination of daily practice of the exercises in this volume, the speaking of straightforward yet well-written literary passages, and the use of your new speech habits in your daily life are excellent preparations for integrating new habits of speech into the creative process of acting. This comprehensive approach to speech-study will increase your range of expression, which will in turn make you more available to the dynamics of a play and give you new confidence in your ability to enter the world of a script.

HOW TO PRACTICE THE WARM-UP EXERCISES ON PAGES 30-35

After your physical and vocal warm-ups, do some of the articulation exercises that begin on page 33. In addition to having fun with rhythms, repeated sounds and silly words, your over-all aim in these exercises and tongue-twisters is to achieve relaxation and opening of the lower jaw; activation of the lips; forward placement of tone on vowel and diphthong sounds; and clean, efficient articulation of consonant sounds (especially the tip-of-the-tongue ones). It is important that you use these exercises to integrate these aspects of Good Speech. It is no good to repeat "can't you won't you don't you" with a relaxed lower jaw but a splashy "t" sound, just as it is equally pointless to rattle off the "Peter Piper" exercise with a tight, immobile jaw. YOU ARE WORKING FOR MAXIMUM CLARITY WITH MINIMUM TENSION. Do not aim for speed-at-all-cost; speed will eventually come about, but as a result of agility and clarity.

Work in a comfortable standing position, with your feet just slightly apart and your arms relaxed at your sides. Focus your awareness on your breath. Notice the ebb and flow of your breath and center your attention on the coolness of the breath as you inhale and the warmth of the breath as you exhale. Let your body remain open to the flow of breath.

Maintain an easy and relaxed flow of breath during the following loosening and stretching exercises. Coordinate your breath with the physical movements; do not "hold" your breath.

It is also important to learn to energize specific muscles, areas of the body and designated articulators without unnecessary involvement of neighboring muscles. For instance, as you knit your eyebrows into a frown, maintain the relaxation of your tongue, lower jaw and throat—all the other areas of your face.

Do not hurry and never try to force results. Be deliberate, even if you have only a short time at your disposal.

1   **EXERCISES FOR THE FACIAL MUSCLES**

◆ Knit your eyebrows into a frown.	Let go.
◆ Lift your eyebrows.	Let go.
◆ Wrinkle your nose.	Let go.
◆ Lift both cheeks into a big smile.	Let go.
◆ Pull the corners of your mouth downward.	Let go.
◆ Relax your jaw wide open and point the tip of your tongue straight out.	Let go.

2   **EXERCISES FOR THE NECK AND SHOULDERS**

◆ Going clockwise, trace imaginary circles on the ceiling with the top of your head, beginning with tiny circles that gradually increase in size. Once you have achieved easy, large circles, begin to make them smaller again until they are minute and your head feels gently poised on top of your neck. Repeat the exercise making counter-clockwise circles.

◆ Maintain an easy and relaxed flow of breath and an easy alignment of your neck and spine as you trace imaginary, clockwise circles just in front of you with the tip of your nose. DO NOT REACH FORWARD with your nose or chin. Begin with tiny circles that gradually increase with size. Then once you have achieved easy, large circles, begin to make them smaller until they are minute and your head is finally at rest. Repeat the exercise making counter-clockwise circles..

◆ Inhale as you raise your shoulders toward your ears; exhale as you let go. Repeat several times.

◆ Inhale as you float your hands and arms toward the sky; exhale as you let go. Repeat several times.

◆ Inhale as you rotate your shoulders forward and up; and then exhale as you let the shoulders drop back and down. Allow your hands and arms to remain relaxed as you make several shoulder circles in one direction, then in the opposite direction.

3   **EXERCISES FOR THE LOWER JAW**

◆ Still standing, drop your head forward, bending your knees slightly. Allow some space between your upper and lower teeth. As you exhale, gently shake your head from side to side and allow your relaxed lower jaw, tongue and cheeks to flutter with the shaking.

4   **EXERCISES FOR THE SOFT PALATE**

◆ Standing upright, imagine the feeling of a yawn in your throat and encourage yourself to yawn several times.

◆ Allow your lower jaw to hang in a relaxed fashion and the tip of your tongue to rest against the back of your lower teeth. Look in a small mirror and observe your soft palate. Lower and lift the soft palate several times by alternating the sounds "ng," as in the word "sing," and "ah," as expressed in a sigh of relief.

Avoid any involvement or movement of your lower jaw during the following exercise:

◆ Using a "modified" yawn, you will stretch and release the interior of your throat and mouth. Allow your lower jaw to remain relaxed and your lips to touch each other lightly while inducing the "feeling" of a yawn. Let the stretch occur IN the mouth and throat while your lips stay in contact with each other.

5   **EXERCISES FOR THE LIPS**

◆ Blow air through your lips, allowing them to flutter. Repeat by blowing vibrated (voiced) air through the lips.

◆ Repeat the following sounds lightly and easily, feeling a crisp movement with a minimum of tension:

wee-wee-wee-wee-wee-wee-wee-wee-wee-wee   *wiː*

waw-waw-waw-waw-waw-waw-waw-waw-waw-waw   *wɔː*

wee-waw-wee-waw-wee-waw-wee-waw-wee-waw

6   **EXERCISES FOR THE TONGUE**

◆ With your lower jaw relaxed, opened and kept still, point the tip of your tongue:

straight out — relaxed in — straight out — relaxed in — etc.

right — left — up — down — right — left — up — down — etc.

left — right — down — up — left — right — down — up — etc.

◆ In a smooth rhythm, like the second hand of a clock, make a big perfect circle with the tip of your tongue, first inside your mouth and then outside your mouth.

◆ Shake out your tongue by blowing air over the tip and allowing the tip to flutter against the gum ridge. Repeat using vibrated air. These two sounds will resemble the trilled Italian "r"; the first one will be voiceless and the second fully voiced.

7   **NEAPOLITAN ICE CREAM EXERCISES**

◆   Just as the individual flavors in Neapolitan ice cream seamlessly adjoin one another yet do not melt into one slushy mush, the vowel and diphthong sounds in these sequences smoothly flow into one another yet do not become an indistinct, undifferentiated vocal mass. Keep each sound "flavor" distinct, yet do not glottalize, waste air or add a *j* or *w* between sounds. Allow the tip of your tongue to remain relaxed behind your lower teeth during the entire sequence:

i:	*u:*	*ɔ:*	*u:*								
ee	oo	aw	oo	ee	oo	aw	oo	ee	oo	aw	oo

u:	*ɔ:*	*a·ĭ·*	*i:*								
oo	aw	ai	ee	oo	aw	ai	ee	oo	aw	ai	ee

8   **EDITH'S FAVORITE**

a:	*e·ĭ·*	*i:*	*a·ĭ·*	*o·ŭ·*	*u:*
MAH	MAY	MEE	MY	MOH	MOO
NAH	NAY	NEE	NIGH	NOH	NOO
LAH	LAY	LEE	LIE	LOH	LOO

◆   The following syllables may be spoken in a variety of configurations and rhythms. Note that the capitalized, underlined syllables are the stressed syllables in the repeated rhythms of the exercises:

<u>MAH</u> may me <u>MY</u> moh moo <u>MAH</u> may me <u>MY</u> moh moo etc.
<u>NAH</u> nay nee <u>NIGH</u> noh noo <u>NAH</u> nay nee <u>NIGH</u> noh noo etc.
<u>LAH</u> lay lee <u>LIE</u> loh loo <u>LAH</u> lay lee <u>LIE</u> loh loo etc.

muh muh <u>MAH</u> muh muh <u>MAY</u> muh muh <u>MEE</u> muh muh <u>MY</u> muh muh <u>MOH</u> muh muh <u>MOO</u> etc.

nuh nuh <u>NAH</u> nuh nuh <u>NAY</u> nuh nuh <u>NEE</u> nuh nuh <u>NIGH</u> nuh nuh <u>NOH</u> nuh nuh <u>NOO</u> etc.

luh luh <u>LAH</u> luh luh <u>LAY</u> luh luh <u>LEE</u> luh luh <u>LIE</u> luh luh <u>LOH</u> luh luh <u>LOO</u> etc.

9   **EXERCISES FOR ARTICULATION**

◆   Repeat for CLARITY of articulation. Work for PRECISION with a MINIMUM of TENSION. AFTER you have accurately mastered the phrases for clarity, work for SPEED in repetition:

puh puh <u>PAH</u> buh buh <u>BAH</u> tuh tuh <u>TAH</u> duh duh <u>DAH</u> kuh kuh <u>KAH</u> guh guh <u>GAH</u>, etc.

guh guh <u>GAH</u> kuh kuh <u>KAH</u> duh duh <u>DAH</u> tuh tuh <u>TAH</u> buh buh <u>BAH</u> puh puh <u>PAH</u>, etc.

titititititititi-<u>TAH</u> dididididididi-<u>DAH</u>   nininininininini-<u>NAH</u> lilililililili-<u>LAH</u>, etc.

EXERCISES FOR ARTICULATION, Cont.

10   ALTERNATE THE FOLLOWING PHRASES:

      paper poppy (4 times)   baby bubble (4 times)

11   Peter Piper the pickled pepper picker picked a peck of pickled peppers.

      A peck of pickled peppers did Peter Piper the pickled pepper picker pick.

      Now if Peter Piper the pickled pepper picker picked a peck of pickled peppers,

      Where is the peck of pickled peppers that Peter Piper the pickled pepper picker

      picked?

12   Yolanda was yearning to yodel.

      She'd   YAH yah yah   YAH yah yah   YAAAAH   a lot

      and   LAY lee lo LAY   as often as not.

      YOH duh duh   LAY-dee-oh   LAY-dee-oh   LAY

      Yolanda would yodel all night and all day.

13   If a Hottentot tot taught a Hottentot tot

      To talk ere the tot could totter,

      Ought the Hottentot tot be taught to say aught,

      Or what ought to be taught her?

14   A tutor who tooted the flute

      Tried to tutor two tooters to toot.

      Said the two to the tutor,

      "Is it harder to toot or

      To tutor two tooters to toot?"

15   REPEAT QUICKLY THREE TIMES EACH:

      can't you won't you don't you

      did you would you could you

ADDITIONAL ARTICULATION EXERCISES

REPEAT EACH OF THE FOLLOWING PHRASES OVER AND OVER. ACCURACY FIRST, THEN SPEED!

1   kinky cookie

2   giggle gaggle (don't swallow ℓ)

3   lilli lolli lilli lolli

4   lilli lolli looli lawli

5   Culligan and calla lily

6   philological ability

7   eleven benevolent elephants

8   li-te-_ra_-lly   li-te-_ra_-ry

9   will you William will you William

10   _b_rilliant Italian William

11   Topeka Topeka Topeka

12   Bodega Bodega Bodega

13   Topeka Bodega Topeka Bodega Topeka Bodega

14   _r_ubber baby buggy bumpers

15   diga _r_iga diga _r_iga diga _r_iga doo

16   _r_ed leather yellow leather

17   _r_u-_r_al _r_idicule

18   minimal animal minimal animal

19   (wh)ther (wh)ch way

ADDITIONAL ARTICULATION EXERCISES, Cont.

20   lemon liniment

21   unique New York $nju\ 'j\supset \breve{\partial}k^{h}$

22   toy boat

23   Peggy Babcock

24   girl gargoyle, guy gargoyle

25   abominable abdominals

26   sushi chef

27   choose o-range shoes

28   garlic gargle, gargle with garlic

29   Massine's machine

green fields
fleeing sheep

big city
imagine enough

Ethel and Emma
a merry American

Ann's hand
Harry's character

I can't dance
ask the class

Colonel Burr stirring
her first rehearsal

voluntary secretary
comfortable sofa

wonderful constable
thoroughly encouraged

school shoes
fruit juice
reducing student
absolute opportunity

pull wool
good book

obey Olivia

Paul paused
water for daughter

John's office
horrible horror

calm father
alms for the garage

engage the stage
eighty-eight

nine lives
mighty knight

boys toil
noisy voyage

home alone
Roman coat

how now
mountain house

merely weary
fair-haired Mary
surely a poor rural tour
four-door
far car

desire fire
our hours

Say each phrase three times VERY RAPIDLY without pausing:

will you William
did you would you could you William
can't you won't you don't you William

You may find it helpful to make a recording of the way you sound as you begin your studies and then make a comparison recording every six to twelve months. The Survey Phrases for Recording on the preceding page and the Survey Sentences for Vowel, Diphthong and Difficult Consonant Sounds that follow will prove useful for this exercise, since each phrase or sentence targets a particular speech sound. By recording these phrases and sentences, you will be able to listen to your speech and also hear how you combine sounds. You may want to compare the sounds you record with those of the speaker on the *Speak with Distinction* practice tape. Above all, remember that you are not in competition with anyone else and that you will progress at your own rate.

1   These people feel that they can guarantee the suite for sweet Phoebe.

2   It's a miracle that the ability of the English actress had been debated so belatedly.

3   King Kong will sing a jingle for the King of England in the spring.

4   Ethel spent twenty-seven cents to get many of the best eggs and vegetables.

5   Fancy! That fascinating character Harry McCann married Anne Hammond.

6   The athletic man catches ants in his handkerchief for Harriet.

7   Angry gangs thanked the bank manager, then sang languidly of tangled anchors.

8   I can't ask Frances to dance with half the class.

9   The absurd girl is a connoisseur of turtles.

10 The colonel's nurse rehearses words at work.

11 Actually, contrary to customary circumstances in American government, the traitor was offered a secretary by the policeman.

12 I wonder if Murray's mother and brother love the cunning constable.

13 Rude Ruth's two rooms are near the school's pool.

14 Pull the poor Worcester wool from the cruel cook's good cook book.

15 Oblige the notoriously poetic Olympian and obey Othello.

16 All talkative daughters thought they bought straw.

17 Paul paused, then walked awkwardly toward the lawn for water.

18 What horrible foreign correspondent in Washington washed the hot copper coffee pot in Dorothy's office?

19 I want a model modern watch.

20 What was it? It was. It wasn't.

21 Father calmly placed palms near the façade of the drama studio's garage.

22 The eighty-eight sailors from Yale are delayed in jail for aye.

23 Ay, it's time to acquire the entire choir's files.

SURVEY SENTENCES, Cont.

24 Boyish Roister Doister toils and toils for oil.

25 Oh no, Joe, don't go for Mr. Stowell's coal.

26 Wring out the towel as you pronounce the vowels in "How now brown cow."

27 Were the dear, experienced auctioneer and the ideal career cashier really here?

28 Various parents said farewell to airy, fair-haired Mary Carey.

29 Surely poor alluring Stewart endured a rural tour during his cure.

30 More and more, the court ignores encores.

31 Is Barbara's large apartment at Harvard far from the Star Market?

32 On Tuesday, the stupid students at Stuart's Institute introduced the duke's new tune to the studio head.

33 Will you bring that brilliant but peculiar Italian millionaire William Hilliard to evaluate Julia's failures at station WWSW?

34 He thrusts his fists against the posts and still insists he sees the ghosts.

35 The singer with the longest fingers sang a long English-language song on Long Island.

36 Very merry Mary married hairy Harry Harris from Harrisburg.

37 Round the rugged rock the ragged rascal ran.

38 Tom met Tilly Teazle for tea on the two o'clock train to Trenton.

39 Rehearsing makes Horace hoarse, and hoarseness is even more harassing to his humble hobby horse. Now if this hoarseness harasses Horace's horse, how it must affect Horace! Actually, it haunts Horace.

1 ˈðiːz ˈpʰiːpḷ ˈfiːl ðət̚ ðeɪ kən ˌɡærənˈtiː ðəˈswiːt̚ ɬə ˈswiːt̚ ˈfiːbɪ

2 ɪt̚s ə ˈmɪrəkḷ ðət̚ ði əˈbɪləti ɔr ði ˈɪŋɡlɪʃ ˈæk̚t̚rɪs həd bɪn dɪˈbeɪt̚ɪd soʊ bɪˈleɪt̚ɪdlɪ

3 ˈkʰɪŋ ˈkʰɔŋ wɪl ˈsɪŋ ə ˈdʒɪŋɡḷ fə ðə ˈkʰɪŋ əv ˈɪŋɡlənd ɪn ðə ˈspˌrɪŋ

4 ˈeθḷ ˈspʰent̚ ˈt̚wenti ˈsevṇ ˈsent̚s t̚ə ˈɡet̚ ˈmenɪ əv ðə ˈbest̚ ˈeɡz ən ˈvedʒt̚əbḷz

5 ˈfænsɪ ðə ˈfæsəneɪtɪŋ ˈkʰærɪk̚t̚ə ˈhærɪ məˈkʰæŋ ˈmærɪd ˈæŋ ˈhæmənd

6 ði æθˈletʰɪk̚ ˈmæŋ ˈkʰæt̚ʃɪz ˈænt̚s ɪn ɪz ˈhæŋkʰətʃɪf fə ˈhærɪ ɪtʰ

7 ˈæŋɡrɪ ˈɡæŋz ˈθæŋk̚t̚ ðə ˈbæŋk ˌmænədʒə ðen ˈsæŋ ˈlæŋɡwɪdlɪ əvˈtʰæŋɡḷd ˈæŋkʰəz

8 aɪ ˈkʰænt ˈæsk, ˈfrænsɪs tʰə ˈdæns wɪð hæf ðə ˈklæs

9 ðɪ əbˈsɜːd ˈɡɜːl ɪz ə ˌkɒnə ˈsɜː rəv ˈtʰɜ·tɪlz

10 ðə ˈkʰɜːnlz ˈnɜs rɪˈhɜsɪz ˈwɜːdz ət ˈwɜ·kʰ

11 ˈæk.tʃuəlɪ ˈkʰɒntɾəri tʰə ˈkʰʌstəməri ˈsɜ·kʰəmstʰənsɪz
   ɪn əˈmerəkʰən ˈɡʌvənmənt
   ðə ˈtɾeɪtʰə wəz ˈɒfəd əˈsekɾətʰəri baɪ ðə pʰə ˈliːs mən

12 aɪ ˈwʌndə rɪf ˈmʌɾɪz ˈmʌðə rən ˈbɾʌðə
   ˈlʌv· ðə ˈkʰʌnɪŋ ˈkʰʌnstʰəbl̩

13 ˈruːd ˈruːðs ˈtʰuː· ˈruːmːz ə ˈnɪðə ðə ˈskʰuːlːz ˈpʰuːl

14 ˈpʰul̩n· ðə ˈpʰʊ̆ə ˈwʊstʰə ˈwʊlː
   frəm ðə ˈkɾuəl ˈkʰʊks ˈɡʊd ˈkʰʊk ˌbʊkʰ

15 oˈbleɪ̈dʒ ðə noˈtʰɔːrɪəslɪ pʰoˈetʰɪkʰ oˈlɪmpʰɪən
   ənd oˈbeɪ̈· oˈθeloʊ

16 ˈɔːl ˈtʰɔ·kʰə tɪv ˈdɒ·tʰəz ˈθɔ·tn̩ ðeɪ̈ ˈbɔ·t ˈstɾɒː

17 ˈpʰɔːl ˈpʰɔːzd̪n̩ ðen ˈwɔ·kʰ tʰ ˈɔ·k ˌwədlɪ
   ˈtʰɔ̆d̪ ðə ˈlɔːn fə ˈwɔ·tʰə

18 'mɒt, 'hɒrəbl̩ 'fɔrɪn ,kˣɒrə 'spˣɒndəntˣ ɪn 'wɒʃɪŋtˑən

'wɒʃt̩, ðə 'hɒt, 'kˣɒpˣə 'kˣɒfɪ 'pˣɒtˣ

ɪn 'dɒrəθɪz 'ɒfəs

19 aĭ 'wɒntˣ ə 'mɒdl̩ 'mɒdən 'wɒtʃ

20 'mɒt, 'wɒz ɪtˣ   ɪt̩ 'wɒz   ɪt̩ 'wɒzn̩tˣ

21 'ʃaːðə 'kˣaːmlɪ 'p̩leĭst, 'pˣaːmːz

'nɪ̃ə ðə fə'saːd ɒv ðə 'dɹaːmə 'stˌjuːdɪoŭz gə'ɹaːʒ

22 ðɪ 'eĭtˣɪ 'eĭt, 'seĭləz fɹəm 'jeĭˑl

aˑ dɪ 'leĭˑd ɪn 'dʒeĭˑl fɔr 'eĭˑ

23 'aĭˑ   ɪt̩ʂ 'tˣaĭˑm tˣʊ ə'k̩waĭə

ðɪ ɪn'tˣaĭə 'k̩waĭəz 'faĭˑlːz

24 'bɔĭ ɪʃ 'rɔĭ ʂtˣə 'dɔĭ ʂtˣə 'tˣɔĭˑlːz ən 'tˣɔĭˑlːz fɔr 'ɔĭˑl

25 'oˑŭ 'noˑŭˑ 'dʒoŭˑ   'doŭnt, 'goŭˑ fə 'mɪʂtˣə 'stˣoŭəlz 'kˣoˑŭˑl

26 'rɪŋː 'aŭt̩, ðə 'tˣaŭ əl   əzjʊ pˌɹo'naŭnʂ ðə 'vaŭəlz

ɪn 'haŭˑ 'naŭˑ 'braŭn 'kˣaŭˑ

27 wɜ ðə ˈdɪ̆ə̆r̲ ɪk, ˈspʰˌɪ rɪ ənɹtʰ ɔk, ʃə ˈnɪ̆ə̆r̲

ən̩ ðɪ aɪ ˈdɪ̆əl kʰə̆ˈr̲ɪ̆ə̆ kʰæ ˈʃɪ̆ə̆ ˈr̲ɪ̆ə lɪ ˈhɪ̆ə̆

28 ˈvɛ̆ə̆r̲ɪ əɹ ˈpʰɛ̆ə̆r̲ ənt, ɹ ˈsed ʄɛ̆ə̆ ˈwel:

tʰʊ ˈɛ̆ə̆r̲ɪ ˈʄɛ̆ə̆ ˌhɛ̆əd ˈmɛ̆ə̆r̲ɪ ˈkʰɛ̆ə̆r̲ɪ

29 ˈʃʊ̆ə̆lɪ ˈpʰʊ̆ə̆r̲ əˈljʊ̆ə̆r̲ɪŋ ˈɹt̩ˌjuˑ ətʰ

ɪnˈdjʊ̆əd ə ˈr̲ʊ̆ə̆r̲əl ˈtʰʊ̆ə̆ ˈdjʊ̆ə̆r̲ɪŋ ɪz ˈkˌjʊ̆ə̆

30 ˈmʊ̆ə̆r̲ ən ˈmʊ̆ə̆ ðə ˈkʰɔ̆ə̆tʰ ɪʄ ˈnʊ̆ə̆z ˈɒŋkʰɔ̆ə̆z

31 ɪz ˈbɑ̆ə̆br̲əz ˈlɑ̆ə̆dʒ əˈpʰɑ̆ə̆t̩ˌmənt ʰ ət, ˈhɑ̆ə̆ vəd

ˈʄɑ̆ə̆ ʄr̲əm ðə ˈɹtʰɑ̆ə̆ ˈmɑ̆ə̆kʰɪtʰ

32 ɒn ˈtʰˌjuːzdɪ ðə ˈɹt̩ˌjuˑpʰ̩d ˈɹt̩juːdn̩t, ɹ ət, ˈɹt̩juˑət, ɹ

ˈɪnɹtʰə̆t̩ˌjutʰ ˈɪntˌrə djuɹt̩, ðə ˈdjuˑk, ɹ ˈnjuː ˈtˌjuːn

tʰə ðə ˈɹt̩ˌjuːdɪ ʊ̆ ˈhed

33 ˈwɪlː jʊ ˈbr̲ɪŋː ðæt, ˈbr̲ɪljənt, bət, pʰˈkˌjuːljə r̲

ɪˈtʰæljən ˈmɪljənĕə ˈwɪljəm ˈhɪljəd tʰʊ ɪˈvæljʊeɪ̆t,

ˈdʒuːljəz ˈʄeɪ̆ljəz ət, ˈɹteɪ̆ʃn̩ ˈdʌbl̩ˌju ˈdʌbl̩ ju

ˈeɹ ˈdʌbl̩ ju

34 hi ˈθrʌstˌs ɪz ˈfɪstˌs əˈgenstˌn̩ ðə ˈpʰoʊstˌs

ən ˈstˀɪlː ɪnˈsɪstˌs i ˈsiːz ðə ˈgoʊstˌs

35 ðə ˈsɪŋə wɪð ðə ˈlɒŋgɪstˌ ˈfɪŋgəz

ˈsæŋː ə ˈlɒŋː ˈɪŋglɪʃ ˈlæŋgwɪdʒ ˈsɒŋː

ɒn ˌlɒŋː ˈaɪlənd

36 ˈveɹɪ ˈmeɹɪ ˈmɛə̆ɹɪ ˈmæɹɪd ˈhɛə̆ɹɪ ˈhæɹɪ ˈhæɹɪs

frəm ˈhæɹɪsˌbɜːg

37 ˈraʊ̆n̩d ðə ˈrʌgɪd ˈrɒk, ðə ˈræɡɪd ˈraskˌl̩ ˈrænː

38 ˈtˀɒmː ˈmet, ˈtˀɪlɪ ˈtˀiːzl̩ fəˈtˀiː

ɒn̩ ðə ˈtˀuː əˈkˌlɒk, ˈtˀreɪ̆n tˀə ˈtˌrentˀən

39 rɪ ˈhɜˑsɪŋ ˈmeɪ̆ksˌs ˈhɒɹəs ˈhɒə̆s

ənd ˈhɒə̆snɪs ɪz ˈiːvn̩ ˈmɒə̆ ˈhæɹəsɪŋ

tˀu ɪz ˈhʌmbl̩ ˈhɒbɪˌhɒə̆s

ˈnaʊ̆ ɪf ˈðɪs ˈhɒə̆snɪs ˈhæɹəsɪz ˈhɒɹəsɪz ˈhɒə̆s

ˈhaʊ̆ ɪt, məstˀ əˈfekˌt, ˈhɒɹəs

ˈækˌtʃuəlɪ ɪt, ˈhɒˑntˌs ˈhɒɹəs

CHAPTER TWO

THE VOWEL SOUNDS

◆ TO THE STUDENT: ◆
HOW TO USE CHAPTERS TWO, THREE AND FOUR

The practice material for the vowel, diphthong and consonant sounds of Spoken English are presented in Chapters Two, Three and Four in the traditional phonetic order. You may practice the sounds in that sequence; however, your teacher may design a program of study and perhaps even design a program particular to each student.

You may also find it helpful to make a recording of the way you sound as you begin your studies and then make a comparison recording every six to twelve months. The Survey Phrases for Recording on page 36 and the Survey Sentences for Vowel, Diphthong and Difficult Consonant Sounds on pages 37-38 will prove useful for this exercise, since each phrase or sentence targets a particular speech sound. By recording these phrases and sentences, you will be able to listen to your speech and also hear how you combine sounds. You may want to compare the sounds you record with those of the speaker on the *Speak with Distinction* practice tape. Above all, remember that you are not in competition with anyone else and that you will progress at your own rate.

DESIGNATED SOUNDS

The chapters are divided into sections, each of which begins by identifying one speech sound and associating it with a KEY WORD. This key word is then used consistently throughout the textbook to refer to its corresponding sound. The phonetic letter for the sound is also given. Memorize the phonetic letter and practice writing it over and over; the phonetic letter is a wonderful shorthand for the sound and it will also "become" the sound itself in your mind's ear. When you make yourself as familiar with the phonetic letter as you are with the "ABC's," you will actually improve your ear:

The vowel sound *i:* as in "L*ee*."

◆ Representative spellings for each sound are also given, to help you identify the sound and to demonstrate that in English, the spelling of a word is not necessarily an indication of how it is to be pronounced:

we	see	dece*i*ve	sp*ea*k	p*eo*ple	k*ey*=q*ua*y
mach*i*ne	f*ie*ld	C*ae*sar	ph*oe*nix	debr*is*	

◆ A description of the production of the sound is given:
Relax your lower jaw and allow the tip of your tongue . . .

◆ An image or suggestion of the quality of the sound may be given:
A clean, forward and brilliant quality characterizes this sound.

◆ Information for recommended USAGE of the sound may be given.

WORDS FOR PRACTICE

The lists of Words for Practice are organized according to the position of the designated sound in the word and according to the sound that follows next within the word. This arrangement for the study of Spoken English is used because the sound that follows the designated sound may determine its length and may influence its placement and clarity.

Vowel and Diphthong Sounds

◆ A glance at the subheadings in Words for Practice for $\dot{i}$: on pages 58-59 will demonstrate that the Five Long Vowel Sounds are listed in groups of Long, Half-Long and Short. Basically, each Long Vowel and Long Diphthong sound is first listed in words that have the stressed syllable in FINAL POSITION, such as "Lee" and "pay." It is important that you use these words to establish the clarity and forward placement of the sound, as well as to sustain breath. With all the vowel and diphthong sounds, Words for Practice proceeds according to the consonant sound that follows, in the order of MANNER OF ARTICULATION (plosives, nasals, the lateral consonant sound, fricatives, and affricates). This arrangement provides the opportunity to practice follow-through of tone for the final voiced consonants (TONE ENDINGS) and to use accurate and efficient articulation of the final voiceless consonants.

◆ In Words for Practice note that each new group of vowels and diphthongs begins with the sound in INITIAL POSITION, followed by words with the sound preceded by the consonant sound h . This provides an opportunity to practice smooth initiation of tone by eliminating the GLOTTAL STOP that can often occur when the sound is in initial position:

ex="X"	hex	excellent hexagon	echo	Hector
exit[2]	hectic	Eccles	heckles	

This order of practice is an extension of the program to Eliminate Glottal Attacks of Vowel and Diphthong Sounds introduced on pages 55-56.

Consonant Sounds

The drill material for each consonant sound features the sound in initial, medial and final positions; in CLUSTERS with other consonant sounds; and in important consonant combinations. Words for Practice of Consonant Sounds are listed according to the sound(s) within the word that follows the consonant sound under study. When followed by a vowel or diphthong sound the order is: front vowels; mid vowels; back vowels; long diphthongs; short diphthongs of "r"; and triphthongs.

When practicing single words, you need not be concerned about the melody or inflection you are using. Still, it may be useful occasionally to practice a word on each of three basic inflections:

falling inflection, or making a statement: Go.   (finished thought)

rising inflection, or asking a question: Go?   (unfinished thought)

level inflection, or sustaining or suspending the word: Go . . .   (unfinished thought)

The lists in Words for Practice contain many unusual words and proper nouns. These are in-cluded not only because they contain important sounds and combinations for practice, but also be-cause these words are often found in plays, especially those by Shakespeare. Aside from the desig-nated sound to be practiced, the full pronunciation and meaning of the word are left to you to discover by using your dictionaries. This will give you some mental stimulation and fun, as well as a chance to exercise your knowledge of phonetics.

PHRASES AND SENTENCES FOR PRACTICE

After the lists of Words for Practice, sounds are explored through short Phrases for Practice and longer Sentences for Practice. When appropriate, the Phrases and Sentences for Practice are grouped according to the length of the particular sound. For instance, phrases and sentences for the vowel sound *i:* as in "Lee" are found in groups of Long, Half-Long and Mixed (Long, Half-Long and, sometimes, Short) lengths:

i:	*i:*	*i·*	*i·*	*i*	*i·*	*i:*
dream of a beam		sleek physique		Leander's secret seas		

In the phrases and sentences for the vowel and diphthong sounds, the first phrases feature the vowel or diphthong in initial positions, for which a smooth initiation of tone must be achieved. The phonetic letter for the glottal attack *ʔ* precedes the phrase or sentence as a reminder to avoid glottalization:

ʔ eager eels and eagles

NOTATIONS USED IN PRACTICE MATERIAL

◆ In Words for Practice, an "equals" sign (=) is used to indicate that the words are HOMONYMS—that they are pronounced identically, but spelled differently:

dear=deer

◆ Occasionally in Words for Practice, a word is followed by (sf), to signify the Strong Form of the word, or by (wf) to indicate the Weak Form of the word. The word "can" is listed as follows in two sections of the book:

—in the *æ* section: can (sf)   —in the *ə* section: can (wf)

◆ Often a small, raised 2 or 3 follows a word to indicate that there are two or three correct and acceptable pronunciations of that word:

either[2]   ˈiːðə   or   ˈaɪðə

vase[3]   ˈvɑːz   or   ˈveɪ·z   or   ˈveɪs

◆ Throughout the textbook the following notations are used to identify the PARTS OF SPEECH, when two words spelled identically are pronounced differently:

noun (n)   verb (v)   adjective (adj)   adverb (adv)

◆ CAPITAL LETTERS may be used to note the STRESSED SYLLABLE of a word:

OBject (n)   obJECT (v)   i-<u>RR</u>Evocable

<u>R</u>Ebel (n)   <u>r</u>eBEL (v)   LAmentable

PERfuME (n)   perFUME (v)   perDIE

PERfect (adj)   perFECT (v)   chauFFEUR

Of course, capital letters are used traditionally to begin proper nouns.

◆ A brief definition or identification of a word may be provided in parentheses, especially when this will clarify the usage of a particular pronunciation. For instance, the word "bourbon" is listed in two sections of the book:

—in the $3\colon$ section: bourbon (n; a drink)

—in the $U\breve{\vartheta}$ section: Bourbon (French royal family)

◆ To help you identify the correct sounds of a particular word, phonetic letters will occasionally be found over the written word. Words that may be spoken with the vowel sound $\mathcal{a}$ are so marked, and all words with "wh" in the spelling of the word, to be spoken with $\mathcal{m}$, are indicated by circling "(wh)." It is suggested that you write phonetic letters above words as a reminder of the correct sound.

◆ Note that in Words for Practice, each line on the page is numbered, as is each pair of words, phrase or sentence in Phrases and Sentences for Practice. In the classroom this system should help the teacher and student quickly find the appropriate item for practice.

GUIDES TO PRONUNCIATION

◆ In most of the vowel and diphthong sections, there is a subsection headed "Words for Clarity of [the sound] Prior to . . ." This is one of the most important and challenging points of pronunciation to be found in *Speak with Distinction*. The need for clarity is highlighted by printing such words with a hyphen that separates the vowel sound from the consonant r:

$æ$
a-<u>r</u>id   ha-<u>rr</u>ied   a-<u>rr</u>ow   Ha-<u>rr</u>ow   a-<u>rr</u>ogant   ha-<u>r</u>icot

◆ Throughout the practice material the letter "r" in the spelling of a word is underlined to indicate that here the pronunciation is $\mathfrak{r}$, the consonant r. This occurs ONLY when the letter "r" in the spelling of a word is followed by a vowel or diphthong sound:

<u>r</u>ed   <u>rh</u>yme=<u>r</u>ime   <u>wr</u>ite=<u>r</u>ight=<u>Wr</u>ight=<u>r</u>ite   b<u>r</u>eak=b<u>r</u>ake   me-<u>rr</u>y   Ma-<u>r</u>y   ma-<u>rr</u>y

- When the letter "r" in the spelling of a word is not underlined, this indicates that the sound is one of the two vowel, five diphthong or two triphthong sounds of Spoken English. Even when spoken with r-coloring, or hard r's, the sounds still are relatively open and therefore still considered vowel and diphthong sounds, not consonant ṟ sounds:

3:	ə	ɪə̆	ɛə̆	ʊə̆	ɔə̆	ɑə̆	ɑ̆ɪə̆	ɑ̆ʊə̆
sti̱r	surpri̱se	here's	their	poor	ore	car	hire=higher	flower=flour

FOR A SUMMARY OF SPOKEN USAGE OF THE LETTER "R" IN WRITTEN ENGLISH, SEE PAGES 344-345.

- There are many sections headed "Match the . . . " that feature pairs (and occasionally trios) of words in which the vowel or diphthong sounds MUST MATCH EXACTLY. The vowel sound in the first word of the pair is the more stable of the two and is to be used as a model for the vowel sound in the second. For example, when saying "mat - man," where "man" is likely to be nasalized and "mat" is not, the two are to be spoken with the same short vowel sound:

æ	æ		æ	æ		æ	æ
mat - man			chat - channel			static - stand	

- Under the heading "Comparison of . . . " sets of words are arranged to show similarities and differences of sounds. Sometimes the words are arranged to suggest the stability of a sequence of sounds that are similar but should not be confused with one another:

tʰ	d		tʰ	d		tʰ	d
teen - dean			heating - heeding			beat - bead	

i·	ɪ	e	ɛə̆	æ	ɑ
cṟeep	cṟypt	cṟept	-----	cṟass	cṟaft

The five dashes (-----) indicate that a suitable word for use in a series of comparisons does not exist in Spoken English. For instance, no word in Spoken English contains the combination k̩rɛə̆ .

The sets also comprise words in which the sounds are often confused and must be spoken precisely to set off the contrast between them:

ʊə̆	ɔə̆		ʊə̆	ɔə̆			
poor — pour=pore			Moor — more				
θ	ð		θ	ð		θ	ð
theme — thee			ether — either[2]			teeth — teethe	

- The sets headed "Exercises for Distinguishing Between . . . " may be those in which one sound is often incorrectly substituted for another in certain American dialects or foreign accents:

ɪ	e		ɪ	e
pin - pen			Minnie - many	
ð	z		ð	z
seethe - seize			bṟeathe - bṟeeze	

♦ The consonant sections include practice material for "Comparison of . . ." two consonant sounds that are made in the same place of articulation but employ other, contrasting phonetic features:

s   and   *z*   or   *ʍ*   and   *w*

The pairs of consonant sounds are given in initial, medial and final positions of the words, with each word on a line sharing the same vowel or diphthong in its stressed syllable, the vowel or diphthong occasionally noted at the left of the line. They are to be practiced in horizontal groups and in vertical groups:

s	*z*		*s*	*z*			*s*	*z*
1a sit	- zit		1b whist	- whizzed			1c kiss	- his
2a send	- Zen		2b pressing	- president			2c "S"	- Des
3a sand	- Zan		3b passel	- Basil			3c ass	- as (sf)
4a Sioux	- zoo		4b abusive	- amusing			4c use (n)	- use (v)
5a sane	- Zane		5b Macy	- Maisie			5c pace	- pays

In using *Speak with Distinction*, it is important to consult the following frequently:
♦ Chart of IPA and Non-IPA Signs. (See pages 380-383.)
♦ Glossary of Terms. (See pages 384-398.)

◆ INFORMATION ABOUT THE VOWEL SOUNDS ◆

VOWEL SOUNDS

Openness

A vowel sound is made with an uninterrupted and unobstructed breath stream through the mouth. Since there is no stoppage or interruption of the vibrated breath for the duration of the sound, a vowel sound is often referred to as an OPEN SOUND. Vowel sounds carry the tones of a language and are to some its heart and soul.

Purity

It is of primary importance that a vowel sound be produced by a single shape of the oral passage, with no movement or change in the articulators during production. For this reason, each vowel sound is called a PURE SOUND, and the slightest movement or change in any of the organs of speech during the formation of a vowel will mar its purity, resulting in DIPHTHONGIZATION. In Good Speech, diphthongization of a pure vowel sound is to be avoided.

Placement

Making a vowel sound is not so much a matter of articulation as it is a matter of forming a single shape through which the breath can pass. For each pure vowel sound in Spoken English, the shape of the oral passage involves the arch of the tongue, the position of the lower jaw and the position of the lips.

◆ THE TIP OF THE TONGUE IS RELAXED BEHIND THE LOWER FRONT TEETH. For released vocal energy and forward placement of tone, this tip-of-the-tongue relaxation is imperative. When relaxed, the tip will touch the back of the lower front teeth.

◆ With the tip of the tongue relaxed behind the lower front teeth, the primary articulator or shaper of a vowel sound is the ARCH OF THE TONGUE. The vowel sounds are classified according to this arching:

Tongue-arch: HIGH ————————————————————————> LOW

FRONT VOWELS: The FRONT of the tongue is arched in relation to the HARD PALATE:

iː	ɪ	e	ɛ		æ	a
Lee	wɪll	let	[fair]		Pat	pass.

MID VOWELS: The MIDDLE of the tongue is arched in relation to the MIDDLE of the PALATE:

ɜː	ə	ʌ
Stir	the surprise	cup.

BACK VOWELS: The BACK of the tongue is arched in relation to the SOFT PALATE:

uː	ʊ	o	ɔː		ɒ	ɑː
Who	would	obey	all		honest	fathers?

◆ The lower jaw, WHICH SHOULD ALWAYS BE FREE OF TENSION, opens to various degrees and is instrumental in determining the acoustic quality of each vowel sound:

	iː	ɪ	uː	ʊ		
The least open vowel sounds are:	Lee	wɪll	who	would		

	æ	a	ʌ	ɒ	ɑː
The most open vowel sounds are:	Pat	pass	cut	honest	fathers

◆   The lips assume various positions that contribute to the formation of the vowel sounds:

The FRONT VOWELS require slightly spread or smiling lips, but it is important to avoid the side-to-side tension of the corners of the mouth known as LATERALIZATION;

The MID VOWELS and the BACK VOWEL sound $a:$ as in "fathers" call for relaxed or neutral lips;

The BACK VOWELS with the exception of $a:$ require rounded lips. The degree of rounding varies according to the position of the lower jaw. For instance, the relatively closed vowel sound $u:$ as in "who" demands closed lip-rounding, while the open vowel sound v as in "honest" calls for open lip-rounding.

The information on placement is summarized in the VOWEL CHART. (See page 11.)

Oral Sounds

In Good Speech, ALL vowel sounds are oral sounds, to be made with the soft palate raised. Thus the breath flows out through the mouth only, rather than through the mouth and nose.

If the soft palate is lazy, hanging down during the production of a vowel sound, the air will go out through both the mouth and nose. This is called NASALIZATION and, in well-spoken English, is to be avoided.

Voiced Sounds

In most languages, including Spoken English, ALL vowel sounds are voiced, that is, made with the vibration of the vocal folds. Of course, this is not true when you whisper.

Lengths

Vowels are classified according to their length or duration. Since a vowel sound is made by a single articulatory shape or position, in theory each and every vowel sound in every language of the world can be produced in a wide variety of lengths, ranging from a mere second to as long as the breath can last. However, in practice, the lengths of vowels—and indeed all sounds—are an intrinsic part of the sound structure of a language and the most important factor in the creation of its rhythms.

In Spoken English, FIVE vowel sounds are known as THE LONG VOWEL SOUNDS because they are found in a variety of lengths, depending upon their positions in stressed or unstressed syllables and upon the kind of sound that follows them within a word. (See page 19.)

$i:$	$3:$	$u:$	$ɔ:$	$a:$
Lee	stir	who	all	fathers

For practical purposes these five vowel sounds are classified, notated and studied in THREE LENGTHS:

	$i:$		$i•$		i
LONG	Lee	HALF-LONG	leak	SHORT	Leander

NINE vowel sounds in Spoken English are known as THE SHORT VOWEL SOUNDS because they are AL-WAYS SHORT, regardless of their phonetic environment or the degree of emphasis they receive:

I	e	$æ$	a	$ə$	$ʌ$	$ʊ$	o	v
will	let	Pat	pass	the	cup	would	obey	honest

EXCEPTION: One front vowel sound, $ɛ$, never exists as a pure vowel sound used in a word. It is found ONLY as the first element of the diphthong sound $ɛə$ as in "fair."

◆ PROGRAM FOR ELIMINATING GLOTTAL ATTACKS ◆
OF THE VOWEL SOUNDS

A glottal attack of vowel and diphthong sounds is a sudden and undesirable interruption in the flow of breath as it passes through the GLOTTIS (the space between the vocal folds) while producing a sound. It gives the sound of a "pop" in the throat, or a scratch, to the first moment of vowel production and generally gets things off to a tense, bad start. An efficient use of breath, and relaxation of the vocal mechanism—especially the throat, lower jaw and back of the tongue—are essential for eliminating glottal attacks. The following exercises provide a way of coordinating the breath and the involuntary movement of the vocal folds to achieve a smooth initiation of sound.

Use the voiceless consonant sound h (in initial position in the first two words of the sentences in the left column); relate that open feeling to the subsequent words, each of which begins with a vowel or diphthong sound. Avoid wasting air on the h sound.

1a Heathens heal each evening.

1b Evening heals each heathen.

2a His hyste-ria indicates individuality.

2b His individuality is hyste-rical!

3a Heavens! A he-ritage established Esther.

3b Establish a he-ritage for Esther.

4a Hannah happily advertised apples.

4b "Happy apples," advertised Hannah.

5a Half-built hasps are the answer.

5b The answer's a hasp.

6a Herb hurled earth and herbs.

6b Earl hurled herbs into the earth.

7a Hush, Hulce! Who's under us?

7b Hulce, with the ulcer, hushed us.

8a Hawes halted awful authors.

8b Did the authors halt awful Hawes?

9a Minnehaha said, "Ah! Amish almonds!"

9b Aha! Halle's a-ria is in Afrikaans.

10a Hail Hazel's ailing age.

10b Hail ailing Hazel's age.

11a High time to hire I-ra.

11b Hire I-ra. It's high time.

12a Ahoy! Oysters in oil.

12b Hoyle's oysters are in Hoyt's oil.

13a Hold holy old olios.

13b Only hold olios holy.

14a Hounds howl at our owls.

14b Howling owls are in our house.

15a Here! Here are earmarked ea-rrings.

15b Here's an e-ra of earmarked ea-rrings.

16a Ha-rem hair is aired, A-ryan.

16b The ha-rem airs heirlooms.

17a Horgon's horn had ornate ornaments.

17b Hortense ordered Horton an oar.

18a Hardly a heart-felt artifice, Arnie!

18b Arnie's heart-felt artifice was hearty.

Think the initial vowel sound as you inhale through the position for that sound. Feel the coolness of the air as you inhale, and sense the LIFTING OF YOUR SOFT PALATE. Allow the inhalation to flow into the exhalation. Take care that there is no break, catch, tension, or waste of breath in the transition to exhalation, and produce the initial vowel sound on the exhalation. Repeat the inhalation process and produce the corresponding phrase on the exhalation.

✓ *Reminder*

> **The concept of inhaling through the vowel position is useful for learning to produce vowels and diphthongs without a glottal attack, but should be employed only in the following practice material and not developed as an habitual way of breathing.**

1	i	easily even "ee's"	12	ʊ	honŏ-rable occupations
2	ɪ	it's Isabel's imitation	13	ɑ	Allah's a-ria
3	e	evidently envious	14	eɪ	alienate Amy
4	æ	amateur anchorman	15	aɪ	ideal ideas
5	ɑ	afternoon answer	16	ɔɪ	oily ointments
6	ɜ	earthly urchins	17	oʊ	open only
7	ə	abandoned accounts	18	aʊ	outcast owls
8	ʌ	understated uttĕ-rance	19	ɪə	ee-rie e-ra
9	u	oozing Oolong	20	ɛə	air heirlooms
10	o	O'Neill's ovation	21	ɔə	orderly oarsman
11	ɔ	always awesome	22	ɑə	ardent a-rias

Each of the following sentences contains at least one word that begins with the consonant *h* . Notice the places where a consonant from the end of a word may be lightly linked to the initial vowel of the next word and notice the places where the link is from a vowel sound to a vowel sound.

23 i   Oh, Eaton! He'd even heave eels for Edith Healy!

24 ɪ   My intuition says his incision is itchy.

25 e   Hey, Emma! Help Ellen to head Edward to Ellis Island.

26 æ   Why Andy, Ha-rry and Alice have had adequate HA-rassment!

27 ɑ   Oh, Auntie half-answered after all.

28 ɜ   I'd say Ernestine hurt Irv and irked Ernie.

29 ʌ   The usher uttered, "Otherwise, get up!"

30 u   Who'd "oooh and ah" and who'd hoot?

31 ɔ   Hawn's awning needs altĕ-rations. It's really awful.

32 ʊ   Obviously, honor obligations HOspitably. I'll try, honestly!

33 eɪ   Hey, Amy. Hale's ailments amaze me!

ELIMINATING GLOTTAL ATTACKS, Cont.

1 ăĭ Hi! I'd like a Heineken over ice, Hypatia.

2 ɔĭ Hoity-toity oil-men cried "Hoicks ahoy."

3 oŭ Hold the hokum with Annie Oakley, O.K.?

4 aŭ How outrageous are our hours?

5 ɪə̆ My ea-rring hurts my hea-ring.

6 ɛə̆ Tell that hei-ress to dry her hair in the air.

7 ɔə̆ Don't horde ordina-ry oars, Orville.

8 aə̆ Arvin was ardent about an arbor near the harbor.

Each of the following sentences begins with a vowel sound in initial position. THINK the vowel sound as you inhale. SPEAK the initial word on the exhalation without a glottal attack and without any waste of breath.

9 i Each evening, Eve eats eels in East Eden.

10 ɪ Individuality is an electrify-ing issue.

11 e Every excellent effort ends with egg on my elbow.

12 æ Ann's anxious to advertise the angry ancho-rite.

13 a Ask Aunt Aftra to answer.

14 ɜ Irv urged her to buy urban herbs.

15 ʌ Up, up and away. Uncle Uxbridge undulated toward Ulster.

16 u Oolong is oozing out of the umiak?

17 ʊ O'Connell omitted potatoes au gratin.

18 ɔ Augustine will alternate with all the aldermen in Albany.

19 ɒ Honestly. This optical ope-ration is obsolete.

20 ɑ Alms for Allah, the atman and Ali.

21 eĭ Abe and Aisne aimed for A's.

22 aĭ Ida idolized Ike's ideas for the icons.

23 ɔĭ Ointment made from oyster oil annoys me.

24 oŭ Oh, did that old ogre just open his Oldsmobile?

25 aŭ Owls are out-and-out outsiders.

26 ɛə̆ Aa-ron, give that Airedale from Ayre some air!

27 ɔə̆ Order in the court! Order in the court!

28 aə̆ Arthur argued with the architect and the artist.

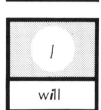

Lee

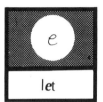

will

The FRONT VOWELS are those vowel sounds in which the FRONT of your tongue is arched in relation to the hard palate. For each of the front vowel sounds your lips are slightly spread, in the feeling of a smile.

let

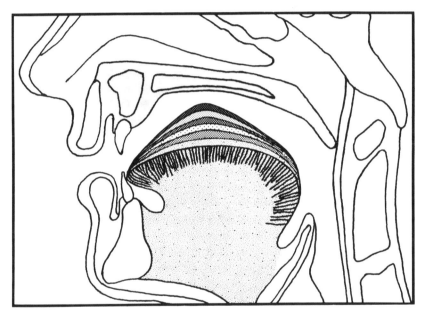

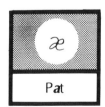

fair*

◆ Your Lower Jaw is Relaxed

◆ Tip of your Tongue Touches Lower Teeth

◆ Soft Palate is Raised

◆ The Sounds are Voiced

Pat

pass.

* In Spoken English, this vowel sound, slightly lower in tongue arch than e , is never used by itself as a pure vowel in a word. It is found only as the first element of the diphthong sound:

◆ THE VOWEL SOUND i: AS IN "Lee" ◆

Represented by the spellings:

we	see	dece*i*ve	sp*ea*k	p*eo*ple	k*ey*=q*uay*
mach*i*ne	f*ie*ld	C*ae*sar	ph*oe*nix	debr*is*	

This sound is the highest FRONT VOWEL SOUND in Spoken English.

✓ *Reminder*

Height refers to the arch of the tongue.

Relax your lower jaw and allow the tip of your tongue to rest behind your lower front teeth. Arch the FRONT of your tongue high toward your hard palate until the front is almost touching the gum ridge. Allow your lips to spread SLIGHTLY in the feeling of a smile, while avoiding lateralization, or excessive side-to-side tension at the corners of your mouth.

A clean, forward, brilliant quality characterizes this sound.

WORDS FOR PRACTICE USING i: LONG

◆ In a STRESSED SYLLABLE when the vowel is the last sound of a word

◆ In a STRESSED SYLLABLE when the vowel is followed by one or more voiced consonants

1 "E" he (sf) pea bea=Bea tea=tee perDIE key=quay ski knee Lee=lea=Leigh alee
2 Galilee plea glee flee=flea fee see=sea emcee garnishee Ma-rie debris tree Cree
3 agree free three STRONG FORMS (sf) of: he she me we thee be

4 Eby Ebro Hebrew ebriate plebe glebe Phoebe Thebes Theban Sheba

5 Edith heeded Eden hedonist Oedipus impedes bead deeds keyed skied mead=Mede
6 medium Nedar leader plead bleed feed seed cedar succeeded read=reed=rede greedy

7 eagle eager Aegle beagles Deegan league legal illegal regal Regan

8 Eames he-man beam team=teem steam esteem deem redeems Nimes gleams femur
9 theme seam=seem regime reams bream extreme dreams cream screams Gremio

10 e'en Heanor penal bean pristine dean keen mean demeanor leaned fiends convene
11 Venus seen obscene sheen se-rene preens green wean queen Eugene Agenor

12 eel heal=heel=he'll (sf) peal=peel steal=steel ordeals keels meal kneel
13 unaneled=unannealed feel reveal sealed shield reels wheel wield squeal congeal
14 Ealing healing Ely Healey appealing mealy Ophelia revealing ceiling Sheila freely

15 Eve heave peeve thieves weave sheaves leave grieve believes receives cleaves

16 seethe sheathe teethe either² wreathe breathes heathen bequeath

17 ease he's (sf) pease appease bees wheeze teased knees fleas seizes Jesus Jesu

18 prestige leisure² seizure lesion freesia anaesthesia Artesian Tunisia

19 aegis liege legion allegiance Fiji siege Regis regent region egregious ouija

WORDS FOR PRACTICE USING /ˑ HALF-LONG

◆ In a STRESSED SYLLABLE when the vowel is followed by one or more voiceless consonants
◆ In a STRESSED SYLLABLE when the vowel is followed by another vowel sound within the same word

1 peep weep deep seeps heaped sheep reap keep creeped people clepe steep

2 eat heat peat=Pete beat=beet teat petite Keaton meat=meet=mete neat liter feat=feet
3 fetus Thetis seat sheet sweet=suite wheat cheat discreet completely quietus

4 eke peak=peek beak beaker teak antique meek unique leak=leek fecal seek physique
5 chic reek=wreak freakish Eu-reka Costa Rica creak=creek speak cheek

6 beef motif apé-ritif leaf=lief belief relief beliefs fief thief sheaf Moncrieff

7 ether heath teeth Menteith Keith 'neath beneath lethal Lethe sheath wreath

8 Easter Hesiod east peace=piece obese Matisse decent geese niece lease police
9 feast thesis Theseus cease Rhys recent grease=Greece greasy inCREASE (v) priest

10 leash appreciate quiche hashish pastiche Tahitian nouveau riche Grecian completion

11 each peach beach=beech teach Nietzsche leach=leech bleach feature reach reechy

12 be-ing tee-ing see-ing free-ing agree-ing flee-ing ski-ing gua-ran-tee-ing

13 eon=aeon paean=peon Fleance Kō-rea Medea Egeus Aegean Creon Freon brio preamble

WORDS FOR PRACTICE USING /i SHORT

◆ In all UNstressed SYLLABLES, including WEAK FORMS of words (See pages 21-25.)

14 meander Leander methinks Aegean Egeus INcrease (n)

15 WEAK FORMS (wf) of: he she me we thee be

PHRASES FOR PRACTICE

Long /iː	Half-Long /iˑ	Mixed Lengths
16 ʔ eager eels and eagles	25 ʔ Easter ether	34 ʔ eat eels
17 Caesar's seizures	26 people's peepholes	35 chiefs achieve
18 repeal Dee's deals	27 discreet cheating	36 feeling piqued
19 Eden's easier edicts	28 neat geese teeth	37 appealing thief
20 green fields	29 flee-ing sheep	38 beastly bees
21 feel free on the sea	30 be-ing sleepy	39 breathe deeply
22 dream of a beam	31 sleek physique	40 Leander's secret seas
23 easy Eve is relieved	32 release the chief	41 be-ing mean
24 the se-rene team grieves	33 heated quiche	42 breathe to speak

SENTENCES FOR PRACTICE

Long i:

1 I dreamed of green fields.
2 You'll feel free on the sea.
3 We're dreaming of clean streams.
4 Legions of bees laid siege to the trees.

5 The machine's fatigued wheels squealed.
6 Even eagles teethe on weeds, my liege.
7 They received meals of veal and eel.
8 Their cuisine leans toward green beans.

9 How do you feel, Mr. O'Neill?
10 He revealed a good deal of zeal.
11 The seal kneeled before the eels.
12 Reams and reams have been seen on that theme.
13 Ma-rina's teal blue tu-reen ca-reened.
14 The old meany screamed, "It's me!"
15 These steaming machines are the Queen's.
16 See the quay along the freezing sea?

Half-Long i·

17 The flee-ing sheep are leaping.
18 Be-ing sleepy causes heaps of grief.
19 Each Easter they eat pizza.
20 Each wreath reeks of grease.
21 Release the teeth when free-ing the jaw.

22 Her sleek physique's quite agreeable.
23 I'm eating wheat and cheap beef.
24 Creon reached the creeping priest.
25 Stop agree-ing with that human be-ing!
26 The peak creaked as Pete was ski-ing.

Mixed Lengths

27 ? Each Easter edict eased the eager Easterners' grief.
28 ? Edith and Edie and even Eva eagerly retreated to East Eden.
29 ? Eating eels on Easter depleted Esau's egotism.
30 ? Ethan's Eate-ry at Avenue E and East Street is extremely neat.
31 We'll meander through the green fields before we meet on the mead.
32 Oedipus, Aeschylus, Aesop, and Caesar seized the street.
33 Ski-ing seemed to heal Regan's weak knees. It redeemed her physique.
34 I don't appreciate a sweet apé-ritif. Vino for me!

◆ THE VOWEL SOUND | AS IN "will" ◆

Represented by the spellings:

*i*n myth bu*i*ld b*u*sy nak*e*d *i*mage w*o*men

capt*ai*n dais*ie*s br*ee*ch*e*s b*e*cause Chels*ea*

Relax your lower jaw and rest the tip of your tongue behind your lower front teeth. Arch the FRONT of your tongue high toward your hard palate, almost in the same position as for *i:* . Allow your lips to spread SLIGHTLY in the feeling of a smile, while avoiding lateralization.

Because of its brilliance, this bright, crisp vowel has been called "the diamond of good speech." Let the clean, simple line of the phonetic letter itself be a reminder of that quality.

The vowel sound | is used

◆ as a single vowel sound in stressed syllables of words

◆ frequently in weak syllables of prefixes and suffixes

◆ as the second element of the diphthongs *eĭ· aĭ· ɔĭ·* (See pages 140-155.)

◆ as the first element of the falling diphthong *ɪə̃* (See pages 169-170.)

◆ as the first element of the rising diphthong *ĭə* (See pages 189-190.)

WORDS FOR PRACTICE USING |

1 Ipswich hips pip tip dip nip lip Philip=fillip sip zip ship r̲ip trip (wh)ip clip

2 Ibsen Hibbert bib Biblical Tybalt dibble nib libe-r̲ate glib fib Sybil r̲ib cr̲ib

3 it hit pit bit titter ditty kit mit knit lit little fit vitr̲iolic sit (wh)it
4 wit chit jitney cr̲itic pr̲etty Br̲itish flit fr̲itter slit grit Sanskr̲it

5 id hid idiot hideous bid did kid Gideon middle amid amidst lid Sid r̲id grid
6 widow Yiddish chid skid Madr̲id pý-r̲amid video

7 Ichabod hick pick tickle Dick Dixon kick Michaelmas knickers lick slick garlic
8 fix vixen thick sick Chiswick Urswick R̲ick Wa-̃rwick wick quick chick tr̲ick

9 igloo higgle igno-r̲ant Higgins pig big Antigonus dig niggardly fig r̲ig (Wh)ig wig

10 image him=hymn Pim=Pym Tim dim Nym limb vim Sims r̲im (wh)im Jim=gym
11 br̲im gr̲im swim scr̲im scr̲immage thimble nimble limber

12 in=inn India hinder pinned bin=been tin din kin Lynn Linda fin thin sin shin
13 win chin gin pr̲ince tint mince Vince convince Gwyn hé-r̲oine genuine mountain

14 England Hingle ink Hinckley Bing tingle sting king kink Ming cling thing nothing
15 anything something sing single sink shingle r̲ing=wr̲ing r̲ink br̲ing spr̲ing str̲ing
16 cooking be-ing mã-r̲ry-ing pu-r̲ring do-ing dr̲aw-ing stay-ing dy-ing enjoy-ing go-ing

17 ill hill ilk hilt pill bill till='til until still dill kill skill Gil mill nil
18 Lil fill=Phil sill shill r̲ill will chill Jill billion million vermillion br̲illiant
19 Iliad hilly pillage Billy utility Dylan=Dillon lilly villain village silly willing

20 if Biff tiff differ̲ent miffed nifty lift sift shift r̲ift (wh)iff cliff gryphon

WORDS FOR PRACTICE USING ɪ , Cont.

1 bivouac Tivoli dividend divot give live olive livid vivid sieve chivalry trivial

2 ɪθ Ithaca pith pithy Me-redith kith myth monolith sith moveth Asquith sixtieth

3 ɪð (wh)ther wither zither thither slither with withal within without stithy smithy

4 isthmus hiss Istanbul histo-ry biscuit Dis kiss miss goodness lissome bliss this
5 edifice sister cyst insist wrist (wh)st wist gist Christmas frisked tryst

6 is his Islam Israel isn't Islington busy 'tis dizzy mizzen Liz fizz visible
7 visage Thisbe risen frizz (wh)z wizard Wiz always vizard

8 issue apish bishop Tisch dish Gish mission ignition fish fission official
9 vicious musician Mau-ritius wish magician swish knish banish Turkish fetish relish

10 vision precision de-rision elision decision incision Trigère

11 itch hitch pitch capitulate bitch habitual ditch niche Greenwich Litchfield
12 Fitch fichew situation rich (wh)ch witch Chichester stitch twitch Ipswich breeches

13 pigeon midge image fidget vigilant deciduous ridge widgeon luggage rummage college

WORDS FOR CLARITY OF ɪ PRIOR TO r

✓ *Reminder* ───────────────────────────────────────

> **Make a clearly defined ɪ sound and begin the following syllable with a clean-cut consonant r . In doing so, you will avoid marring the clarity of the ɪ sound with r-coloring.**

14 i-rascible i-rritate i-rrational i-rregular I-roquois i-rrelevant e-rase e-ruption
15 I-ran i-RREpa-rable E-ros i-RREvocable e-rosion pi-ranha Py-rrhus Py-rrhic py-ramid
16 pe-riod impe-rious pi-rouette empi-rical Pi-randello Hype-rion Hispe-ria be-reaved
17 be-reft be-rate Be-rowne ty-ranny Ty-rrel ty-rannical sati-ric mate-rial wiste-ria
18 di-rect de-rive de-rision di-rigible mi-racle mi-rage mi-rror ly-ric ly-rical li-ra
19 vi-rago vi-rile gi-raffe se-rene si-rrah sy-rup Sy-ria he-roic he-redita-ry spi-rit
20 sti-rrup

WORDS FOR PRACTICE USING ɪŋ

DO NOT TENSE AND NASALIZE ɪ IN ɪŋ ENDINGS; DO NOT SUBSTITUTE ĩŋ OR ĩn :

21 Ming dreaming gleaming beaming scheming seeming teeming trimming stemming slamming
22 squirming firming worming humming drumming coming dooming booming fuming bombing
23 calming embalming aiming taming naming timing miming climbing homing roaming

24 meaning leaning weaning cleaning preening sinning winning hemming tanning manning
25 turning burning earning cunning running stunning mooning dawning fawning donning
26 raining remaining gaining pining dining mining joining owning moaning Downing
27 crowning drowning warning ironing

28 ɪɪŋ cá-rry-ing má-rry-ing ra-lly-ing ta-lly-ing (wh)-nny-ing pi-ty-ing rea-dy-ing
29 ⌣ pá-rry-ing hû-rry-ing scú-rry-ing dir-ty-ing

MATCH THE VOWEL SOUND / IN EACH OF THESE SETS

DO NOT PINCH AND NASALIZE / BEFORE η :

1 ick	— England	— ink	9 fix	— finger	— fink
2 pick	— ping	— pink	10 thick	— thing	— think
3 Bic	— Bing	— Binkley	11 sick	— sing	— sink
4 tick	— tingle	— tinker	12 Rick	— ring	— rink
5 Dixon	— dingle	— dinky	13 wick	— wing	— wink
6 kick	— king	— kink	14 jig	— jingle	— jinx
7 Mick	— Ming	— mink	15 click	— cling	— clink
8 lick	— linger	— link	16 brick	— bring	— brink

PHRASES FOR PRACTICE USING /

17 ʔ it's icky, it's itchy
18 ʔ illegal and illegitimate illusions
19 ʔ i-RREvocable e-ruptions in I-ran
20 lingered in England
21 delicious chocolate chip dip
22 itchy damaged skin

23 ʔ indispensable individuals
24 ʔ intensely i-rrational
25 ʔ Ithaca's English inn
26 Turkish luggage bills
27 chilled garlic aspic
28 pick (which) sacrilege you wish

SENTENCES FOR PRACTICE USING /

29 ʔ I-rregular instances of i-rrational i-rritations e-rupted in Ipswich.
30 ʔ Imagine thick ink in England.
31 ʔ Incidentally, Inga invited intimacy.
32 Phil Killian's interested in mythology.   ˈɪn tᵊrɪstᵻd
33 A pill for the ill will fill the bill.
34 Brilliant Italian William will kill for dill.
35 Tim gives tin kings to indigent children.
36 Give a little bit, Mr. Biddle!
37 It's been a bit dim in the garbage bin.
38 Let's have Sunday school on Monday.
39 Jimmy lived with vim and vigor.
40 Behold the po-et's imagery in this po-em.
41 Lily's ability to sing in English is pitiful, unfortunately.
42 Stop pi-ty-ing him. He's ma-rry-ing English nobility.
43 There's sy-rup on my sti-rrup, si-rrah.   ˈsɪrə
44 We're in dim spi-rits, Mi-rabel.
45 "Pick pink," said the ubiquitous Binkley.
46 Rick will ring the rink in a wink.
47 I'm thinking of bringing the psychic king.
48 Mr. Minny hid mints from Ms. Ginny.
49 Lynn's twin, Lydia, indicated a bit of lecithin for her sister's skin.
50 An individual's id informs intimacy.

SENTENCES FOR PRACTICE USING *I* , Cont.

1 INcreased bits of lint in the print indicated gritty recriminations.
2 Simply sitting and tippling gin is imminent for him.
3 Lincoln's grin is impish.
4 Sid's sinfully wicked if he's had a hit of gin.
5 Minnie invoked a hymn to industry.
6 Did the din limit the winning a bit?

The vowel sound *I* is used in the following UNstressed prefixes and suffixes.

Use *I* in the unstressed syllable of the word "believe." *bɪ'li:v*

◆ DO NOT use the sloppy, careless "buh-" *bə -*
◆ DO NOT use the pedantic, affected "bee-" *bi -*
◆ DO NOT use a spelling pronunciation "beh-" *be -*

PREFIXES USING *I*

7 imagine enough illegal epistle ebullience embalm embark emerge eternal emote
I — 8 emba-rrass embitter emotion employ illicit illite-rate elect y-clept Yvonne
9 engaged envision invade indeed enliven ensnare endeavor invite entice

Ir- 10 I-ran e-radicate e-rase e-rode i-rrational e-rotic i-RREvocable e-rect I-raq

Ik,s- 11 expand expense expect expenditure expe-rience explicit explode exceed excel

Igz- 12 exact exagge-rate examine example executive exhaust exist exult exotic

bɪ- 13 beloved between believe before begin behave behold behind belief belong
14 because beware beyond bewitch be-reft be-rate be-reaved Be-rowne

dɪ - 15 debate decay deceive deny deceased diseased decide decline deCREASE (v) decry
16 defeat defend delicious delight deliver denote di-rect de-ride de-ranged

sɪ - 17 severe seCREtive[2] seclude secu-rity sedition seduction se-rene si-rocco

rɪ - 18 retire return receive receipt reception recite reduce recover remain reform
19 rehearse release relieve remark remember replace Republic Rinaldo rebellious

prɪ,prɪ- 20 preclude prescription prescribed predict precede prefer precursor pre-rogative

SUFFIXES AND WORD ENDINGS USING *I*

21 happy choppy chirpy soapy harpy giddy shoddy baby maybe hobby city pretty
- I 22 piety ability poetry indivisibility possibility safety velocity timidity unity
23 dignity eternity hockey piggy soggy coffee savvy navvy navy pithy swarthy
24 missy messy Percy Battersea racy Chelsea easy daisy reechy edgy clergy

-mɪ 25 enemy balmy seamy dreamy shimmy Jimmy Miami mommy gloomy roomy Tommy
26 economy infamy sesame hammy chamois Hermy squirmy

SUFFIXES AND WORD ENDINGS USING I , Cont.

-nɪ
1 any Henny penny many ty-ranny destiny company money honey sunny harmony
2 mutiny calumny Danny gluttony bonny cranny symphony cacophony phony larceny

-lɪ
3 steely Billy silly hilly angrily fa-mi-ly readily really belly tally rally
4 early Burleigh=burly sully duly holly Raleigh daily smiley goalie surely

-rɪ
5 ee-rie=Erie dea-rie tea-ry ve-ry me-rry Ma-ry ma-rry Ha-rry fu-rry
6 cu-rry hu-rry glo-ry so-rry sa-ri dow-ry chee-ry fai-ry hoa-ry sta-rry

-ɪd
7 faded hated blessed (adj) contented crooked crowded hundred limited ma-rried
8 naked parted ragged spi-rited interested

NOTE: In verse, when an "-ed" ending is meant to have a beat of its own in the rhythm of a line, this syllable is pronounced (as with other "-ed" endings) as - ɪd . DO NOT pronounce such endings -ed :

Hence banished is banish'd from the world , (*Romeo and Juliet*, III.iii.19)

My best beloved and approved friend, (*The Taming of the Shrew*, I.ii.3)

-ɪtʰ
9 limit basket ba-ronet bonnet bracket ticket bullet cabinet carpet sherbet
10 closet posit deposit po-et market scarlet Hamlet credit inhe-rit me-rit
11 private immediate alternate (n; adj) affectionate effeminate elabo-rate (adj)
12 fortunate agate conglome-rate (n; adj) pi-rate lite-rate

-ɪstʰ
13 cheapest coldest busiest darkest deepest earnest=Ernest nea-rest dea-rest

-lɪs
14 careless breathless blameless reckless endless lawless spotless Arliss Alice

-nɪs
15 goodness baldness brightness bitterness blackness boldness highness anise
16 fearlessness carelessness loneliness
17 NOTE ALSO: empress princess goddess hostess

-ɪm
18 passim maxim Pilgrim victim po-em verbatim goyim homonym

-ɪn
19 Latin Martin linen women satin coffin Helen mountain captain villain
20 fountain Chamberlain chaplain=Chaplin Athens o-rigin Brooklyn fo-reign E-rin

-ɪŋ
21 skipping webbing leaving teething buzzing hitting running ringing

-ɪv
22 motive captive creative missive decisive explosive exclusive positive negative

-ɪθ
23 Edith monolith Me-redith fiftieth sixtieth lieth moveth proveth sta-reth

-sɪz
24 creases ceases misses blesses glasses purses fusses paces prices voices
-zɪz
25 breezes diseases oozes pauses phases prizes Moses roses houses rouses
-ɪz
26 ma-rriages images cities pities abilities fa-mi-lies harmonies enemies va-ries

-ɪdʒ
27 image pri-vi-lege college baggage manage cleavage ravage savage pillage
28 average beverage leve-rage cou-rage ma-rriage ca-rriage dispa-rage po-rridge

COMPARE THE USE OF / IN UNSTRESSED SYLLABLES WITH ɛ IN STRESSED SYLLABLES:

UNstressed	Stressed	
1 SUBject (n)	subJECT (v)	Please don't subJECT me to a new SUBject.
2 PROject (n)	proJECT (v)	Try to proJECT all the way to the housing PROject.
3 OBject (n)	obJECT (v)	I obJECT to be-ing treated as a sex OBject.
4 PERfect (adj)	perFECT (v)	You've managed to perFECT this. It's PERfect!

Note that the "-day" endings of the days of the week have two acceptable pronunciations:

"Monday" may be pronounced ˈmʌndɪ or ˈmʌndeɪ
The first is preferable.

Tuesday ˈtjuːzdɪ   Wednesday ˈwɛnzdɪ   Thursday ˈθɜːzdɪ

Friday ˈfraɪdɪ   Saturday ˈsætədɪ   Sunday ˈsʌndɪ

PHRASES FOR PRACTICE USING / PREFIXES AND SUFFIXES

5 ʔ image of anxiety
6 ʔ embittered emotions emerged
7 selfishness and carelessness
8 college pri-vi-le-ges
9 eternally happy
10 behold the eternal
11 an i-RREvocable remark
12 exagge-rated ability
13 because of necessity
14 images of diseases
15 between receptions
16 interesting endeavors
17 Lily's creative ability
18 hila-rious he-roics
19 e-rase ty-ranny

20 ʔ imagine enough interest   ˈɪntₗrɪstʰ
21 ʔ exhausting existing exams
22 severe coldness
23 largest spinet
24 debate the possibilities
25 limited tickets
26 intelligible Philip
27 develop expe-rience
28 enchanted fo-rest
29 positive knowledge
30 any money for honey
31 possibly Monday and Tuesday
32 English singing
33 a gloomy enemy
34 Thursday's the twentieth

SENTENCES FOR PRACTICE USING / PREFIXES AND SUFFIXES

35 ʔ Illicit individuals imagined an illegal examination of existing expenditures.
36 ʔ The i-rregula-rity of the ensuing endeavors seemed inevitable.
37 ʔ Incidentally, illegal epistles emba-rrass individual employees.
38 ʔ Imagine! Eternal evasion of emotion!
39 ʔ It's illegal to embalm employers.
40 ʔ Eleven illite-rate Episcopalians enlisted.
41 I believe in eternity.
42 She began to behave believably.
43 Behind every beginner is belief.
44 Between receptions, we debated defense.
45 Before we rehearse, let's review page eleven.
46 Elaine expe-rienced severe depression.

SENTENCES FOR PRACTICE USING / **PREFIXES AND SUFFIXES, Cont.**

1 Electric lights illuminated the exposure.
2 "Despair and die," declared Delilah.
3 I can't deny it was delicious.
4 Which design do you desire?
5 Remember the Republican press releases?
6 Expand the executive suite, for example.
7 Exactly! Examine the entire estate.
8 The mutiny on the *Bounty* was an extremely explosive situation.
9 They prefer to predict rather than prescribe.
10 The pretender prefers his own prescription. It's his pre-rogative.
11 How ve-ry seCREtive of you, Cecile!   ʃɪ 'k͵rɪ· t̂ɪʋ
12 This city is empty on Sundays.
13 I'm skipping the party on Saturday, honey.
14 Is the symphony play-ing on Tuesday?
15 Surely Lilly was me-rry.
16 Really, what a pity!   'rɪɜ lɪ
17 The wicked witness interested me.
18 What an interesting rate of interest.   'ɪnt͵rɪʌt̂ʰ
19 Don't be silly; it's my responsibilty.
20 He did his duty with dignity.
21 Many many bears need honey, including Winnie.
22 Tommy, we're nearly to the enemy.
23 The gloomy economy left Sammy clammy.
24 Ty-ranny led to mutiny.
25 It's my destiny to be sunny.
26 He ma-rried Bunny for her money.
27 Do you have any money, honey?
28 The harmony enchanted the nobility.
29 He enlisted with studied dignity.
30 It's not just whimsy, it's necessity.
31 We pitied the ma-rried ba-ronet.   'bærə nɪt̂ʰ
32 Hamlet, are you seCREting away a SEcret?   ʃɪ 'k͵rɪ· t̂ɪŋ
33 A deposit, was it?
34 It's mere carelessness, Your Highness.
35 Goodness, but they like kindness.
36 His darkest fears were endless.
37 The eldest sister was the dea-rest.
38 Show it to the po-et.
39 The enemies sing harmonies breathlessly.
40 The fo-reign captain hails from Athens.
41 Cou-rage! Ma-rriage will bring knowledge.
42 This city is filled with ghastly, beastly diseases.
43 The festivities featured two divinities.

◆ THE VOWEL SOUND e AS IN "let" ◆

Represented by the spellings:

led=lead   dead   leopard   heifer   bury=berry

guest   said   any   Thames (English river)

Relax your lower jaw and allow the tip of your tongue to relax behind your lower front teeth. Arch the FRONT of your tongue half-high, just slightly lower than for i: and I . Your lips are VERY SLIGHTLY smiling, in an almost neutral position.

Because of its clarity and bright, forward placement, this crisp ALWAYS SHORT vowel has been called "the emerald of good speech." By keeping the arch of your tongue high and forward, you can avoid the lax, dull placement known as "fallen arches of the tongue."

WORDS FOR PRACTICE USING e

1 Epps hep epsilon heptagon Epworth Hepworth epilogue epic epoch pep tepid
2 step=steppe kept leper leopard leapt slept y-clept=y-cleped septic shepherd
3 repertó-ry strep prep threepence³ threepenny³ weapon jeopardy

4 ebb ebony Hebrides Eben=ebon hebanon deb Lebanon Februa-ry REbel (n) web

5 et Hetty etiquette heté-rodox Etna hetman pet bet septet debt kettle get met
6 metal=mettle net let fetid veté-ran set brochette courgette rheto-ric ba-rette
7 whet wet yet Chet jet

8 Ed head Edgar headgear pedant bed Ted dead medal=meddle Ned led=lead bled
9 fled fed feoda-ry said shed red wed

10 "X" hex excellent hexagon echo Hector exit² hectic Eccles heckles execrable
11 peck beckon Aztec textile deck gecko heck lexicon feckless perFECT (v) vex sects
12 sex wrecks=Rex check=Czech reJECT (v) obJECT (v) subJECT (v)

13 egg Hegg exaltation Hegarty peg beg beggar integrity degradation keg Meg
14 negligent leg segment regular

15 Emma hem empathy hemp embassy Hemingway temper Thames condemn memo-ry
16 nemesis lemon alembic phlegm feminine them (sf) semblance resemble remedy
17 Wembley gem stem

18 end hen ensign Henson ENtrance (n) pen bend ten den Kent again men many
19 commend lends Leonard cleanse cleanly defend venture then thence sends sense
20 scents=cents transcends rend when Wednesday yen gently agenda

21 Engels penguin Stengel dengue length strength

22 ell hell compel bel reBEL (v) tell dell Miguel Mel knell=Nell fell velvet
23 cell=sell gazelle shell mo-rel overwhelm well quell yell gel
24 Ellen Helen Ellis hellish elephant Hellenist pellet belly telegram delicate Kelly
25 mellow fellow cellar=seller zealot relish Wellington yellow cello jealous

26 effort heifer deaf definite Neff left cleft enfeoffed theft Cephalus zephyr
27 be-reft heft weft Jeffrey=Geoffrey

WORDS FOR PRACTICE USING *e* , Cont.

1 Evan heaven ever heavy Evelyn bevy beverage devil Devon ,endeavor Kevin never

2 Neville leaven eleven levé-rage seven sever chevron revel i-RREvocable revolution

3 Ethel=ethyl Heth ethics ethnic Macbeth death method lethargy Seth=saith breath

4 heather Heatherton tether leather nether feather brethren (whether weather

5 Esther Hester pessimist best bestial test destitute desecrate guess mess Nestor

6 celestial Lester=Leicester blessed confess vessel thespian assess zest rest

7 behest west quest yes chess jest=gest suggest

8 Ezra hesitate peasant embezzle desert (n) lesbian fez Bethesda says resonate

9 present (n) presentation resident president

10 Esham Hessian Bangladesh mesh confession cession=session concession procession

11 creche impression fresh Cheshire

12 cortege measure leisure² pleasure treasure Brezhnev Jesuit

13 etch Hetch petulant tetchy=techy ketch sketch lecher leche-ry fetch vetch

14 retch=wretch treaché-ry stretch

15 edge hedge schedule ledge pledge vegetable sedge register regicide dredge wedge

WORDS FOR CLARITY OF *e* PRIOR TO ɾ

✓ *Reminder* ————————————————————————————————————

> Make a clearly defined *e* sound and begin the following syllable with a clean-cut consonant ɾ . In doing so, you will avoid marring the clarity of the *e* sound with r-coloring.

16 E-ric He-rrick e-rror He-rod e-rrant he-rring E-rebus he-retic e-remite he-ritage

17 e-rudite² Pe-rry pe-ril pe-rish be-rry=bu-ry Be-ring Be-resford Te-rence te-rror

18 te-rro-rize te-rrible te-rrify te-rrier te-rrapin te-rrace te-rrito-ry te-rrito-rial

19 De-rry de-relict de-rrick=De-rek de-rogate de-rring-do de-rivation Ke-rry ke-rosene

20 ke-ratin me-rry me-rrier me-rriment me-rit Ame-rica Me-rriam Me-rrill gene-ric

21 cele-rity fe-rry fe-rret Fe-rris fe-rrous fe-reto-ry fe-rrate fe-rric ve-ry

22 ve-rily ve-rify ve-ritable se-rry ce-remony se-raph se-renade CE-rebral she-rry

23 She-ridan Che-ryl he-roine=he-roin he-roism he-rald He-reford he-resy (whe-rry

24 che-rry che-rish che-rub Je-rry Ge-rald Ge-raldine ge-rund Hespe-rides Spe-rry

25 prospe-rity ste-rile auste-rity ste-reo hyste-ric sphe-rical the-rapy

e

MATCH THE *e* SOUNDS IN THE FOLLOWING PAIRS OF WORDS:

1 stretch — strength	8 "X" — eggs	15 inEXpiable — inEXplicable
2 elect — length	9 Beck — beg	16 REquisite — EXquisite
3 peck — penguin	10 peck — peg	17 DEstiny — DEspicable
4 echo — Engels	11 elect — leg	18 mess — measure
5 plenty — twenty	12 Becker — beggar	19 tread — treasure
6 conSENT — abSENT (v)	13 set — get	20 ledge — leisure[2]
7 relent — freQUENT (v)	14 said — saith=Seth	21 pledge — pleasure

PHRASES FOR PRACTICE USING *e*

22 ʔ Epworth and Edward etched
23 ʔ excellent Ethel and Emma
24 ʔ Esther ended every echo
25 many me-rry me-rits
26 bu-ry the be-rries
27 se-renade She-ridan's he-roine
28 elect for what length
29 too selfish to settle
30 ten condemned bestial men   'best∫əl
31 "Get it," said Seth.
32 mark an "X" on the eggs

33 ʔ Ethel's elegant elements
34 ʔ Edward's EXquisite EXit   'ek,sk,wı zıℓ
35 ʔ E-ric's e-rrant e-rrors
36 Ame-rican me-rits
37 Teddy's te-rrible te-rrier
38 ve-rify gene-ric he-rring
39 the strength of the penguins
40 a peck of pegs
41 a mess to measure
42 red metal medal
43 the REquisite EXquisite echo

SENTENCES FOR PRACTICE USING *e*

44 ʔ Eddie executed an EXquisite exit.
45 ʔ Execute exiled enemies.
46 ʔ Ethel and Emma ended excellently.
47 ʔ Engel inspected every egg without exception.
48 Beth never intended to catch the wretched strep.
49 Many men intended to lend gems to Ms. Menza.
50 The inEXplicable expert was commended.
51 The apprentice tenor trembled with tension.
52 The gene-ric Ame-rican cheddar was EXquisite.
53 Memo-ries of Je-rry meant endless upset.
54 It's excellently well-penned.
55 He measured the length and strength.
56 You'll become DEspe-rate in this DEspicable DEsert.   'desṕik̀əbℓ
57 Excellent eggs come from penguins.
58 Quentin freQUENTed Penny's tent to beg eggs from the beggar.   frı'k,wentid
59 "E-rror in the bill," saith the teller to the me-rry Ame-rican.
60 The be-rries bu-ried in De-rry me-rit your attention.
61 When do you get any? You'll never get any ever again!
62 Is Led Zeppelin the nonpa-reil of heavy metal?   ,nɒn ṕə'reℓ:
63 Let's settle on the metal kettle, Mr. Messing.
64 The inEXpiable crime was inEXplicable.   ın'ek,sp̀lik̀əbℓ
65 Someone measure this REquisite but less-than-EXquisite mess. I've requisitioned it myself.

SENTENCES FOR PRACTICE USING e **, Cont.**

1 Will you conSENT to be FREquently ABsent?
2 Let him abSENT himself from our pending gathĕ-ring.
3 Quentin must freQUENT Lenten festivities FREquently!   *frı 'k,wĕntˇ* (v)

EXERCISES FOR "PIN-PEN" SUBSTITUTION

For words pronounced en do not substitute the sequence $ın$ incorrectly turning the word "pen" into "pin."

MATCH THE VOWEL SOUNDS IN THE FOLLOWING SETS:

e		en		e		e		en		e		e		en
4 Pet	— pe	— pen	7 debt	— de	— den	10 Ed	— e	— end
5 bet	— be	— bend	8 met	— me	— many	11 Eddie	— e	— any
6 septet	— te	— ten	9 Ted	— te	— attend	12 set	— se	— send

13 Has "Mister Ed" ended yet?
14 Seen Etta, anyone?
15 This is my pet pen.
16 I bet it'll bend.
17 It's that wretched red wren again.
18 He wedded the wench.
19 Jed is a genuine gentleman.
20 Ted attended then, did he?
21 Fred, let's be friends.

22 I said send it!
23 The Mets met mány men.
24 I'm indebted to my dentist.
25 Yes, I've a yen for that yenta.
26 Ed, ănyone dead in the den?
27 Heads up, Henry!
28 You got wet when, Wendall?
29 The vet invented venison dentures.
30 That sled you sent me is so slender!

e	em		e	em		e	em
31 ever	— ember	34 every	— embryo	37 elevate	— emanate
32 ebony	— Eme-ry	35 evident	— eminent	38 tepid	— Thames *tĕm:z*
33 Eppy	— empty	36 treble	— tremble	39 Trevor	— tremor

40 Does everyone remember MTV?
41 Jed's gems were genuine.
42 Mel remembered dreadful tremors.
43 Show Efrem the Empress Emily emblem.
44 Incredibly, the Kremlin trembled again.

45 Eppy, Emily, and Zelda resemble Zen monks.
46 It's evident in the embryo, Emmett.
47 Zagreb's gremlins hemmed dresses.
48 Every eminent member eats M&M's.
49 Let Eme-ry assemble the best members.

EXERCISES FOR DISTINGUISHING BETWEEN $ı$ **AND** e

$ın$	en		$ın$	en		$ım$	em
50 pin	— pen	59 hint	— enter	68 imp	— empty
51 bin=been	— Ben	60 thin	— then	69 Tim's	— Thames
52 tin	— ten	61 Lind	— lend	70 dimple	— Dempsey
53 kin	— Ken	62 mint	— meant	71 Jim=gym	— gem
54 sinned	— send	63 wind (n)	— wend	72 imminent	— eminent
55 tinder	— tender	64 fin	— fen	73 trimmer	— tremor
56 Min	— men	65 gin	— genĕ-rous	74 ever	— empĕ-ror
57 Minnie	— many	66 begin	— again	75 simple	— semblance
58 "inny"	— any	67 tint	— tent	76 timber	— temper

e

SENTENCES FOR DISTINGUISHING BETWEEN /ɪ/ AND /e/

1 ImPRESS him with the presence of EMpress Emmeline.

2 Ben's been in his tent with a tin of beans.

3 The wench remembered him with a grin and a big tumbler of gin.

4 Ben had a yen for Zen and a ⟨wh⟩im for hymns.

5 Attention! The feminist benefit will begin again at ten!

6 It was destined to play on the Fringe but not in the West End.

7 I intended to remember Emily's eminent friend.

8 Lincoln Center presents . . . **ANYTHING GOES!**

9 Minnie met many men way back then in Denver.

10 Amends inevitably follow grim recriminations.

11 Tempu-ra tends to be endemic in Memphis, Tennessee.

12 Is it Tennyson's wren that says, again and again, "Nevermore?"

13 Hand me the tin of pins and the ten tin pens. No, first hand me the ten tin pens

14   and then ten tin pins from the tin pin tin. No, only one tin pin from the tin pin tin

15   and rather than the ten tin pens, just hand me one tin pen and one more tin pin

16   from the tin pin tin.

PRACTICE SENTENCES USING *en* AND *em*

17 Tennessee's tennis men went again.

18 Ben's pen has a bent end.

19 Kenny's gentle kennel is in Denver.

20 Many censured wenches attended.

21 End tenure for the tenors!

22 Be content with elementa-ry Zen.

23 We've rented our tents for mere cents.

24 Ken invented identities for the men.

25 Did many men get any bread on Wednesday?   ˈwenz dɪ

26 Emma remembered those temperamental lemons.

27 But gems are so feminine, Empe-ror!

28 Remember to tend the embers, Dempsey.

29 She emulated an eminent femme fatale.

30 Emily's memo-ry resembles Clementine's.

31 "Temper, temper," emanated from the embassy.

32 The anti-temperance league tempo-ra-rily remedied the trembling victims' tremors.

33 *The Tempest* tempted me to emigrate.

♦ THE VOWEL SOUND æ AS IN "Pat" ♦

Represented by the spellings:

      h**a**m   pl**ai**d   g**ua**rantee

    Relax your lower jaw and rest the tip of your tongue behind the lower front teeth. Arch the FRONT of your tongue low in your mouth. The gently arched body of the tongue is practically flat. Your lips are VERY SLIGHTLY smiling, in an almost relaxed, neutral position. Good oral resonance of this tidy, compact vowel sound requires, as do all vowel and diphthong sounds, a RAISED SOFT PALATE.

    æ   can, in poor speech, be one of the most tense, diphthongized and nasalized vowels in Spoken English. The challenge of this vowel sound is to produce a freely open and forward sound that is rhythmically clean and crisp. It is ALWAYS SHORT.

WORDS FOR PRACTICE USING æ   æ   æ

1 apple happen apt hap pap tap dapple cap gap map nap=knap lap slap vapid sap
2 zap rap=wrap trap shrapnel perhaps yap chap Japanese

3 abbot habit babble tab dab cab gab Mab nab lab labý-rinth slab fabric Sabbath
4 shabby Rabb rabbit drab crab grabs inhabitant jabbed

5 at (sf) hat attic hatter pat bat tatters tattoo cat begat mat=Matt Nat=gnat Latin
6 latter late-ral fat vat that (sf) sat rat brat á-ristocrat Manhattan chat

7 add had (sf) pad bad=bade forbade tadpole dad cad egad mad gonad lad clad
8 ladder fad Thaddeus sad radical Chad

9 act hacked ax hacks accent zodiac pack back attack cackle maximum knack lack
10 lax plaque black flaxen flaccid vaccinate Thacke-ray sack Saxon shack rack=wrack
11 whack WAC wax yak Jack

12 Aggie hag agate haggard bag tag dagger gag maggot lag blackguard nag faggot
13 vagabond sag zigzag shag rag braggart dragged wag jagged

14 am (sf) ham ample hamper Hampshire pamper bamboo tam dam=damn camp
15 gamble=gambol ma'am mammal enamel lamb LAmentable fa-mi-ly vampire Sam
16 examine sham ram cram yam champ Cham jam

17 Ann=an (if) an (sf) and (sf) hand Andover Hanover anvil Pan ban tan exTANT Dan
18 can (sf) CAnnot began man Nancy land fan van Thanatos than (sf) sand Zanzibar
19 ran bran Chan Januá-ry roMANCE

20 angle hang anchor hanker pang bang tang dangle canker gang mangle Lang lank
21 language fang vanquish thank sang sank shank rang rank wangle Yankee jangle

22 Al Hal Albert halberd Al's halcyon pal cabal Cal gal The Mall (London) canal Val
23 Sal shall (sf) mo-rale co-rral Ralph Italian stallion galleon galleasses valiant
24 pallid ballad talon dally California gallon GAllant (n ; adj) malice fallacy valor

25 Africa "have to" (must) aphrodisiac baffle Stafford daffodil cafe gaff Mafeking
26 Lafcadio saffron Shafalus raffle traffic chaffinch Jaffe

WORDS FOR PRACTICE USING æ , Cont.

1 avid havoc ave_rage Haversham Avalon have (sf) avā-_rice haversack avenue
2 MacTavish davit cavern cavil gavel mavĕ-_rick navvy lavender Faversham savage
3 _ravage _raven (v) _ravening _Ravenspurgh²

4 Athens hath Athol Athabasca atheNAEum ath-lete athletic psychopath Bathsheba
5 Bathurst bathysphere Cathy=Kathy Kathĕ-_rine mathematics math Lathbŭ-_ry _Rathbone

6 Cather gather Mather blather slather fathom

7 ass hassle acid hassock aster=Astor "has to" (must) poetaster passive passenger
8 bastard tassel dastardly casque Casca castigate gas mass Nast lass fascinate
9 vacillate sassy Shasta mŏ-_rass Fortinbr_as chastity Jasper

10 as (sf) has (sf) Asbŭ-_ry has-been asthma hasn't topaz Basil=basil Tasmania dazzles
11 chasm gazetteer Lază-_rus plasma pizzazz _razzle chasuble jazz

12 ash hash Ashley Ashland passion bashful abashed stash mouSTACHE dash cash gash
13 mash Nash=gnash lash splash Fascist sash _rash _ration br_ash tr_ash cr_ash

14 azure azŭ-_rite casual

15 Acheson hatchet patch ba-che-lor attach Datchet catch match natŭ-_ral snatch latch
16 thatch satŭ-_rate _ratchet br_ach scr_atch congratulate congratulations

17 agile hadji Agincourt pageant badge Plantagenet gadget imagine fadge vaginal

WORDS FOR CLARITY OF æ PRIOR TO ɾ

✓ *Reminder* ———————————————————————————

> **Make an open, clearly defined æ sound and begin the following syllable with a clean-cut consonant ɾ . In doing so, you will avoid marring the clarity of the æ sound with r-coloring.**

18 a-_rid ha-_rried a-_rrow Ha-_rrow a-_rrogant ha-_ricot A-_riadne Ha-_rry a-_rras HA-_rass

19 A-_rab a-_rable A-_ragon a-_ristocracy A-_rizona Ha-_rold Ha-_rris ha-_rrowing Ha-_rriet

20 Ha-_rrod's pa-_rry pa-_rallel pa-_rable pa-_rachute pa-_ragrăph appa-_rent appa-_rel Pa-_ris

21 pa-_ramour pa-_rish pa-_rrot pa-_radox pa-_rasol compa-_rison capa-_risoned pa-_rasite

22 pa-_rody pa-_radise pa-_ragon Ba-_rry=Ba-_rrie ba-_ron=ba-_rren ba-_rrow ba-_rrel ba-_rricade

23 ba-_ritone ba-_rrier ba-_rricuda ta-_rry ta-_rantella ta-_rragon Da-_rrow Da-_rrell=Da-_rryl

24 ca-_rry ca-_rry-ing ca-_rried ca-_rriage ca-_rol=Ca-_rroll cha-_racter ca-_rat=ca-_rrot

25 ca-_ravan ca-_rrion Ca-_riBBEan Ca-_rolina ca-_ricature Ga-_rry gua-_rantee ga-_rret ga-_rish

26 ga-_rrulous ga-_rrison Ga-_rrick ma-_rry ma-_rry-ing ma-_rried ma-_rriage ma-_rrow ma-_ribou

27 ma-_rathon ma-_rigolds ma-_riner ma-_ritime na-_rrate na-_rration na-_rrator na-_rrative

WORDS FOR CLARITY OF æ PRIOR TO r , Cont.

1 na-rrow La-rry la-rynx la-ryngitis ala-rum la-riat hila-rity singula-rity

2 regula-rity Fa-rrow Fa-rrell Fa-raday Fa-rragut fa-rrier Pha-ramond pha-risee

3 Va-rrius Sa-ratoga Sa-racen cha-rabanc cha-rity cha-ritable cha-riot cha-rioteer

4 Cha-ring Ja-rrett spa-rrow dispa-rage cla-ret cla-rity cla-rify cla-rion Cla-rence

MATCH THE æ SOUNDS IN THE FOLLOWING PAIRS OF WORDS:

5 mat	— ma-rry	13 cat	— ca-rry	21 sat	— Sa-racen
6 apt	— a-rrow	14 cat	— cha-racter	22 hat	— Ha-rry
7 attic	— a-rrogant	15 gap	— ga-rish	23 hack	— HA-rass 'hæɹəʌ
8 pat	— Pa-ris	16 mat	— ma-rrow	24 chat	— cha-riot
9 pack	— pa-rish	17 gnat	— na-rrow	25 spat	— dispa-rage
10 bat	— ba-rrister	18 lap	— La-rry	26 clap	— cla-rify
11 tat	— ta-rry	19 fat	— Fa-rrell	27 mat	— ma-rry
12 dad	— Da-rrow	20 vat	— va-ricose	28 act	— a-rras

PHRASES FOR PRACTICE USING æ

29 ʔ Alice's alibi	44 ʔ acting angry	59 ʔ anxious actress Aggie
30 ʔ athletic African acrobat	45 ʔ addled adolescent	60 ʔ avalanche action
31 ʔ act a-rrogantly	46 ʔ actually advertised	61 ʔ adequate admi-ral
32 handy plaid hanger	47 bag and baggage	62 Kathy's cha-racter
33 Ha-rry's ca-rriage	48 Sally in the alley	63 sacrifice singula-rity
34 catch the band wagon	49 dramatic fashion	64 appa-rent ma-rigolds
35 ma-rry Ann Anderson	50 flaccid flaxen flags	65 na-rrate the ta-rantella
36 Anne's hand in ma-rriage	51 ran the ma-rathon rapidly	66 a catch-as-catch-can match
37 we CAnnot can yams	52 thou canst not tan	67 branded as a bastard
38 fancy the silly ass	53 LAmentable lambs	68 glad to be bad
39 Sam's candy stand	54 Ca-riBBEan raccoon	69 Latin tattoo
40 man and the masses	55 a ragged hag	70 the tramp's tragedy
41 Macbeth and Banquo	56 Hank's in fact a Yankee	71 lacking in languor
42 ma-rry, I will	57 HA-rass Ha-rriet	72 thank the bank
43 ta-rry a while	58 gua-ranteed ca-rat	73 Ha-rold's pa-rasol

SENTENCES FOR PRACTICE USING æ

74 ʔ Agatha's angry accusations aggravated Adam's a-rrogance.

75 ʔ Acting angry is actually an act of anguish. 'æk,t,ʃʊəli

76 ʔ "Apples for the ath-letes," added Astor.

77 ʔ Andrew Anson agitated for African asters.

78 Ann's hand is bandaged and CAnnot be handled.

79 Canned ham and rancid lamb have been banned.

80 The actress na-rrated for the National Ballet in a casual fashion.

81 Ha-rold has to have handfuls of aspi-rin on hand for his wracking hangovers.

82 We CAnnot and they CAnnot. Canst thou? 'kʰænɒtʰ

83 Thou canst not tan in Anchó-rage in Januá-ry.

10-15 line dialogues w/ all 4 right sound phonetically

SENTENCES FOR PRACTICE USING æ, Cont.

1 Laminate those LAmentable lambs.   *'læmənt'əbl*
2 Dad's glad to be sad.
3 The good and the bad bäde farewell to the lad.
4 The tattoo's actually in graphic Latin.
5 Actually, actors began the fad.
6 Pam scrambled a man-sized basil sandwich for Basil Rathbone.   *'bæzl*
7 The ragged hag staggered with her baggage.
8 "Yes, I am, I am," stammered the ham actor.
9 Prince Hal cö-rralled his pal Al in an alcove.
10 They trashed his flashy mouSTACHE and dashing fashions.   *mə'stæʃ*
11 Max has played Macbeth, Macduff and Banquo.
12 Chaplin's tramp is a classic tragic cha-racter.   *'kæ̱rɪk,t'ə*
13 Actually, the actual avalänche was an accident.
14 The actor anchored off South Africa.
15 The man's roMANCE is a phantom of his own fancy.   *r̲o'mænʂ*
16 That hat of Ha-rry's natu-rally matches his appa-rel.
17 Pat appa-rently is back in A-rizona.
18 This passion for pa-radise is tantalizingly tangible.
19 Make no compa-rison to the Ba-ron's ca-rriage.
20 Mack ma-rried into the Athabascan a-ristocracy.
21 Let's pack off to Pa-ris in a ca-ravan with Janet and Dan.
22 Ta-rry awhile, Cla-rence Da-rrow!
23 The ma-riner na-rrated a ga-rish pa-rable.
24 There's hila-rity with regula-rity on Grandview Avenue.
25 Ha-rry Ha-rris was HA-rassed by Ca-rol Ca-rroll.   *'hærəʂt'*
26 Let's have a candid chat about cha-rity.
27 We bäde adieu to Ba-rry and Ma-rilyn.   *ə'dɟuː*
28 They forbäde us to banquet on mangoes.
29 Are these amicable applicants' applications APPlicable?

EXERCISES FOR OPENING THE VOWEL SOUND æ AND ELIMINATING NASALIZATION PRECEDING ⁿ AND ᵐ

MATCH THE VOWEL SOUND æ IN THE FOLLOWING PAIRS OF WORDS:

æ	æn	æ	æn	æ	æn
30 at (sf)	— Ann=an (if)	38 lad	— land	46 daddy	— dandy
31 add	— and (sf)	39 fat	— fan	47 fat	— fancy
32 pat	— pant	40 that (sf)	— than (sf)	48 scat	— scan
33 tat	— tan	41 sat	— sand	49 bad=bade	— band=banned
34 dad	— Dan	42 rat	— ran	50 fad	— fanned
35 cat	— can (sf)	43 hat	— hand	51 plaid	— planned
36 mat	— man	44 chat	— channel	52 static	— stand
37 Nat=gnat	— Nancy	45 begat	— began	53 glad	— gland

EXERCISES FOR OPENING THE VOWEL SOUND æ **AND ELIMINATING NASALIZATION PRECEDING** n **AND** m **, Cont.**

	æ	æm		æ	æm		æ	æm
1	apt	— ample	7	scrapple	— scramble	13	dapper	— damper
2	pap	— Pam	8	tap	— tam	14	sap	— Sam
3	rap	— ram	9	cap	— camp	15	jab	— jam
4	Shapp	— sham	10	lap	— lamb	16	fab	— fa-mi-ly
5	map	— ma'am	11	chap	— champ	17	nap	— Su-rinam
6	hap	— ham	12	gabble	— gamble= gambol	18	vapid	— vamp

FOR æŋ **DO NOT SUBSTITUTE** ɛ̃ŋ **—, MAKING "BANK" BECOME "BENK" OR "BAYNK"**

MATCH THE VOWEL SOUND æ IN THE FOLLOWING GROUPS OF WORDS:

	æk	æŋ	æŋk		æk	æŋ	æŋk		æk	æŋ	æŋk
19	pack	— pang	— Pancras	22	tack	— tang	— tank	25	back	— bang	— bank
20	lack	— Lang	— lank	23	rack	— rang	— rank	26	sack	— sang	— sank
21	hack	— hang	— hank	24	clack	— clang	— clank	27	act	— anger	— anchor

	æk	æŋ
28	act	— anger angry angle angular anxious anchor Ancho-rage
29	pack	— pang panky St. Pancras Pangloss Pangbourne
30	back	— bang bank bangle Bangor bankrupt banquet Banquo
31	attack	— tang tangle entangle tank tango Tanganyika Tancred
32	Dack	— dang dangle dank
33	cackle	— canker kanga-roo
34	gag	— gang gangster gangly gangrene
35	mack	— mangle Mangan mango mangrove
36	lack	— Lang Langham language languid languish languor lank lanky
37	fact	— fang newfangled
38	vaccinate	— vanquish vanquisher
39	Thacke-ray	— thank thanks Thanksgiving
40	sack	— sang sanguine sank Sanka sanga-ree
41	rack=wrack	— rang wrangle me-ringue ha-rangue rank rancor
42	hack	— hang hank handkerchief
43	yak	— yin-yang yank Yankee
44	jack	— jangle

CONSONANT COMBINATIONS:

45 plank blank blanket clank flank spangled spank stank prank crank drank frank
46 shrank sprang Mustang

SENTENCES FOR PRACTICE USING æ WITH ŋ

1 ʔ An angular a-rrow anchored the apple to the a-rrogant a-ristocrat. ˈæ rɪ ʌ tˀə ˌkˌræt

2 Back to the bank, Banquo!

3 He lacked the language of roMANCE.

4 Van vaccinated the vanquished Yankees.

5 The sack sank into the mi-raculous me-ringue.

6 The hack actor hanged himself with a handkerchief. ˈhæŋ kˀə t,ʃɪ ʃ

7 Thacke-ray thanks you for the black blanket.

8 Dracula drank drams of plasma, as planned.

9 They did a tacky tango on a tank.

10 "Anchors away!" the angry banker sang from the gangplank.

11 Thank you, Banquo, for the Thanksgiving banquet.

12 Hank was anxious to vanquish the Yankees from the dank and ranco-rous bank.

13 Angry gangs thanked the bank manager, then sang languidly of the tangled anchors.

14 Mangoes in me-ringue were the hit of the whole shebang.

15 Sack the newfangled fandango and bring back the tango!

16 Frankly, entanglements make me anxious.

17 La-rry, cla-rify the cha-racters' language in Act Two.

18 I'd be happy with a fancy, newfangled Mustang.

19 It's a fact that Pam gambles with gangsters at the track.

20 Just a shack in Shangri-La would make me glad.

21 Ha-rry hates HA-rassment. It makes him angry.

22 Frank's pranks drove Ma-rilyn batty.

SENTENCES COMPARING æ WITH ɒ

23 Nice tam, Tom. Got it at Gatwick?

24 Don and Dan took a jab at the job offer.

25 Blond is bland, but black is blockbuster.

26 A pox upon thee, Mr. Paxton!

27 Oddly enough, it added up in the end.

28 Put the box back in the closet, Cassie.

29 What was that crash across the canal?

30 Put your socks in the sack or you'll be so-rry.

This is the so-called INTERMEDIATE "A." Represented by the spellings:

ask   aunt

This sound is a LOW, FRONT-OF-THE-TONGUE vowel with respect to the arch of the tongue. It has become known as the INTERMEDIATE "A" vowel because its position is often perceived as intermediate between the vowel sound $æ$ as in "Pat" and the vowel sound a: as in "father."

Let your lower jaw lie wide open, relaxed; allow the tip of your tongue to rest behind your lower front teeth. Allow your lips to spread VERY SLIGHTLY in the feeling of a smile. Arch the FRONT of your tongue low and forward as the jaw opens to its widest position for any front vowel.

One way to arrive at, or at least to approximate, the correct Intermediate "A" vowel sound is to sing the word "my." Notice the first part of the sung word, which will sound something like "ma-." Once again sing a good, long, extended "my," but this time notice that you are in fact sustaining a long pure vowel sound "maaaaaaa-." FEEL and HEAR this pure vowel sound and then say: "ma- mask," "ma- mast," "a- ask."

a is the first element of the diphthong sound $a\cdot \breve{i}\cdot$ as in "my."

As a pure vowel sound a is ALWAYS SHORT and is used ONLY in the so-called "ASK-LIST" of words. The Ask-List is a compilation of the words in Spoken English, such as "ask," that have three standards of pronunciation for the letter "a" in the spelling of a word, depending on the standard of Spoken English being used at the time. (A complete Ask-List is given on pages 81-83.) Beyond a reliance on this list, it is a good idea when using proper names or referring to particular places to turn to local sources for the correct pronunciation.

The three standards of pronunciation for words that comprise the Ask-List are given in *A Pronouncing Dictionary of American English*, by John S. Kenyon and Thomas A. Knott. For the actor, of course, the choice of which of the three to use will be determined by the play and by the character. Take the word "ask," for instance:

$æ$ 1 THE SHORT "A" is used in General American pronunciation and is employed by a majority of North Americans in ordinary speech. This is the vowel sound that occurs in the name "Pat" in North American English and in Received Prounuciation (RP) of British English;

a 2 THE INTERMEDIATE "A" is the American pronunciation listed in Webster's *Third New International Dictionary*. This is also the Theater Standard for Good Speech in classic texts and the Eastern American Standard given in Kenyon and Knott's *Dictionary;*

a: 3 THE BROAD "A" or ITALIAN "A" is the British Standard for Received Pronunciation (RP) as given in *Everyman's English Pronouncing Dictionary*, by Daniel Jones. This is the vowel sound that occurs in the word "father" in both North American English and British RP.

There are no rules for determining whether a particular word is on the Ask-List. Usage in the living language influences a word's pronunciation, and it is this usage that over centuries has governed the words of the Ask-List. No one person, group, class, region, or country has invented the list.

To illustrate that no rules exist for determining an Ask-List word, take a look at the following words. Those in the left column are on the Ask-List; each has three standards of pronunciation. Those on the right are NOT on the Ask-List; each has only one standard in both North American pronunciation and British Received Pronunciation.

ASK-WORDS: three standards æ ɑ ɑː :	NOT ASK-WORDS: one standard æ only
1 pass, passable, Passover	passage, passenger, passive
2 can't	can (n; v), can (sf of auxiliary verb), CAnnot, cant (jargon)
3 class, classy	classic, classical, classify
4 path	psychopath, pathological
5 graph, telegraph	graphic, telegraphic
6 pass, class, brass, grass	bass (fish), Cass, mass, lass, crass
7 lather, rather	gather, blather, slather

This should demonstrate that there are no spelling or phonetic rules for determining Ask-List words; nevertheless, the Ask-List words are all followed by certain consonant sounds. Below is a partial listing of the most common Ask-List words, grouped according to the consonant sounds that follow them. (Again, the complete Ask-List is on pages 81-83.)

-f
   8 abaft aft after afternoon behalf calf chaff craft "-craft" endings daft
   9 distaff draft=draught epitaph gi-raffe graft graph "-graph" endings half
  10 laugh raft rafter shaft staff waft cenotaph

-θ
  11 bath lath path wrath

-nt
  12 advantage aunt can't chant enchant grant plant shan't slant supplant
  13 vantage

-nd
  14 chandler command commander demand Flanders reprimand slander
  15 countermand

-nt,ʃ
  16 avalanche blanch=Blanche branch planch stanch stanchion

-ns
  17 advance answer chance chancel chancellor chancé-ry dance enhance France
  18 Frances=Francis glance lance prance trance

-s
  19 aghast alas ask bask basket blast brass cask casket cast=caste castle
  20 caster=castor clasp class disaster fast fasten flabbergast flask flasket
  21 gasp ghastly glass grasp grass hasp last mask=masque mast master mastiff
  22 nasty pass passable Passover past pastime pastor pasture plaster rascal
  23 rasp repast task vast alabaster

-z
  24 raspbe-rry (This is the only Ask-List word with z .)

-mp,l
  25 example sample sampler

-v
  26 calves halve salve (ointment)

-ð
  27 lather rather paths baths laths

THE ASK-LIST OF WORDS

These words have three standards of pronunciation:

a In Good Speech in classic texts   *æ* In General American   *a:* In British RP

abaft	blasted	chaff, -s	classmate
advance, -s	blasting	chaff-cutter, -s	classmen
advanced	blast-furnace, -s	chaffed	classroom, -s
advancement, -s	blastment, -s	chaffer, -s (n)	classwoman
advancing	blast-pipe	[chaffer (v) *æ*]	classwomen
advantage, -s	branch, -es	chaffiness	classy
advantaged	Branch	chaffing, -ly	command, -s
aft	branched	chaffless	commanded
after	branching	chaffy	commander, -s
"after-" prefixes	branchless	chance, -s	commanding, -ly
aftermath, -s	brass, -es	chanced	commandment, -s
afternoon	brass-band, -s	chancel, -s	commando, -s
afterward, -s	brass-founder	chancelle-ries	counterblast, -s
aghast	brass-hat, -s	chancelle-ry	countermand, -s
alabaster	brassie, -s (golf)	chancellor, -s	countermanded
Alabaster	brassier (more brassy)	Chancellor	countermanding
alas (*æ* in RP)	brassiest	chancellorship, -s	craft, -s
answer, -s	brassy	chancer	craftier
answe-rable	broadcast, -s	chance-ries	craftiest
answe-rably	calf	chance-ry	craftily
answered	calf's-foot	Chance-ry	craftiness
answe-rer, -s	calf-skin	chancier	craftsman, -men
answe-ring	calve, -s	chanciest	"-craft" suffixes
ask, -s	calved	chancing	daft
[ask newt *æ*]	calves'-foot	chancy	dafter
asked	calve-skin, -s	chandler, -s	daftest
asking	calving	Chandler	daftly
aunt, -s	can't	chant, -s	daftness
auntie, -s	cask, -s	chanted	dance, -s
autograph, -s	casked	chanter, -s	Dance
avalanche, -s	casket, -s	chantey	danced
avast	casking	chanties	dancer, -s
bask, -s	cast, -s	chanting	Dancer
basked	castaway, -s	Chantrey	dancing
basket, -s	caste, -s	chantries	deathmask, -s
basketball,-s	caster	chantry	demand, -s
basketful, -s	Castelnau	Chantry	demanded
basketry	casting, -s	chanty	demanding
basket-work	casting-net, -s	clasp, -s	disadvantage, -d, -s
bath, -s	casting-vote, -s	clasped	disaster, -s
bath-brick, -s	cast-iron	clasping	disastrous, -ly
bath-chair, -s	castle, -s	clasp-knife, -ves	disastrousness
bathroom, -s	Castlebar	class, -es	distaff, -s
behalf	Castlerea (gh)	classed	downcast
blanch, -es	Castleton	classier	downdraught, -s
Blanche	castoff, -s	classiest	draft, -s
blanched	castor, -s; Castor	classiness	drafted
blanching	castor-oil	classing	drafter, -s
blast, -s	cenotaph, -s	classman	drafting

THE ASK-LIST OF WORDS, Cont.

draftsman, -men
draught, -s
"draught-" prefixes
draughtier
draughtiest
draughtily
draughtiness
draughty
draughtsman, -men
encephalograph, -s
enchant, -s
enchanted
enchanter, -s
enchanting
enchantment
enchantress, -es
enclasp, -s
enclasped
enclasping
engraft, -s
engrafted
engrafting
engraftment
enhance, -s
enhanced
enhancement, -s
enhancing
ensample, -s
entrance, -s (v)
entranced, -ly
epigraph, -s
epitaph, -s
everlasting, -ly
everlastingness
example, -s
exampled
exampling
Falstaff
fast, -s
fasted
faster, -s
fastest
fasting
fastness
fast-day, -s
fasten, -s
fastened
fastener, -s
fastening
fastness, -es
"-fast" suffixes
flabbergast, -s
flabbergasted

flabbergasting
Flanders
flask, -s
flasket, -s
forecast, -ed, -ing, -s
forecaster, -s
France
Frances
Francies
Francis
freelance, -s, -d
gasped, -s
gasped
gasping
ghastlier
ghastliest
ghastliness
ghastly
gi-raffe, -s
glance, -s
glanced
glancing, -ly
glass, -es
glass-blower, -s
glass-blowing
glass-cutter, -s
glassful, -s
glass-house, -s
glassier
glassiest
glassily
glassiness
glass-paper, -s
glassware
glass-work, -s
glasswort
glassy
graft, -s
"-graft" suffixes
grafted
grafter, -s
grafting
grant
Grant
granted
grantee, -s
granting
grantor, -s
graph, -s
"-graph" suffixes
Grasmere
grasp, -s
grasped

grasper, -s
grasping, -ly
grass, -es
grass-cutter, -s
grassed
grass-green
grasshopper, -s
grassier
grassiest
grassing
grass-land
grass-widow, -s
grass-widower, -s
grassy
half
"half-" prefixes
halve, -s
halved
halves
halving
handicraft, -s
hasp,-s
hasped
hasping
headmaster, -s
he-reafter
impassable, -bly
implant, -s, -ed
indraught, -s
lance, -s
Lance
lanced
lance-corpo-ral, -s
lancer, -s
lancet, -s
Lancet
lancing
Lancing
last, -s
lasted
lasting, -ly
lastly
lath, -s
lather, -s
lathered
lathe-ring
lathwork
lathy
laugh, -s
laughable
laughableness
laughably
laughed

laugher, -s
laughing, -ly
laughing-gas
laughing-stock, -s
laughter
mask, -s
masked
masking
masque, -s
mast, -s
master, -s
"master-" prefixes
"-master" suffixes
mastered
masterful, -ly
masterfulness
maste-ring
masterpiece, -s
maste-ry
mast-head, -s
mastiff, -s (æ in RP)
mischance, -s
mooncalf
mooncalves
nastier
nastiest
nastily
nastiness
nasty
outcast, -s
outcaste, -s
outcasted
outcasting
outclass, -es
outclassing
outlast, -s
outlasted
outlasting
overcast
overglance, -d, -s
overtask, -ed, -ing, -s
pa-ragraph, -s
pa-ragraphed
pa-ragraphing
pass, -es
passed
passable, -ness
passably
pass-book, -s
passer, -s
[passer sparrow æ]
passer-by
passers-by

THE ASK-LIST OF WORDS, Cont.

passing	prancing	sampler, -s	tasked
pass-key, -s	quaff, -s*	sampling	tasking
passman, -men	quaffed *	schoolmaster, -s	taskmaster, -s
Passover, -s	quaffer, -s *	shaft, -s	task-mistress, -es
passport, -s	quaffing *	Shaftesbu-ry	telecast, -s
pass-word, -s	raft, -s	shan't	telegraph, -s
past	rafted, -s	slander, -s	telegraphed
pastime, -s	rafter, -s	slandered	telegraphing
past-master, -s	raftered	slande-rer	the-reafter
pastor, -s	rafting	slande-ring	topmast[2]
pasto-ral, -s	rascal, -s	slande-rous, -ly	trance, -s
pasto-ralism	rascalities	slande-rousness	transplant, -s
pasto-rate, -s	rascality	slant, -s	transplantable
pastu-rage	rascally	slanted	transplanted
pasture, -s	rasp, -s	slanting, -ly	transplanting
pastured	rasped	slantwise	trespass, -es [2]
pastu-ring	rasping	staff, -s	trespassed
path, -s	raspbe-rries	staffed	trespasser, -s
pathfinder, -s	raspbe-rry	staffing	trespassing
Pathfinder	raspiness	stagecraft	unstanch
pathless	raspy	stanch, -es	unsurpassed
pathway, -s	rather	stanched	upcast, -s
perchance	recast, -s	stanching	vantage, -s
blanch, -es	recasting	stanchion, -s	vast
blanchette, -s	repass, -es	statecraft	vaster
plant, -s	repassed	steadfast, -ly	vastest
planted	repassing	steadfastness	vastly
planter, -s	repast, -s	stedfast	vastness
planting	repasture	supplant, -s	vasty
plaster, -s	reprimand, -s	supplanted	waft, -s
plastered	reprimanded	supplanter, -s	waftage
plaste-rer, -s	reprimanding	supplanting	wafted
plaste-ring	salve, -s ** (anoint)	surpass, -ed, -es	wafting
prance, -s	salved **	surpassing, -ly	witchcraft
Prance	salving **	taft, -ed, -s	wrath (𝒟 or ꞇ˙ in RP)
pranced	sample, -s	tafting	wrathful, -ly
prancer, -s	sampled	task, -s	

* In North American speech and in British RP, "quaff" and its derivatives usually are pronounced ˈkˌwɒf but often in verse must rhyme with an Ask-Word, in which case they, too, become Ask-Words.

** In British RP, "salve" (anoint; soothe) and its derivatives are pronounced: ˈsæl:v

For proper names and places not listed above, it is best to check local pronunciation and the dictionaries if you suspect it may be an Ask-Word.

In British RP the words on the Ask-List are pronounced with $a:$ as in "father." In addition to these words, there are a few words pronounced with $a:$ by many British RP speakers, while $æ$ as in "Pat" is used by other RP speakers as well as virtually all North Americans. With such words, most characters in North American plays will use $æ$; for characters in British plays it is advisable to investigate factors such as regional, class and educational backgrounds, to determine which vowel sound should be used. Some of these words are:

Alexander bastard bastardized bastardy contrast contrasting exaspe-rate exaspe-rating

haft ranch rancher "trans-" prefixes moustache masque-rade

PHRASES FOR PRACTICE USING ɑ

1. ʔ Auntie asked after
2. castle in France
3. fast dancing
4. demand the flask
5. slander Flanders
6. the last master
7. ask the class
8. chant the epitaph
9. glass full of grass
10. unsurpassed slander
11. wrathful telegraph
12. handicrafted laths

13. ʔ after answers, alas
14. vasty fields of France
15. a brass casket
16. a drafty raft
17. path to the bath
18. pigeons on the grass, alas
19. a chance advantage
20. rather ghastly
21. raspbe-rry branch basket
22. halved samples of salve
23. recast the gasping dancer
24. reprimanding taskmaster

25. ʔ afternoon aftermath
26. I can't dance
27. a disastrous avalanche
28. I ask you for an answer
29. enchanting witchcraft
30. a masterful cast
31. on behalf of the calf
32. at last I've passed
33. classroom draftsman
34. grass-green grasshopper
35. disadvantaged drafter
36. outlast the outclassed outcast

SENTENCES FOR PRACTICE USING ɑ

37. ʔ Auntie asked for an answer after advancing.
38. The commander demanded an alabaster casket. ˈæləˈbæstə
39. Reprimands from the taskmaster are examples of his wrath.
40. Castleton's calf-skins were classy castoffs.
41. Auntie was aghast after the nasty afternoon answers.
42. Aunt Blanche had the last laugh.
43. It was a vast castle in France.
44. Ask the class for the answers.
45. The rascal demanded the flask.
46. Francis slandered Flanders.
47. They chanted epitaphs over the casket.
48. Good afternoon, Mr. Gi-raffe.
49. At last I've passed!
50. The masterful cast led the dance.
51. I can't dance, Aunt Frances.
52. On behalf of the calf, I'd like to invite you to the pasture.
53. A disastrous avalanche spoiled my chances.
54. I shan't be taking a bath after all.
55. I'd rather fast than eat raspbe-rries.
56. After the dance, let's board the craft.
57. She enchanted me with her witchcraft.
58. The last pa-ragraph was ghastly.
59. It's half past five in the afternoon.
60. Did the staff take advantage of the planter?
61. I demand an answer now!
62. This cask, for example, is made of brass.
63. Grant me a better vantage, I command you.
64. That nasty commander went into a trance.
65. Pass me the glass, Pastor Francis.

SENTENCES FOR COMPARISON OF æ ə **AND** ɑ:

1 ʔ Ann asked Allah.

2 Patty made a pass at papa.

3 The band took a bath in balmy weather.

4 The damsel had a dance with Dante.

5 This cant can't fool Kahn.

6 Matt mastered the armada.

7 She gladly glanced at Glamis. 'glɑːmːz

8 Do we have to have half the hallah?

9 I gather you would rather lather, father.

10 Mi-raculously, the rascal was a mi-rage.

11 The man commanded the armada.

12 CAnnot this cast be calm?

13 The ant's aunt gave alms.

14 Nat knew a nasty sonata.

15 The passenger passed out under a palm.

16 The gas is ghastly on the Gaza Strip.

17 Sam had a sampling of the samba.

18 The lass rode the last llama.

19 Kathe-rine Castleton was calm.

20 Maddy mastered her mama.

21 Tad, your task is tacos.

22 Fanny fancied fasteners on the façade.

23 Andy's aunt is a debutante.

24 Chas thought it chancy to cha-cha.

25 Masticate in a mask, Masha.

26 Some savvy savage gave salve to the Slav.

27 Gas that asp, you ghastly iguana!

28 Fancy, she advanced to Nirvana.

29 Ann, sir, answered with nuance.

30 The asters were a disaster on the plaza and

    the Astors were a disaster at the Plaza.

31 Exaspe-rated, Jasper had a disastrous massage.

	i:	*ɪ*	*e*	*ɛɚ*	*æ*	*ɑ*
1	deed	did	dead	dared	dad	daft
2	teams=teems	Tim's	Thames	tears (rips)	tams	task
3	keen=Kean	kin	ken	cairn	can, cant	can't
4	green	grin	Grendel	agra-rian	grand	grant
5	glean	glint	glen	glare	gland	glance
6	dean	din	den	dare	Dan	dance
7	demeaned	mint	mend	mare	manned	demand
8	leave	live (v)	leaven	lair	lavish	laugh
9	bean	bin=been	Ben	bairn	ban	bath
	i·	*ɪ*	*e*	*ɛɚ*	*æ*	*ɑ*
10	eat	it	et	airtime	at (sf)	ask
11	"eef"	if	effort	air-fare	Africa	after
12	east	is't	Esther	airsick	aster=Astor	asked
13	peat=Pete	pit	pet	pair=pear	pat	path
14	beat=beet	bit	bet	bare=bear	bat	bath
15	liter=litre	litter	letter	lair	latter	last
16	meats=meets	mits	Mets	mare's	mats	mast
17	reef	riff	reft	rare	raffle	raft
18	leafed	lift	left	lair	lavish	laugh
19	grease=Greece	gristle	regress	grega-rious	crass	grass
20	feast	fist	fest	fair=fare	fascinate	fast
21	reach	rich	wretch	rare	ratchet	rascal
22	Keats	kit	kettle	care	cat	cast
23	clepe	clip	y-clept	Clare	clap	clasp
24	Meese	miss	mess	mares	mass	mask=masque
25	creep	crypt	crept	-----	crass	craft
26	pieced	pistol	pest	pairs=pares	pasty (pie)	past
27	peep	pip	pep	pear pie	pap	path
28	antique	tick	Tech	tear (rip)	attack	task
29	reap	rip	rep	rare	rap=wrap	rasp

SENTENCES FOR PRACTICE USING FRONT VOWEL SOUNDS IN ORDER

1 ʔ Even if every airline advertises afterwards?

2 Bea is letting hai-ry Ha-rry answer.

3 She will help Ma-ry ma-rry the rascal.

4 Please give the pets a pair of passes.

5 Dreamers drink the dregs of rare drams of draught.

6 Indeed, it did dent a fair share of the damaged rafters.

7 Dean didn't dare Dan to dance.

8 Beat a bit of your best pear batter, Blanche.

SENTENCES FOR PRACTICE USING FRONT VOWEL SOUNDS IN MIXED ORDER

9 ʔ Even an iffy airfare to Africa demanded effort.

10 The wretch reached for a rare ratchet to resist the rascal.

11 Aleta littered the lair with a letter too lavish to last.

12 Brenda Brindle, the branch libra-rian, was branded a bastard.

13 Felice has a flair for fittingly fettered, flashy fasteners.

14 His hai-ry head needs only half a hat.

15 I shan't take even a share in a shanty on Shaftesbu-ry Avenue this September.

16 Clare cleaned the band's bathroom in a fitful frenzy.

SENTENCES FOR PRACTICE USING THE FRONT VOWEL SOUNDS PRIOR TO CONSONANT R

17 ʔ It's an e-ra of e-rrors, due to A-riel's a-rrogance.

18 ʔ I was i-rritated by an e-rrant ai-ry a-rrow.

19 In this pe-riod, the pe-ril of be-ing a pa-rent is appa-rent.

20 The py-ramid that Pe-rry is repai-ring is a pa-ragon of style.

21 Sibe-rian be-rries for the overbea-ring ba-ron!

22 The ty-ranny of te-rrible te-rrors is tea-ring apart Ta-rrytown.

23 Ki-ri put ke-rosene into Ka-ren's cha-racterless ca-rriage.

24 It's a mi-racle me-rry Ma-ry ma-rried.

25 Ve-ra ve-rified the va-rious reports on Va-rrius.

26 Se-riously, se-renade Sa-rah in Sa-ratoga.

27 Only the he-roic he-ralded hai-ry Ha-rold.

28 The he-retical he-roine's ha-rem hired the ha-rridan.

The MID, or CENTRAL, VOWELS are those vowel sounds in which the MIDDLE of your tongue is arched in relation to the place where the hard and soft palates meet. For each of the mid vowel sounds your lips are relaxed, or neutral.

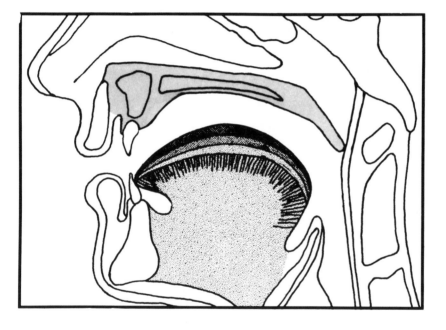

St*ir*

th*e* su*r*prise

c*u*p.

◆ Your Lower Jaw is Relaxed

◆ Tip of your Tongue Touches Lower Teeth

◆ Soft Palate is Raised

◆ The Sounds are Voiced

◆ THE VOWEL SOUND 3: AS IN "stir" ◆

Represented by the spellings: 3ʳ   3ʳᴸ

b**er**th=b**ir**th   s**ir**   h**ur**t   M**yr**tle   att**or**ney   reh**ear**se

c**our**teous   connoiss**eur**   k**er**nel=c**olo**nel

("Colonel" is the only word in the English language that is pronounced with an "r"-like sound, but has no letter "r" in the spelling.)

Let your lower jaw relax to a half-open position and rest the tip of your tongue behind your lower front teeth. Arch the MIDDLE of your tongue about half-way toward the middle of your hard palate. Your lips should be relaxed and neutral. It is essential that the tip of your tongue remain relaxed behind and touching the back of your lower front teeth for the duration of the sound.

The free resonance and eerie quality of this vowel sound require the combined relaxation of lips, jaw, tongue, and throat. The quality is similar to that of the consonant r, but is a softer murmur.

This is called THE STRONG VOWEL OF "R" because it is usually found in STRESSED SYLLABLES.

The first mid vowel sound 3: and the second mid vowel sound ə (when the word has a letter "r" in the spelling) have two acceptable standards of pronunciation:

3: WITHOUT R-COLORING: The tip of your tongue is relaxed behind and touching the back of your lower front teeth. The sound is free and forward.

3ᶜ: WITH R-COLORING: The tip of your tongue is tensed up and over, the body of your tongue is retracted. The sound is tense and back.

R-COLORING is also known as INVERSION, RETROFLEXION, HARD R'S, and WESTERN R'S.

The relaxation of tongue, lower jaw and throat that is necessary for the production of 3: without r-coloring make it an excellent sound to use in developing elasticity and ease of tone and tension-free production of the voice. For this reason it is recommended that in singing and in Good Speech for classic texts, this strong vowel of "r", and the other vowel and diphthong sounds of "r," be made WITHOUT R-COLORING.

For a summation of the consonant, vowel, diphthong, and triphthong sounds associated with the letter "r" in the spelling, see pages 344-345.

WORDS FOR PRACTICE USING 3: LONG

◆ In a STRESSED SYLLABLE when the vowel is the last sound of a word
◆ In a STRESSED SYLLABLE when the vowel is followed by one or more voiced consonants

1 err her (sf) purr burr inter (v) amaTEUR[2] stir cur occur de rigueur myrrh demur
2 blur fur=fir chauFFEUR aver sir (sf) connoiSSEUR shirr monsieur (wh)rr were (sf)

3 herb Herb urban herbal superb bourbon (n; a drink) perturbed Durban curbs Gerber
4 blurb refurbished verb Thurber Serb sherbet gerbil

5 erred heard=herd hurdle purred Perdita bird=Byrd interred curd occurred gird
6 guerdon murder nerd preferred Ferdinand verdant third absurd shirred (wh)rred word

7 ergo purgatoᵊ-ry Burgundy Bergdorf's gurgle Ferguson Virgo

8 ermine Herman Irma hermit permanent sperm Birmingham terms dermal skirmish murmur
9 Myrmidon firm vermin thermal sermon Sherman worm squirm German=Jermyn

10 earn=urn=ern Hearn=Herne Ernie hernia earnest=Ernest Calpurnia burned turn=tern Dern
11 kernel=colonel Gurney inurned learn ferns Verne concerned yearns churn journey

WORDS FOR PRACTICE USING LONG, Cont.

1 earl hurl pearl=purl burl=Berle curl girl Merle Aumerle furl (whirl) world churl
2 early Herlie Erlynne hurling pearly burly=Burleigh curling girlish Merlin furlough
3 Thurlow surly Shirley Sherlock (whirling) Worley swirling churlish

4 Irving Irvine PERvert (n) dervish curves scurvy Merv nerves fervor verve served
5 reserves swerve Gervase

6 further furthest worthy Worthing burthen murther

7 errs hers purrs Pursey spurs burrs inters concurs Curzon demurs Mersey blurs
8 firs=furs=furze confers avers Thursday sirs (wh)rrs

9 Persian excursion version inversion reversion aversion

10 urge urgent purge burgeoning turgid sturgeon dirge scourge regurgitate merge
11 splurge verge Verges virgin surge=serge surgeon

WORDS FOR CLARITY OF 3: PRIOR TO r

✓Reminder ────────────────────────────────

Make a relaxed, clearly defined 3: sound and begin the following syllable with a
clean-cut consonant r. In doing so, you will avoid marring the clarity of the 3:
sound with r-coloring.

12 e-rring pu-rring inte-rring sti-rring sti-rrer cu-rrish concu-rring demu-rring blu-rring

13 blu-rry fu-rry infe-rring ave-rring shi-rring (wh)-rring

WORDS FOR PRACTICE USING 3· HALF-LONG

◆ In a STRESSED SYLLABLE when the vowel is followed by one or more voiceless consonants
◆ In a STRESSED SYLLABLE when the vowel is followed by a voiced consonant that is then followed by a voiceless consonant within the same word
(3: is never followed by another vowel sound within the same word.)

14 Earp herpes Erpingham purpose burp interpret slurp usurp serpent ProSERpina sherpa
15 chirp

16 hurt pert Burton Laertes dirt curt=Kurt courtesy curtsey skirt girtle Gertrude
17 Merton inert alert flirt fertile avert overt thirty assert certain certes=Surtees
18 dessert=desert (v) shirt wert squirt Yertle Chertsey

19 irk Herkimer irksome Hercules Urquhart perk Turk turkey Dirk Kirk gherkin Mercu-ry
20 murky mercantile smirk lurk firkin circus berserk shirk work quirk=Quirke jerkin

21 Herford PERfect (adj) PERfume (n) Burford turf curfew Murphy serf=surf=Cerf

22 earth Perth birth=berth dearth girth mirth firth worth

23 Erse hearse ers(wh)le Hearst Ursula hirsute rehearse coerce purse Percy person
24 Perseus reimburse burst terse durst curses curst=cursed (v) immerse graMERcy nurse
25 first thirst thyrsus Circe worse worst=worsed

WORDS FOR PRACTICE USING 3ˑ HALF-LONG, Cont.

1 Hirsch Herschel Pershing Gershwin immersion commercial inertia assertion worship

2 urchin perch birches kerchief merchant nurture lurch virtue searched reSEARCH (v)

3 Ernst burnt learnt weren't (one syllable)

WORDS FOR PRACTICE USING ʒ SHORT

◆ In all UNstressed SYLLABLES, including WEAK FORMS of words (See pages 21-25.)

4 urbane herbaceous herbivo-rous Hermione hermetic EXpert (n) Hepburn

5 Berlin (Germany) Terpsicho-re Thersites INsert (n) Mercutio

6 WEAK FORMS (wf) of: were her sir

PHRASES FOR PRACTICE

Long 3:	Half-Long 3ˑ	Mixed Lengths
7 ʔ earn e-rring urges	14 ʔ irksome earthy urchin	21 ʔ Erpingham erred
8 sti-rring with a sti-rrer	15 worship dirt	22 Earl heard the urchin
9 squirming worms	16 irksome merchants	23 murmu-ring Merce
10 whirling words	17 the hurt turkey	24 immerse the murde-rer
11 the girl's world	18 reSEARCH the purpose	25 an amaTEUR chauFFEUR
12 Pearl began to purr	19 certainly perfect	26 the earth's curves
13 churlish Merv's nerves	20 a PERfect PERfume	27 an EXpert connoisseur

SENTENCES FOR PRACTICE

Long 3:

28 Colonel Burr served kernels.

29 He's sti-rring with a sti-rrer.

30 Squirming worms are heard early.

31 Whirling words are hurled upon the virgin.

32 The girl's world is filled with churls.

33 Ermine burns, ergo turn to other furs.

34 You worm, you cur, you murmu-rer!

35 Pearl unfurled the world-famous curls.

36 An amaTEUR chauFFEUR? How absurd!

37 They journeyed further to murder birds.

Half-Long 3ˑ

38 The first rehearsal was certainly jerky.

39 We must work to worship virtue.

40 Irksome urchins hurt the turkey.

41 The nurse reSEARCHED the perfect birth.

42 Mercy, her PERfume gets worse and worse.

43 Thirteen chirping turkeys are on alert.

Mixed Lengths

44 ʔ Irma irked earnest Earl with her ermine.

45 The whirling dervishes rehearsed in a circle with Hotspur.

46 Hermione yearned to learn the verse before her first rehearsal.

47 Follow the turn of the earth's curves, monsieur. məˈsjɜː

48 Earl heard the hurt bird's urgings.

49 "Murde-rer," he burst out imperfectly.

50 A certain person had reverted to averting.

51 The concerned nurse urged the girl toward church.

52 What's worse than burnt curd, Merle?

53 Monsieur Ferdinand's chauFFEUR worships courtesy.

54 He heard that Irving Berlin's works are perfect.

55 Did an EXpert inSERT these blu-rry INserts?

56 Thirty persons were irked by those fu-rry, pu-rring Persians.

Represented by the spellings:

al*i*ve	sof*a*	tel*e*phone	th*e* (wf before a consonant)	poss*i*ble	*o*ppose
purp*o*se	mel*o*dy	t*o* (wf before a consonant)	*u*pon	s*u*ppose	chor*us*
lab*y*rinth	sirr*ah*	nat*io*nal	gorg*eou*s	vic*iou*s	por*ous*	Confuc*ius*

AND

bast*ard*	sug*ar*	asc*er*tain	fath*er*	grand*eur*	tap*er*=tap*ir*
stubb*om*	act*or*	cupbo*ard*	s*u*rprise	sulph*ur*	pict*ure*	mart*yr*

(For these and similar words from the "r-spelling" branch of the ∂ family, see page 102.)

Relax your lower jaw and your lips, and relax the tip of your tongue behind your lower front teeth. The only active element of articulation is the body of the tongue, the MIDDLE of which is arched slightly lower than it is for ɜ: . This position is a little lower than the position that the tongue assumes when at rest. In fact, if you merely part your lips, relax and let go your lower jaw and tongue, then vocalize, you will tend to get the correct sound.

This weak, neutral vowel sound seems to have an indeterminate quality and is ALWAYS SHORT because it is ALWAYS FOUND IN UNSTRESSED SYLLABLES:

a-ME-ri-ca   ∂'me r∂kʰ∂

This is the most relaxed sound, as well as the most frequently used vowel sound, in Spoken English. It is sometimes referred to as "the schwa" or "the neutral vowel."

This vowel sound ∂ is the sound that all vowels tend to become in unstressed syllables and in WEAK FORMS of words. The words that may use ∂ in their WEAK FORMS are:

a	an	the (before a consonant sound)	am	can	could	do	does	had
has	have	must	shall	should	was	would	some	them	us	at
from	into	to	of	and	as	but	that	than		(See pages 21-25.)

WORDS FOR PRACTICE USING ∂ IN INITIAL POSITION

✔ *Reminder* ——

∂ **is found ONLY in UNstressed SYLLABLES.**

1 a (wf) The indefinite article is, almost without exception, spoken as ∂ . In EXTREMELY RARE instances of contrastive emphasis or intensified stress, it may be pronounced in its STRONG FORM 'e·ĭ· .

2 uh (American) er (British) (These interjections of vocalized hesitation are prounounced ∂ .)

3 apart appease upon oppose apply appliance appeal app*ro*priate opp*ro*brious

4 abet abate about absorb above abscond obJECT (v) objection observe obscure

5 at (wf) attempt attentive attack attune atomic Atlanta Atlantic at*ro*cious

6 ado adieu adapt addiction admit adˍvantage admire adhere Adonis administer

7 akin account Achilles o'clock occult acknowledge Achitophel accede accept

8 again against agˍhast agog agape ago agree o'G*ro*at Agrippa

WORDS FOR PRACTICE USING ∂ **IN INITIAL POSITION, Cont.**

1 am (wf) amid amends Ame-ṛica amaze amok=amuck among amuse ammonia Amyntas

2 an (wf) anemic anele=anneal analysis anathema anew annuity until annoy and (wf)

3 allow ally (v) allied (v) alǎs Alonso allude allusion allay Aleppo

4 affect affective affied affianced aphasia affair afṛaid afloat afoot afar

5 of (wf) avidity avenge averse avuncular avaunt avail Avoca avoid avow avouch

6 Athena Athenian athanasy athirst athwart Athene

7 us (wf) ascent=assent assimilate aspersion acidity assiduous askew assay acetic

8 as (wf) azalea Azusa Azores (British)

9 ashore ashamed Ashanti

10 ahead ahoy Ahearn=Aherne ahorse Ahithophel ahungered

11 awhile

12 awash await awake away=aweigh aware award

13 achieve Achin

14 agility agenda ajar adjacent adjoin adjourn adjust adjudicate Agenor

WORDS FOR CLARITY OF ∂ **PRIOR TO** ɾ

✓ *Reminder*

Make a clearly defined ∂ **sound and begin the following syllable with a clean-cut consonant r. In doing so you will avoid marring the clarity of the** ∂ **sound with r-coloring.**

15 a-ṛena a-ṛithmetic o-ṛiginal a-ṛṛest o-ṛography A-ṛachne A-ṛabian a-ṛṛange a-wry

16 a-ṛṛive a-ṛise a-ṛight A-ṛion=O-ṛion a-ṛoma a-ṛose a-ṛoint a-ṛṛears

WORDS FOR PRACTICE USING ∂ **IN MEDIAL POSITION**

17 pathetic potato police Potomac Pomona panache palaver palatial pollute Paducah
18 sympathy hypocṛite capable competent hippodṛome epitǎph opposite capitol=capital

19 balloon banana basilica Bassanio buffoon botanical bacchante Bahamas Bologna
20 Eben=ebon ebony sabotage sibilant inhabitant shibboleth Lebanon Thibodaux

21 tomato tonight today together tomŏ-ṛṛow taboo[2] Tacoma Tahiti
22 attitude centipede cǎstaway automatic photogṛǎph artifice stṛategy stṛatosphere

23 Duluth Dolŏ-ṛes Dahomey Damascus Dakota dominion
24 additive adamant manicure sedative modify codify meditate pedigṛee ṛoundabout

WORDS FOR PRACTICE USING ə IN MEDIAL POSITION, Cont.

1 collision capacity commence commit collect cabal cadaver chameleon catharsis
2 comprise compose combine (v) compare component competitive comBAtive
3 conclude condition contend convey conDUCT (v) convention convenient control
4 succotash vacancy fricative recognize academic provocative Maccabeus sycophant

5 galore galoshes guffaw gavotte gazelle gazette Goliath Galatians galactic
6 megaphone monogamous antagonize vagabond legacy brigadier bigamy

7 maternal massage malignant molecular monopoly monsieur molasses Munro mouSTACHE
8 harmony comedy commentator Termagent permanent calamitous Emily stamina Pamela

9 nativity[2] Napoleon Natal Natrona Navarre Nathaniel
10 analyst vanity economy anonymous enemy canopy unicorn penetrate phonograph minimum

11 laboᵒ:-rious LeBeau Lafeu Latrobe latrine Lanier lapel lasagna lascivious Latona
12 telegram mollify holiday syllable halibut melody California elephant illustrate

13 fanatic facility phonetic fallopian fallacious phalanges phenomenon facade
14 taffeta Stephanie cacophony suffocate Antipholus sophomore emphasis

15 voluminous Volumnia Valencia vaGA-ry valise vacuity voluptuous vale'-rian
16 avenue revenue cavity brevity Savona-rola moveable Galveston Navajo

17 Themistocles thalidomide Thalia (muse) θə'l aïə
18 Kathe-rine mathematics Hathaway catheter lithograph pathological aNAthema ethical

19 society salacious satiety suppose succumb sufficient sonoᵒ:-rous solicit Savannah
20 possible passable capacity responsible lassitude discipline gossamer maximum lexicon

21 Zenelaphon Zabriskie Zappoᵒ:-ra
22 feasible Zanzibar Josephine mezzanine marzipan visitor

23 chagrin Shapi-ro chenille shalloon Shallot Shamokin chamade Chanel chemise
24 pe-rishable Haversham Esham national rational fictional professional nonchalant

25 rapacious Rapunzel rabbinical Ramona rapidity rococo Ravenna ravine rappel
26 protect produce (v) pronounce traduce introduce instrument centralize synchronize

27 ce-remony te-rrible ho-rrible te-rrapin pa-rable ba-ronet ae-roplane tho-roughly

28 habitual habiliment hallucinate Havana Hawaii inhalation

29 Chamoᵒ:-rro Chapultepec
30 bachelor Tehachapi

31 Japan japonica Jamaica Jakarta Jacoby[2] jalopy
32 imagination imagina-ry vigilant tragedy longitude regional regiment regurgitate

WORDS FOR CLARITY OF MEDIAL ∂ PRIOR TO ŗ

✔ *Reminder*

> Make a relaxed, clearly defined ∂ sound and begin the following syllable with a clean-cut consonant ŗ . In doing so, you will avoid marring the clarity of the ∂ sound with r-coloring.

1 pa-ṟiah Pa-ṟisian pa-ṟole pe-ṟuke pe-ṟusal Pa-ṟolles pa-ṟishioner   pa-ṟade

2 ba-ṟonial ba-ṟṟage ba-ṟouche Ba-ṟabbas (Amer) ba-ṟoque ta-ṟantula Ta-ṟentum To-ṟonto

3 ca-ṟeer Ko-ṟea cha-ṟisma Co-ṟona Ka-ṟiba cou-ṟageous co-ṟṟupt ca-ṟouse co-ṟṟal

4 ga-ṟage go-ṟilla=gue-ṟilla ga-ṟotte ga-ṟṟulity Ma-ṟia me-ṟingue ma-ṟina ma-ṟoon

5 ma-ṟaud Ma-ṟengo Ma-ṟie mo-ṟel Mo-ṟosco la-ṟyngeal fa-ṟṟago fa-ṟina fa-ṟouche

6 fe-ṟocious fo-ṟensic va-ṟiety va-ṟiola Tho-ṟeau so-rō̃-ṟity pso-ṟiasis su-ṟṟeal

7 su-ṟṟound su-ṟṟender so-ṟites cha-ṟade che-ṟoot ha-ṟangue Ha-ṟa̅ː-re Ge-ṟonimo

8 drape-ṟy snobbe-ṟy histo-ṟy mise-ṟy Grego-ṟy eate-ṟy cele-ṟy sala-ṟy facto-ṟy

9 satisfacto-ṟy contradicto-ṟy valedicto-ṟy summe-ṟy=summa-ṟy gunne-ṟy canne-ṟy mumme-ṟy

10 suga-ṟy machine-ṟy senso-ṟy Flanne-ṟy sorce-ṟy mamma-ṟies nunne-ṟy (See page 348.)

11 live-ṟy leve-ṟage i-ṟṟeve-ṟent i-ṟṟeve-ṟence ava-ṟice Calva-ṟy cove-ṟing cove-ṟage

12 ṟecove-ṟy discove-ṟy Ave-ṟy knave-ṟy savo-ṟy=savou-ṟy Bova-ṟy carve-ṟy

NOTE: The following words do NOT have a schwa sound prior to the consonant r: every=ev'ry.

13 eve̱ry beve̱rage seve̱ral ṟeve̱rend ṟeve̱rence ave̱rage mave̱rick savage̱ry sove̱reign ivo̱ry

14 favo̱rite=favou̱rite (It may be necessary in verse to add a schwa sound for the scansion.)

ENUNCIATE CLEAN SYLLABLES IN -∂ rə bļ ENDINGS

15 con-si-de-ṟa-ble ho-no-ṟa-ble COM-pa-ṟa-ble in-COM-pa-ṟa-ble in-EX-o-ṟa-ble

16 i-nnu-me-ṟa-ble i-ṞṞE-pa-ṟa-ble in-se-pa-ṟa-ble in-su-ffe-ṟa-ble in-to-le-ṟa-ble

17 mea-su-ṟa-ble plea-su-ṟa-ble mi-se-ṟa-ble un-al-te-ṟa-ble un-u-tte-ṟa-ble

18 ve-ne-ṟa-ble vul-ne-ṟa-ble

ENUNCIATE CLEAN SYLLABLES IN −∂ r∂ ENDINGS

19 blun-de-ṟer con-que-ṟor char-te-ṟer em-pe-ṟor ha-mme-ṟer Klem-pe-ṟer u-su-ṟer

20 la-bo-ṟer loi-te-ṟer lin-ge-ṟer mur-de-ṟer mur-mu-ṟer mea-su-ṟer pa-pe-ṟer

21 plå-ste-ṟer plun-de-ṟer su-ffe-ṟer sor-ce-ṟer sta-mme-ṟer tṟea-su-ṟer u-tte-ṟer

22 wan-de-ṟer wa-ve-ṟer (wh)i-spe-ṟer ad-ven-tu-ṟer phi-lan-de-ṟer fin-ge-ṟer

MEDIAL ∂ IN COMMON WORD ENDINGS

23 gallop=Gallup shallop salop scallop dollop wallop tṟollop=Tṟollope sy-ṟup sti-ṟṟup

24 chĕ-ṟub Ǣ-ṟab scǣ-ṟab

MEDIAL ∂ IN COMMON WORD ENDINGS, Cont.

1 ballot harlot zealot Ascot gamut ducat abbot ca-rrot=carat but (wf) that (wf)

2 method salad synod ballad He-rod Ha-rrod's could (wf) would (wf) had (wf)

3 hammock stomach hillock epoch eunuch paddock havoc Lenox ca-rrack ba-rracks

4 column solemn Malcolm venom atom Adam madam=madame phantom kingdom
5 wisdom handsome winsome gingham ha-rem quo-rum fo-rum ala-rum Hi-ram
6 some (wf) them (wf) from (wf)

7 open happen deepen ripen weapon steepen happened sharpened Chippendale*

8 Eben=ebon carbon bourbon ribbon riband Durban turban incumbent *

9 bacon weaken chicken beacon vacant second jocund fecund beckoned reckoned*
10 can (wf)

11 wagon Regan flagon dragon shenanigan Ba-rrigan Logan Hogan Termagant brigand*

12 wanton Brenton Lenten Trenton Hampton inhabitant repentent penitent COMbatant
13 Charleston Brixton Livingstone Gladstone Boston Princeton Galveston

14 London Brendan Ogden Dresden Camden tendon pendant dependent attendant

15 woman gentleman=gentlemen Herman Harmon Hymen common lemon omen
16 Roman summon

17 payment government raiment argument dormant garment adamant pavement judgment
18 diamond Hammond Raymond Drummond summoned Lomond

19 Lennon Lebanon Brennan cannon pennon Tynan phenomenon Shannon
20 tenant covenant imminent eminent component continent

21 Phelan Allan=Allen Dylan gallon Galen MacMillan Milan (in The Tempest) 'mɪlən
22 gallant talent repellant vigilant virulent

23 By-ron he-ron Sha-ron Ka-ren ba-ron=ba-rren Cu-rran Wa-rren
24 e-rrant pa-rent a-rrant appa-rent cu-rrent=cu-rrant to-rrent ty-rant
25 e-rrand ge-rund reve-rend Te-rence igno-rance reve-rence tole-rance

26 audience twopence sixpence halfpence sentence acquaintance repentance circumstance
27 attendance independence penance balance influence violence vigilance affianced

28 minion onion canyon banyan convenient Stanyan Bunyan poignant
29 million mullion scallion valiant Ophelia stallion ebullient Italian brilliant

30 paean=peon Ca-riBBEan Fleance Aegean miscreant McGoohan fluent truant Ryan
31 Dion=Dian pliant client viand scion Zion Hesione Bryant Cohen doyen[2] buoyant

32 vow-el Pow-ell bow-el tow-el MacDow-ell Cow-ell How-ell du-al=du-el renew-al
33 fu-el Sew-all gru-el jew-el cru-el di-al vi-al tri-al roy-al loy-al Low-ell

*Some experts consider these to be syllabic: -p,n   -bn   -k,n   -gn

MEDIAL ∂ IN COMMON WORD ENDINGS, Cont.

1 mammoth Sabbath behemoth Monmouth Plymouth Dartmouth Klamath Goliath

2 famous Amos anonymous furnace menace purpose porpoise trespass[2] nimbus Thomas

3 breakfast Plautus carcass focus windlass callous=Callas solace Wallace palace

4 mischievous grievous voluminous ballast mollusk precious vicious Brutus Cassius[2]

5 a-rras I-ras Py-rrus emba-rrass humo-rous dange-rous amo-rous adulte-rous Ho-race

6 glamo-rous treache-rous HA-rass

7 us (wf) must (wf) (ALSO −∂z in wf: does has was)

8 en-vi-ous Sil-vi-us te-di-ous co-pi-ous hi-la-ri-ous Ca-ssi-us[2] pi-te-ous

9 hi-de-ous se-ri-ous de-vi-ous im-pi-ous The-se-us Per-se-us Or-phe-us

10 He-rri-ot Che-vi-ot cha-ri-ot I-sca-ri-ot Ma-rri-ott

11 my-ri-ad pe-ri-od I-li-ad dry-ad He-si-od

12 te-di-um o-pi-um de-li-ri-um li-no-le-um i-di-om sta-di-um pan-de-mo-ni-um

13 cra-ni-um com-pen-di-um E-ly-si-um Or-phe-um

14 me-di-an Sy-ri-an Vi-vi-en a-vi-an Da-mi-an Char-mi-an A-ra-bi-an

15 re-me-di-al con-vi-vi-al me-ni-al fi-li-al A-ri-el ma-te-ri-al vi-tri-ol

WORDS FOR PRACTICE USING ∂ IN FINAL POSITION

16 idea panacea dia-rrhea Ko-rea Ma-ria Crimea Althea Pia onomatopoeia Cythe-rea

17 in-som-ni-a me-di-a A-ra-bi-a O-lym-pi-a a-ne-mi-a tri-vi-a cor-ne-a se-pi-a

18 Volumnia Calpurnia mania forsythia Cynthia Nige-ria Estonia hyste-ria mala-ria

19 India cornucopia Arcadia Austria Zambia utopia Hermia Olivia Bohemia Columbia

20 tibia fibia ano-rexia diphthe-ria suburbia phobia

21 Van-ya Son-ya=Son-ia Lib-ya E-mil-ia Ce-cel-ia Ca-li-forn-ia Vir-gin-ia

22 azalea gardenia petunia Celia Pennsylvania Saturnalia Britannia Australia Titania

23 alleluia hallelujah Westphalia span-iel Nathan-iel Dan-iel

24 pa-riah Je-remiah papaya Ma-ria (British) Maya jambalaya O-resteia Goya soya

25 pa-ranoia boa Samoa Joshua Nashua

26 Napa Zappa sherpa papa Mazeppa Eu-ropa Tampa Agrippa

27 Cuba tuba Manitoba Sheba Elba rumba samba soba Hecuba scuba

28 taffeta Perdita Alberta fermata pasta data Lysistrata Minnesota Dakota stigmata

29 Rita Anita Greta Calcutta Sparta Hrotswitha to & into (wf before a consonant sound)

30 Linda Leda Candida Canada Flo-rida Hedda panda Amanda armada cicada soda Nevada

31 Ame-rica Alaska Inca e-rotica Casca Rebecca Lorca Africa Monica Bianca Corsica

WORDS FOR PRACTICE USING ə IN FINAL POSITION, Cont.

1 Aga saga mega Riga Vega conga omega

2 comma stigma asthma drama Alabama Oklahoma diploma cha-risma gamma Lima Burma

3 a-rena Nina stamina ma-rijuana oca-rina Anna Louisiana Savannah Helena Vienna

4 Ravenna Dinah Diana manna henna China banana Ca-rolina Dana ma-rina balle-rina

5 vanilla Pella novella impala gala flotilla Ursula go-rilla=gue-rilla Viola cola

6 formula koala Dracula Manila Scilla Venezuela Godzilla Pamela gladiola Angola

7 sofa loofah Haifa

8 Java Eva ova diva Ava Godiva Danilova Jehovah Tovah guava

9 Martha A-retha naphtha Tabitha Samantha Siddhartha Eartha

10 the (wf before a consonant sound)

11 Sousa Lisa Ibiza pizza salsa balsa Ursa Xhosa mimosa Formosa

12 Portia=Porsche Masha Nova Scotia Hypatia Russia pasha inertia fascia acacia Natasha

13 Persia Asia euthanasia amnesia freesia anesthesia aphasia

14 Georgia raja maha-raja ganja ninja

WORDS FOR PRACTICE USING —rə

✓ Reminder

Make a clearly defined vowel sound and begin the following syllable with a clean-cut consonant r . In doing so, you will avoid marring the clarity of the vowel sound with r-coloring.

15 si-rrah e-ra Ve-ra li-ra Ta-ra epheme-ra came-ra tho-rough[2] au-ra Lau-ra

16 flo-ra Au-ro-ra Ma-ra

PHRASES FOR PRACTICE USING ə

17 ? atrocious a-roma

18 ? accept an objection

19 ? Atlanta attempted it

20 opposed pathetic potatoes

21 together tonight at eight

22 tomo-rrow at ten o'clock

23 sabotage the balloon

24 collect chameleon cadavers

25 inconVENiently inCONtinent

26 monogamous gazelles galore

27 Monsieur's mouSTACHE

28 loy-al Pow-ell's tow-el

29 du-al cru-el jew-els

30 ? adieu, Achilles

31 ? upon the hono-rable A-rabian

32 ? a-rrange a-rrivals

33 Madame's bourbon sy-rup

34 epoch of weakened stomachs

35 saTIety is aNAthema

36 recognize the introduction

37 the bachelor sophomore

38 su-rround To-ronto

39 ha-rangue Pa-risian pa-riahs

40 the nunne-ry's hi-sto-ry

41 inCOMpa-rably mi-se-ra-ble

42 an em-pe-ror and a con-que-ror

PHRASES FOR PRACTICE USING ə , Cont.

1 the renew-al of vow-els
2 a ducat for the eunuch
3 Livingstone and Gladstone
4 an ill-shapen halfpence ˈheïpˀəns
5 existence on sixpence
6 sentence the repentent
7 cǽ-rrots, lettuce, celeə-ry

8 in-EX-ə̌-ra-ble amendments
9 ve-neə̌-ra-ble u-su-rers
10 COM-pǎ-ra-ble COMbatants
11 i-RRE-pǎ-ra-ble i-RRE-veə̌-rence
12 the adventu-rer's mur-deə̌-rer
13 DAmask from DaMAscus ˈdæməʂkʰ

SENTENCES FOR PRACTICE USING ə

14 Amidst the middle of Ame-rica is an inCOMpǎ-rable sofa.
15 China's account of the elephant holiday is a saga of great drama.
16 Today, tonight and tomoᴅ̆-rrow—it's Azusa!
17 That idea is a roy-al annoy-ance to the recognized tri-al attorney.
18 Napoleon's voluminous vanity was se-ri-ous-ly te-di-ous to the me-di-a.
19 Life in a utopi-a leads to hy-ste-ri-a, pǽ-ra-noi-a and tri-vi-al de-li-ri-um.
20 Wallace found solǎce in mischievously trespassing in the hi-de-ous sta-di-um.
21 Hallelujah! Cecelia's brilliant azaleas and forsythia have won the Italian medallion.

POLYSYLLABIC ENDINGS WITH - -ə r ı

Some polysyllabic words ending in "-ary," "-ery," "-ory," and "-berry" have TWO acceptable standards of pronunciation in North American English and a THIRD standard in British English.

For example, a word such as "secretary" may be pronounced three ways:

ˈsek,rətˀə rı   THEATER STANDARD FOR GOOD SPEECH IN CLASSIC TEXTS
"SEK-ruh-tuh-ry": the weak vowel sound ə   is in the unstressed penulti-mate syllable, prior to the consonant r;

ˈsek,rə,tˀe rı   STANDARD FOR GENERAL NORTH AMERICAN SPEECH
"SEK-ruh-TE-rry": a strong vowel e   is in the penultimate syllable, which has a secondary stress;

ˈsek,rı t,rı   STANDARD FOR SOME BRITISH-ENGLISH SPEAKERS
"SEK-ri-tri": eliminate the vowel sound altogether, which means that an entire syllable is lost.

22 apotheca-ry arbitra-ry auxilia-ry elocutiona-ry imagina-ry tempǒ-ra-ry ordina-ry
23 prelimina-ry prima-ry missiona-ry Februa-ry volunta-ry dictiona-ry necessa-ry
24 libra-ry lite-ra-ry sanita-ry secreta-ry solita-ry stationa-ry=statione-ry statua-ry
25 contra-ry commenta-ry contempo-ra-ry culina-ry customa-ry he-redita-ry honǒ-ra-ry

26 barbe-rry strawbe-rry raˊspbe-rry baybe-rry cranbe-rry bluebe-rry goosebe-rry

Similarly, a word such as "repertory" may have three standards of pronunciation:

ˈrepˌə tˈə rɪ   THEATER STANDARD FOR GOOD SPEECH IN CLASSIC TEXTS

ˈrepˌə ˌtɔ: rɪ   STANDARD FOR GENERAL NORTH AMERICAN SPEECH

ˈrepˌə tˌrɪ   STANDARD FOR SOME BRITISH-ENGLISH SPEAKERS

1 audito-_ry_ explanato-_ry_ exclamato-_ry_ inflammato-_ry_ invento-_ry_ obligato-_ry_ observato-_ry_
2 offerto-_ry_ o-_ra_-to-_ry_ prePA-_rato_-ry promisso-_ry_ purgato-_ry_ te-_rrito_-ry dedicato-_ry_
3 declamato-_ry_ dormito-_ry_ lavato-_ry_ reformato-_ry_ reperto-_ry_ conservato-_ry_ laborato-_ry_

Some polysyllabic words ending in "-ony" have TWO standards of pronunciation; "ceremony," for instance:

ˈsɛ rə ˌmoŭ nɪ   STANDARD IN ALL KINDS OF NORTH AMERICAN SPEECH
"SE-ruh-MOH-ny": uses a short diphthong oŭ in the penultimate syllable, which has a secondary stress.

ˈsɛ rɪ mə nɪ   STANDARD FOR BRITISH ENGLISH (RP)
"SE-ri-muh-ni": uses the weak vowel ə in the unstressed penultimate syllable.

4 ce-_re_mony testimony mat_ri_mony pat_ri_mony alimony ac_ri_mony parsimony

PHRASES FOR PRACTICE USING – ə rɪ **AND** – ə nɪ

5 extraordina-_ry_ vocabula-_ry_
6 imagina-_ry_ ce-_remony_
7 explanato-_ry_ o-_ra_-to-_ry_
8 elocutiona-_ry_ valedicto-_ry_
9 contra-_ry_ to customa-_ry_ circumstances
10 prima-_ry_ commenta-_ry_
11 lite-_ra_-ry libra-_ry_
12 a reperto-_ry_ company
13 just an ordina-_ry_ observato-_ry_
14 a tempo-_ra_-ry secreta-_ry_
15 audito-_ry_ laborato-_ry_
16 _The Imagina-ry Invalid_ in reperto-_ry_
17 contempo-_ra_-ry promisso-_ry_ notes
18 what an extraordina-_ry_ dictiona-_ry_
19 ac_ri_mony in mat_ri_mony leads to alimony

20 Februa-_ry_ is like purgato-_ry_
21 off to the reformato-_ry_
22 the Ame-_rican_ Conservato-_ry_ Theatre
23 an inflammato-_ry_ o-_ra_-to-_ry_
24 an obligato-_ry_ smile
25 an auxilia-_ry_ lending libra-_ry_
26 arbitra-_ry_ prelimina-_ries_
27 cranbe-_rry_ sauce and goosebe-_rries_
28 a culina-_ry_ laborato-_ry_   ˈkˌjuː lə nə rɪ
29 contempo-_ra_-ry statua-_ry_
30 O true apotheca-_ry_
31 strawbe-_rries_ are necessa-_ry_
32 a solita-_ry_ missiona-_ry_
33 raspbe-_rry_ confectione-_ries_
34 volunta-_ry_ milita-_ry_ testimony

INTRUSIVE "R"

If there is no "r" in the spelling of a word, do not insert a consonant r after the vowel sound when this is followed by another vowel or diphthong sound that begins the next word. The spaces in the following sentences are marked with an arc, ⌢ , to help you proceed properly from one word to the next and avoid an INTRUSIVE "R" sound. Keep the tip of your tongue relaxed behind and touching the back of your lower front teeth as you make the transition from one word to the next:

SAY: the idea⌢of it   NOT: the idear of it

1   Amé-rica⌢ended the war with China⌢on May eighth.
2   Alaska⌢Airlines serves soda⌢and crackers on flights to Asia⌢and Africa.
3   The idea⌢of Cuba⌢asking Alabama⌢amazes me.
4   The sofa,⌢ottoman and china⌢all ended up in the A-rizona⌢office.
5   The panda⌢ate food from China⌢and Taiwan.
6   Will Emma⌢ever get her sofa⌢upholstered?
7   Anna⌢Anderson claimed to be the cza-rina⌢of Russia,⌢I believe.
8   Dana⌢eased onto the sofa⌢and gave Bianca⌢a kiss.
9   Amanda⌢and Jeffrey ate banana⌢ice cream.
10 Tana⌢acted the roles of Hedda⌢and Candida⌢astonishingly well.
11 Going from Lima,⌢Ohio, to Lima,⌢Pe-ru, is my idea⌢of culture shock.
12 NASA⌢announced today that Viola,⌢Olivia⌢and Bianca⌢are reviving their conga⌢and rumba⌢act.
13 The A-rena⌢ended its season with *Lysistrata*⌢and *Anna⌢and the King of Siam.*
14 A llama⌢is play-ing the harmonica⌢at the corner of Ventu-ra⌢and Sepulveda.
15 Santa⌢entered the cabaña⌢on his sleigh.
16 Suburbia⌢is encroaching on the Napa⌢industries.
17 Attila,⌢is all the data⌢in?
18 The new formula⌢only made the baby koala⌢angrier.
19 Linda⌢allowed Puddha⌢and Kasha⌢a single muffin.
20 The sangria⌢at this cantina⌢is delicious.
21 Co-rona⌢ached to have a pizza⌢oven in its plaza⌢a-rea.
22 Stella⌢attained a diploma⌢in the study of Africa⌢and its vanilla⌢industry.

ELIMINATE THE INTRUSIVE "R," THEN USE THE CORRECT LINKING "R" IN WORDS ENDING WITH AN "R" IN THE SPELLING

23 The china⌢is on the table, so dinner is served.
24 Corsica⌢and Cuba⌢are always hotter in summer.
25 The plaza⌢opened on December eleventh.
26 In yoga,⌢a mantra⌢is chanted to enter into Nirvana.
27 Was Dinah⌢in the diner in China?
28 The tuba⌢honestly grew a tuber on its side!
29 Helena⌢and Eleanor elbowed their way in.
30 "Ca-rolina⌢in the Morning" is the finer a-ria⌢of the two.
31 The scuba⌢equipment a-rrived in Cuba⌢on the schooner at noon.

INTRUSIVE "R" FOLLOWING

Do not insert a consonant r after the vowel sound ɔ: when it is followed by another vowel or a diphthong sound either within the same word or in the next word of the phrase. Keep the tip of your tongue relaxed behind your lower front teeth:

SAY: I saw͡ it.   NOT: I sawr it.

1 Mr. McGraw͡ assisted the law͡ and order candidate.
2 Thaw͡ out the chicken and the cole slaw,͡ Alice.
3 "I saw͡ it, I saw͡ it," Shaw͡ asserted.
4 Was Fido's paw͡ injured in the macaw͡ accident?
5 I saw͡ into the gaping maw͡ of the whale.
6 Let's withdraw͡ all the bear claw͡ entries from the draw-ing.
7 The sound of saw͡-ing is gnaw͡-ing away at my nerves.
8 My jaw͡ aches from the raw͡ oysters.

ELIMINATE THE INTRUSIVE "R" AND USE THE CORRECT LINKING "R" WITH "R" IN THE SPELLING OF A WORD

9 Are you sore about the chainsaw͡ attack?
10 You can see every pore on his paw͡ in this shot.
11 Evelyn Waugh͡ always wore all my ove-ralls.   'i:vlɪn 'wɔ:
12 Quit paw͡-ing me! There's a daw͡ at the door and it's pou-ring rain, Isado-ra!
13 There's a flaw͡ in the bone that you're gnaw͡-ing on the floo-ring, so start igno-ring it.

When the vowel sound ə occurs with the letter "r" in the spelling of a word, the sound is known as the

WEAK VOWEL SOUND OF "R" ə AS IN "surprise"

This branch of the ə family, as introduced on page 92, is represented by the spellings:

bastard sugar ascertain father grandeur affirmation tapir stubborn actor cupboard
surprise sulphur picture martyr

The position of ə , the WEAK VOWEL OF "R," has been described earlier in this section, on page 92, but the information bears repeating here.

Relax your lower jaw and your lips and relax the tip of your tongue behind your lower front teeth. The only active element of articulation will be the body of the tongue, the MIDDLE of which is arched slightly lower than it is for ɜ:. This position is a little lower than the position that the tongue assumes when at rest. In fact, if you merely part your lips, relax and let go your lower jaw and tongue, then vocalize, you will tend to get the correct sound.

This sound is called THE WEAK VOWEL OF "R" because it is ALWAYS FOUND IN UNSTRESSED SYLLABLES.

This Weak Vowel of "r" ə and the Strong Vowel of "r" ɜ: (see page 89) have two acceptable standards of pronunciation:

ə   WITHOUT R-COLORING: The tip of your tongue is relaxed behind and touching the back of your lower front teeth. The sound is free and forward.

əc   WITH R-COLORING: The tip of your tongue is tensed up and over, the body of your tongue is retracted. The sound is tense and back.

R-COLORING is also known as INVERSION, RETROFLEXION, HARD R'S, and WESTERN R'S.

In singing and in Good Speech for classic texts, it is recommended that this Weak Vowel of "r" and the other vowel and diphthong sounds of "r," be made WITHOUT r-coloring.

For a summation of the consonant, vowel, diphthong, and triphthong sounds associated with the letter "r" in the spelling, see pages 344-345.

ə   is used in the WEAK FORMS of: are   were   her   for   or   nor   sir (See pages 21-25.)

WORDS FOR PRACTICE USING ə IN INITIAL POSITION

ə   with the letter "r" in the spelling rarely occurs in INITIAL POSITION.

WORDS FOR PRACTICE USING ə IN MEDIAL POSITION

1 purport particular perturbed pertain perDIE Purdue perFECT (v) perFUME (v) perSEver
2 repertò-ry appertain opportunity leopard shepherd=Shepard Lupercal

3 Bermuda BerNARD[2] Albert liberty cupboard clapboard halberd flabbergàst stubborn
4 Osborn=Osbourne Claiborn=Claibourne Cockburn=Coburn Holborn hibernate neighborly

5 chatterbox pestered bastard dastardly accoutered=accout'red Saturday eastern western
6 Saturn subaltern bitterly Chesterfield butterfly interval Battersea

7 pandered standard murdered=murd'red wonderful modern underling wanderlust

8 curtail curmudgeon record (n) Packard lacquered handkerchief

9 beleaguered haggard sluggard Hungerford

10 cummerbund hammered Somers=summers performers dormers

11 monarch unmannerly enervate energy pennyworth ˈpíʌenəθ

12 Willard Ballard mallard dullard collard=collared particularly curlers twirlers

13 forbid forbǽde forlorn forget offertò-ry effort Stafford confirmation com-for-ta-ble

14 vermilion Virginia virginity vernacular Waverly government COvert (n) culvert
15 discovered Malvern severs perSEvers endeavors=endeavours lovers divers overwhelm

16 thermometer Petherbridge Atherton authors

17 Wetherby mothered smothered southern northern brotherly southerly bothersome

18 surprise surmount surVEY (v) survival ascertain pàssersby

19 Azerbaijan desert (n) wizard hazard mazzard reservation

20 fisherman pressured fishers=fissures threshers rashers

21 measured treasured measurements leisurely seizures pleasures treasures

22 billiards Villiers[2] failures vineyard tenured pṍniard

23 pilchard pictured Richard Pritchard Hatchard's Wycherley

24 legerdemain badgered mergers

25 iron ˈaɪ͡ən   ironing ˈaɪ͡ə nɪŋ   (CONTRAST: i-rony   envi-ronment)

∂

WORDS FOR PRACTICE USING ∂ IN FINAL POSITION

1 cree-pi-er ha-ppi-er stea-di-er fu-nni-er su-nni-er doer wooer sewer chewer fewer
2 soothsayer purveyor conveyer buyer dyer Meyer liar prior briar dryer friar=fryer cryer

3 SOME WORDS THAT MAY ALSO BE TRIPHTHONGS: power bower tower dower cower Gower

4 kipper simper (wh)mper leper dapper supper paper taper=tapir torpor

5 Cibber timber Wilbur amber timbre tabor neighbor labor saber=sabre Tiber arbor

6 theater=theatre victor debtor center=centre elector actor attar hatter sátyr
7 senator visitor sowter=souter suitor otter pia mater traitor Tartar martyr
8 Easter sister Mr. jester Nestor Lester=Leicester Wooster=Worcester Foster Gloucester
9 leader breeder elder candor=candour co-rridor rudder nadir seder raider bolder

10 liquor rancor hander succor=sucker euchre Oscar conquer acre fakir

11 eager beleaguer meager=meagre beggar Edgar burger=burgher sugar lager tiger ogre

12 -ŋə slinger singer hangar=hanger Langer

13 -ŋgə linger finger anger languor

14 lemur femur glimmer tremor clamor=clamour glamor=glamour murmur armor=armour

15 dinner tenner=tenor manner=manor governor Elinor=Eleanor miner=minor

16 pallor valor curler twirler color=colour particular trailer parlor
17 settler Tatler rattler butler Midler medlar Adler Sadler=saddler hurdler

18 reefer pilfer heifer zephyr gaffer surfer Christopher Lucifer suffer sulphur

19 beaver Cleaver perSEver never Denver Oliver favor=favour savor=savour survivor Ivor

20 ether author

21 either² neither² breather zither dither (wh)ther wither tether nether leather
22 feather heather (wh)ther weather Cather gather Mather further other mother smother
23 another brother bother father

24 mixer elixir flexor tenser=tensor confessor professor Vassar officer racer e-raser

25 freezer scissor razor appraiser laser Lazar visor adviser=advisor supervisor

26 fisher=fissure thresher pressure censure usher gusher pusher tonsure glacier
27 "-shire" endings: Hampshire Wilshire Worcestershire Gloucestershire Wa-rwickshire

28 seizure leisure² measure pleasure treasure azure Hoosier ozier Frazier

29 tenure familiar failure

30 feature creature teacher bleacher reSEARcher Thatcher future suture venture
31 investiture lite-rature poacher voucher

WORDS FOR PRACTICE USING ə IN FINAL POSITION, Cont.

1 -p₁ t₁ʃə scripture rapture capture rupture

2 -k₁ t₁ʃə picture lecture fracture structure architecture conjecture tincture

3 -s t₁ʃə gesture pasture mixture fixture

4 ledger badger merger Niger dodger Bodger Folger soldier

WORDS FOR PRACTICE USING -r ə

✓ Reminder ───

> Make a clearly defined vowel or diphthong sound and begin the following syllable with a clean-cut consonant r . In doing so, you will avoid marring the clarity of the vowel or diphthong sound with r-coloring.

5 mi-rror e-rror te-rror sti-rrer con-que-ror em-pe-ror la-bo-rer loi-te-rer

6 mur-de-rer mur-mu-rer mea-su-rer pa-pe-rer sor-ce-rer trea-su-rer u-su-rer wan-de-rer

7 (wh)-spe-rer ad-ven-tu-rer phi-lan-de-rer Cu-rrer ho-rror dea-rer nea-rer Shea-rer

8 hea-rer clea-rer bea-rer fai-rer sha-rer ra-rer wea-rer sta-rer poo-rer su-rer

9 pu-rer procu-rer pou-rer

PHRASES FOR PRACTIC USING ə

10 perFECT the reperto-ry

11 Senator Claibourne

12 Mr. George BERnard Shaw

13 treasure pleasures

14 a comfortable interval

15 the neighbor's daughter

16 picture the coward

17 thy brother's brother

18 permit liberty

19 Albert, the happier beaver

20 the traitor Sir Peter

21 perSEver to endeavor

22 pressured the survivors

23 nea-rer and dea-rer

24 ho-rror of ho-rrors

25 an e-rror with a sti-rrer

26 a failure at billiards

27 familiar to Willard

28 a ruptured structure

29 lectures on scripture

30 capture her gestures

31 a fixture of the pasture

32 enraptured conjecture

33 Folger's merger with Sadle-'s

SENTENCES FOR PRACTICE USING ə

34 Father, mother, sister, brother, run for cover!

35 The Centre Theatre Group's cha-racter actors were treasured players.

36 I never, never miss "Creature Feature," "Chiller Theater" and "The Saturday Ho-rror Pictures."

37 Will we ever perfect our manners in this uncomfortable trailer?

38 It's a pleasure to enter the theater to see *Measure for Measure*.

39 Elinor was a traitor to the governments of Leicestershire and Worcestershire.

40 In that architecture, the actual structures were a mixture of raptu-rous conjecture and familiar pasto-ral gestures.

41 Supper's in the cupboard, Mother Hubbard, and it's particularly meager.

42 The i-rony of ironing in Gloucestershire was lost on Mr. Thatcher.

43 The co-rridor's a particularly standard and familiar center for murders.

◆ THE VOWEL SOUND ∧ AS IN "cup" ◆

Represented by the spellings:

much   come   **tou**ch   fl**oo**d   d**oe**s

Relax your lower jaw wide open and relax the tip of your tongue behind your lower front teeth. The MIDDLE of your tongue is arched low in your mouth. Your lips are relaxed and neutral.

The quality of this open vowel sound is direct, crisp and very bright. It is ALWAYS SHORT.

∧ is usually in stressed syllables, but occasionally it is found in unstressed syllables, particularly in compound words:

teacup   butternut   oxblood   handcuff   income

WORDS FOR PRACTICE USING ∧

1 up pup tup twopence twopenny cup hiccough Muppet comeuppance nuptial sup supple
2 _r_upture ab_r_upt th_r_eepence[3] yuppie

3 hub pub bubble Beelzebub tub stub dub double cub nub lubber subaltern _r_ub
4 t_r_ouble g_r_ub chubby

5 utter hut utmost Putney sputter butt=but (sf) Tut cut gut mutt mutter clutter
6 glut flutter slut Sutter _r_ut _R_utland chutney jut

7 udder huddle puddle bud stud Dudley cuddle mud muddle Lud blood flood befuddled
8 thud sudden _r_udder Judson

9 Uckland huckster Uxb_r_idge Huxley Puck Buckingham Buxton tucks=tux duck muck
10 amok=amuck knuckle luck Biloxi luxŭ-_r_y[2] deluxe plucked suck shuck _r_uck t_r_ucks
11 st_r_uck inst_r_uct f_r_uctify chuck juxtapose

12 ugly hug pug bugs tug dug=Doug mug lug slug luxŭ-_r_y[2] thug _r_ug d_r_ug chug

13 umber humble umb_r_ella hum umb_r_age Humph_r_ey pommel bum tumble stomach stump dumb
14 come income compass gum mum mumble numb lumber plum=plumb Blum glum slum fumble
15 sum=some (sf) summit conSUmmate (adj) summer _r_um d_r_ums grumble chum jumble jump

16 under hunter Hun pun bundle ton stun dun=done dungeon cunning guns Monday month
17 nun=none London Lunt lunge plunge blunder blunt=Blount fun thunder sun=son shun
18 _r_un _r_unt t_r_undle won=one wonder "un-" prefixes (e.g., undone unloved undiscovered)
19 IN SHAKESPEARE: CONjure (juggle, invoke a spirit) constable

20 hung bung tongue stung dung among lung slung flung clung sung _r_ung young
21 Unger hunger bungle fungus jungle "-monger" suffixes (e.g., warmonger fishmonger)
22 uncle hunk punk puncture bunk dunk skunk monk nuncle lunk plunk slunk clunk
23 flunk avuncular sunk sunken t_r_unk d_r_unk d_r_unken sh_r_unk chunk junk juncture

24 hull bulb bulge dull indulge cull skull gulls seagull mull annul lull divulge

25 ullage Tully dullard culling Culligan Gulliver mulling lulling lullaby sullied

26 -∧l̯jə- ebullient scullion mullion

WORDS FOR PRACTICE USING $\bigwedge$, Cont.

1 ulcer Hulce Ulster ultimate ultra ulna ulte-rior hulk pulp pulchritude pulse
2 impulse repulse compulsive bulk adult adulte-ry culprit culpable cult occult
3 culminate culture gulf gulp gulch emulsion tumultuous TUmult fulcrum Vulcan
4 revulsion vulture vulne-rable consult sulk result exult

5 huff puff buff tough Macduff duffel cuff muffle enough luff bluff
6 slough (shed skin) suffer shuffle rough=ruff ruffle scruff truffle chuff=chough

7 oven hover above dove coven covey covet cover covenant covert (n) discovers
8 govern love plover gloves shoved

9 Uthwatt Arbuthnot doth Cuthbert Kornbluth Guthrie nothing

10 other Hotham t'other mother smother another Sutherland southern=Sothern southerly
11 southron Southwark Sotheby's Rutherland Ruthrieston brother

12 us (sf) hustle pus bus bust bustle busk tusk dust=dost dusk cusp discuss disgust
13 gusset muss must (sf) musk muscle muster lust fustian thus sustenance SUspect (n)
14 rust truss trust crust just justice

15 puzzle buzz does (sf) dozen doesn't cousin coz cozier guzzle muzzle nuzzle fuzz
16 Chuzzlewit
17 IN SHAKESPEARE: hussy hussif=huzzif=huswife=housewife $'h\Lambda z i \mathcal{f}$

18 usher hush percussion gush mush lush luscious blush flush rush brush crush
19 thrush

20 hutch touch Dutch duchess duchy escutcheon much clutch such crutch

21 pudgy budge cudgel curmudgeon nudge bludgeon fudge trudge drudge grudge judge

WORDS FOR CLARITY OF $\bigwedge$ PRIOR TO $\curlyvee$

✔ *Reminder* ——————————————————————————————

> **Make an open, clearly defined $\bigwedge$ sound and begin the following syllable with a clean-cut consonant $\curlyvee$. In doing so, you will avoid marring the clarity of the $\bigwedge$ sound with r-coloring.**

22 bu-rrow=bo-rough tu-rret Du-rham dhu-rrie cu-rry cou-rage encou-rage discou-raged

23 Cu-rrier Cu-rran cu-rrant=cu-rrent cu-rrency occu-rrence Mu-rray Mu-rrow mu-rri-on

24 mu-rrain nou-rish nou-rishment fu-rrow fu-rrier (dealer in furs) tho-rough

25 tho-roughly Su-rrey su-rrogate hu-rry hu-rried hu-rriedly hu-rricane wo-rry

26 wo-rried wo-rry-ing flou-rish flu-rry scu-rrilous

Λ

MATCH THE Λ SOUNDS IN THE FOLLOWING PAIRS OF WORDS:

1 cŭp — cŏu-rage
2 cut — cu-<u>rr</u>y
3 buck — bo-<u>r</u>ough=bu-<u>rr</u>ow
4 tuck — tu-<u>rr</u>et

5 cut — occu-<u>rr</u>ence
6 muck — Mu-<u>rr</u>ay
7 mutt — mu-<u>rr</u>ain
8 Canuck — nou-<u>r</u>ish

9 fun — fu-<u>rr</u>ow
10 suck — Su-<u>rr</u>ey
11 Huck — hu-<u>rr</u>y
12 luck — flou-<u>r</u>ish

PHRASES FOR PRACTICE USING Λ

13 b<u>r</u>other stunned mother
14 *Suddenly Lăst Summer*
15 cunning constable
16 flooded with money
17 humble judge
18 doves took the funds
19 lust among the young
20 such fun in the sun
21 conSUmmate sums
22 she doesn't <u>r</u>un enough
23 culture vulture
24 <u>r</u>epulsively indulgent

25 conjure with a compass
26 he loves the d<u>r</u>ums
27 buttercups in the sun
28 TUmult and thunder
29 shun the young
30 the dull gulls
31 exulting adultĕ-<u>r</u>er
32 on a hund<u>r</u>ed f<u>r</u>onts
33 yes, coz, he does love
34 wonder just once
35 just among the young
36 an impulsive adult

37 tho-<u>r</u>oughly discou-<u>r</u>aged
38 cut up the cu-<u>rr</u>ency
39 hu-<u>rr</u>y, you hussif!
40 enough nou-<u>r</u>ishment
41 twopence in the tu-<u>rr</u>et
42 we won, so don't wo-<u>rr</u>y
43 a mutt named Mu-<u>rr</u>ay
44 the Lunts in *Love for Love*
45 that dumb sun
46 she suns in the buff
47 a younger warmonger
48 compulsive consultant

SENTENCES FOR PRACTICE USING Λ

49 Ŭ Ugly Uncle Unger hung up on us.
50 Mu-<u>rr</u>ay's cousin loved jitterbugging at Sunday functions.
51 The loving cup was such fun to muck up.
52 B<u>r</u>other stunned mother lăst summer with his impulsive stunts.
53 She was flooded with fun and money.
54 Justice Justin, just one moment!
55 Much thunder dŭ-<u>r</u>ing the hu-<u>rr</u>icane wo-<u>rr</u>ied Gus.
56 The plumber encou-<u>r</u>aged the young fu-<u>rr</u>ier to hu-<u>rr</u>y to Su-<u>rr</u>ey.
57 <u>R</u>usty was a glutton for butternut fudge at potluck suppers.
58 Yucca is among the youngest succulents in One-Gun Gulch.
59 Let's see *A Month in the Country* in London.
60 Those dull gulls <u>r</u>epulsed the adults.
61 It's a wonder that one dozen turtledoves and a hund<u>r</u>ed buttercups we<u>r</u>e enough.
62 He hung up his gloves with a discou-<u>r</u>aged sh<u>r</u>ug.
63 T<u>r</u>ust Bud to encou-<u>r</u>age gluttony and d<u>r</u>ug-<u>r</u>unning at the supper club.
64 Consult a culture vulture for <u>r</u>esults in a hu-<u>rr</u>y.
65 The Bucket of Blood is a conSUmmate London pub. *k̆ən bʌmĭtʰ*
66 Love and lust lulled my hulking bulk.
67 I wonder if there's much nou-<u>r</u>ishment in a twopenny bun? *'tʰʌp, n̩ɪ*
68 Yes, coz, to dust thou dost <u>r</u>eturn.
69 The younger warmonger conjured up twopence for the housewife. (=hussif=huzzif=huswife)

'tʰʌpʰənɹ

ɜː	ə		ʌ
Eerie, soft murmur	Weak, neutral sound		Open, crisp sound
Usually in STRESSED SYLLABLE	Always in UNstressed SYLLABLE		Usually in STRESSED SYLLABLE
1 err	er (hesitation)	uh=a	up
2 sir (sf)	surprise	suppose	sup
3 fur	gopher	sofa	fun
4 burrs	berserk	bazooka	buzz
5 cu-rrish	acre	co-rral	cou-rage
6 conCUR	CONquer	commence	come
7 Turk	otter	Tacoma	tuck
8 dirge	odor	soda	duck
9 MURder	MUR-der	Duluth	dull
10 earn=urn	slattern	until	untilled
11 demur	femur	ma-rine	mu-rrain
12 verve	ever	ve-racious	Vulcan
13 occur	ochre	cocoon	cuckold
14 gird	ogre	go-rilla	Gussow

SENTENCES FOR PRACTICE USING ɜː , ə AND ʌ

```
    3: ə    ə ə ʌ
15 Earn a pattern of fun.
    ə  ɜ·     ɜ:        ə  ʌ  ə ə 3· ə    ʌ ə              ʌ
16 The cursing Colonel, never much of a curser, is cu-rrently making cu-rry.
        ə  ɜ·    ə ə      ʌ  ə ə ə       ə
17 Ought a Turkish otter to take Tucker to Tacoma?
    ə         ə ə      ʌ  ə  3:
18 I suppose it's a surprise supper, sir?
    3:  ə ə    ə ə    ə    ə ʌ            ʌ
19 Infer that an infe-rence from the fu-rrier might be fun.
    ə    ə  ʌ  3: ə    ə    ə  3:
20 A gopher "fun fur" was offered to Fern.
    ʌ    ə         ə ə  3: ə  ə           ə
21 Come! Commence to conCUR and to CONquer.
    ʌ ə ə         3: ə   ə   ə
22 Must a ma-rine demur to femur inju-ry?
```

SENTENCES FOR PRACTICE USING THE THREE MID VOWEL SOUNDS FOLLOWED BY THE CONSONANT ɾ

✔ *Reminder* ──

Make a clearly defined vowel sound and begin the following syllable with a clean-cut consonant ɾ . In doing so, you will avoid marring the clarity of the vowel sound with r-coloring.

     ə 3:   ə ə ə   ə ʌ
1 The pu-<u>rr</u>ing empe-<u>r</u>or was in a hu-<u>rr</u>y.

      3:        ə ɔ ə ʌ
2 It's bu-<u>rr</u>y in the labo-<u>r</u>ers' bo-<u>r</u>ough.

    ə 3:   3: ə ə ə ʌ
3 The my-<u>rr</u>hic murmu-<u>r</u>er was Mu-<u>rr</u>ay.

    ə 3:   ə ə   ə ʌ
4 The (wh)-<u>rr</u>ing wande-<u>r</u>er made us wo-<u>rr</u>y.

    ə 3:   ə ʌ ə   ə ʌ
5 The fu-<u>rr</u>y thing was cove-<u>r</u>ing the fu-<u>rr</u>ow.

      ə 3:   ə   ə ʌ
6 She was sti-<u>rr</u>ing batte-<u>r</u>ies in the tu-<u>rr</u>et.

    ə 3:   ə ə   ʌ
7 The cu-<u>rr</u>ish conque-<u>r</u>or had cou-<u>r</u>age.

     ə 3: ə ə   ə ɑ ə ə ə   ʌ
8 Are the sti-<u>rr</u>er and the plaste-<u>r</u>er from Su-<u>rr</u>ey?

    ə 3:   ə ə ə   ʌ ə
9 The pu-<u>rr</u>ing stamme-<u>r</u>er could barely stutter.

      3:     3: ə ə   ʌ ə   ə ʌ
10 "You cu-<u>rr</u>ish murde-<u>r</u>er," she uttered with a flu-<u>rr</u>y.

     ə   3:   ə   ə ə   ə ə ə ə ʌ ə ə ʌ ə
11 She was infe-<u>rr</u>ing that he was a philande-<u>r</u>er and a scu-<u>rr</u>ilous hustler.

Wh**o**

The BACK VOWELS are those vowel sounds in which the BACK of your tongue is arched in relation to the soft palate. For each of the back vowel sounds, with the exception of *α:* as in "fathers," your lips are rounded. For *α:* your lips are relaxed, or neutral.

w**ou**ld

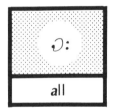

obey

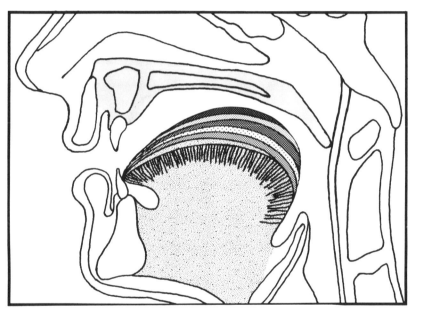

all

◆ Your Lower Jaw is Relaxed

◆ Tip of your Tongue Touches Lower Teeth

◆ Soft Palate is Raised

◆ The Sounds are Voiced

h**o**nest

f**a**thers?

◆ THE VOWEL SOUND *u:* AS IN "wh*o*" ◆

Represented by the spellings:

r*u*de   bl*ue*=bl*ew*   fr*ui*t   d*o*   *oo*ze   s*ou*p   sh*oe*

thr*ough*=thr*u*=thr*o'*=thr*ew*

Of all the back vowel sounds in Spoken English, this one calls for the arch of the tongue to be in its highest and farthest-back position. It also calls for the most lip-rounding of any sound in Spoken English.

Relax your lower jaw and rest the tip of your tongue behind your lower front teeth. Arch the BACK of your tongue high toward your soft palate and round your lips into a circle.

A dark ominous quality is characteristic of this sound. The close lip-rounding should bring the awareness of a pure and forward placement of tone.

This vowel sound is frequently preceded by the consonant sound *j* , producing a combination *ju:*, commonly known as "Long U" or "Liquid U." Here are a few examples of words containing the combination *ju:* :

you=ewe   pew=Pugh   beauty   tune   duke   cue=Kew=queue   argue   mute   new=knew

lute[2]   few   view   thews   assume[2]   Zeus   hue=hew=Hugh

In the words, phrases and sentences in this section, *ju:* will be given only in initial position. An extensive section with this combination in medial and final positions may be found on pages 310-311.

WORDS FOR PRACTICE USING *u:* LONG

◆ In a STRESSED SYLLABLE when the vowel is the last sound of a word

◆ In a STRESSED SYLLABLE when the vowel is followed by one or more voiced consonants

1 Pooh shampoo boo taboo ca-ribou two=too Timbuctoo virTU Xanadu coo goo moo
2 loo=Lou Waterloo blue=blew clue=clew glue flew=flue=flu slew=slough (marsh) canoe
3 rendezvous Sioux zoo shoe rue kanga-roo Prue brew true drew crew accrue grew
4 threw=through=thru=thro' strew misconstrue screw who woo you=ewe chew Jew

5 STRONG FORMS (sf) of: do   you   to   who (relative pronoun)
6 NOTE: The prepositions "into" "onto" "unto" usually have their first syllables stressed, but frequently in verse the second syllable is stressed, with a long *u:* : inTO onTO unTO.

7 Poo-Bah boob Doobie goober looby Schubert=Shubert rube rubric Reuben rhubarb
8 A-ruba che-rubic troubadour shrew Eubie jubilant Jubal

9 oodles who'd (sf) poodle booed doodle cooed kudos mood=mooed noodles
10 clewed=clued included occlude conclude glued food voodoo rude=rued=rood rudiments
11 prude prudent brood=brewed intrude protrude Drood crude=crewed strewed
12 misconstrued strudel wooed you'd (sf) chewed Judas adjudicate judo Jude Judy

13 bougainvillea Dougan Dougal Coogan googly beluga nougat Chattanooga Kruger frugal

14 oomiak=umiak boom tomb Khartoum doom combe loom plume bloom gloom zoom
15 room=rheum rumor=rumour ruminate broom groom whom womb Youmans

WORDS FOR PRACTICE USING ʊː LONG, Cont.

1 Oona kahuna harpoon spoon boon=Bohun (in G.B. Shaw) baboon cartoon Doone
2 Muldoon cocoon schooner Scone (*Macbeth*) tycoon goon drăgoon lagoon moon noon loon
3 balloon typhoon buffoon soon Zuni zounds shoon rune mă-roon Be-rowne=Bi-ron
4 prune poltroon croons strewn wound swounds unify universe fortune (British only) June
5 Juneau=Juno Junius

6 oolong who'll (sf) hooligan pool Istanbul tool stool Dooley cool school ghoul
7 fool Missoula rule drools Yule=Yul=you'll (sf) Jules Julius Julie julep Juilliard

8 move moving removes unmoved louver effluvium prove proven improved approve
9 reprove groove behove Hoover hooves (esp. British) you've (sf) juvenile=Juvenal

10 booths smooth smoothed soothe soothes truths youths

11 ooze=Ouze whose=who's ousel=ouzel Ousey=Uzi ouzo booze two's Duse Jacuzzi moos
12 lose Toulouse blues clues glues floozy snooze zoos shoes ruse=rues pĕ-ruse
13 bruise=brews Druse cruised woozy use (v) choose=chews Jews

14 Hoosier conclusions exclusion malocclusion rouge intrusion protrusion

15 stooge Fuji Scrooge

WORDS FOR PRACTICE USING ʊˑ HALF-LONG

◆ In a STRESSED SYLLABLE when the vowel is followed by one or more voiceless consonants
◆ In a STRESSED SYLLABLE when the vowel is followed by another vowel sound within the same word

16 oops hoops poop nincompoop Boop stoops coop=coupe recoups coupon snoop
17 Snoopy loop blooper sloop soup Rupert troop=troupe drooping croup Scroop scruples
18 unscrupulous groups grouper regrouped upsilon whooping=hooping swoop Jupiter

19 boot toot moot loot Pluto Plutarch Klute glutinous snooty footle footling
20 souter=sowter zoot shoot root=route che-root brute=bruit brutal Brutus recruit
21 crouton fruit hoot cahoots Utah Ute Jute

22 spook Buchă-rest toucan kook snooker palooka glucose fluke Fă-rouk euchre jukebox

23 oof pouf spoofed Tartuffe goof Goofy aloof loofah roof Rufus rueful proof
24 reproof hoof (esp. British) woof (weaving) euphony

25 booth booth's tooth tooth's couth uncouth vermouth Duluth sleuth sooth forsooth
26 soothsayer Ruth ruthless truth youth youth's euthanasia

27 papoose caboose twosome couscous goose moose=mousse noose loose loosen
28 conclusive reCLUSE[2] exclusive sluice Azusa roost rooster Proust spruce Bruce
29 truce intrusive obtrusive abstruse trousseau crucify gruesome hoosegow Hoosic
30 juice use (n) used to (was accustomed to)

31 cartouche ablution sushi ruche ruching bă-rouche crucial excruciating

WORDS FOR PRACTICE USING $u\cdot$ HALF-LONG, Cont.

1 pooch duce (Italian) Gooch mooch smooched hooch Chattahoochee

2 bowie knife Louie chewy ruin fluid Druid cruet incongruity truant fluent doer
3 wooer brewer gluing doing mooing booing chewing shrewish Jewish roué luau

WORDS FOR PRACTICE USING u SHORT

◆ In all UNstressed SYLLABLES, including WEAK FORMS of words (See pages 21-25.)

4 boutique Bhutan toupee plutocracy routine prudential brutality brunette throughout
5 ubiquitous unique euphonious judicious cashew bijou statue statute virtue nodule
6 WEAK FORMS (wf) of: do you who (relative pronoun)
               to into onto unto (before a vowel or diphthong sound)

PHRASES FOR PRACTICE

Long u:	Half-Long $u\cdot$	Mixed Lengths
7 ˀ oozing ousels	18 Oops! Oof!	29 ˀ ouzo has oomph
8 school shoes	19 fruit juice	30 whose room do you use
9 the Moody Blues	20 a moose, forsooth	31 use Ruth's rouge
10 a cool pool	21 the brute's route	32 rumors on the roof
11 gloom of the tombs	22 the youth's boot	33 routinely soothe Bruce
12 move to the moon	23 the use of fruit	34 remove Ruth's booze
13 whose spoon	24 a loose noose	35 glu-ing the stool
14 whose school shoes	25 regroup in Duluth	36 a brutish tycoon
15 choose two schools	26 loose root	37 cool grapefruit juice
16 snooze on the cruise	27 recoup the loot	38 the truth, you brute
17 improved pool rules	28 uncouth Ruth	39 Tartuffe's boot boutique

SENTENCES FOR PRACTICE

Long u:

40 Whose shoes did Julie use?

41 Pooh's school shoes are cool.

42 The gloom and doom in the room threw me.

43 I'll zoom through school 'til Yule.

44 The Moody Blues are truly moving and grooving.

45 The pool rules are made by fools.

46 We flew to the Missoula Zoo.

47 Who'll use a spool in the pool?

Half-Long $u\cdot$

48 Fruit juice is a useful fluid.

49 The moose looped the loop, forsooth.

50 Add vermouth to the rooster soup.

51 What are we doing on the roof, Rufus?

52 The drooping troupe changed route.

53 And Ruth's aloof to boot!

SENTENCES FOR PRACTICE, Cont.

Mixed Lengths

1 ʔ Oodles of ouzels and oomiaks oozed oomph.
2 Ruth shooed the two roosters and the loose goose out of the pool.
3 Choose between fruit juice, prune soup and mousse.
4 Rules improved the school's afternoon routine.
5 You'll find him crude, rude and abusive.
6 It behoves you to prove yourself a fool.
7 The brunette's trousseau was from the boutique in Duluth.
8 Who was so rude and crude as to snooze through Bruce's conclusion?
9 The uncouth brutal ghoul had no use for the truth.
10 Booze won't improve Pluto's afternoon blues.
11 You're through, you brute . . . and not a moment too soon!
12 Remove the blue plume and ruching from Lulu's tutu.
13 I'm in no mood to be wooed by Tartuffe.
14 Junius Booth's lack of tooth decay was conclusive proof of his youth.
15 All too soon, a brutal typhoon will strew sloops and schooners throughout Altoona.
16 Rude Ruth's rooms are ruined by blue and ma-roon roofing.
17 Rupert, do this soon, and by June you'll be cruising to A-ruba on a sloop.
18 It may prove prudent to use chicken soup to prevent croup and whooping cough. ˈhuːpɪŋ
19 The two jubilant juveniles from Buchá-rest used a foolproof ruse against the troops.
20 In his youth, Scrooge proved conclusively to be a truly smooth tycoon.
21 By Jupiter, they're shooting a movie on the moon!
22 Lord Scroop's unscrupulous moves in Shrewsbú-ry were misconstrued by the moody dragoons.
23 The true-blue sleuth's Waterloo was his rendezvous with a loose floozy in a caboose.

$ju:$

◆ **THE CONSONANT-VOWEL SOUND** $ju:$ **AS IN** *"you"* ◆

Represented by the spellings:

> **you**=ewe h**ue**=h**ew**=H**ugh** b**eau**ty t**u**ne c**ue**=K**ew**=q**ueue** v**iew** Ze**us**

This combination is popularly known as "Long U" or "Liquid U" It is found frequently in initial position and also following most of the consonant sounds of Spoken English.

$ju:$ is optional when following the sounds *s* and *l* within the same syllable:

> suit *'sju·t^h* or *'su·t^h*   lute *'lju·t^h* or *'lu·t^h*

As with all words that have an optional pronunciation, these words are noted in this textbook by the placement of a small, raised ² following them:

> suit²   lute²

$ju:$ NEVER occurs after certain consonant sounds and consonant combinations within a word. Examples of these, which call for the pure vowel sound $u:$ include:

'p‚lu‚m	*'blu:*	*'k‚lu:*	*'glu:*	*'flu:*	*'slu:*	*'ɪʃu*
plume	blew=blue	clue	glue	flew=flue	slew	issue

'ru:d	*'p‚ru:d*	*'bru:*	*'t‚ru:*	*'st‚ru:*	*'dru:*	*ə'k‚ru:*
rude	prude	brew	true	strew	drew	accrue

'sk‚ru:	*'gru:*	*'fru·t^h*	*'θru:*	*'ʃru:*	*'tʃu:*	*'dʒu:*
screw	grew	fruit	threw	shrew	chew	Jew

WORDS FOR PRACTICE USING $ju:$ LONG

◆ In a STRESSED SYLLABLE when the vowel is the last sound of a word

◆ In a STRESSED SYLLABLE when the vowel is followed by one or more voiced consonants

1   ewe=you (sf) pew=Pugh imbue debut stew dew=due adieu subdue residue cue=Kew=queue
2   skew askew mew new=knew=gnu avenue revenue retinue lieu² few
3   view review=revue thew sue=Sue² ensue² pursue² hew=hue=Hugh

4   Eubie puberty buboes tube Tubal tuber tubular dubious indubitable cube
5   cubic Cuba lugubrious nubile Nubian Newbe-rry lubricate² salubrious ²
6   exube-rant² Hubie Hubert hubris

7   Udall Udimore you'd (sf) imbued Tudor attitude platitutde beatitude latitude
8   rectitude gratitude etude studious student cued=queued argued mewed nude renewed
9   lewd² prelude² ludicrous² allude² elude² delude² feud feudal
10   viewed sued² suda-ry² exude²

11   fugue Hugo Huguenot

12   Yuma Youmans puma spume albumen tumor TUmult costume cumulus=cumulous
13   cumulative accumulate nume-ral nume-rous Newman illuminate² luminous²
14   luminescent² aluminum² voluminous² fume fumigate perFUME (v) assume² consume²
15   resume² exhume² presume² human humanoid humor=humour Hume
16   humo-rous=hume-rus humid Yuma Youmans

17   unit uniform universe Eunice impugn puny tune tuna opportunity tunic dune
18   cuneiform immune lunar² lunacy² lunatic² fune-ral hewn

WORDS FOR PRACTICE USING $ju:$ LONG, Cont.

1 Yule=Yul=you'll (sf) eulogy eulogize pule puling vestibule tulip duly ridicule
2 culina-ry gules mule mulish Newley=newly Hewlitt

3 uvula you've (sf)

4 use (v) pew=Pugh's spews imbues abuse (v) Tuesday dues cues=queues accuse
5 muse=mews amuse amusing new=gnus renews sinews newspaper curlews[2] purlieus[2]
6 fuse refuse refusal confused fusilier views thews enthused enthusiasm
7 sues=Sue's[2] Susan[2] ensues[2] pursues[2] hews=hues=Hugh's

8 usual usually usu-ry usu-rer contusion illusion[2] allusion[2] collusion[2]
9 fusion profusion confusion infusion

10 pugilist Nugent deluge huge hugely hugeous

WORDS FOR PRACTICE USING $ju\cdot$ HALF-LONG

- ◆ In a STRESSED SYLLABLE when the vowel is followed by one or more voiceless consonants
- ◆ In a STRESSED SYLLABLE when the vowel is followed by another vowel sound within the same word

11 pupil stupid dupe duplicate duplex Cupid recupe-rate[2] cupola lupine[2]
12 Lupercal[2] supine[2] super[2] supe-rintendent[2] supervise[2]

13 Ute Utah pewter putrid repute computer Butte beauty tutor tutelage astute
14 institute destitute duty duteous dutiful Deute-ronomy cute acute cuticle mute
15 commute mutant mutiny newt neuter neutral neutron Newton nutriments miNUTE (adj)
16 lute[2] salute[2] ABsolute[2] REsolute[2] DIssolute[2] refute futile suit[2]
17 suitor[2] pursuit[2]

18 euchre ukulele puke rebukes Dubuque Pentateuch duke ducal cucumber mucous=mucus
19 nuclear nucleus Luke[2] lucrative[2] LUcrece[2] Fuchs sucrose[2]

20 euphony Beaufort (South Carolina) Buford NewfoundLAND

21 youth youth's euthanasia

22 use (n) Euston puce abuse (n) abusive obtuse deuce introduce deduce reproduce
23 induce conducive Cusack mucilage nuisance hypotenuse lucid[2] Luce[2] Lucifer[2]
24 elusive=illusive[2] fusillade fuselage effusive Zeus[2] Houston (Texas)

25 Lilliputian contribution institution constitution elocution Mercutio minutiae
26 Aleutian[2] solution[2] Lucius[2] revolution[2] fuchsia Confucius

27 mutual future suture[2]

28 spewing Stuart=Stewart steward stewing du-el=du-al duo Dewey=dewy new-el
29 re-new-al nuance Newark ingenuity annuity Lewis[2] fu-el suicide[2] suet[2]

WORDS FOR PRACTICE USING ju SHORT

◆ In all UNstressed SYLLABLES, including WEAK FORMS of words (See pages 21-25.)

1 unique unite ubiquitous euphonious euthanasy Eugene pudendum bubonic bucolic
2 bulimia tuberculosis tumescent tuition CONtumely stupendous stupidity duet Dumain
3 duplicitous Duquesnes cupidity cubiculo Cunard museum mutation nume-rical nutrition
4 lieutenant[2] purlieu[2] nephew fune-real PERfume (n) Thucydides superb[2] supreme[2] superlative[2]
5 humane humunculous humanity humiliate
6 WEAK FORMS (wf) of: you you'd you'll you've

For more practice material on ju: , see pages 310-311.

PHRASES FOR PRACTICE

Long ju:	Half-Long $ju\cdot$	Mixed Lengths
7 use a new attitude	12 stupid pupils and tutors	17 refuse the duke's views
8 the usual dubious reviews	13 refute astute institutes	18 acute TUmult and enthusiasm
9 pursue new avenues	14 reproduce minute nutrients	19 a museum for Tudor cos-tumes
10 amused at the news	15 absolutely beautiful	20 introduce Stewart to Hugh Newley
11 assume an attitude	16 salute the dutiful duo	21 salute the lewd lieutenant

SENTENCES FOR PRACTICE

Long ju:

22 What's the new news at the new court? (*As You Like It*, I.i.95-96)
23 We humans presume that we're immune to news from the indubitably huge universe.
24 Much to our amusement, allusions to lunacy were pursued with enthusiasm.
25 The student newspaper was deluged with the usual profusion of platitudes. $'del_iju$:
26 On Tuesdays Mr. Hewlitt usually eulogizes nume-rous Tudor pugilists. ju: $zu \partial l$,

Half-Long $ju\cdot$

27 The pursuit of nuclear fu-els is acutely futile and stupid.
28 The duke introduced astute and lucrative resolutions into the institute.
29 Cupid reputedly makes a nuisance of himself in the execution of his elusive duties.
30 They can't be induced to duplicate the minute nuances of beautiful elocution.
31 That stupid tutor has no future with the ukulele, let alone the lute!

Mixed Lengths

32 The reviews of the duke's new tune were unusually abusive.
33 It's lunacy to view the universe as conducive to universal computer use.
34 The tutor's bemused attitude amused the studious pupils.
35 His nephew's stupendous stupidity eluded Zeus.
36 The ubiquitous duo introduced another superb culina-ry contribution to the lieutenant.
37 I assume she bade adieu to her exube-rant suitor in Newark and took the tube to New York.
38 In my view, it's an indubitably abusive, stupid and deluso-ry institution.
39 You accuse me of reproducing the Tudor illumination? How ludicrous!

For words distinguishing the pure vowel sound u: and the combination ju:, see page 310, lines 1-11.

◆ THE VOWEL SOUND U AS IN "would" ◆

Represented by the spellings:

book wolf could pull worsted

Relax your lower jaw and rest the tip of your tongue behind your lower front teeth. Arch the BACK of your tongue high toward the soft palate, almost as high as for the position of $u\colon$ (this sound bears the same relation to $u\colon$ as I does to $i\colon$.) Closely round your lips and keep the sound focused well forward through them.

This rich, rounded sound is ALWAYS SHORT. Though crisp, it has a weighty quality that comes from the active use of the lips to focus the tone forward and out. Let the clean, simple curve of the phonetic letter itself be a reminder of its short, round nature.

The vowel sound U

◆ Does not occur in initial position, except in foreign words and names

◆ Is found in final position only in weak forms (wf) of words (See pages 21-25.)

◆ Is found frequently in the sequence jU in unstressed syllables: "reputation" (See page 311.)

◆ Is the second element of the diphthong sounds $o\cdot\breve{U}\cdot$ and $a\cdot\breve{U}\cdot$ (See pages 157-167.)

◆ Is the first element of the falling diphthong sound $U\breve{\partial}$ (See pages 174-176.)

◆ Is the first element of the rising diphthong sound $\breve{U}\partial$ (See pages 189-190.)

WORDS FOR PRACTICE USING U

1 put input kaput sputnik foot footing barefoot soot

2 pudding Buddha ombudsman stood withstood could (sf) couldst good goody Gudrun
3 noodnik should (sf) shouldst hood boyhood hoodwink hoodlum[2] wood=would (sf)
4 wouldst 'twould rosewood

5 book took mistook cook cuckoo cookie nook Mukden Chinook looks=luxe fuchsine
6 Succoth forsook shook rook rookie brook Brooklyn Bolingbroke Pembroke crook
7 Cruikshank hook hooker hookah

8 boogie-woogie sugar

9 umlaut cum laude Lumumba Kuala Lumpur woman
10 Bundestag Bu-rundi Kunde-ra Kundry nuncio[2] wunderkind Sunni junta

11 Munch (Edvard) $'m\upsilon\eta k^h$

12 pull pulpit pulmona-ry[2] bull bulwark bullion Bulganin Bulga-ria[2] bulbul
13 gulden full fulsome fulfill wool Woollcott wolf=Woolf Wolseley Wolsey Wolsingham
14 pustule schedule
15 pulley pullet Pulitzer bully bullet Bullock Bulawayo Lully fully Fuller Fulham
16 wooly woolen Woolwich

17 poof woof (dog's bark) woofer

18 puss pussywillow schuss Anschluss Wooster=Worcester Worcestershire worsted (yarn)

19 Uzbek bosom goosebe-rry

WORDS FOR PRACTICE USING *U* **, Cont.**

1 push pushing Pushkin bush bushy ambush Flatbush cushion cushy Cushing

2 putsch butch butcher

3 - *Uəl* cr̲u-el jew-el IN-flu-ence e-fflu-ent a-fflu-ent Gar-gan-tu-a vir-tu-ous

4 -*U r*- luxu-r̲ious r̲u-ral hu-r̲rah ho-r̲izon ju-r̲y inju-r̲ious conju-r̲ation

5 WEAK FORMS (wf) of: do you your
6 WEAK FORMS (wf) before a vowel or diphthong sound: to into onto unto

PHRASES FOR PRACTICE USING *U*

7 pull wool	13 pull the pulpit	19 took it to Worcester (=Wooster)
8 good book	14 cook the cuckoo	20 the butcher's bosom
9 fully worsted woolens	15 withstood the bull	21 barefoot r̲ookie
10 hu-r̲rah for ho-r̲izons	16 good sugar cookies	22 by hook or by cr̲ook
11 cook the goosebe̲-rries	17 the cr̲ook was cr̲u-el	
12 push and pull	18 a good-looking jew-el	

SENTENCES FOR PRACTICE USING *U*

23 Pull the wood f̲rom the wooden hook, woman!
24 He pulled the good book f̲rom the pulpit.
25 We would if we could, but should we?
26 The cook put her foot down and shook it.
27 The butcher cooked the cuckoo.
28 Should the jew-el be good-looking?
29 He withstood the bull for his full boyhood.
30 The hooker took the hookah to Worcester. '*wʊʌt'ə*
31 Look! Look! A Chinook on the ho-r̲izon!
32 He took sugar cookies and pudding to B̲rooklyn.
33 The cr̲ooked cr̲ook Cr̲uikshank was cr̲u-el.
34 Butch looked fo̲r a woman's woolen pullover with a worsted-woolen hood. '*wʊʌt'ɪd*
35 Could the Sunni wunderkind cook up a junta in B̲ŭ-r̲undi?
36 By hook or by cr̲ook we'll set foot in Flatbush, B̲rooklyn.
37 Should the ju-r̲y be fulsome, 'twould be good to be pushy and influence them.
38 B̲olingbr̲oke forsook an affluent boyhood fo̲r a virtuous one with Buddha. '*bɒlɪŋ brʊk'*
39 Let's boogie on down to Bulawayo fo̲r a good look at their luxu-r̲ious little nook.
40 I'm hooked on goodies such as puddings, sugar cookies, bullion, and goosebe̲-rries.

COMPARE $u{:}$ **WITH** υ

$u{:}$	υ		$u{:}$	υ		$u{:}$	υ
1 footling	— footing		8 toucan	— took		15 wooed	— wood= would (sf)
2 souter	— soot		9 fluke	— look		16 pouf	— poof
3 stooge	— stood		10 mȧ-rooned	— Bŭ-rŭndi		17 roof	— woof (dog's bark)
4 kook	— cook		11 pool	— pull		18 rooster	—Worcester= Wooster
5 cooed	— could (sf)		12 fool	— full		19 booze	— bosom
6 shoed	— should (sf)		13 tabouli	— bully		20 pooch	— putsch
7 who'd (wf)	— hood		14 papoose	— puss		21 cru-et	— cru-el

In classic texts, use the consonant-vowel combination ju , rather than the more contemporary $j\partial$, in unstressed syllables of words:

22 reputation deputy copulate opulent computation nebula nebulous ambulance
23 pe-rambulate somnambulism occupy calculate Dracula muscular truculent o-racular
24 spectacular particular oculist mi-raculous articulate argument regular regulate
25 coagulate jugular stimulant communist emulate monument

NOTE: In all standards of Spoken English, use the ju combination when the "u" in the spelling of the word is followed by a vowel or diphthong sound. Some examples of this are found in:

26 arduous innocuous insinuate sinuous attenuate tenuous manual annual

◆ THE VOWEL SOUND ◯ AS IN "obey" ◆

Represented by the spellings:

*o*bey   *au* gratin

Relax your jaw and relax the tip of your tongue behind your lower front teeth. Arch the BACK of your tongue half-high and round your lips so that they form a perfect "o" shape.

This clean, round vowel sound is ALWAYS SHORT. Its energy comes from the very definite, rounded form of the lips for the brief duration of the sound.

The vowel sound ◯ is

◆ Used as a pure vowel sound ONLY in UNstressed SYLLABLES

◆ Usually found in the first syllable of a word

◆ The first element of the diphthong sound $O \cdot \breve{U} \cdot$ (See pages 157-160.)

◆ NOT found at the ends of words. There the diphthong $O\breve{U}$ is invariably used:

window ˈwɪndoŭ   fellow ˈfɛloŭ   elbow ˈɛlboŭ

◆ Often replaced, in casual conversation, with the weak mid vowel ∂. Words listed below that may also use ∂ are marked with a small, raised [2] following the word:

possess [2]

WORDS FOR PRACTICE USING ◯

1 opaque opine au pair oppress[2] oppression[2] opinion[2]

2 obedient obese obeisance obitua-r̠y auberge obey Obion oblique oblivion[2]

3 *Otello* (Verdi opera) O'Toole otologist

4 Odysseus Odetta Odets Odessa odometer O'Day

5 O'Connell Ocala occasion[2] occasional[2] occult[2] occu-r̠rence[2]

6 au gr̠atin O'Gr̠ady

7 omittance omit[2] omission[2]

8 O'Neill Oneida

9 Olympia Olivia Olivier O'Lea-r̠y Olympics[2]

10 Ophelia offend[2] offensive[2] official[2] officious[2]

11 overt Auvergne ovation

12 Othello[2]

13 Osaka Osi-r̠is

14 ozonic

15 O'Shea

16 O'R̠yan O'R̠ourke O-r̠ion[2]

WORDS FOR PRACTICE USING ○ , Cont.

1 O'Hä-ra Ohio O'Hare

2 oasis

3 poetic pomander polemic[2] potential[2] possess[2]

4 Boethius Bohemian Boccaccio bolometer

5 totalita-ri̯an tonality tova̱-ri̯ch

6 domaine docility donation Doheny doNAtor Domitius[2] domestic[2] dominion[2]

7 coeval coadjutor coagulate coerce coercion coope̯-rate koala Copernicus coquette
8 cocotte cocaine coVERT (adj) Covina cosignato̯-ry co-ri̱val cohabit

9 Mobile motel momentum momentous mosaic motet modiste moderne Moline Mohican
10 monastic[2]

11 novella novitiate noto̱-ri̯ous nobility November notation Nogales novena nomadic
12 Nobel

13 locale locality loquacious locution Lautre̱c Lothä-ri̯o Slovakian Slovenia

14 foment Fokine phonetic[2]

15 vocation vocabula̯-ry̱[2] vocife̯-rou̱s[2]

16 Somalia Sophia soJOURN (v) sobri̱ety[2] solemnity[2]

17 zodiacal

18 ro̱bust ro̱tund ro̱tunda ro̱tation ro̱MANCE ro̱mantic Ṟomania Ṟochelle

19 pro̱boscis pro̱bation pro̱cra̱stinate pro̱fane pro̱SERpina pro̱-saic pro̱-ro̱gue pro̱hibit
20 pro̱genitor pro̱fess[2] pro̱fessor[2] pro̱ceed[2] pro̱TEST (v)[2] pro̱claim[2]
21 pro̱cured[2] pro̱duce (v)[2] pro̱cession[2] pro̱found[2] pro̱lific[2] pro̱phetic[2]
22 pro̱trude[2] pro̱nounce[2]

23 bro̱chure bro̱cade bro̱chette

24 cro̱quet Cro̱atian

25 gro̱tesque

26 hotel holistic Hokkaido Homé-ri̱c hosannah Hó-ra̱tio[2]

27 Yosemite

28 Joanne Jocasta jocose jocosity Johannesburg

PHRASES FOR PRACTICE USING O

1 ʔ obey Olivia
2 Olympia hotel
3 romantic oppression
4 mosaic in the rotunda
5 grotesque oasis
6 Bohemian cocaine

7 ʔ officially omitted
8 loquacious coquette
9 Othello's otologist
10 November obitua-ry
11 notȯːrious novella
12 a robust ovation

13 ʔ occasionally opaque
14 profoundly proTEST
15 a momentous occasion
16 a prolonged ovation

SENTENCES FOR PRACTICE USING O

17 ʔ Obey Othello on this official occasion, Ophelia.
18 ʔ Officially omit Ohio's offensive ovation.
19 A "moderne" mosaic in Mobile is a potential donation.
20 You've overtly omitted the poetic tonalities in the official notation.
21 Ophelia procured her probation in November.
22 Notȯːriously, oppression is fomented in that robust locality.
23 The poetically romantic hotel was like an oasis in their nomadic proceedings.
24 The totalitā-rian oppressor cohabits a motel room with an obese member of the nobility.
25 In my opinion, it's an overtly oblique angle.
26 Prolonged processions are profoundly grotesque.
27 Vocifé-rous Bohemians romanticized Jocasta's holistic hotel.

COMPARISON OF THE PURE VOWEL O (UNstressed SYLLABLES)
WITH THE DIPHTHONG o·ŭ· (USUALLY IN STRESSED SYLLABLES)

O	oŭ	O	oŭ	O	oŭ
28 poetic	— poet	32 overt	— over	36 obey	— Obie
29 proTEST (v)	— PROtest (n)	33 cocaine	— coke	37 nobility	— noble
30 robust	— robe	34 motel	— moat	38 offend	— oafish
31 location	— local	35 momentum	— moment	39 Homé-ric	— Homer

NOTE: Many common words with an "o" spelling always have the weak vowel sound ə :

40 oppose polite police potato tomato tonight tomo-rrow together commend command
41 comedian molasses provoke promote introduce melody innocent

◆ THE VOWEL SOUND ɔː AS IN "all" ◆

Represented by the spellings:

draw   flaunt   talk   ball   **ou**ght   chorus

Relax your lower jaw and relax the tip of your tongue behind your lower front teeth. Arch the BACK of your tongue half-low toward your soft palate. Round your lips into an oval shape. Keep the sound pure for its duration.

A rich, warm, velvety quality is characteristic of this sound. The egg shape of the phonetic letter itself should be a reminder of the oval shape and focus of your lips, necessary for good placement of the vowel sound. It is an excellent choice for voice practice, if the tone is placed forward through rounded lips and the articulation is steady.

The vowel sound ɔː

◆ Must be kept pure

◆ Is the first element of the diphthong sound ɔˑɪˑ (See pages 154-156.)

◆ Is the first element of the diphthong sound ɔə̃ (See pages 177-179.)

WORDS FOR PRACTICE USING ɔː LONG

◆ In a STRESSED SYLLABLE when the vowel is the last sound of a word

◆ In a STRESSED SYLLABLE when the vowel is followed by one or more voiced consonants

1 awe haw paw taw daw caw macaw geegaw maw gnaw law claw flaw slaw thaw saw
2 Shaw raw craw McGraw draw withdraw straw Waugh squaw chaw jaw

3 auburn hauberk Aubrey bauble daub rawboned Traubel

4 awed hawed Auden audience pawed bawd bawdy tawdry dawdle caudle=caudal Cawdor
5 gawds gaudy Maud maudlin=Magdalen (Oxford University) gnawed laud applaud
6 clawed=Claude Claudius flawed guffawed vaudeville[2] thawed sawed ma-raud broad
7 fraud jawed

8 auger augu-ry August Augustine

9 aumbry Maugham

10 awning Hawn pawn pawned spawns bawn tawny dawn leprechaun lawn laundry fawns
11 fawning Vaughan Shauna prawn brawny drawn yawn jaundice

12 all=awl hall=haul always alderman Haldeman Albany pall=Paul Paula appalling
13 ball=bawl tall stall calls cauldron scald gall=Gaul mall=maul small lawless fall
14 fallen withal Saul Salisbu-ry shawl Rawls sprawled brawls scrawl enthrall Raleigh
15 walls squall

16 awes hawse pause=paws daws cause=caws because causal gauze geegaws maws
17 nausea[3] gnaws laws applause plausible clause=claws Santa Claus flaws thaws saws
18 Shaw's straws draws hawser chaws jaws

19 lawyer Sawyer

$\mathcal{O}$ː

WORDS FOR CLARITY OF $\mathcal{O}$ː PRIOR TO $\underline{r}$

✓ *Reminder* ———————————————————————————

Make an open, clearly defined $\mathcal{O}$ː sound and begin the following syllable with a clean-cut consonant $\underline{r}$. In doing so, you will avoid marring the clarity of the $\mathcal{O}$ː sound with r-coloring.

1 au-<u>ra</u> au-<u>reate</u> au-<u>reole</u> Au-<u>rō</u>-<u>ra</u> o-<u>ral</u>=au-<u>ral</u> O-<u>rient</u> labo-<u>rious</u> To-<u>ry</u> Victo-<u>ria</u>

2 victo-<u>rious</u> noto-<u>rious</u> Tau-<u>rus</u> sto-<u>ry</u> Isado-<u>ra</u> cho-<u>rus</u> cho-<u>ral</u> deco-<u>rum</u> cho-<u>rine</u>

3 mo-<u>ron</u> memo-<u>rial</u> Lau-<u>ra</u> lau-<u>reate</u> glo-<u>ry</u> glo-<u>rious</u> flo-<u>ra</u> fo-<u>rum</u> Sho-<u>reham</u> quo-<u>rum</u>

WORDS FOR PRACTICE USING $\mathcal{O}^{\bullet}$ HALF-LONG

♦ In a STRESSED SYLLABLE when the vowel is followed by one or more voiceless consonants

♦ In a STRESSED SYLLABLE when the vowel is followed by a voiced consonant that is then followed by a voiceless consonant, within the same word

♦ In a STRESSED SYLLABLE when the vowel is followed by another vowel sound

4 pauper

5 ought=aught haughty autumn auto bought taught=taut daughter caught cauté-<u>rize</u>
6 nought=naught naughty nautical Laughton slaughter onslaught fought thought sought
7 <u>wr</u>ought <u>br</u>ought <u>fr</u>aught water

8 Auckland auction hawk awkward balk bauxite talks stalked caulking caucus gawky
9 mawkish Fawkes Faulkner falcon² Salk <u>r</u>aucous walk chalk

10 Alton halt Halston Balkan Dalton malt Malta falcon² Falstaff falchion salt
11 assault exalt <u>R</u>alston Gib<u>r</u>altar Walter waltz

12 paunch taunt staunch Staunton daunt undaunted gaunt launch Launce flaunt vaunting
13 avaunt saunter <u>r</u>aunchy jaunt

14 awful Kaufman lawful

15 author Hawthorne authō-<u>rized</u>

16 awesome auspices Aust<u>r</u>ia Austin=Austen paucity Dawson caustic mausoleum nausea³
17 Lawson Slauson faucet sauce saucy sausage exhaust exhaustion

18 caution

19 debauch

20 paw-ing claw-ing gnaw-ing thaw-ing saw-ing d<u>r</u>aw-ing with-d<u>r</u>aw-al
21 d<u>r</u>aw-er (one who draws)

WORDS FOR PRACTICE USING ʊ SHORT

◆ In all UNstressed SYLLABLES, including WEAK FORMS of words (See pages 21-25.)

1 audition audacious autumnal autocracy automaton Augustus augment Aumerle almighty
2 albeit alright already Aufidius authentic autho-rity Australia austere Paulina
3 Caucasian Mau-reen glaucoma fo-rever Esau Warsaw scrimshaw
4 WEAK FORMS (wf) of: or for nor

PHRASES FOR PRACTICE

Long ɔː | **Half-Long ɔ·** | **Mixed Lengths**

5 ʔ always in awe
6 broadly bawdy Cawdor
7 because of Dawn's cause
8 a glo-rious cho-rus
9 Lau-ra is a Tau-rus
10 applaud bawdy Maud
11 Paul's enthralling brawl
12 Santa Claus fraud
13 withdraw the law's clauses
14 all applaud Shaw

15 ʔ awkward author
16 walking and talking
17 haunting autumn
18 the author's thoughts
19 fought for naught
20 flaunted faults
21 awkward walk
22 faulty automatic faucet
23 nautical daughter
24 *The Maltese Falcon*

25 ʔ autumnal awning auction
26 a saucy bawd
27 the law was awesome
28 enthralling draw-ing
29 call it small talk
30 prawns in sauce
31 small hawks and falcons
32 Saul's audacious yawn
33 autumnal walking jaunts
34 Esau saw Waugh's daughter

SENTENCES FOR PRACTICE

Long ɔː

35 ʔ August always awes me.
36 Paul paused in the hall.
37 Dawn caused the laws to be withdrawn.
38 It was appallingly broadly drawn, Cawdor.
39 We called Paul to the awning to laud him.
40 The sprawling cho-rus enthralled all.

41 ʔ All the awnings for the Allman's?
42 Shawn yawned at the small flaws.
43 Mr. Vaughan saw small fawns on the lawn.
44 Thaw that slaw before it falls.
45 The cause! Because of the cause!
46 Lau-ra clawed at it and gnawed on it.

Half-Long ɔ·

47 ʔ Authors! Ought we to automate?
48 They fought until they caught the author.
49 True or false: the faults are paltry.
50 We stalked the haunted slaughter house.
51 Avaunt, thou saucy, taunting daughter!

52 ʔ Awesome authors auctioned autos.
53 They brought water to my daughter.
54 The awkward fought for naught.
55 The paucity of chalk is awesome.
56 Ought authors to have raucous thoughts?

Mixed Lengths

57 ʔ All awful automatic awnings ought always to be altered in August.
58 The applause brought tall Audrey's waltz to a halt.
59 It was a broad draw-ing of an autumnal dawn.
60 Shaw bought it and brought it to Paul.
61 Mau-reen's audacity always awed the mo-ronic Caucasians.
62 Lau-ra's maudlin talk caused Shawn to yawn and Dawn to applaud.
63 The exhausted mother-in-law said nought but, "Pshaw."
64 Paul taught "Talk the talk and walk the walk."
65 Talk to a Tau-rus because they're always authentic.

SENTENCES FOR PRACTICE, Cont.

1 Withdraw all of Aubrey's draw-ings from the mall.
2 You ought not to call Esau at dawn.
3 They applauded the lawyer's causes, but not her naughty thoughts.
4 Faulkner's falcons have already launched themselves into the vaulted autumn sky.
5 Altogether now: "Withdraw the laws!"
6 The jaundiced pauper saw the tawny fawn and stalked it until dawn.
7 August's daughter sought summer in Austin and autumn in Austria.
8 Victo-ria's glo-rious sto-ry received the Lau-reate's Memo-rial Prize.

For sentences to eliminate Intrusive "R" after the vowel sound ɔː , see pages 101-102.

◆ THE VOWEL SOUND ɒ AS IN "honest" ◆

Represented by the spellings:

w**a**tch d**o**ck l**au**rel squ**a**sh L**aw**rence=L**au**rence Gl**ou**cester bur**eau**cracy

This is the lowest back-of-the-tongue vowel sound that has lip-rounding.

Relax your lower jaw wide open and relax the tip of your tongue behind your lower front teeth. Arch the BACK of your tongue to a low position, nearly flat in your mouth. Your lips are rounded, which, given the openness of the jaw, gives the mouth the shape of a large circle.

A sharp, tart quality is characteristic of this rounded, open vowel sound. The large round shape of the phonetic letter itself can be a reminder of the shape of your mouth required to make the sound. It is ALWAYS SHORT. It is very important to keep it crisp and pure, since this sound tends to become pinched, nasalized, diphthongized, and otherwise distorted in various dialects and accents.

WORDS FOR PRACTICE USING ɒ

1 opt hopped ope̯ra Hopper opposite Hopalong optical opulent pop popular poplar

2 bebop top topography stop copper copulate cops=copse mop Knopf lop flop sloppy

3 fop sop shops proper property tropics dropped crops chop

4 obsolete Hobbes obelisk hobble OBject (n) obsequies obvious Bob nabob cob cobbled

5 gobbles Gobbo mob mobster nob=knob snob lob lobby slob fob sobbed sobs rob

6 Robert Robin probably throb wobbles squab Chobham job

7 Ott hot otter hotter Otto pot Potsdam spotted bottom bottle tot totter dot cot

8 cottage cotton Scot got begotten forgotten motley motto not=knot CAnnot lot allot

9 Launcelot (American) plot blot clotted flotsam slot sot shot rot rotten trot throttle

10 what whatnot wot=watt squat cumquat yacht jot

11 odd hod odyssey oddity pod body Todd toddler toddy Dodd dodd**ǝ**-ring cod codify

12 God gods goddess modern modify model modicum plod clod nod fodder sod shod rod

13 prod trod wad swaddling squad jodhpurs

14 ox hocks occupy hockey occident Hoxton octet pocket pox Spock box tock toxic

15 intoxicate stock dock=doc doctor pa̯-r**æ**dox cock peacocks Cox mock smock knocks=Knox

16 noxious locks=lox fox Vauxhall sock Socrates shocked rock rocket proxy sprocket

17 bu̯-reaucracy Troca**e**dé-ro crock frock Throckmorton wok chock chocolate jockey jocund

18 Ogden hog bog toggle dog cog cognate agog pedagogue synagogue Mogs smog noggin

19 log catalogue dialogue prologue epilogue clog flog fog soggy progress (n) frog

20 omelette homily ominous homonym pompous POMpey bomb abominable Tom Thomas

21 stomped dominant domicile intercom comment comedy COMp**ǝ**-rable mom nomimal

22 nominate Lombardy aplomb conglom**ǝ**e-rate vomit somber zombie rhomboid prom from (sf)

23 trombone Cromwell grommet romp wombat swamp Yom Kippur chomp

24 on Honda onyx Honolulu honor honest upon pond poniard respond response Hellespont

25 bonfire bond tonic don con confident condor constant gone gondola monsters

26 Montana demonstrative monitor Monaco anon nonny Lonny Avalon fond Von ma**æ**-rathon

27 shone (Canadian & British) Ron Brontë frond wan wand wander want yon beyond John

WORDS FOR PRACTICE USING ɒ , Cont.

1 ping-pong bong bonkers tongs Minnetonka donkey Kong conquer gong mongrel long
2 longing prolong belongings oblong elongate longer longest Fong thong diphthong
3 song wrong prong strong stronger throng Hong Kong honk jonquils

4 doll dolphin Adolphus golf moll loll volcano volume evolve involve revolve
5 menthol Sol solve pä-rasol dissolve resolve absolve

6 Ollie holly Oliver holiday Holland polyp politic polish Bolingbroke tolĕ-rant
7 stolid dollar college collar=choler scholar golly mollify Smollett knowledge lolling
8 follow follicle volley volunteer solid solemn solitä-ry Solomon trollop=Trollope
9 frolic Wally wallow wallet swallow squalid squalor Cholly jolly

10 off Hoffman often Hofstra office officer offal boffo toff toffee A-ristophanes
11 doff cough coffee coffin scoff Gough Moffat loft Karloff soft sophomore Zoffany
12 profit trough Croft quaff Joffrey

13 Ovid ovulate of (sf) poverty Covent Garden Coventry the-reof (thereof) ðɛ ə 'rɒv
14 whe-reof (whereof) he-reof (hereof) provender province provident provocation

15 Othello (British) apothecä-ry Bothnia Bothwell Goth Goths Gotham gothic moth cloth
16 tablecloth's sloth Sothcott Roth=wroth Rothschild broth brothel troth (American) froth

17 pother bother moths cloths tablecloths Rothermere Frothingham

18 ossify hostile=hostel hospice HOspitable possible posse boss Boston toss docile
19 dossier cost moss prognosticate loss lost gloss Gloucester floss foster fossil
20 isosceles Ross E-ros rostrum prosper Prospĕ-ro process cross across frost throstle
21 wasp wast wassail jostle

22 Oz Osric Osmond Ozzie=Aussie posit positive Boz cosmos cosmic cosmopolitan gosling
23 Moslem nozzle lozenge Rosalind Roz was (sf) wasn't 'twas

24 Oshkosh posh bosh mackintosh nosh sloshed frosh wash Washington squash Joshua

25 botch botulism Scotch hopscotch notch splotch crotch watch Sasquatch

26 podgy Bodger stodgy dodge codger homogenous nodule lodge misogynist Roger=Rodger
27 e-rogenous progeny Hodges hodgepodge

WORDS FOR CLARITY OF ɒ PRIOR TO r

✓ Reminder _____

> Make an open, clearly defined ɒ sound and begin the following syllable with a clean-cut consonant r . In doing so, you will avoid marring the clarity of the ɒ sound with r-coloring.

28 o-range ho-rror o-racle ho-rrible o-rigin ho-rrid o-rris Ho-race o-rotund ho-rologe

29 o-racle Ho-rrocks o-risons abho-rrence o-rifice ho-roscope O-regon Ho-rowitz o-rator

30 o-rato-rical o-rato-ry po-rridge po-rringer bo-rrow Bo-ris to-rrid to-rrent

WORDS FOR CLARITY OF ɒ PRIOR TO r , Cont.

1 histo-<u>ri</u>cal Do-<u>ro</u>thy Do-<u>ri</u>s Do-<u>ri</u>cles Do-<u>rri</u>tt co-<u>ra</u>l co-<u>rre</u>spond Co-<u>ri</u>n co-<u>ro</u>nation

2 co-<u>ro</u>nets inco-<u>rri</u>gible Go-<u>re</u>ll Go-<u>rri</u>nge mo-<u>rro</u>w tomo-<u>rro</u>w mo-<u>ra</u>l Mo-<u>rri</u>s=Mau-<u>ri</u>ce

3 No-<u>rri</u>s mino-<u>ri</u>ty lo-<u>rry</u> Law-<u>re</u>nce=Lau-<u>re</u>nce lau-<u>re</u>l Flo-<u>ri</u>da flo-<u>ri</u>st Flo-<u>ri</u>zel

4 flo-<u>ri</u>d Flo-<u>re</u>nce Flo-<u>ri</u>mel flo-<u>ri</u>n fo-<u>re</u>st fo-<u>rei</u>gn fo-<u>re</u>head *florid* fo-<u>ra</u>ge

5 fo-<u>ra</u>y autho-<u>ri</u>ty so-<u>rry</u> so-<u>rri</u>er so-<u>rre</u>l Zo-<u>rro</u> wa-<u>rra</u>nt wa-<u>rri</u>or Wa-<u>rwi</u>ck

6 qua-<u>rre</u>l qua-<u>rre</u>ler qua-<u>ra</u>ntine qua-<u>rry</u> Yo-<u>ri</u>ck senio-<u>ri</u>ty majo-<u>ri</u>ty

MATCH THE VOWEL SOUNDS ɒ IN THE FOLLOWING PAIRS OF WORDS:

7 oxen	— o-<u>ra</u>nge	13 cot	— co-<u>ra</u>l	19 hot	— ho-<u>rro</u>r
8 opposite	— o-<u>ri</u>gin	14 Mott	— tomo-<u>rro</u>w	20 lot	— Law-<u>re</u>nce
9 pottage	— po-<u>rri</u>dge	15 mop	— mo-<u>ra</u>l	21 flop	— Flo-<u>ri</u>da
10 box	— bo-<u>rro</u>w	16 fop	— fo-<u>re</u>st	22 wok	— wa-<u>rri</u>or
11 tot	— to-<u>rri</u>d	17 sot	— so-<u>rry</u>	23 quad	— qua-<u>rre</u>l
12 dot	— Do-<u>ro</u>thy	18 hop	— ho-<u>rri</u>ble	24 jot	— majo-<u>ri</u>ty

EXERCISES FOR OPENING THE VOWEL SOUND ɒ AND ELIMINATING NASALIZATION BEFORE m n ŋ

MATCH THE VOWEL SOUNDS ɒ IN THE FOLLOWING PAIRS OF WORDS:

ɒ	ɒm	ɒ	ɒn	ɒ	ɒŋ
25 opposite	— ominous	37 odd	— on	49 pickpocket	— ping-pong
26 pop	— pomp	38 odyssey	— honesty	50 box	— bongs
27 bop	— bomb	39 pod	— pond	51 tock	— tong
28 top	— Tom	40 dot	— don	52 dock=doc	— donkey
29 Dobbs	— dominant	41 got	— gone	53 cock	— Congo
30 cop	— comment	42 modern	— monster	54 mock	— mongrel
31 nob=knob	— nominal	43 nod	— anon	55 lock	— long
32 plop	— aplomb	44 fodder	— fond	56 lox	— pro<u>lo</u>ngs
33 sob	— somber	45 wad	— wander	57 sock	— song
34 hobble	— homily	46 watt=wot	— want	58 <u>ro</u>ck	— <u>wro</u>ng
35 c<u>ro</u>p	— C<u>ro</u>mwell	47 jot	— John	59 p<u>ro</u>xy	— p<u>ro</u>ng
36 chop	— chomp	48 hot	— Honda	60 St<u>ro</u>ck	— st<u>ro</u>ng

FOR CORRECT PRONUNCIATION, MATCH THE *ɒ* SOUNDS IN THE FOLLOWING PAIRS OF WORDS. MAKE SURE
THAT THE VOWEL SOUND OF EACH WORD IN THE SECOND COLUMN EXACTLY MATCHES THE VOWEL SOUND OF
ITS PARTNER IN THE FIRST COLUMN. EACH PAIR WILL BE ASSONANT:

1 watt=wot — want	15 copy — coffee	29 tot — toss
2 watt=wot — what	16 hospice — office	30 cot — cost
3 hot — what	17 coxswain — coffin	31 lot — loss
4 got — God	18 lot — loft	32 lots — lost
5 chop — chocolate	19 sot — soft	33 rot — Ross
6 hock — hog	20 ovulate — of (sf)	34 crock — cross
7 dock=doc — dog	21 their ox — the-reof (thereof)	35 a crock — across
8 lock — log	22 where Ron — whe-reon (whereon)	36 wasp — wast
9 fox — fogs	23 mop — moth	37 Oz — was (sf)
10 frock — frog	24 clot — cloth	38 lozenge — wasn't
11 prom — from (sf)	25 oxen — often	39 deposit — Was it?
12 dot — doll	26 rot — Roth	40 Boz — 'twas
13 got — golf	27 Brock — broth	41 wasp — wash
14 ox — off	28 box — Boston	

PHRASES AND SHORT SENTENCES FOR PRACTICE USING *ɒ*

42 ? odd ominous opera
43 honest John's office
44 Honest to God, it's not.
45 hot copper coffee pot
46 The hot watt is WHAT?
47 What is it you want?
48 Boz, I'm positive it was.
49 intoxicated jockey
50 autho-rity of God

51 ? Osmond often ope-rates.
52 somewhat like rot
53 Bob CAnnot watch yachts.
54 It was. It wasn't.
55 What are you positive of?
56 hot chocolate
57 Tom lost his job.
58 ho-rrible ho-rror
59 ho-rribly hot fo-rehead –rid

60 ? Oxen offered o-ranges.
61 prolong a song
62 What was it? A deposit?
63 Don wandered on.
64 God, what is wrong?
65 wash in Washington
66 the wa-rrior Wa-rwick
67 What wattage is lost?
68 Foster, meet Gloucester.

SENTENCES FOR PRACTICE USING *ɒ*

69 ? Osmond often offered Otto obviously odd opportunities.
70 The mo-ral majo-rity is wrong.
71 We wot not what it was that you wanted.
72 What was it? It was. It wasn't.
73 Foster's modern model was boxed in Boston.
74 Thomas Watt, what are you honestly thinking of now?
75 Honest John wanted a coffee shop near the college.
76 Is the coffee pot hot, Ho-race?
77 This whatnot is not what you want, Mr. Fox.
78 It was the Wizard of Oz! It was!
79 Rosalind, are you positive it was?
80 What was it, a hot closet?

SENTENCES FOR PRACTICE USING ꞷ **, Cont.**

 1 I like kumquats some(what).
 2 The HOspitable Aussie, Ozzie Osbert, is positive it wasn't a lozenge. *ˈhɒspɪtəbl̩*
 3 Ovid, (what) are you thinking ᴼf?
 4 Okay, Ovid, (what) ᴼf it?
 5 Those provinces have got to be gotten rid ᴼf.
 6 (What) street in London are you thinking ᴼf, Ovid? Ovington Street?
 7 Not that I know ᴼf.
 8 I don't know him, but I know ᴼf him.
 9 Bob went to Bombay, but saw nothing ᴼf Bombay there.
10 A comet? Far frᴼm it!
11 Cromwell, (which) prom are you frᴼm?
12 Mom, (where) do you come frᴼm?
13 Lot lost his hot chocolate at the loft.
14 Holly, are you honestly honᵃ-ring the majo-rity?
15 Foster and Gloucester lost her, so Don wandered on and on. *ˈglɒstə*
16 Wanda wanted a monstrously modern watch.
17 Officer, doff your hat and get off!
18 Are you really Thom Thomas from Thomas Road in Thomas, Pennsylvania? Be honest!
19 That's Ovid, but it's not a ve-ᵉry good picture of him.   ꞷʊɪm
20 That rotten tot dropped his cloth into a pot of broth.
21 Bob's yacht is dry-docked just beyond the convent's pond.
22 The intoleᵃ-rably jolly collie swallowed some alcohol.
23 It's ho-rrible and intoleᵃ-rable, Solomon!
24 In college he led a solitaᵃ-ry, squalid, but knowledgeable life.
25 Boston WASPs don't bother to wash in Washington.
26 A wok is wanted for the wa-rrior, Wa-rwick. *ˈwɒrɪkʰ*
27 Doc's dog opted for the o-ranges.
28 I wa-rrant that tomo-rrow Do-rothy will mop up the po-rridge.
29 A pox upon thee, Flo-ᵃrence, for thy motley mo-rals.
30 God's authᵃ-ᴼrity is strong and prolonged.
31 Prolong that diphthong for a long, long time!
32 Hoss found the hospital HOspitable
33 The commune was inCOMpaᵃ-rably HOspitable.
34 Yes! Tom Peacocke's o-rotund ᴼ-ratᵃ-ry was wa-rranted by the fo-reign o-racle's o-risons.

◆ THE VOWEL SOUND *a:* AS IN "fathers" ◆

Represented by the spellings:

    f**a**thers   **a**lms   hurr**ah**

Relax your lower jaw wide open and rest the tip of your tongue behind your lower front teeth. The BACK of your tongue has a very low arch, so that the body of the tongue is almost flat. Your lips are in a relaxed, neutral position.

The production of this vowel sound requires absolute relaxation of the lower jaw, tongue and lips, which is why so many speech and singing exercises employ it as the basis for developing forward placement of tone. A glance at the Vowel Chart on page 11 will confirm that *a:* is the most forward in placement of the back vowel sounds, besides being the only back vowel sound made with relaxed, neutral lips.

A mellow, warm quality in the manner of a sigh characterizes this vowel sound. Interestingly enough, it is one of the least common vowel sounds found in North American English.

The vowel sound *a:*

◆ Is the first element of the diphthong sound *aŭ·* (See pages 161-165.)

◆ Is the first element of the diphthong sound *aǝ̌* (See pages 180-182.)

WORDS FOR PRACTICE USING *a:* LONG

◆ In a STRESSED SYLLABLE when the vowel is the last sound of a word

◆ In a STRESSED SYLLABLE when the vowel is followed by one or more voiced consonants

1 aha pa paPA (British) spa Pooh-Bah Bogota Dada maMA (British) Panama Shangri-La

2 blah shah Zsa Zsa Ra hŭ-rrah bra (Mardi) Gras Wawa cha cha

3 baba kebab Zimbabwe

4 façade Baden (German) enchilada avocado Mikado armada Mahdi

5 Aga Iago gaga lager Lagos[2] Wagner (German) saga raga Prague Braga fa-rragǝ vi-ragó

6 Amish Ahmed ò-rigami MAma (American) Vietnam llama Glamis samba diò-ramǝ Ramy

7 Brahms Brahmin drama pyjamas

NOTE that the following words have no *l* sound, though they have an "l" in the spelling:

8 alms ("ahmz") almond palm palmistry napalm balm balmy embalm calm calmly

9 Malmesbŭ-rǝy malmsey psalms halm qualms

10 Anna[2] Hanukkah autobahn Tanya Titania[3] Kahn gymkhana Afrikaans Ghana Gandhi

11 Milan Nirvana Bassanio lasagna Pisanio pi-ranha mahǝ-rani prana Tranio iguana

12 Allah Halle koala Ali Baba impala Bali Stalin Dali Kali Mahler finale Marsala (Taj) Mahal

13 Pavlov lava Slav Slavic Yugoslavia bravo Mojave suave Jahveh Chavez Java Zouave

14 father fatherly

15 Gaza Mazda plaza vase[3] tabula rasa

16 gǝ-ragé mi-ragé bǝ-rragé camouflage espionage badinage massage corsage La Cage

WORDS FOR PRACTICE USING $a:$ LONG, Cont.

1 <u>R</u>ahway Jahweh

2 Taj (Mahal) adagio mahá̃-<u>r</u>aja

WORDS FOR CLARITY OF $a:$ PRIOR TO r

✓ *Reminder* ─────────────────────────────────────

Make an open, clearly defined $a:$ sound and begin the following syllable with a clean-cut consonant r . In doing so, you will avoid marring the clarity of the $a:$ sound with r-coloring.

3 a-<u>ri</u>a Ba-<u>ri</u> Hata-<u>ri</u> calama-<u>ri</u> scena-<u>ri</u>o La-<u>ra</u> Phila-<u>ri</u>o safa-<u>ri</u> Lotha-<u>ri</u>o sa-<u>ri</u>

4 Cesa-<u>ri</u>o Saha-<u>ra</u> (Mata) Ha-<u>ri</u> tia-<u>ra</u>

✓ *Reminder* ─────────────────────────────────────

Use $a\breve{\partial}$ in words such as those in line 5, which are derived from root words that contain that diphthong sound.

5 spa-<u>rr</u>ing ba-<u>rr</u>ing ta-<u>rr</u>ing sta-<u>rr</u>ing sta-<u>rr</u>y ma-<u>rr</u>ing fa-<u>r</u>away ja-<u>rr</u>ing

WORDS FOR PRACTICE USING $a\cdot$ HALF-LONG

◆ In a STRESSED SYLLABLE when the vowel is followed by one or more voiceless consonants

◆ In a STRESSED SYLLABLE when the vowel is followed by a voiced consonant that is then followed by a voiceless consonant within the same word

6 PApa (American) tapas gestapo capo <u>g</u>rappa

7 atman Mahatma Zapata Bata Katya <u>r</u>egatta Bugatti Mata (Hă-<u>ri</u>) fermata Sina<u>tr</u>a Nazi

8 sonata fata (morgana) kẵ-<u>r</u>ate

9 akvavit Pachelbel Bach taco khaki (British) Cuernavaca Saki saké

10 pasta basta basso Nastassja Hadassah casa Picasso Lhasa Las Vegas Vasco

11 pasha Natasha pistachio mustachio kasha Masha Vash Sasha <u>R</u>ashi

12 hibachi dacha macho nachos

13 debutante Dante <u>R</u>enaissance

WORDS FOR PRACTICE USING a SHORT

◆ In all UNstressed SYLLABLES of words

14 Minnehaha nuance blasé Swahili (Muhammad) Ali

$a{:}$

PHRASES FOR PRACTICE

Long $a{:}$	Half-Long $a^{\cdot}$	Mixed Lengths
1 calm father	8 Masha and Natasha	15 blasé drama
2 alms for the Shah	9 a macho Nazi	16 mama and papa (Amer)
3 mi-rages on the Saha-ra *a:*	10 nachos and tacos	17 a Bach a-ria
4 massage at the spa	11 Masha the debutante	18 Mata Ha-ri's mama
5 embalm the armada	12 pistachios and saké *ʃaˑkʰeï*	19 Tranio's kasha
6 drama of the Dalai Lama	13 the pasha's pasta	20 Minnehaha's father
7 palms on the plaza	14 a fermata in the sonata	21 calming nuances

SENTENCES FOR PRACTICE

Long $a{:}$

22 ʔ Aha! Ali gave alms to Ahmed.
23 Calmly, father, calmly.
24 Hŭ-rrah for the iguanas of Panama!
25 Bassanio's gă-rage is camouflaged.
26 Tranio saw a façade of palms in Java.

27 ʔ Ah! Avocados and almonds!
28 The Shah had a massage at Tanya's spa.
29 Is the saga of the armada a drama?
30 Iago was embalmed under palms in the Saha-ra.
31 Almond balm calmed the pyjama-clad Hahn.

Half-Long $a^{\cdot}$

32 Masha and Natasha ate pistachios.
33 The macho Sinatra met Zapata in a dacha.

34 Dante, your PApa eats tacos and pasta.
35 The Bach sonata is post-Renaissance.

Mixed Lengths

36 ʔ Ah! Alms for Ali and avocados for A-ri's Aga!
37 Ali Baba's saga has fathered a drama in Swahili.
38 Mata Ha-ri's mamma was a real vi-rago.
39 Father, have no qualms about the Bach a-ria.
40 Minnehaha had qualms about serving iguana and pi-ranha to the debutante.
41 Enchiladas and avocados were forbidden at Zapata's Lake Tahoe spa.
42 Dante's saga of espionage at the Taj Mahal lacked drama.
43 Mr. Kahn and Nastassja Hahn sipped saké at the Plaza's Palm Court.
44 The balmy winds in Ghana calmed papa.
45 There was too much rubato in the Brahms sonata and the Wagner a-ria.
46 Masha read aloud the saga of "Mama Koala and Papa Llama."
47 Vasco da Gama had a bă-rrage of massages at a spa in Zermatt.
48 Did you see Sinatra in *The Mikado* in Panama, Zimbabwe or Malmesbŭ-ry? *'maːmzbərɪ*
49 Gandhi found his atman through mindfulness of prana.
50 Iago put pasta on the hibachi with a dash of grappa and saké.
51 Ramy, the Ali Baba of the Gaza Strip, looked suave in his Bugatti.
52 The debutante was ma-rring her sa-ri as her father recited a psalm.
53 "Camouflage that ja-rring Picasso," cried the Slavic gestapo Pooh-Bah.
54 The basso's Lhasa Apso ate tapas and pasta dŭ-ring the Wagner a-ria.
55 André is spa-rring with Muhammad Ali in Rahway.
56 Here's the scena-rio: Mata Ha-ri opens a gă-rage in the Saha-ra and meets a calm Lotha-rio.

	ɔː	ɒ	ɑː		ɔ·	ɒ	ɑ·
1	awe	ox	ah	41	awesome	ossify	arse
2	audit	odd	Aden	42	ought	otter	atman
3	all	Ollie	Allah	43	pauper	popper	PApa (Amer)
4	pawed	pod	palm	44	balks	box	Bach's
5	appalling	Apollo	impala	45	talk	tock	taco
6	bawling	Bolingbroke	Bali	46	daunt	Don	Dante
7	Maugham	bomb	balm	47	mawkish	mock	Mako
8	bawdy	body	Baden (Ger)	48	naughty	knotty	Nazi
9	tall	Tom	Tahoe	49	Salk	sock	Saki; saké
10	tawny	tonic	Tana	50	auto	Otto	atman
11	cawed	cod	calm	51	Kaufman	coffee	Kafka
12	leprechaun	con	Kahn	52	taunt	tontine	dilettante
13	calling	collie	Kali	53	caustic	accosted	Picasso
14	caller	choler	Ocala	54	caution	Oshkosh	kasha
15	Maugham	mom	MAma (Amer)				
16	Maud	modern	armada		ɔ·	ɒ	ɑː
17	maul=mall	mollify	Mahler	55	Dalton	dolly	Dali
18	lawless	lolling	llama	56	daughter	dotted	Dada
19	fawned	fond	father	57	falcon	folly	father
20	sawed	sod	façade	58	sought	sot	saga
21	Shaw	shot	shah	59	sauce	somber	samba
22	raw	Roger	raja	60	raucous	rockers	mi-rages
23	hall	holly	Halle	61	Mohawk	hock	Mojave
24	wall	wallet	Wahwah	62	walk	wok	ma-rijuana
25	squall	squalid	suave	63	brought	broth	Brahms
26	drawn	drop	drama	64	chalk	chock	cha cha
27	trawl	Trollope	tra la la	65	awful	offal	Aga Kahn
28	jaundice	John	Java	66	onslaught	slot	Slavic
29	spawn	respond	spa	67	jaunt	majo-rity	ja-rring
30	jaw	jot	pyjamas	68	gaunt	gone	Ghana
31	O-rient	o-risons	a-ria	69	Walter	Wally	koala
32	labo-rious	Bo-ris	Ba-ri	70	stalling	stolid	Stalin
33	Tau-rus	to-rrid	ta-rring	71	August	Ogden	Aga
34	sto-ry	histo-ric	sta-rry	72	applaud	plod	Palladio
35	cho-ral	co-ral	sca-rring				
36	mo-ron	mo-ral	ma-rring				
37	sno-ring	mino-rity	scena-rio				
38	Lau-ra	Law-rence	La-ra				
39	fo-rum	fo-reign	fa-raway				
40	soa-ring	so-rry	sa-ri				

PHRASES AND SHORT SENTENCES FOR COMPARISON OF THE LAST THREE OPEN BACK VOWELS

ɔː	ɒ	ɑː

1 Paul wants calm.
2 Has Paul gone to Palm Springs?
3 Dawn stopped the Shah.
4 The chŏ-rus lost the llama.
5 Maud's song is a psalm.
6 The squaw washed the mă-rijuana.
7 Hawes bombed the gă-rage. *gə'rɑːʒ*

ɔˑ	ɒ	ɑː

8 She bought an odd a-ria.
9 Is paucity possible in Palm Springs?
10 I thought the dog liked drama.
11 He bought the bomb and balm.
12 a sauce of butterscotch and almond
13 Waltzes are wanted by Minnehaha.
14 Walking properly is calming.

ɒ	ɑː	ɔː

15 The fond father falls.
16 The prop is drama's pawn.
17 pots of palms at Paul's
18 Rotten Iago is a fraud.

ɒ	ɑː	ɔˑ

19 The odd almond is awful.
20 The songs from *La Cage* were faultless.
21 Thomas shot his father's hawk.
22 The doctor's qualms were for naught.
23 Lau-rence met La-ra and Launce.

ɑː	ɔː	ɒ

24 Koalas are always costly.
25 Mahler's jaw dropped.
26 The guava with prawns bombed.
27 Hŭ-rrah! Raw rockfish!
28 Kali called the collie.
29 Only the suave will draw the swan.

ɑː	ɒ	ɔː

30 "Façade" wăs oddly inaudible.
31 Psalms soften the fall.
32 drama of the common macaw
33 The almond wăsn't raw.
34 Bah rot and pshaw!
35 The Shah chronically crawled.
36 Massage the monster's paw.

ɑː	ɒ	ɔˑ

37 The llama wasn't slaughtered.
38 Father watched his talk.
39 embalming the hot haunts
40 the spa's tonic water
41 avocado chopped in sauce
42 enchiladas in hot sauce
43 Kahn contacted the author.

ɑː	ɔː	ɒ

44 The Shah's shawl was shoddy.
45 The Dalai Lama's laws are lost. *'dɑːlaĭ*
46 The koala's ball is a bomb.
47 the calm of Magdalen College (Oxford University) *'mɔːdlɪn*

ɑː	ɔˑ	ɒ

48 Iago fought a cough.
49 Tanya thought it common.
50 The raja halted in Boston.
51 façades ŏf false confidence
52 The armada fought mo-rally.

ɑː	ɔˑ	ɒ

53 The Brahmin's launch has been modernized.
54 A mi-rage taunted Don.
55 Tanya taught tots.
56 Iago balked at honesty.
57 That's Dali's daughter Dolly.
58 Cesa-rio sauntered onward.

CHAPTER THREE

THE DIPHTHONG AND
TRIPHTHONG SOUNDS

DIPHTHONGS

A diphthong sound is such a close blending of two vowel sounds that they are perceived as a single phonetic unit. When a diphthong is spoken, the articulators begin in the position of one vowel sound and move so smoothly toward the position of another vowel sound that it is impossible to tell where the first vowel ends and the second begins.

Movement

Even if it is slight, the movement, or glide, of the articulators required by each diphthong sound can be seen, heard and felt.

✓ *Reminder* ─────────────────────────────────────

A vowel sound is pure, requiring no movement or change in the articulators.

The rule of thumb is: If it's absolutely still, it's a vowel; if it moves, it's a diphthong.

Elements

Each of the two vowels that make up a diphthong sound is called an ELEMENT. The first element is the starting point for the diphthong sound, and the second element is the direction in which the movement is made.

Prominence

In most languages, the vibrated breath of one element of each diphthong sound has greater PROMINENCE or SONORITY (carrying power; resonance), while the vibrated breath of the other element has weaker prominence or sonority. In phonetic transcription, the WEAK ELEMENT is noted by placing a small curve over the phonetic letter:

Falling Diphthongs

When the first element of a diphthong is more prominent, and the second element is weaker, the sound is called a FALLING DIPHTHONG because it contains a fall or decrease of sonority. In transcribing this, the small curve denoting weaker sonority is placed over the SECOND element. With two exceptions, which are used only in verse, all of the diphthong sounds of Spoken English are falling diphthongs.

Rising Diphthongs

When the first element of a diphthong is weaker, and the second element is more prominent, the sound is called a RISING DIPHTHONG because it contains a rise or increase of sonority. In transcribing this, the small curve denoting weaker sonority is placed over the FIRST element. There are two rising diphthong sounds in Spoken English, but in North American speech they are found only in verse and in song lyrics.

Placement

There are FIVE "LONG" DIPHTHONGS and FIVE "ALWAYS-SHORT" DIPHTHONGS of "R" in Spoken English. Each of these ten is a falling diphthong sound and each is a CLOSING DIPHTHONG, since the movement proceeds from a more open to a more closed vowel sound. The diphthongs are grouped and studied according to their second elements:

$$e\cdot\breve{i}\cdot \quad a\cdot\breve{i}\cdot \quad \mathfrak{o}\cdot\breve{i}\cdot$$

◆ Three diphthong sounds move toward   /   as in "will":   **Pay my boy.**

$$o\cdot\breve{u}\cdot \quad a\cdot\breve{u}\cdot$$

◆ Two diphthong sounds move toward $\cup$ as in "would":   **Go now.**

◆ Five diphthong sounds move toward $\quad i\breve{\partial} \quad \varepsilon\breve{\partial} \quad u\breve{\partial} \quad \mathfrak{o}\breve{\partial} \quad a\breve{\partial}$
   the neutral vowel sound ∂ as in "su**r**prise": H**er**e's th**eir** p**oor** **ore** c**ar**.

Because the second element ∂ is a mid (or central) vowel, these five are sometimes called CENTER-ING DIPHTHONGS.

◆ Since each of the ten diphthong sounds is comprised of two vowel sounds, certain features of vowel placement also apply to the diphthong sounds: a) THE TIP OF THE TONGUE IS RELAXED BE-HIND THE LOWER FRONT TEETH; b) In Good Speech, the diphthongs are ORAL sounds, with the SOFT PALATE RAISED. Nasalization is to be avoided; c) In Spoken English, all diphthong sounds are VOICED.

Lengths

Diphthong sounds are classified according to the length or duration of the sound. In theory each diphthong sound may be sustained for as long as breath can last, but due to the intrinsic structure of the language, certain lengths and rhythmic features are found.

◆ Five diphthongs are found in a wide variety of lengths, depending upon their positions in stressed or unstressed syllables, the position of a syllable within the word and the kind of sound that follows them within the word. (See page 20.). For practical purposes these diph-thongs are classified, notated and studied in just two lengths.

$$e\cdot\breve{i}\cdot \quad a\cdot\breve{i}\cdot \quad \mathfrak{o}\cdot\breve{i}\cdot \quad o\cdot\breve{u}\cdot \quad a\cdot\breve{u}\cdot$$

LONG: **Pay my boy. Go now.**

$$e\breve{i} \quad a\breve{i} \quad \mathfrak{o}\breve{i} \quad o\breve{u} \quad a\breve{u}$$

SHORT: **Kate l**i**kes o**ysters. **P**o**king ab**ou**t.**

◆ The five diphthongs associated with the letter "r" in the spelling are ALWAYS SHORT.

$$i\breve{\partial} \quad \varepsilon\breve{\partial} \quad u\breve{\partial} \quad \mathfrak{o}\breve{\partial} \quad a\breve{\partial}$$

ALWAYS SHORT: **H**e**re's th**eir** p**oor** **ore** c**ar**.**

In verse and in song lyrics, it is frequently necessary to pronounce certain two-syllable sequences as one syllable. In some cases this may involve the use of a TRIPHTHONG SOUND, while in others it may involve the use of a rising diphthong sound.

TRIPHTHONGS

A triphthong sound is one in which three vowel sounds are blended so closely that they are used and perceived as a single phonetic unit consisting of ONE syllable.

Words such as "hire" and "flower" are commonly pronounced in TWO syllables, with a diphthong in one syllable and the weak neutral vowel sound ə as in "surprise" in the next syllable:

hi-re=high-er   aɪ̯ ə   flow-er=flou-r aʊ̯ ə

However, when the rhythm of a line in verse demands that these two-syllable sequences be elided into ONE syllable, the three vowel sounds are blended into triphthong sounds:

hire=higher   aɪ̆ə̆   flower=flow'r=flour aʊ̆ə̆

The two triphthong sounds are ALWAYS SHORT and, with the exception of the weak form of the pronoun "our," used only as required in verse and in song. (See pages 21-25.)

RISING DIPHTHONGS

Words such as "tedious" and "influence" are commonly pronounced using sequences of two distinct vowel sounds that form TWO distinct, unstressed syllables:

TE-di-ous   ɪ ə   IN-flu-ence   ʊ ə

However, when the rhythm of a line in verse or song demands that such two-syllable sequences be elided into ONE syllable, the two vowel sounds are blended smoothly to form two new diphthong sounds:

TE-dious   ɪ̆ə   IN-fluence   ʊ̆ə

What makes these diphthongs "new" and unique (not to mention distinct from ɪə̆ as in "here" and ʊə̆ as in "poor") is that the first element is weak and the second more prominent. In phonetic transcription the small curve placed over the weak FIRST element indicates a RISING DIPHTHONG. In Spoken English, these occur ONLY in unstressed syllables, and ONLY as required in verse or song. (See pages 189-190.)

Three falling diphthong sounds have I as in "i͟s" as their second, weak element. Two falling diphthong sounds have U as in "w**ou**ld" as their second, weak element. These five diphthong sounds may be pronounced in various lengths in Spoken English, although each is described and notated in only two lengths, LONG and SHORT.

Pay	*e·ĭ·*
my	*a·ĭ·*
b**oy**.	*ɔ·ĭ·*
G**o**	*o·ŭ·*
n**ow**.	*a·ŭ·*

♦ **THE DIPHTHONG SOUND** *e·ĭ·* **AS IN "pay"** ♦

Represented by the spellings:

  *a*te=*ei*ght r*ai*n=r*eig*n=r*ei*n pr*ay*=pr*ey* gr*ea*t=gr*a*te

  g*au*ge clich*é* ball*et* matin*ée*

Relax your lower jaw to just below a half-closed position and relax the tip of your tongue behind your lower front teeth. Arch the FRONT of your tongue half-high for the first element *e* and from that position glide your tongue-arch upward, or make a vanish, toward the position of *ɪ* , the weak second element. During this glide of the tongue-arch, your lower jaw moves upward slightly, and your lips are spread SLIGHTLY. The movement, though subtle, can be seen and felt as the two vowel elements blend into a single new sound, the diphthong *e·ĭ·* .

Comprised of the "emerald" and "diamond" of Good Speech, the diphthong *e·ĭ·* demands brilliance, clarity and forward placement of tone. Even at its longest, this sound must retain its bright quality, avoiding the lax, lazy placement known as "fallen arches of the tongue."

WORDS FOR PRACTICE USING *e·ĭ·* LONG

♦ In a STRESSED SYLLABLE that is the FINAL syllable of a word, when the diphthong is also the last sound of the word

♦ In a STRESSED SYLLABLE that is the final syllable of a word, when the diphthong is followed by one or more voiced consonants

1 ay=aye (ever) hay=heigh pay bay obey stay day cay=Kaye risqué gay may dismay
2 nay=neigh matinée lay=lei play clay flay slay delay relay (v) fey=Fay convey
3 survey (v) ₔinveigh they (sf) say assay Shea=Shay sashay=sachet cachet cliché négligé
4 ray=Rea a-rray pray=prey bray tray betray dray McCrea gray=grey fray (wh)ey
5 way=weigh yea Che jay

NOTE:The STRONG FORM of the indefinite article "a" is *'e·ĭ·* , but its use is extremely rare. It is almost invariably used in its WEAK FORM, which is simply *ə* .

6 Abe babe McCabe Gabe Rabe

7 aid=aide=ade Haid paid spayed=spade bayed stayed=staid Dade blockade brigade
8 maid=made dismayed neighed colonnade lemonade laid played blade glade flayed Slade
9 fade invade surveyed conveyed purveyed=pervade they'd (sf) shade sashayed raid
10 cha-rade pa-rade brayed=braid trade betrayed grade afraid weighed=wade swayed=suede
11 persuade jade

12 aim hame tame dame came games maim=Mame names lame blame claim
13 proclaims reclaim fame same shames ashamed Rhames frames James

14 Aisne Haynes pain=pane Spain urbane ta'en obtain stained Dane=deign disdains
15 cane=Kane=Cain skein gain main=mane domain remained inane lain=lane plane=plain
16 MacLean's slain fain=feign vane=vein=vain thane sane Zane rain=reign=rein brains
17 trained drain crane=Craine grain engrained refrain wane=Wayne chains Jane

18 ale=ail hale=hail pale=pail bale=bail tale=tail curtail stale dale kale=Kael scales
19 gale=Gail male=mail nail snail flails failed vale=vail prevails sale=sail assailed
20 shale rail Braille trails Grail frail (wh)ales Wales=wails quail Yale jail=gaol

WORDS FOR PRACTICE USING $e\cdot\breve{\imath}\cdot$ LONG, Cont.

1 behave pave stave Dave caves gave knave=nave lave slave they've (sf) saves shaved
2 rave depraved brave architrave drave craves graves waves

3 bathes scathe lathe swathe enswathe

4 "A's" Hayes=haze pays spays bays obeys stays days=daze Kaye's=cays gaze maize
5 amaze neighs lays=laze delays plays glaze flays slays phase=faze=Fay's conveys
6 inveighs vase[3] assays Shea's=chaise sachets=sashays rays=raise=raze
7 praise=prays=preys brays=braise betrays crazed graze phrase=frays ways sways jays

8 beige

9 age aged (v) page stage caged engaged gauge preSAGE (v) rage enraged wage assuage

WORDS FOR PRACTICE USING $e\breve{\imath}$ SHORT IN ALL OTHER CASES

◆ In a STRESSED SYLLABLE followed by a voiced consonant that in turn is followed by a voiceless consonant

◆ In a STRESSED SYLLABLE followed by one or more voiceless consonants

◆ In any syllable but the last syllable of a word

◆ In all UNstressed SYLLABLES, including WEAK FORMS (wf) of words

10 paint taint cam'st mayn't complaint faint=feint saints

11 ape halfpence *'heĭpᵻəns* apricot halfpenny *'heĭp, nɪ* papist papal
12 taper=tapir stapled cape capon escaped gaped maple nape Vapians vapor sapient
13 shapes rape traipsed crêpe scrape grapes Chapin jape

14 abel=Abel Abraham habeus baby tabor table stable cable gable maybe neighbor nabob
15 labial Claibourne fable sable saber=sabre rabies

16 ate=eight hate=Haight eighty=Ate Haiti pate bait abate debate Tate potato state
17 status[2] date data datum Kate Caitlin skate gate=gait mate tomato Maitland
18 innate late relate plate slates inflate fate theta sate rate appâ-ratus[2]
19 be-rate prate calibrate trait Drayton crate grateful freight weight=wait equate

20 aiding Hades Adrian Hadrian Baedeker Arcadia cicada nadir laden Palladium fading
21 invader sadist shadings raided upbraided trader degrading wading jaded

22 ache hake Aiken acorn opaque spake baked bacon takes stake=steak Dakin cake make
23 Jamaica naked snake lake placates Blake flakes fake fakir vacant sake Zakes
24 shake rake brake=break mandrake fracas wake quake Jacques (*As You Like It*)

25 ague pagan bagel Nagel Lagos[2] flagrant Fagin vaguely vagrant inveigle sago
26 Ragin=Reagan Hegel San Diego

27 Amos Hamish Aamon Haman Amiens amiable payment taming Damian Cambridge
28 gamester maiming naming lamely famous Samos shamus Raymond framing Jamie

WORDS FOR PRACTICE USING *eĭ* SHORT, Cont.

1 anus heinous ancient container dainty canine Hyrcanian gainful mania planer=plainer
2 feigning ḍü-ranium brainy trainer refraining waning wainscot Chaney Janus Sejanus

3 Ailey Hayley alien palings bailiff Taylor=tailer daily=Daly Caleb Gaelic mailing
4 inalienable echolalia failure Thalia (woman's name) salient sailing raillé-ry
5 pralines trailer (whaling) wailing Waylon Yalie jailer=gaoler

6 aphid playful safe Rafer Dreyfus[2] waif wafer wayfa-rer chafe

7 Avon haven pavement Octavius David Mavis maven navy navel=naval knave-ry flavor
8 slavish favor savior=saviour Xavier shaving raven (n) craven gravy waving quaver

9 atheist pathos Carpathian bathos Caithness Nathan natheless Latham Lathrop
10 plaything faith wraith Galbraith Braithwaite

11 bathing lather (lathe-worker)

12 aced haste pace space pastry base=bass (music) taste stasis case mace freemason
13 Mason griMACE[2] nascent lace place=plaice complacent face vase[3] race e-rase
14 brace trace grace Thrace waist=waste persuasive chaste=chased Jason

15 Azenburg hazing diapason Basingstoke daisy gazes amazing nasal laser complaisant
16 phases raisin appraisal brazen grazing phrases

17 Haitian Hypatia patient spatial herbaceous station sedation application purgation
18 cremation emaciated nation palatial glacier facial salvation conversation Alsatian
19 civilization nä-rration gracious Thracian

20 Asian Anastasia euthanasia Malaysian glazier aphasia invasion ḷEu-rasian abrasion
21 Frazier persuasion

22 "H" paycheck Bache nature Vachell=Vachel Rachel

23 agent aged (adj) paging Beijing contagious stagey Cajun gauges Magi preSAges (v)
24 raging Trajan wages assuaging

25 pay-ing stay-ing dismay-ing neigh-ing survey-ing say-ing pray-ing=prey-ing bray-ing
26 portray-ing gray-ing fray-ing weigh-ing payable Bayard Cataian dais archaic chaos
27 Ā-ramaic layer Menelaus laic conveyer rayon pray-er (one who prays) crayon

28 Aonian aorta élan peyote payola Bayonne forte (loud) début chaotic gainsay-ing
29 Laertes ballet Feydeau Seychelles Galbraith enervate appreciate deviate (verb)
30 WEAK FORMS (wf) of: may they

PHRASES FOR PRACTICE

Long e·ĭ·   **Short** eĭ   **Mixed Lengths**

1 ↗ Abe aimed at the aide
2 hail Yale's females
3 portray the Dane on stage
4 engage Dave the Knave
5 gave aid to Ames
6 remain engaged for ay *e·ĭ·*
7 save the (whales)
8 page the males for mail
9 a delayed vague phase

10 ↗ able apes ate apricots
11 eighty-eight sailors
12 a pastry-tasting date
13 a fake faith healer
14 fading daily
15 griMAces of FAces
16 play-ing the hateful rake
17 hate wasted space
18 saints of faint faith

19 ↗ aid the amazing aviators
20 tasteful veils for sale
21 save hate mail for later
22 ashamed of naming names
23 an enraged great Dane
24 wave to the waif
25 make my day
26 bathe in Jamaica Bay
27 stale atheistic say-ings

SENTENCES FOR PRACTICE

Long e·ĭ·   **Short** eĭ

28 ↗ Ale ailed and aged the aide.
29 ↗ Ames and Abe aim to get "A's" for ay. *e·ĭ·*
30 Yea, the Thane hath ta'en the stage.
31 Regale Yale's males with pails of ale.
32 The slave craved to regain his name.
33 It's insane to remain in the shade today.
34 Fame is the name of the game, Craig.
35 Save the (whales) from the crazed males.

36 ↗ Eight apricots abate aches.
37 ↗ Amiable angels ate acres of acorns.
38 The saints were stay-ing near the railroad.
39 Mailer is waiting for a tailor from Haiti.
40 Kate's makeup faded (when) she griMACED.
41 Amazingly, a naked atheist waited at the gate.
42 Was Laertes able to make a date at CarNEgie?
43 She's making her début in a famous ballet.

Mixed Lengths

44 ↗ Ada and Ames alienated Abe the atheist (when) they aimed at angels.
45 Dale failed to nail the available sails dŭ-ring the gale.
46 The neighbors were enraged to be awakened by the wailing babe.
47 They say that Craig makes a great mate for Kate Hale.
48 The graciously laid table displayed an ə-rray of azaleas.
49 This appə-ratus will aid the survey and ə-rrange the data.
50 Jane wasn't able to pace her gait, and so abstained from the painful race.
51 Wade waded (while) he waited for ways to weigh (whales).
52 Make my day by saving hate mail from the blaze.
53 We all prayed in vain for Dave's great break.
54 Hŭ-rray! Both male and female sailors made the grade!
55 The rain in Spain mainly makes me crazy.
56 I'm late for an important date with James Mason.
57 The remaining players ate up the stage. (What) a mistake!
58 Thou hast ta'en the day, o great fakir!
59 They may stay away a day or two, or they may take a belated paid vacation.
60 Brave mates, make haste to save your favorite Ā-rabians for the pə-rade.

EXERCISES FOR DISTINGUISHING BETWEEN *el* **AND** *e·ĭ·l*

el	*e·ĭ·l*	*el*	*e·ĭ·l*	*el*	*e·ĭ·l*
1 El	— ale=ail	15 shell	— shale	29 Keller	— Caleb
2 lapel	— pale=pail	16 mŏ-<u>r</u>el	— <u>r</u>ail	30 gelding	— <u>r</u>egaling
3 bell	— bale=bail	17 hell	— hale=hail	31 Mellor	— Mailer
4 tell	— tale=tail	18 (whĕlp	— (whāle	32 felon	— failure
5 pastel	— stale	19 well	— wail	33 selling	— salient
6 dell	— dale	20 yell	— Yale	34 cellar	— sailor
7 <u>R</u>aquel	— kale=Kael	21 gel	— jail=gaol	35 Zeller	— azalea
8 Miguel	— gale=Gail	22 Elliot	— alien	36 <u>r</u>elish	— <u>r</u>ailroad
9 Mel	— male=mail	23 Ellie	— Ailey	37 t<u>r</u>ellis	— t<u>r</u>ailing
10 Nell	— nail	24 p<u>r</u>opeller	— paler	38 Helen	— Van Halen
11 fell	— fail	25 belly	— Bailey	39 hellish	— Hayley
12 <u>R</u>avel	— vale=vail	26 <u>r</u>ebellion	— Balliol	40 hellion	— Mahalia
13 Thelma	— Thalia *ˈθeiljə* 27 teller	— tailer=Taylor			41 welling	— wailing
(woman's name)					
14 sell=cell	— sale=sail	28 deli	— daily=Daly	42 jealous	— jailers= gaolers

SENTENCES FOR PRACTICE

43 Ms. Pell will pay eels to look pale.

44 Mel Bell tied bay eels into bales.

45 This pastel ca̅n't stay, Elia. It's stale.

46 Is that <u>R</u>ay Ealing <u>r</u>ailing at the <u>r</u>ailroad?

47 Cant<u>r</u>ell will port<u>r</u>ay Ely on the t<u>r</u>ail.

48 At the deli that day, Eli saw Daly.

49 I heard him yell, "Yea! Eli got into Yale!"

50 It's well and good that you weigh elands, Waylon.

51 You <u>r</u>eceived an "A," Lee, in Ailey's cla̅ss.

52 That's the day Lee saw dailies.

53 Add a bay leaf, Bailey.

54 Wellington doesn't like the way Ling-Ling's wailing.

55 Ellen, is the name "A. Leono͟re" alien to you?

56 Hey, Lee, it's hailing!

◆ THE DIPHTHONG SOUND $æ\breve{\imath}\cdot$ AS IN "my" ◆

Represented by the spellings:

I=eye=aye (yes)   tie=Thai   thigh   I'll=aisle=isle

by=buy=bye   guide   height   benign   diamond   fire[2]

Relax your lower jaw wide open and relax the tip of your tongue behind your lower front teeth. Arch the FRONT of your tongue forward and low for the first element $æ$ and from that position glide your tongue-arch, or make a vanish, toward the position of $\imath$, the weak second element. During this glide of the tongue-arch, your lower jaw moves from open to half-open, and your lips are spread SLIGHTLY. The movement of the glide is quite distinct and can easily be seen and felt as the two vowel elements blend to form the single new sound $æ\breve{\imath}\cdot$.

This sound should be one of the most bright, open sounds in Spoken English and one that has a good deal of movement. This openness is especially crucial in the words in which this sound is SHORT in length. This sound is also susceptible to tight, swallowed placement; therefore, a relaxed aw is a must.

WORDS FOR PRACTICE USING $æ\breve{\imath}\cdot$ LONG

◆ In a STRESSED SYLLABLE that is the FINAL syllable of a word, when the diphthong is also the last sound of the word

◆ In a STRESSED SYLLABLE that is the FINAL syllable of a word, when the diphthong is followed by one or more voiced consonants

1 eye=aye=ay (yes) hi=hie=high pie=pi spy by=buy=bye alibi tie=Thai sty die=dye
2 Mordecai sky guy nigh deny lie=lye July rely ply reply apply Bly=Bligh fly sly
3 fie defy vie thigh sigh=Cy shy rye=wry pry spry try dry cry descry fry=Frye
4 why "Y"=Wye Kwai
5 STRONG FORMS (sf) of: I by my thy

6 imbibe vibes bribe tribe diatribe scribes ascribe described circumscribed

7 eyed=I'd (sf) hide=Hyde Ides hides pied spied bide tide=tied died=dyed guide
8 denied snide lied elide allied collide plied Clyde glide slide confide provide
9 sighed=side reside shied ride pried=pride bride tried dried cried wide chide

10 I'm (sf) time=thyme dimes mime lime sublime climbed slime enzyme rhyme=rime primed
11 crimes chimes

12 eyne hind pine opine spine combine (v) bind tine dined condign kind mined=mind
13 nine benign line malign blind declined fined=find refined vines thine sign resign
14 designed shine Rhine rind brine grind whine wine winds (v) entwined

15 aisle=isle=I'll (sf) pile compiled bile tile stile=style crocodile Kyle guile
16 beguile mile mild smiles Nile Lyle=lisle file defiled vile reviles reconcile
17 riled while awhile wiles wild child Giles

18 I've (sf) hive Ives hives dive archives knives lives (n) Clive five revives rive
19 de-rived drives contrived thrive shrive wive chives jive gyves

20 Rotherhithe tithe lithe Blythe=blithe scythe writhes

WORDS FOR PRACTICE USING aĭ LONG, Cont.

1 eyes hies=highs pies despise buys alibis ties advertise dies=dyes skies catechize
2 disguise guise=guys surmise denies canonize lies realize plies flies defies revise
3 thighs sighs=size shies rise a-rise prize=pries surprised tries dries cries
4 descries fries (why)'s wise eulogize

WORDS FOR PRACTICE USING aĭ SHORT IN ALL OTHER CASES

◆ In a STRESSED SYLLABLE followed by a voiced consonant that is in turn followed by a voiceles consonant

◆ In a STRESSED SYLLABLE followed by one or more voiceless consonants

◆ In any syllable but the last syllable of a word

◆ In all UNstressed SYLLABLES, including WEAK FORMS of words

5 pint Mainz (German) shin'st (whilst) smil'st

6 hype hypochondriac pipe piper typed stipend sniper viper ripe ripen tripe stripe
7 gripes wipe swipes

8 ibis hibernate Bible imbiber Tiber Khyber Nyberg libel libra-ry fiber fibrous
9 vibrant vibrate cybernetics tribal

10 item heighten height despite bites tight Dighton Aphrodite indict kite mite=might
11 night=knight nightingale delight enlighten plight blight flight slight fight vitamin
12 vital sight=site=cite exciting rite=write=Wright play-wright brighten trite Crichton
13 frighten (white) wight Wytham

14 Ida Haydn I'd (wf) idle=idol=idyll Heidelberg biding tidings Dido guidance Midas
15 snidely glider Fido Poseidon riding bridal trident strident Dryden Friday widen

16 Ike hike icon haiku pike spikes bike tyke dike Michael microphone Nike like
17 like=lichen ficus Viking psychic cycle Riker's Wyken

18 bygone tiger taiga Steiger geiger migrant migraine Sligo

19 I'm (wf) Hymen timing stymie diamond miming Lima (Ohio) climate climax slimy Simon
20 Ziman rhyming primal Wyman chiming

21 Ina's highness pineapple bina-ry tiny dynasty kindly gynecologist minor=miner mynah
22 ninety Linus reclining final findings vinyl sinus signing designer shining rhino
23 (whining) wining entwining China angina

24 I'll (wf) highly islander highlander pilot Tyler Thailand stylus stylish Schuyler
25 beguiling mileage Milo Nilus lilac defiling reviling asylum Silas xylophone Riley

26 Eiffel hyphen bifurcate typhoid stifle knife life fife syphon cipher rife rifle
27 trifle strife Dreyfuss[2] wife midwife housewife (Amer)

28 I've (wf) ivy ivory Ivan Stuyvesant diving divers (n; adj) Godiva MacGyver
29 conniving lively enliven revival survival rival privacy striving driving thriving

WORDS FOR PRACTICE USING aĭ SHORT, Cont.

1 tithing blithely <u>wr</u>ithing

2 iced heist icicle Pisces bison enticing dice mice nice lice spliced suffice
3 feisty vice advice <u>pr</u>ecise concise Zeisler <u>r</u>ice <u>pr</u>ice <u>tr</u>ice Ch<u>r</u>ist th<u>r</u>ice

4 Eisen despises kaiser geyser miser advising sizing <u>r</u>ising hŏ-<u>r</u>izon <u>r</u>ep<u>r</u>isal wisest

5 hygiene Niger Elijah

6 spy-ing buy-ing dy-ing de-ny-ing ly-ing <u>r</u>e-ply-ing fly-ing sigh-ing <u>tr</u>y-ing <u>fr</u>y-ing

7 Iowa ions pious bias Dionysus Dion=Dian Caius Mayan maniacal lion affianced
8 viand scion cyanide Zion <u>r</u>iot=<u>r</u>yot <u>R</u>yan B<u>r</u>yant <u>tr</u>iumph Wyatt quiet elegiac giant

9 di-al di-a-lect de-ni-al vi-al Vi-o-la <u>tr</u>i-al

10 papaya O-<u>r</u>esteia Jedediah Maya jambalaya de Falla Messiah playa Mă-<u>r</u>i-a (British)

11 pyre Sti-ers dire admire lyre=li-ar fire sire pli-ers <u>fr</u>i-ar=<u>fr</u>y-er
12 ire hire=high-er Ireland hireling spire expire byre=buy-er Tyre=tire <u>r</u>etire
13 mire=Mey-er fli-er desire shire=shy-er b<u>r</u>i-ar d<u>r</u>y-er=d<u>r</u>i-er c<u>r</u>i-er=C<u>r</u>y-er wire
14 Dwy-er choir inquire=enquire inqui-ry MacGuire gyre
    NOTE: In verse, these may also be pronounced in one syllable, as TRIPHTHONGS. (See pages 186-187.)

15 idea ideal idyllic identity hyena binomial typhoon Tibē-<u>r</u>ius Diana dynamic
16 Chimē-<u>r</u>a cayenne myopic Nigē-<u>r</u>ia licentious Lysander Libē-<u>r</u>ia lib<u>r</u>ă-<u>r</u>ian vitality
17 citation Cheyenne <u>r</u>hinocĕ-<u>r</u>os p<u>r</u>ivation C<u>r</u>imea Wyoming quietus gigantic
18 WEAK FORMS of : I'd I'm I'll I've by my

WORDS FOR CLARITY OF aĭ PRIOR TO r

✓Reminder
> Make an open, clearly defined aĭ sound and begin the following syllable with a clean-cut consonant r . In doing so, you will avoid marring the clarity of the aĭ sound with r-coloring.

19 I-<u>r</u>ene i-<u>r</u>onic i-<u>r</u>ate I-<u>r</u>is I-<u>r</u>as i-<u>r</u>ony Hi-<u>r</u>am hy-<u>r</u>ax pi-<u>r</u>ate papy-<u>r</u>us Pi-<u>r</u>aeus

20 aspi-<u>r</u>ant spi-<u>r</u>al By-<u>r</u>on Bay-<u>r</u>euth ty-<u>r</u>ant ti-<u>r</u>ade Cai-<u>r</u>o (Egypt) My-<u>r</u>a vi-<u>r</u>us

21 envi-<u>r</u>onment thy-<u>r</u>oid Osi-<u>r</u>is si-<u>r</u>en gy-<u>r</u>oscope

EXERCISES FOR OPENING AND FORWARD PLACEMENT OF a AND aɪ̆·

a	aɪ̆·	aɪ̆·	aɪ̆	aɪ̆	aɪə	OR	aɪə̯
Always					**Two**		**Triphthong:**
Short	**Long**	**Long**	**Short**	**Short**	**Syllables**		**One Syllable**
1 ask	eyes	aisle=isle	I'll (wf)	ice	ire		ire
2 pass	pies	pile	espi-als	pike	pyre		pyre
3 bath	bind	bile	By-ron	bite	byre=buy–er		byre=buyer
4 task	time	tile	ty-rant	tyke	tire=Tyre		tire=Tyre
5 dance	dine	crocodile	di-al	indict	dire=dy-er		dire=dyer
6 master	mind	mile	May-an	Michael	mire=Mey-er		mire=Meyer
7 nasty	denies	Nile	de-ni-al	nice	-----		-----
8 laugh	lives (n)	Lyle	Ly-all	likely	lyre=li-ar		lyre=liar
9 fast	find	file	de-fi-ant	suffice	fire		fire
10 vast	revive	vile	vi-al	vice	-----		-----
11 rascal	rise	rile	tri-al	frighten	fri-ar=fry-er		friar=fryer
12 half	high	high school	highlander	height	hire=high-er		hire=higher

PHRASES FOR PRACTICE

Long aɪ̆·

13 ꭓ aye, an eye for an eye
14 nine lives
15 a child's eyes
16 advised to hide her thighs
17 wine and dine at nine
18 five crimes on the Ides
19 a sign of the times
20 compile fines and bribes

Short aɪ̆

21 ꭓ idylls of the ayatollah
22 the price is right
23 childish dislikes
24 precise advice
25 nineteen finalists
26 pi-rates and ty-rants
27 retired choirs
28 I-rene's desires

Mixed Lengths

29 ꭓ Ives' ice-cream
30 a wild Gemini child
31 idolized Ives
32 biding my time
33 cry-ing with a smile
34 de-ny-ing lies
35 Viola and Ma-ria thrive
36 fie upon retirement

SENTENCES FOR PRACTICE

Long aɪ̆·

37 His nine lives were wild.
38 The child's eyes beguiled me.
39 He imbibed five fine Rhine wines.
40 I see miles and miles of smiles.
41 The ties that bind have revived me.
42 Why disguise the sublime scythes?
43 The bride takes pride in her designs.
44 Hie thee to the mines, Giles.
45 Unrefined slime defiled the Nile.
46 That's why the maligned crocodile writhes.

Short aɪ̆

47 What mighty knight is fly-ing a kite?
48 The pi-rate, that ty-rant, was defiant.
49 I spiked that tyke on the turnpike.
50 I'm try-ing and try-ing to quit buy-ing.
51 Cease sigh-ing, sire, or you'll expire.
52 Let's hike right up to Pike's Peak.
53 Stop cry-ing over the dy-ing lice.
54 I idolize the Viking dynasty.
55 Don't hire the uptight, i-rate buyer.
56 Fire-fighting will tire the idle scion.

SENTENCES FOR PRACTICE, Cont.

Mixed Lengths

1 Aye, I've an idea Ives is idealistic, isolated and idle.
2 Michael has rightly realigned the icons in his triumphant designs.
3 The guide's itiné-ra-ry supplied precise mileage for the entire hike.
4 The diet is comprised of white Rhine wine and fried rice with thyme.
5 Ike was fired with a desire to acquire the lyre, sire.
6 I-rene exercised wisely to acquire the desired rightly-sized thighs.
7 Invite the feisty finalists to try to describe their lives.
8 There are times when they thrive on whining, cry-ing and conniving.
9 I defy you to retire in the twilight of your wild life.
10 You'll see five fine bright young lights this Friday night at the fights.
11 I'm as high as a kite on dry white wine and Key Lime pie.
12 The climax was an exciting diatribe against a child's life in the diamond mines.
13 Pass me some pie and a pint of spiked papaya juice.
14 Fasten it and you'll find you're likely to survive tonight's fire.
15 The vast, vile vi-al is a Viking find from Iceland.
16 Half got high, took a mile-high hike to the Heights, and got hired as guides.
17 You'd be daft to dive from divers dikes in such dire times.
18 Ask me if I like life in Ireland, Ike.
19 That rascal will rise to the heights of a life of crime and then do time on Riker's Island.

◆ **THE DIPHTHONG SOUND** ɔ˙ɪ̆˙ **AS IN "b*oy*"** ◆

Represented by the spellings:

    *oy*ster   *oi*l   b*oy*   b*uoy*ant   Fr*eu*d

    Relax your lower jaw to a half-open position and relax the tip of your tongue behind your lower front teeth. Arch the BACK of your tongue half-low for the first element ɔ   and from that position glide your tongue-arch forward and upward, or make a vanish, toward the position of ɪ   , the weak second element. During this glide of the tongue-arch, your lower jaw moves to a high position and your lips move from a rounded to a SLIGHTLY spread position. The two vowel elements are blended into a single, new sound, the diphthong ɔ˙ɪ̆˙ , by movement of the tongue, jaw and lips that can be seen and felt.

    This sound, the only diphthong sound in Spoken English that moves from a BACK VOWEL to a FRONT VOWEL, utilizes more movement than any other sound in the language.

    The diphthong sound ɔ˙ɪ̆˙ should be a plush, full-bodied sound. It must begin with a generous opening of the mouth, and the glide, or vanish, must be smoothly executed.

WORDS FOR PRACTICE USING ɔ˙ɪ̆˙ LONG

    ◆ In a STRESSED SYLLABLE that is the FINAL syllable of a word, when the diphthong is also the last sound of the word

    ◆ In a STRESSED SYLLABLE that is the FINAL syllable of a word, when the diphthong is followed by one or more voiced consonants

1   oy   ahoy   poi   boy=buoy   toy   coy   goy   annoy   Illinois   Loy   aLLOY (v)   hoi polloi   ploy
2   employ   cloy   Foy   Savoy   soy   Roy   cordu-roy   Troy   destroy   St. Croix   joy   enjoy

3   buoyed=Boyd   toyed   annoyed   pa-ranoid   humanoid   Lloyd   aLLOYED (v)   Floyd   void   avoid
4   trapezoid   destroyed   android   Freud   enjoyed

5   Poins   coin   coins   Burgoyne   Des Moines   loins   purloin   groin   join   joins   conjoin
6   enjoined   adjoin

7   oil   Hoyle   spoil   boil=Boyle   toils   toiled   Doyle   coil   recoil   turmoil   foil=Foyle
8   trefoil   voile   soil   soiled   roil   broil

9   hoise   poise   boys=buoys   toys   noise   annoys   aLLOYS (v)   ploys   cloys   Foy's   Roy's   Troy's
10   joys   enjoys

WORDS FOR PRACTICE USING ɔɪ̆ SHORT IN ALL OTHER CASES

    ◆ In a STRESSED SYLLABLE followed by a voiced consonant that is in turn followed by a voiceless consonant

    ◆ In a STRESSED SYLLABLE followed by one or more voiceless consonants

    ◆ In any syllable but the last syllable of a word

    ◆ In all UNstressed SYLLABLES

11   point   appoint   disappoint   annoint   a-roint   joint   disjoint   spoilt

12   Hoyt   Boito   doit   Coit   goiter   reconnoiter   Beloit   loiter   Voit=Voight   Reuters   Detroit

13   hoyden=hoiden   avoidance   embroider   Croyden   Freudian

WORDS FOR PRACTICE USING ɔĭ SHORT, Cont.

1 hoicks boycott tṛoika pĕ-ṛestṛoika yoicks

2 Bṛeughel

3 Pacoima employment enjoyment

4 ointment pointer pointless appointment poignant Boynton Toynbee coinage purloining
5 joining joiner conjoining adjoining jointure disjointed

6 oily spoiling spoiler spoilage toiling toilet doily=D'Oyly uncoiling foiling
7 soybean bṛoiler Tṛoilus fṛäulein joyless

8 coif (cap)

9 oyster hoist boiste-ṛous moist moisten noisome cloister foist voice voiced
10 voiceless Ṛoyce Ṛoister choice Joyce ṛejoiced joist

11 poison Boise boysenbĕ-ṛry noisy foison

12 buoy-ing toy-ing annoy-ing employ-ing cloy-ing destṛoy-ing enjoy-ing

13 boy-ish goy-im moi-e-ty voy-age doy-en buoy-ant Sä-ṛoy-an Goy-a annoy-ance
14 pä-ṛa-noi-a soy-a Hoy-a loy-al loy-al-ty ṛoy-al ṛoy-al-ty

15 Moyers foyer enjoyer

16 poinsettia envoy borzoi Bolshoi alloy (n) Ṛoyale

EXERCISES FOR FORWARD AND OPEN PLACEMENT OF ɔ: AND ɔ·ĭ·

ɔ:	ɔ·ĭ·	ɔĭ	ɔ:	ɔ·ĭ·	ɔĭ
17 awe	— oil	— oyster	23 caw	— coy	— coif
18 paw	— poised	— point	24 geegaw	— goy	— goiter
19 bawl=ball	— boil	— boiste-ṛous	25 maw	— Des Moines	— moist
20 tall	— toil	— toilet	26 gnaw	— noise	— noisome
21 daw	— Doyle	— doit	27 haw	— ahoy	— hoist
22 dṛaw	— Tṛoy	— Detṛoit	28 jaw	— join	— joint

PHRASES AND SHORT SENTENCES FOR PRACTICE

Long ɔ·ĭ·	Short ɔĭ	Mixed Lengths
29 ? Oy! Oil!	36 ? oysters in oily ointment	43 ? oysters in oil
30 Boys toil and toil.	37 loy-al to ṛoy-al-ty	44 employ-ing boiling oil
31 destṛoy Tṛoy	38 a boiste-ṛous voice	45 a joyful "Ahoy!"
32 oil fṛom the soil	39 joylessly poisoned	46 cloy-ing Poins
33 Noise destṛoys her poise.	40 boycott appointments	47 pä-ṛanoid choice
34 too coy to enjoy	41 embṛoidered doilies	48 enjoyed Detṛoit and Des Moines
35 avoid the Savoy	42 joyous boyish foibles	49 ṛoy-al-ty avoids St. Cṛoix

SENTENCES FOR PRACTICE

Long ɔ˙ɪ̆˙

1 Ahoy, boys! Noise from Savoy!
2 They toiled and toiled in the soil.
3 Avoid oil and employ soy, Miss Lloyd.
4 Destroy the spoils of Troy.
5 Their loins are poised to enjoy St. Croix.

6 Oil, oil, on my vé-ry own soil.
7 Here's a coil. We'll boil in oil.
8 Each spoiled boy avoids joy.
9 The hoi polloi destroyed the humanoid.
10 No more toys for Roy. He's be-ing spoiled.

Short ɔɪ̆

11 "A poignant choice," rejoiced *The Voice*.
12 Are you loy-al to roy-al-ty, Troilus?
13 Her boisté-rous voice poisoned the foyer.
14 The point is that employers aren't loy-al.
15 Point your voice toward Detroit, Joyce.
16 A moi-e-ty was foisted on Hoyt.

17 A noisy voy-age is my first choice.
18 Their exploitation of Goya is annoy-ing.
19 He's enjoy-ing the roy-al treatment.
20 Hoist anchors, you moist oysters!
21 Even the ointment was cloy-ing.
22 Rejoice! They're destroy-ing the loy-a-lists!

Mixed Lengths

23 ʎ Avoid oyster-oil ointment.
24 Joyce employed his loy-al foils.
25 Noise from the hoi polloi is annoy-ing.
26 Are you enjoy-ing the Rolls Royce, Roy?
27 It was pointless to avoid the unemployed.
28 Joyce was overjoyed at the appointment.
29 His boy-ishness was poignant but coy.
30 The alloys in these toys must be oiled.

31 Oy! His pa-ranoia is a roy-al disappointment.
32 Spoiled poi poisoned Boyd.
33 The roy-al poinsettias have been purloined.
34 Floyd avoided *Ralph Roister Doister*.
35 Will the Bolshoi employ the boy-ish envoy?
36 Doyle destroyed the adjoining cloisters.
37 Fräulein Freud foiled the turmoil in Boise.
38 Burgoyne was appointed to reconnoiter Troy.

◆ THE DIPHTHONG SOUND $O\cdot\breve{U}\cdot$ AS IN "go" ◆

Represented by the spellings:

    s*o*=s*ew*-s*ow* (seed)   s*oul*=s*ole*=S*eoul*   c*oa*t   d*oe*=d*ough*   m*au*ve

    b*eau*=b*ow* (weapon; violin; knot)   y*eo*man   br*oa*ch=br*oo*ch

    Relax your lower jaw to just below a half-closed position and relax the tip of your tongue behind your lower front teeth. Round your lips into a circle. Arch the BACK of your tongue half-high for the first element O and from that position glide your tongue-arch upward, or make a vanish, toward the position of U , the weak second element. During this glide, your lips will become slightly more rounded and your lower jaw will move slightly upward. These movements, though subtle, can be seen and felt as you blend the two vowel elements into a single new sound—the diphthong $O\cdot\breve{U}\cdot$.

    This dark, rich sound must have a gently firm rounding of the lips to insure a resonance that is focused and clear. It is imperative that a lip-lazy production of the sound be avoided and that, for the North American speaker, the so-called "British 'oh'" $\partial\breve{U}$ be avoided as well.

WORDS FOR PRACTICE USING $O\cdot\breve{U}\cdot$ LONG

- ◆ In a STRESSED SYLLABLE that is the FINAL syllable of a word, when the diphthong is also the last sound of the word

- ◆ In a STRESSED SYLLABLE that is the FINAL syllable of a word, when the diphthong is followed by one or more voiced consonants

1 O=oh=owe hoe Poe=Po beau=Bo=bow (weapon; violin; knot) tow=toe plateau stow

2 bestow dough=doe go mow=Moe no=know=Noh snow low=lo below blow glow

3 flow=Flo slow=sloe foe though=tho' although sew=so=sow (seed) Zoe[2] show=shew

4 <u>r</u>oe=<u>r</u>ow (line; oar) p<u>r</u>o t<u>r</u>ow c<u>r</u>ow f<u>r</u>o th<u>r</u>ow (wh)oa woe Joe=Jo

5 Hobe lobe=Loeb globe <u>r</u>obe p<u>r</u>obes Lat<u>r</u>obe Job

6 ode=owed hoed Spode bode abode toad=towed bestowed code goad mode commode

7 node snowed load=lode=lowed explode glowed flowed slowed sewed=sowed

8 showed=shewed <u>r</u>oad=<u>r</u>owed Joad

9 Hoag Pogue Moog vogue <u>r</u>ogue=<u>R</u>oeg b<u>r</u>ogue

10 Om home tome dome combed gnome=Nome loam gloam foam Soames

11 <u>R</u>ome=<u>r</u>oam ch<u>r</u>ome

12 own hone pone bones tone entoned stones condone cone=Kohn moaned known

13 lone=loan blown clones flown Sloane phones sewn=sown zone shown=shone (American)

14 <u>r</u>oan=<u>R</u>hone p<u>r</u>one d<u>r</u>ones c<u>r</u>one g<u>r</u>own=g<u>r</u>oan th<u>r</u>own=th<u>r</u>one Joan

15 old hold=holed hole=whole pole=poll bowl=boll toll told=tolled dole coal=Cole cold

16 scold goal gold mole mold knoll foal fold soul=sole=Seoul sold shoals <u>r</u>oll=<u>r</u>ole

17 pa-<u>r</u>ole <u>r</u>olled t<u>r</u>olls d<u>r</u>oll sc<u>r</u>oll cajole

18 hove cove mauve loaves clove Fauve <u>r</u>oves t<u>r</u>ove d<u>r</u>ove g<u>r</u>oves th<u>r</u>ove wove Jove

19 oaths loathe (hate) loathed loathes clothe clothes clothed bet<u>r</u>oth bet<u>r</u>othed

WORDS FOR PRACTICE USING $o \cdot \breve{u} \cdot$ LONG, Cont.

1 owes hoes=hose pose suppose composed repose exposed bows (weapons; violins; knots)
2 toes=tows doze=does (deer) goes mows nose=knows lows blows close (v) glows flows
3 slows foes those sews=sows (seed) shows=shews rose=rows (oars) a-rose prose=pros
4 Ambrose trows crows grows froze throws=throes Shrewsbu-ry[2] woes chose Joe's

5 loge Vosges

6 doge ho-rologe

WORDS FOR PRACTICE USING $o \breve{u}$ SHORT IN ALL OTHER CASES

◆ In a STRESSED SYLLABLE followed by a voiced consonant that is in turn followed by a voiceless consonant

◆ In a STRESSED SYLLABLE followed by one or more voiceless consonants

◆ In any syllable but the last syllable of a word

◆ In all UNstressed SYLLABLES (These are invariably at the ends of words.)

7 don't won't=wont (n: custom; adj: accustomed; apt) bolts colt dolt molt revolt jolt

8 ope hope hoping opal hopeful pope taupe dope copious coping scope moped (v)
9 moped (n) nope lope eloped slopes soap Schopenhauer rope Eu-ropa trope groping

10 Obie=obi Hobie oboe Hoboken Obe-ron Holborn Toby Doberman cobalt Gobelin Moby
11 mobile noble global phobia sober probity Frobisher Okeechobee

12 oat Houghton iota potent boat tote stoat dotes coat=cote Dakota goat moat demote
13 remote noted denote lotus bloated Cloten gloating float vote Minnesota shoat
14 rote=wrote Croat groat quote Choate

15 Odin odalisque odor Podunk Baudelaire toady dodo coded goading pagoda modish
16 loden exploded soda Rhoda rodent Wodan Jody

17 oak hocus-pocus okra poked Poconos spoke bespoke token stoked coke rococo mocha
18 local locusts bloke cloaks Slocum folks forecastle=fo'c'sle focus revoke soaked
19 ba-roque broke trochee croaked woke yoke=yolk choke joke

20 ogle Hogan Hogarth Bogart bogus toga Calistoga Logan fogy Shogun roguish

21 omen Homer Oklahoma coma Tacoma moment nomad Sonoma nomenclature
22 Loman diploma gloaming foaming Roman Romeo bromide Dromio yeoman

23 owning honing owner one-rous pony Bona tonal Daytona intoning donor Coney
24 ce-remony[2] matrimony[2] kimono Pomona lonely loner Bellona phony sonar zoning
25 Co-rona Ve-rona droning cronies groaning Jonah

26 olio holy=wholly Poland bowling tolling cola goalie Angola Nolan lowly Lola
27 Foley foliage Rizzoli's Roland=Rowland Rowley rolling proleta-riat cajoling solely

28 Olsen holster bolster olden Holden holding boldly embolden doldrums coldly colden
29 Molson molding folder Folger soldier Isolde wold

30 oaf tofu gopher loaf loafer loaf's sofa shofar strophe woeful

WORDS FOR PRACTICE USING OŬ SHORT, Cont.

1 ova ovum oval bovine Tovah Segovia nova novocaine cloven clover Soviet rover

2 roving drover Grover woven anchovy jovial

3 oath both Dothan loth=loath (unwilling; reluctant) troth (Brit) growth quoth

4 loathing clothing betrothal

5 ow'st host post boatswain=bosun verbose boast comatose toasts dose docent coast

6 ghost most Formosa know'st close (adj) closely show'st roast gross grocer grocᵊ-ry

7 "supposed to" (expected to)

8 ozone hosing posey suppose dozing Moses noses nosy rosᵊ-ry roses frozen chose

9 chosen Joseph Josephine Joe's

10 ocean potion kosher precocious gauche Goshen motion emotion notion Kenosha lotion

11 cloche Foch devotion social associate Dŭ-rocher quotient Boeotian brioche

12 osier exposure Dozier explosion implosion closure enclosure e-rosion

13 poach coached Loach roach approached broach=brooch encroached

14 doge's cogent sojourn (n) Trojan

15 oyes=oyez ʹoŭ jeʃ

16 NOTE: DO NOT ADD A ᵘ SOUND TO THESE AND SIMILAR WORDS: ow-ing bestow-ing go-ing

17 mow-ing know-ing blow-ing glow-ing flow-ing sew-ing=sow-ing show-ing=shew-ing

18 row-ing wallow-ing swallow-ing go-er low-er blow-er row-er slow-er low-est slow-est

19 Owen po-em po-et po-e-try po-e-sy boa Jĕ-roboam Krakatoa Alcoa Samoa Noah

20 Mauna Loa Lois Rowen=Rowan Baden-Powell Stow-ell bestow-al Low-ell Crow-ell

21 Soho Idaho Navajo Aleppo elbow Mephisto window echo Moscow logo memo winnow

22 Apollo billow Othello Niblo Sappho salvo ǣ-rrow Banquo yoyo macho banjo

PHRASES FOR PRACTICE

Long O·Ŭ·	Short OŬ	Mixed Lengths
23 ⌐ old odes	30 ⌐ only okra and oats	37 ⌐ overly open "O's"
24 no Noh in Rome	31 won't the pope smoke both	38 a soul's holy growth
25 home alone with Joan	32 groaning and moaning	39 Mr. Stow-ell stole
26 stone-cold coals	33 lonesome cronies	40 be loth to loathe
27 be bold with gold	34 colts and poultry	41 we rowed by rote
28 go below the plateau	35 wont to quote both ghosts	42 loading loaves
29 disclose clothes	36 see Moscow from a window	43 Poe's copious notes

SENTENCES FOR PRACTICE

Long O·Ŭ·

44 ⌐ Oh, hold old odes.

45 Roll the dough for the gateau.

46 We owned and sold old homes in Nome.

47 Behold the old gold in the hold.

48 ⌐ You own the whole old hold.

49 Show those toes, you rogue!

50 It's stone cold in the hold.

51 His soul groaned and moaned.

SENTENCES FOR PRACTICE, Cont.

1 Clothes were disclosed in the loaves.
2 <u>R</u>ome has shown no bones in her stones.
3 Moe loathed the <u>r</u>ole of the t<u>r</u>oll.

4 The whole bowl enclosed the coal.
5 Phone home when you know the oaths.
6 Fold the clothes to be sewn.

Short o ŭ

7 ʏ Open only the oats, Otis.
8 These <u>R</u>oman coats are bespoke.
9 She is wont to associate with yeomen
10 The g<u>r</u>oaning and moaning goats are g<u>r</u>oss.

11 ʏ Opie's hoping for oceans of oceans.
12 We <u>wr</u>ote Holt a note f<u>r</u>om Moscow.
13 The soldiers are going to note the poult<u>r</u>y.
14 Opal app<u>r</u>oached the showing hopefully.

Mixed Lengths

15 ʏ Owen owned an ocean-going oaken boat.
16 Dole's goal was to <u>r</u>oll the whole boatload of coal into Oakland.
17 I know it, I'm a po-et!
18 Show him a po-em or some d<u>r</u>oll token of devotion.
19 Mr. Stow-ell stole Low-ell's gold f<u>r</u>om Bā-<u>r</u>on Baden-Pow-ell.
20 The lonesome loners would both be loth to loathe a loan.
    NOTE: "loth" (reluctant) may also be spelled "loath."
21 We're loading loaves onto the boats, and they're going to <u>R</u>ome.
22 O noble <u>R</u>ome, you know you're my only home.
23 No, no, no, it's not a goat!
24 Only Joseph is at home on the hollow th<u>r</u>one of the Holy <u>R</u>oman Empire.
25 Poe took copious notes on vocal folds.
26 I t<u>r</u>ow this is no joke.
27 Idaho potato g<u>r</u>ow-ers sold both loads of homegrown oats by phone.
28 Hold Mr. Holt until Capone's på-<u>r</u>ole has been <u>r</u>evoked.
29 Shoulder those stones and boulders and load them into the hold.
30 The old c<u>r</u>one st<u>r</u>oked her th<u>r</u>oat dolefully, as is her wont.   'woŭnt^h
31 At the moment, Oldman is holding his own against the stoned mogul.

COMPARE THE PURE VOWEL SOUND   o
WITH THE DIPHTHONG SOUND   oŭ·

Always in UNstressed SYLLABLES
Usually in STRESSED SYLLABLES; UNstressed
SYLLABLES at ends of word:; e.g., "window"

o	oŭ	o	oŭ	o	oŭ
32 opaque	— opal	37 momentum	— moment	42 c<u>r</u>oquet	— c<u>r</u>oak
33 odometer	— odalisque	38 locality	— local	43 nobility	— noble
34 overt	— over	39 vocation	— <u>r</u>evoke	44 Joanne	— Joan oŭ·
35 potential	— potent	40 p<u>r</u>obation	— p<u>r</u>obity	45 Bohemian	— elbow
36 Mobile	— mobile	41 b<u>r</u>ocade	— b<u>r</u>oker	46 domain	— window

SENTENCES FOR PRACTICE USING   o   AND   o·ŭ·

47 Odetta <u>wr</u>ote <u>r</u>omantic odes to noted nobility.
48 "Oval opals," opined Ophelia, "are overtly and openly opaque."
49 O'Neill's only notes on Poland are notŏ-<u>r</u>iously polemical.
50 At this low locale, O'Shea can show the ocean's potential.
51 "A <u>R</u>omantic Oasis for Bohemian Nomads," boasted the <u>R</u>oman hotel's b<u>r</u>ochure.

Represented by the spellings:

h*ou*se   b*ou*gh=b*ow* (bend; prow)

Relax your lower jaw wide open and relax the tip of your tongue behind your lower front teeth. Arch the BACK of your tongue to a very low, practically flat position for the first element, a . From that position glide your lower jaw and your tongue-arch upward, or make a vanish, toward the positin of $\cup$, the weak second element. During this glide, your lips move from a relaxed, neutral position for a to a very round position for $\cup$. As you blend the two vowel elements into a single, new sound—the diphthong $a\breve{u}$ —the coordinated movements of the articulators can easily be seen and felt.

If any sound in Spoken English can fit the clichéd term "pear-shaped," this is it. The first element a is the most forward of the back vowel sounds, as well as the one requiring the most fully relaxed lips and an almost fully relaxed tongue-arch. Any physical tension or constriction, and any nasality, will mar the creamy-smooth resonance of this diphthong sound. The placement should be clear and ringing, the glide mellow and smooth.

WORDS FOR PRACTICE USING $a\breve{u}$ LONG

◆ In a STRESSED SYLLABLE that is the FINAL syllable of a word, when the diphthong is also the last sound of the word

◆ In a STRESSED SYLLABLE that is the FINAL syllable of the word, when the diphthong is followed by one or more voiced consonants

1 how anyhow somehow pow bough=bow (prow; bend) cá-*r*abao Tao=Dow endow cow Mao

2 now allow plough=plow Blau slough (mudhole) vow avow disavow thou (v)

3 thou (pronoun, sf) sow (hog) *r*ow (quarrel) p*r*ow b*r*ow F*r*au wow chow

4 bowed Dowd cowed loud allowed plowed cloud vowed avowed p*r*oud c*r*owd
5 sh*r*oud wowed

6 hound pound expound bound towns down gown mound noun *r*enown lounge
7 found sound *r*esound *r*ound b*r*own d*r*own d*r*owned c*r*own ground f*r*owned wound (v; wind)

8 owl howl cowl scowl fowl=foul p*r*owled g*r*owls yowl jowls

9 mouth (v) mouths (v; n)

10 house (v) housed espouse boughs=bows (prows; bends) Dow's cows Mao's=mouse (v)
11 allows plows=ploughs sloughs (mudholes) vows disavows sows (hogs) *r*ouse á-*r*ouse
12 cá-*r*ouse p*r*ows b*r*ows=b*r*owse d*r*owse wows

13 gouge gouged

$\boxed{a \breve{u} \cdot}$

WORDS FOR PRACTICE USING $a\breve{u}$ SHORT IN ALL OTHER CASES

◆ In a STRESSED SYLLABLE followed by a voiced consonant that is in turn followed by a voiceless consonant

◆ In a STRESSED SYLLABLE followed by one or more voiceless consonants

◆ In any syllable but the last syllable of a word

◆ In all UNstressed SYLLABLES

1 ounce pounce bounce count account disCOUNT (v) recounts (v) mount mounch announce
2 pronounced flounced frounce frowns't

3 out pout spout bout about tout stout doubt doubtful redoubtable lookout scout
4 gout snouts lout clout flouts devout shouted rout trout drought grout sprout

5 howdy howdah powder dowdy Gaudi loudly cloudy Saudi[2] rowdy crowded shrouded
6 chowder

7 Baum[2] endowment trauma[2]

8 hounding impounded bounder Townsend Downey accountant countenance scoundrel
9 mountain Mountie flounder foundling sounding roundabout Browning drowning

10 howling howler Dowling cowlick scowling Cowley Fowler Crowley growling yowling
11 jowly foully

12 mouth (n) mouth's south

13 mouthing Crowther

14 oust Houston (New York City street) spouse[2] tousled Towson doused Scouse mouse (n)
15 louse blouse soused roust roustabout Prowse Krauss grouse frowsty joust

16 houses housing espousal bowser Mauser schnauzer lousy blowsy thousand rousing
17 a-rouses cả-rousal browsing drowsy frowsy

18 pouch Boucher couch Goucher slouch vouch voucher crouched grouch

19 Bowe-ry dow-ry cow-rie Low-ry

20 NOTE: DO NOT INSERT A u SOUND INTO THE FOLLOWING WORDS: bow-ing endow-ing allow-ing
21 plough-ing=plow-ing vow-ing MacGowan prowess dowager

22 How-ell Pow-ell bow-el tow-el dow-el MacDow-ell Cow-ell disavow-al row-el trow-el

23 our=hour How-ar Eisenhow-er pow-er pow-er-ful bow-er=Bau-er tow-er dow-er cow-er
24 sour Gow-er Izenour lour=low-er (v; look threatening) Clow-er glow-er flour=flow-er
25 devour sour show-er
   NOTE: Especially in verse, these and similar words may be pronounced in one syllable, with the
   TRIPHTHONG SOUND $a\breve{u}\breve{ə}$. (See pages 186-188.)

26 pow-e-ring tow-e-ring cow-e-ring scou-ring ("skow-uh-ring") flow-e-ry flow-e-ring
27 lou-ring=low-e-ring (adj: frowning; threatening) devou-ring ("di-vow-uh-ring") show-e-ring

28 thou (wf) vouchSAFE powwow

EXERCISES FOR OPENING AND FORWARD PLACEMENT OF $a\colon$ AND $a \cdot \breve{u} \cdot$

$a\colon$	$a \cdot \breve{u} \cdot$	$a \breve{u}$	$\widehat{a \breve{u}} \ni$	OR	$\widehat{a \breve{u} \ni}$
			Two Syllables		Triphthong: One Syllable
Pure Vowel	**Long**	**Short**	**Syllables**		**One Syllable**
1 ah	owl	out	our=hour		our=hour
2 palm	pound	pouch	pow-er		power
3 Casbah	bound	bounce	bow-er		bower
4 Natasha	town	tow-el	tow-er		tower
5 Dada	down	doubt	dow-er		dower
6 calm	cow	count	cow-er		cower
7 gaga	gouge	gout	Gow-er		Gower
8 Shangri-La	allow	louse	lour=low-er		lour=lower (look threatening)
9 vase³	vow	vouch	devour		devour
10 psalm	sow (hog)	south	sour		sour
11 Shah	-----	shout	show-er		shower
12 pa	pow	pout	Pow-ell		
13 bah	bough	about	bow-el		
14 ta	town	tout	tow-el		
15 Dali	down	Dowling	dow-el		
16 calm	cowl	cowlick	Cow-ell		
17 vase³	vows	vouch	vow-el		
18 rah	round	Rowley	row-el		
19 aha	howl	howling	How-ell		

PHRASES FOR PRACTICE

Long $a \cdot \breve{u} \cdot$	**Short** $a \breve{u}$	**Mixed Lengths**
20 ʔ owls in O.U.D.S.*	30 ʔ out in the outhouse	40 ʔ owls ousted from O.U.D.S.*
21 brown owls and ground fowl	31 an ounce of power	41 howling mountain hounds
22 proud to frown and howl	32 shout it out loudly	42 an hour from downtown
23 mouth the vows	33 scour the mountain house	43 resoundingly loud
24 round and a-round	34 a powerhouse of a spouse	44 housed in a brown house
25 impound the hounds	35 doubtlessly a louse	45 vow to count vouchers
26 cows ca-roused	36 a bout with gout	46 the clouds that lour (=lower)
27 astound the crowds	37 devour flowers	47 clowning a-round
28 foul fowl on the prowl	38 about an hour	48 MacDow-ell's jowls
29 bound to scowl and growl	39 Pow-ell's devou-ring power	49 now announce nouns

* Oxford University Dramatic Society $'a \cdot \breve{u} \cdot d z$

a·ŭ·

SENTENCES FOR PRACTICE

Long *a·ŭ·*

1 Brown owls are found a-round the town.
2 We vowed to allow no frowns or scowls.
3 Mouth the vows like a cow with jowls.
4 Round and a-round the foul fowl bounds.
5 Owls and other fowl abound down under.
6 Howl, howl, howl to the crowd.
7 How now, brown cow?
8 My sows sound too loud now.
9 Bow now or bow down, you clown.
10 We're proud to espouse Mao's vows.

Short *aŭ*

11 Get out, thou loutish count!
12 The howling grouch shouted loudly.
13 There's a soused mouse about this house.
14 Take out the louse with a clout on the snout.
15 No doubt her mouth was in a pout.
16 Ouch! I can't get it out of my pouch.
17 About a thousand vow-els were sounded.
18 Get out, go south, you grouse!
19 The army's been routed south of Houston Street.
20 Low-ry's dow-ry is a house on the Bowe-ry.

Mixed Lengths

21 ⸮ Ounce for ounce he's an out-and-out owl.
22 I vow to allow no scowling or shouting now.
23 We're down and out in downtown Goucher.
24 Crowds crouch outside to howl and grouse.
25 You can count on thousands to pounce on the ground within the hour.
26 Powerful dowagers loudly announce devout vows.
27 A house mouse and a ground grouse bound out of the fountain.
28 Thou frown'st upon me, but I disCOUNT thy scowls.
29 Resoundingly loud fowls ousted the proud grouse hourly.
30 Let's douse ourselves with a shower in the lounge now.
31 He was drowned down South in a foul slough (mudhole).
32 The renowned announcer vows there will be clouds and showers.
33 One lousy grouch can bring down a thousand ca-rousing highbrows.
34 Our house is just south of the downtown bounda-ries.
35 With a lou-ring frown he lay soused on the brown couch. *'laŭ ə rɪŋ*

MATCH THE *a·ŭ·* DIPHTHONG SOUNDS IN THE FOLLOWING PAIRS OF WORDS

a·ŭ·	*aŭ*	*a·ŭ·*	*aŭ*	*a·ŭ·*	*aŭ*
1 O.U.D.S.*	— out	10 abound	— about	19 crown	— crouch
2 owl	— oust	11 bow	— bout	20 house (v)	— house (n)
3 pound	— pouch	12 town	— tout	21 gouge	— gout
4 pow	— pout	13 down	— doubt	22 mouth (v)	— mouth (n)
5 expound	— spout	14 cow	— couch	23 jowls	— joust
6 now	— snout	15 loud	— flout	24 thou (sf)	— without
7 clown	— clout	16 ground	— grouse	25 sound	— soused
8 loud	— lout	17 sow	— south	26 chow	— shout
9 dowse	— douse	18 mouse (v)	— mouse (n)	27 vows	— vouch

* Oxford University Dramatic Society *'a·ŭ·dz*

SENTENCES FOR PRACTICE
28 Put a pound note in that pouch and it's bound to come out.
29 Now his snout has given that clown clout.
30 The sow went south to round out the hound's list of houseguests.
31 To find the crown, crouch down by the count's couch.
32 Get out, you lout! I've found out about you and the trout!
33 No doubt her spouse's mouth was in a pout du-ring the joust.
34 Somewhere about this house, a soused mouse is crouching.
35 Why can't that old grouch grouse and shout out his doubts a bit less loudly?
36 Ouch! I can't get this sauerkraut out of my mouth.
37 At the height of the drought, the scout routed the trout from the spouting fountain.
38 The tousled New York roustabout is slouching toward his house on Houston Street.
39 Groucho's about out of vouchers for the much-touted bout.
40 You louse, get out of that mousy blouse. You're too stout.
41 The redoubtably devout lookout downed a few sprouts.

e·ĭ·	*eĭ*	*a·ĭ·*	*aĭ*	*ɔ·ĭ·*
1 ay (ever)	ace	eye=aye	ice	oy
2 aid=ade	ate=eight	Ides	item	ahoy
3 ail=ale	ailing	isle	island	oil
4 hay	haste	high=hie	heist	ahoy
5 pane=pain	paint	pine	pint	Poins
6 pays	pace	pies	spice	poise
7 bathe	bathos	writhe	python	boys
8 bay	Bayonne	buy	biannual	boy=buoy
9 ta'en	taint	tine=Tyne	tiny	toy
10 gay	gait=gate	guy	Guyana	gargoyle
11 main=mane	maintenance	mine	minor	Des Moines
12 inane	ain't	nine	ninety	annoy
13 laid	late	lied	light	Lloyd
14 fail	phalanx	file	filing	foil
15 save	safe	scythe	cipher	soy
16 rage	Rachel	ride	righteous	Roy

ɔĭ	o·ŭ·	oŭ	a·ŭ·	aŭ	
voice	owe=O	oats	ow	oust	1
Hoyt	ode	oat	O.U.D.S.*	out	2
Oilers	old	older	owl	owlet	3
hoist	hoe	host	how	house (n)	4
points	pole=poll	poultry	pound	pounce	5
poison	pose	post	espouse	spouse	6
boiste-rous	loathe (v)	loth (adj)	mouth (v)	mouth (n)	7
Boyet	beau	elbow	bough	bout	8
Toynbee	intone	tony	town	Townsend	9
goiter	go	Goshen	gown	gout	10
moist	moan	moaning	mound	mount	11
annount	known	won't=wont	renown	announce	12
loiter	load	lotus	loud	lout	13
foiling	foal	Foley	fowl=foul	Fowler	14
soya	showed	sofa	sound	south	15
roister	rose	roach	rouse	roust	16

* Oxford University Dramatic Society 'a·ŭ·dʒ

Five falling diphthong sounds are associated with the letter "r" in the spelling of a word. They are called "centering" diphthongs because each one has the mid, or central, vowel sound ∂ , as in "*sur*prise," as its second, weak element.

H*ere*'s	ɪə̆
th*eir*	ɛə̆
p*oor*	ʊə̆
ore	ɔə̆
c*ar*.	ɑə̆

◆ THE ALWAYS-SHORT ◆
DIPHTHONG SOUND $I\breve{\partial}$ AS IN "h*ere*'s"

Represented by the spellings:

h*ere*=h*ear*   d*eer*=d*ear*   p*ier*=p*eer*   w*eir*d   Gloucestersh*ire*[2]

souven*ir*

Relax your lower jaw and rest the tip of your tongue behind your lower front teeth. Arch the FRONT of your tongue high in the position for the first element I , as your lips SLIGHTLY spread in the feeling of a smile. From this position glide your tongue-arch, or make a vanish, toward the relaxed position for the weak second element ∂ , allowing your lips to relax into a neutral position. The coordinated movements of your tongue-arch, lips and jaw can be easily seen and felt as you blend the two vowel elements into the distinctly single diphthong sound $I\breve{\partial}$.

As for all the vowel and diphthong sounds associated with the letter "r" in the spelling of a word, the ALWAYS-SHORT diphthong sound $I\breve{\partial}$ has TWO standards of pronunciation in North American speech:

$I\breve{\partial}$ WITHOUT R-COLORING: The tip of your tongue is relaxed behind your lower front teeth. The sound is free and forward.

$I\breve{\partial}c$ WITH R-COLORING: The tip of your tongue is tensed up and over, the body of your tongue is retracted. The sound is tense and back.

Because of the forward, released vocal energy that comes from keeping the tip of your tongue free of tension, it is recommended that in singing and in Good Speech in classic texts the standard WITHOUT R-COLORING, $I\breve{\partial}$, be used for this lyric, caressing sound.

WORDS FOR PRACTICE

1 ear here=hear peer=pier appear spear bier=beer tier=tear (eyewater) privateer

2 musketeer Mouseketeer frontier racketeer steer austere dear=deer grenadier Kier=kir

3 gear mere Vermeer premier=premiere[2] smear cashmere near veneer souvenir mutineer

4 buccaneer Lanier deNIER sneer Lear=leer gondolier cavalier chandelier blear clear

5 chanticleer fleer fear sphere veer revere sear=sere=seer (prophet) sincere

6 brassiere sheer=shear cashier rear à-rrear cã-reer drear Greer=Grier we're=weir

7 queer year cheer jeer Zaire

8 NOTE: The English county suffix "-shire" may be $-\int\partial$ or $-\int I\breve{\partial}$: Yorkshire Worcestershire

9 peered appeared speared beard tiered geared premiered[2] smeared neared sneered

10 leered cleared feared afeard=afeared veered revered seared sheared reared weird

11 cheered jeered

12 Smirnoff nearness

13 peerless merely nearly fearless Brearley yearly cheerly cheerless

14 NOTE: "Real" and its derivatives are the only words in Spoken English in which the diphthong sound $I\breve{\partial}$ occurs without a letter "r" in the spelling. Needless to say, they must NEVER be uttered with r-coloring.

real $'rI\breve{\partial}l$ really $'rI\breve{\partial}lI$ realtor $'rI\breve{\partial}lt\breve{\partial}$ realty $'rI\breve{\partial}ltI$

15 earphone tearful Deerfield fearful cheerful

WORDS FOR PRACTICE, Cont.

1 pierce Pierson=Pearson Pearsall deerskin Kirsten fearsome hearsay

2 piers=peers appears spears biers=beers tiers=tears steers gears smears nears leers
3 clears fleers fears veers reveres Sears shears a-rrears ca-reers hears years
4 cheers jeers

WORDS FOR CLARITY OF $\breve{\text{ɪə}}$ PRIOR TO r

✓ Reminder ———————————————————————————————

Make a relaxed, clearly defined $\breve{\text{ɪə}}$ sound and begin the following syllable with a clean-cut consonant r . In doing so, you will avoid marring the clarity of the $\breve{\text{ɪə}}$ sound with r-coloring.

5 ea-rring hea-ring he-rein he-reof pee-rage appea-ring Bee-ry tea-ry stee-rage

6 dea-ry=dea-rie endea-ring dea-rer dea-rest Madei-ra Gea-ry Mea-ra nea-ring

7 nea-rer O'Lea-ry lee-ry clea-ring blea-ry clea-rer fea-ring vee-ring reve-ring

8 sea-ring shea-ring Shea-rer a-rrea-rage drea-ry wea-ry chee-ring chee-ry jee-ring

NOTE: The sequence $\underline{\breve{\text{ɪə}} r\text{-}}$ is usually found when a suffix such as "-ing," "-age" or "-er" is added to a root word that ends with the diphthong $\breve{\text{ɪə}}$. In many other words that are not derived from root words, the sequence $\underline{\text{ɪ} r\text{-}}$ occurs but has an optional and equally acceptable pronunciation using $\underline{\breve{\text{ɪə}} r\text{-}}$. Some of these words follow:

$$\underline{\text{ɪ } r\text{-}} \qquad \text{OR} \qquad \underline{\breve{\text{ɪə}} \ r\text{-}}$$

9 ee-rie=E-rie e-ra He-ra he-ro pe-riod impe-rial expe-rience vene-real deli-rious

10 Ve-ra se-rious se-ries se-rial=ce-real

PHRASES FOR PRACTICE

11 r earmarked earphones for the hea-rers
12 a ca-reer at Goodyear
13 my dear, dear Ve-ra
14 all too cavalier and cheerful
15 really se-rious

16 r ee-rie ea-rrings
17 steer clear of the belvedere
18 Lear vee-ring toward Gloucestershire
19 a cashier's ca-reer
20 chee-ring the God-fea-ring

SENTENCES FOR PRACTICE

21 r The ear's ea-rrings are earphones.
22 It's a drea-ry atmosphere, I fear.
23 Se-riously, will the se-ries appear?
24 The rear column is really real.
25 Are you sincere, my dear?
26 The seer predicts dear prices this year.
27 How queer! Lear volunteered a souvenir.

28 Did Ve-ra hear *King Lear* clearly?
29 She's been my nea-rest and dea-rest for years.
30 How severe is the fear you have of beards?
31 The impe-rial musketeers revere beer.
32 "Cheerly to the frontier," sneers the cavalier.
33 The a-rrea-rage brought her near to tears.
34 It's merely a rear view of He-ra by Vermeer.

◆ THE ALWAYS-SHORT ◆
DIPHTHONG SOUND ɛ̆ə̆ AS IN "their"

Represented by the spellings:

> th**eir**=th**ere**=th**ey're**   p**air**=p**ear**=p**are**   p**are**nt   m**are**=m**ayor**
>
> pr**ayer** (supplication)
>
> **air**=**ere**=**e'er**=**heir**=**Ayr**=**Eyre**: Six homonyms, each comprised of one sound and one sound only, the diphthong ɛ̆ə̆ .

Relax your lower jaw and relax the tip of your tongue behind your lower front teeth. Arch the FRONT of your tongue half-low in the position for the first element ɛ (the tongue-arch for ɛ is slightly lower than for e as in "let") and let your lips be SLIGHTLY smiling. From this position let your tongue-arch glide, or make a vanish, toward the relaxed position for the weak second element ə , allowing your lips to relax into a neutral position. The coordinated movements of tongue-arch, lips and jaw can be easily seen and felt as you blend the two vowel elements into the distinctly single diphthong sound ɛ̆ə̆ .

In Good Speech, the vowel sound ɛ is never used as a pure vowel sound. It occurs ONLY as the first element of the diphthong sound ɛ̆ə̆ .

As for all the vowel and diphthong sounds associated with the letter "r" in the spelling of a word, the ALWAYS-SHORT diphthong sound ɛ̆ə̆ has TWO standards of pronunciation in North American speech:

ɛ̆ə̆ WITHOUT R-COLORING: The tip of your tongue is relaxed behind your lower front teeth. The sound is free and forward.

ɛ̆ə̆ɾ WITH R-COLORING: The tip of your tongue is tensed up and over, the body of your tongue is retracted. The sound is tense and back.

Because of the forward, released vocal energy that comes from keeping the tip of your tongue free of tension, it is recommended that in singing and in Good Speech in classic texts the standard WITHOUT R-COLORING, ɛ̆ə̆ , be used for this tender, lyric sound.

WORDS FOR PRACTICE

1 air=ere=e'er=Ayr=Eyre hair=hare pair=pare=pear compare repair spare despair
2 bare=bear forBEAR (v) FOREbear (n) tear (rip) Voltaire solitaire stair=stare dare
3 care scare mare=mayor ne'er extraordinaire debonair lair Blair=blare Claire=Clare
4 glare flair=flare fair=fare their=there=they're corsair share Trigère rare
5 prayer (supplication) where somewhere anywhere everywhere elsewhere wear=ware
6 beware square Yare Molière chair

7 aired=Aird Airedale pared=paired spared bared=Baird stared dared daredevil cared
8 scare Laird blared flared fared shared squared chaired

9 bairn Cairns

10 airless heirloom hairless barely careless fairly

11 bearskin scarce

12 airs=heirs=Ayr's=Eyre's hares pears=pairs compares bears=bares tears (rips)
13 upstairs dares cares scares mares=mayors blares=Blair's glares fares theirs=there's
14 shares prayers (supplications) where's wares=wears squares chairs

WORDS FOR PRACTICE, Cont.

1 e'er(wh)ile

2 airway airwave airworthy fareWELL fairweather (wh)erewithal

WORDS FOR CLARITY OF $\varepsilon\breve{\partial}$ PRIOR TO Γ

✓ *Reminder* ─────────────────────────────────

Make a relaxed, clearly defined $\varepsilon\breve{\partial}$ sound and begin the following syllable with a clean-cut consonant Γ . In doing so, you will avoid marring the clarity of the $\varepsilon\breve{\partial}$ sound with r-coloring.

3 ai-ry=ae-ry=ae-rie=ey-rie hai-ry A-riel=ae-rial A-ryan Ei-re ai-ring Ha-ring

4 ae-roplane ha-rem pa-ring=pai-ring repai-rer pa-rent pa-rentage transpa-rent Spa-rer

5 despai-ring bea-rer bea-ring=Ba-ring forbea-rance tea-ring tea-rable secreta-rial

6 secreta-riat sanita-rium sta-ring da-ring dai-ry ca-ring Ca-rey Ka-ren vica-rious

7 preca-rious sca-ry Ga-ry va-GA-ry Ga-ry's va-GA-ries grega-rious Ma-ry Ma-ryland

8 Ma-rian=Ma-rion na-ry cana-ry hila-rious mala-ria bla-ring Cla-ra gla-ring fai-ry

9 fa-ring fai-rer fai-rest wayfa-rer Pha-raoh va-ry va-rious va-riable va-riant

10 va-rio-rum the-rein the-reon the-reof Sa-ra=Sa-rah commissa-riat sha-ring Sha-ron

11 ra-rer ra-rest ra-rity ra-rified honö-ra-rium prai-rie agra-rian (wh)e-rein (wh)e-reat

12 (wh)e-reunto (wh)e-reupon (wh)e-reon (wh)e-reof wa-ry wea-rer wea-rable Wa-reham

13 wea-ring=Wa-ring swea-ring swea-rer cha-ry chai-ring

PHRASES FOR PRACTICE

14 Γ A-riel's ai-ry heir

15 fareWELL to cares

16 dare to share the questionnaire

17 compare Ayrshire's air to Ei-re's air

18 housewares to be repaired

19 a pair of hai-ry bears

20 Γ ere the A-ryan is on the air

21 fairly va-ried fares

22 Sha-ron and Ka-ren's pa-rents

23 the new pa-rent Ga-ry

24 fairly pear-shaped teddy bear

25 va-rious ra-rities

SENTENCES FOR PRACTICE

26 That mare of Ma-ry's doesn't care for Ka-ren.

27 He made a fair fai-ry but an inva-riably overbea-ring pha-raoh.

28 We dare not swear to share Sha-ron's wares with her grandpa-rents.

29 Some(wh)ere there's a da-ringly transpa-rent pair of chairs.

30 Forbear to stare at the rare family heirlooms on the stairs.

31 I'm in despair! I can't bear my hair!

32 The commissa-riat dared the proleta-riat to prepare for secreta-rial positions.

33 FareWELL to prayer, fareWELL to care.

SENTENCES FOR PRACTICE, Cont.

1 Ere we despair, let's say a prayer to our FOREbears.
2 In the ha-rem there's na-ry a spare copy of Molière.
3 The da-ring wayfa-rer bäde a wa-ry fareWELL to Voltaire.
4 Please be aware that the glare on the prai-rie can be unbea-rable.
5 There, there; they're their chairs.
6 Beware, lest you despair for e'er.
7 The mayor is fair, the fai-ry is fai-rer, but the pha-raoh is fai-rest.

EXERCISES FOR DISTINGUISHING BETWEEN ℮ AND ɛɔ̆ PRIOR TO THE CONSONANT r̆

℮	ɛɔ̆	℮	ɛɔ̆	℮	ɛɔ̆
8 e-rror	— ae-roplane	14 de-rring	— da-ring	20 ve-ry	— va-ry
9 Pe-rry	— pa-ring	15 Ke-rry	— Ca-rey	21 se-rry	— Sa-rah
10 Be-ring	— bea-ring	16 ke-ratin	— Ka-ren	22 she-rry	— sha-ring
11 te-rror	— tea-rer	17 me-rry	— Ma-ry	23 he-rring	— Ha-ring
12 te-rrible	— tea-rable	18 cele-rity	— hila-rious	24 whe-rry	— wa-ry
13 De-rry	— dai-ry	19 fe-rry	— fai-ry	25 che-rry	— cha-ry

SENTENCES FOR PRACTICE DISTINGUISHING ℮r- FROM ɛɔ̆r

26 An e-rror in the ae-rial can be ve-ry sca-ry.

27 Fe-rry the fai-ry with cele-rity to see the hila-rious seafa-ring fe-rret.

28 Pe-rry's cha-ry of repai-ring the te-rribly tea-rable che-rry chair.

29 Ke-rry Ca-rey used a preca-rious ke-ratin and dai-ry lotion to repair De-rry's hair.

30 Sha-ring a little she-rry with Sha-ron's pa-rents, Pe-rry?

◆ THE ALWAYS-SHORT ◆
DIPHTHONG SOUND $\upsilon\breve{\partial}$ AS IN "p*oor*"

Represented by the spellings:

p*oor*   t*our*   s*ure*   j*u*ry   M*oor*=m*oor*=M*oore*

Relax your lower jaw and rest the tip of your tongue behind your lower front teeth. Arch the BACK of your tongue high in the position for the first element υ , as your lips round closely. From this position glide your tongue-arch, or make a vanish, toward the relaxed position for the weak second element ∂ , allowing your lips to relax into a neutral position. The coordinated movements of your tongue-arch, lips and jaw can be easily seen and felt as you blend the two vowel elements into the distinctly single diphthong sound $\upsilon\breve{\partial}$.

As for all the vowel and diphthong sounds associated with the letter "r" in the spelling of a word, the ALWAYS-SHORT diphthong sound $\upsilon\breve{\partial}$ has TWO standards of pronunciation in North American speech:

$\upsilon\breve{\partial}$ WITHOUT R-COLORING: The tip of your tongue is relaxed behind your lower front teeth. The sound is free and forward.

$\upsilon\breve{\partial}^{\iota}$ WITH R-COLORING: The tip of your tongue is tensed up and over, the body of your tongue is retracted. The sound is tense and back.

Because of the forward, released vocal energy that comes from keeping the tip of your tongue free of tension, it is recommended that in singing and in Good Speech in classic texts the standard WITHOUT R-COLORING, $\upsilon\breve{\partial}$, be used .

This rich, weighty sound must have full focus of tone through closely-rounded lips. Lateralization or even relaxation of the lips will destroy the lush energy of this important sound.

WORDS FOR PRACTICE

1 Ur (German) poor Kuala Lumpur spoor boor=Boer tour contour dour Moor=moor=Moore
2 amour pa̱-ramour Koh-i-noor velour=velours Bloor McClure Fluor Cavour sure
3 assure r̲eassure insure b̲rochure du jour R̲uhr abjure conJURE (v; charge solemnly)
4 mature[2] immature[2] pr̲emature[2]: $- t_{,}\int\upsilon\breve{\partial}$ or $- t_{,}j\upsilon\breve{\partial}$

5 Bourbon (French family name)

6 bourdon toured contoured gourd moored Lourdes assured r̲eassured insured abjured

7 gourmet gourmand

8 bourn=bourne=Bourne

9 poorly courlan surely pr̲ematurely

10 bourse

11 boors tours contours Coors Moors=moors=Moore's velours (stage curtains, American)
12 assures r̲eassures insures b̲rochures matures[2] abjures

13 bourgeois (middle class) courgette

WORDS FOR CLARITY OF ʊə̆ **PRIOR TO** r **(You may also use** ʊ **.)**

✓ *Reminder* ————————————————————————————

> Make a rounded, clearly defined ʊə̆ sound and begin the following syllable with a clean-cut consonant r . In doing so, you will avoid marring the clarity of the ʊə̆ sound with r-coloring.

1 U-ri U-ruguay² poo-rer poo-rest boo-rish tou-rist tou-ring contou-ring cou-rier

2 cou-RAGE (*Hamlet* I.iii.65) Agou-ra moo-ring Moo-rish Missou-ri pleu-risy plu-ral

3 su-re-ty assu-ring assu-rance assu-redly reassu-ring insu-rer insu-rance luxu-rious

4 ru-ral pru-rient matu-ring² *mə'tʃʊə̆rɪŋ* or *mə'tʲʊə̆rɪŋ*

5 ju-ry injurious abju-ring conJU-ring (v; charging solemnly)

WORDS FOR PRACTICE USING ʲʊə̆

6 your=you're=Ure pure impure mature² immature² premature² *-tʃʊə̆* or *-tʲʊə̆*
7 endure cure manicure pedicure procure secure obscure immure demure inure manure
8 lure² allure² rotogravure

9 matured² cured secured procured obscured immured inured lured²

10 purely securely demurely

11 yours=Ure's matures² cures secures obscures immures inures lures²

WORDS FOR CLARITY OF ʲʊə̆ **PRIOR TO** r **(You may also use** ʲʊ **.)**

✓ *Reminder* ————————————————————————————

> Make a rounded, clearly defined ʊə̆ sound and begin the following syllable with a clean-cut consonant r . In doing so, you will avoid marring the clarity of the ʊə̆ sound with r-coloring.

12 u-rine U-ranus *ʲʊə̆rənəs* U-ral Eu-rope U-ruguay² Eu-ropa Eu-rasian u-rethra

13 U-riah u-ranium pu-rer pu-rest=pu-rist Pu-ritan pu-rity impu-rity pu-ree spu-rious

14 bu-reau bu-reaucrat Van Bu-ren du-ring endu-ring du-ration endu-rance du-rable

15 unendu-rably Cu-rie cu-ring secu-rity cu-rious cu-riosity cu-rate cu-rio Epicu-rus

16 epicu-rean Mercu-rial obscu-rity mu-ral Mu-riel penu-rious neu-rotic neu-rosis

17 lu-rid² allu-ring² fu-ry fu-rious fuh-rer bravu-ra Thu-rio thu-rible

18 Thu-ringia caesu-ra Zu-rich Hu-ron Hu-rok

PAIRS FOR COMPARISON OF _ひ:∂_ (Two Syllables) WITH ひ$\breve{\partial}$ (One Syllable)

ひ:∂	ひ$\breve{\partial}$		_ひ:∂_	ひ$\breve{\partial}$		_ひ:∂_	ひ$\breve{\partial}$
1 booer	— boor=Boer	5 chewer	— premature	9 fewer	— fu-ry
2 doer	— dour	6 ewer	— Ure=your	10 viewer	— rotogravure
3 shoer	— sure	7 skewer	— obscure		
4 brewer	— Ruhr	8 newer	— inure		

PAIRS FOR COMPARISON OF ひ$\breve{\partial}$ WITH $\supset\breve{\partial}$

ひ$\breve{\partial}$	$\supset\breve{\partial}$		ひ$\breve{\partial}$	$\supset\breve{\partial}$		ひ$\breve{\partial}$	$\supset\breve{\partial}$
11 poor	— pour=pore	14 dour	— door	17 your=you're	— yore
12 boor=Boer	— bore=boar	15 Moor	— more	18 premature	— chore
13 tour	— tore=Tor	16 sure	— shore	19 spoor	— spore

PHRASES FOR PRACTICE

20 the poor boo-rish tou-rist
21 yours and only yours 'jひ$\breve{\partial}$z
22 reassure your pa-ramour
23 assu-redly luxu-rious
24 the poo-rest cou-rier
25 endured the obscure cure
26 Eu-rope du-ring Pu-ritanism
27 unendu-rably fu-rious

28 you can be sure he's insured
29 a dour Moor
30 an immature ju-ry
31 a ru-ral tour   'rひ$\breve{\partial}$ rəl
32 the gourd du jour
33 allu-ringly pru-rient
34 inju-riously cu-rious
35 the fu-ry of the ju-ry

SENTENCES FOR PRACTICE

36 You can be sure he's poor.
37 Assure the bourgeois Moor that his tour will surely be luxu-rious.
38 Isn't this detour a bit premature?
39 Tou-ring the moors is an endu-rance test for the insecure.
40 The epicure's cu-riosity led him to endure the _courgette du jour._
41 Rest assured that a manicure and a pedicure will cure your demure nature.
42 I found the Ruhr Valley too ru-ral and Lourdes not ve-ry allu-ring.   'lひ$\breve{\partial}$d
43 Mu-riel toured the ru-ral contours of Zu-rich, Thu-ringia and obscure parts of Eu-rope.
44 I'll make assu-rance double sure that the planet U-ranus is inured to epicu-reanism.
45 Queen Noor procured the Koh-in-noor diamond to benefit the poor of Eu-rasia. 'kŏひ I nひ$\breve{\partial}$
46 Mu-riel, your mu-ral isn't insured against inju-rious tou-rists.
47 My amour is a pa-ramour of penu-rious secu-rity, I can assure you.
48 The brochure obscured the lu-rid lure of Pu-ritanism.
49 It's your duty to tell them that you're Miss Ure's Eu-ropean cu-rate.
50 I conJURE you to abjure your lu-ridly pru-rient neu-roses.

◆ THE ALWAYS-SHORT ◆
DIPHTHONG SOUND ɔɔ̌ AS IN *"ore"*

Represented by the spellings:

      oar=ore=o'er=or (sf)   d**oor**   p**our**   w**ar**   dinos**aur**

    Relax your lower jaw and rest the tip of your tongue behind your lower front teeth. Arch the BACK of your tongue half-low in the position for the first element ɔ , as you round your lips into an almost oval shape. From this position glide your tongue-arch, or make a vanish, toward the relaxed neutral position for the weak second element ə , allowing your lips to relax into a neutral position. The coordinated movements of your tongue-arch, lips and jaw can be easily seen and felt as you blend the two vowel elements into the distinctly single diphthong sound ɔɔ̌ .

    As for all the vowel and diphthong sounds associated with the letter "r" in the spelling of a word, the ALWAYS-SHORT diphthong sound ɔɔ̌ has TWO standards of pronunciation in North American speech:

ɔɔ̌ WITHOUT R-COLORING: The tip of your tongue is relaxed behind your lower front teeth. The sound is free and forward.

ɔɚ̌ WITH R-COLORING: The tip of your tongue is tensed up and over, the body of your tongue is retracted. The sound is tense and back.

    Because of the forward, released vocal energy that comes from keeping the tip of your tongue free of tension, it is recommended that in singing and in Good Speech in classic texts the standard WITHOUT R-COLORING, ɔɔ̌ , be used for this rich, forceful sound.

WORDS FOR PRACTICE

1 oar=ore=o'er=or (sf) whore=hoar abhor pore=pour rapport spore bore=boar tore=Tor
2 centaur Minotaur store door adore matador core=corps albacore encore decor score
3 gore more ignore nor (sf) Lenore snore lore galore deplore explore implore floor
4 four=fore=for (sf) metaphor carnivore Thor soar=sore dinosaur shore ashore seashore
5 roar drawer (furniture part) wore=war yore chore

6 porpoise torpor torpid torpedo corpse corpulent Thorpe warp

7 orb Corbin Gorboduc morbid forBEAR (v) FOREbear (n) absorbed sorbet Zorba

8 Orton Horton horticulture port report abort retort contorted distorts court=Cort
9 courtesan cortisone mortify mortar Norton fort=forte (n; strong point)
10 for-te (adv; loudly) cavort sort resort short Wharton wart quarter thwart chortle

11 oared=Ord horde order ordinance ordnance ordina-ry poured bored=board toward="tord"
12 stored adored cord=chord reCORD (v) gored mordant ignored lord deplored explored
13 floored Ford afford soared=sword shored roared extraordina-ry ward=warred Jordan

14 orchestra orchid pork torque stork Dorcas cork Gorky Lorca fork O'Rourke quark

15 organ Horgan organize porgy Borge corgie gorgon Morgan Glamorgan mortgage sorghum

16 ormolu hormones TORment (n) torMENT (v) storm dormant doorman dormer
17 Gorman Mormon Norman Normandy normal enormous form FORmidable informed
18 performance formal warmonger Warman swarm

WORDS FOR PRACTICE, Cont.

1 ornate horn ornament hornet pornography born Bournemouth torn adorn corn Cornish
2 morn=mourn morning=mourning forlorn fornicate thorn shorn worn=warn

3 orphan Corfu morphine endomorph Norfolk (wharf) dwarf

4 Orville Torvald

5 orthodox orthography north Northumberland forth swarth

6 northern swarthy

7 Orson whoreson Orsino horse=hoarse porcelain Borstal torso dorsal course=coarse
8 gorse Morse morsel Norse forced source sorce̊-ry sorce̊-rer exȏrcist reSOURCE Warsaw

9 oars whores pours=pores spores bores=boars borzoi stores restores doors cores
10 scores mores ignores deplores implores carnivores Thor's sores=soars shores roars
11 drawers (underpants) wars chores

12 Portia=Porsche portion abortion contortion torsion extortion Gorshen floorshow
13 foreshadow consortium Rorschach warship

14 orchard porch torch torture Storch scorch fortune fortunate

15 orgy Borgia cordial gorge gorgeous forged George
   NOTE: The following words employ the diphthong ɔ̆ə̆ because they each derive from a root word containing that diphthong sound.

WORDS FOR CLARITY OF ɔ̆ə̆ PRIOR TO ɾ

✓ Reminder ——————————————————————————————

> Make an open, clearly defined ɔ̆ə̆ sound and begin the following syllable with a clean-cut consonant ɾ . In doing so, you will avoid marring the clarity of the ɔ̆ə̆ sound with r-coloring.

16 oa-rring who-ring abho-rring pou-ring=po-ring bo-ring sto-ring ado-ring sco-rer go-ry

17 sno-ring deplo-rable explo-rer soa-ring sho-ring roa-ring wa-rring

PHRASES FOR PRACTICE

18 ɾ ordinå-ry orders
19 thou whoreson courtier
20 a warm Northern morning
21 Portia's portion of the fortune
22 ignore corpulent corpses

23 ɾ orthodox orgy
24 order in the court
25 a torMENted orphan
26 TORment and torture
27 deplo-rable wars

SENTENCES FOR PRACTICE

28 Georgia restored order to the extraordinå-ry war-torn morning.
29 We've restored the decor of a gorgeous four-door Ford.
30 The whores oarred toward shore in Singapore, but stayed aboard at San Salvador.
31 Lord, oh Lord, I have no rapport with Seymour, so I ignore him.

ยย

SENTENCES FOR PRACTICE, Cont.

1 The war reporters have warned the born-again Mormon that the fortress is FORmidable.
2 I'm in mourning for my horse, of course.
3 These chores bore me more and more each morning.
4 My organs are sore from the sorce-rer's exorcism.
5 Bjorn scored four hundred forty-four more points than George.
6 Can you please order one more quart from the organic orchard?
7 They poured mortar this morning at Morgan's.

◆ THE ALWAYS-SHORT ◆
DIPHTHONG SOUND aə̆ AS IN "car"

Represented by the spellings:

are (sf)   c**ar**   s**er**geant=S**ar**gent   h**ear**th   gu**ar**d

cat**arrh**   biz**arre**   baz**aar**

Relax your lower jaw and rest the tip of your tongue behind your lower front teeth. Arch the BACK of your tongue low in the position for the first element, a . From this position glide your tongue-arch, or make a vanish, toward the relaxed position for the weak second element ə . Since your lips are relaxed or neutral for both elements, and since the tongue-arch is minimal, the movement that blends the two vowel elements into the diphthong sound aə̆ will primarily be a simple upward movement of the lower jaw.

As for all the vowel and diphthong sounds associated with the letter "r" in the spelling of a word, the ALWAYS-SHORT diphthong sound aə̆ has TWO standards of pronunciation in North American speech:

aə̆ WITHOUT R-COLORING: The tip of your tongue is relaxed behind your lower front teeth. The sound is free and forward.

aə̆ᵣWITH R-COLORING: The tip of your tongue is tensed up and over, the body of your tongue is retracted. The sound is tense and back.

Because of the forward, released vocal energy that comes from keeping the tip of your tongue free of tension, it is recommended that in singing and in Good Speech in classic texts the standard WITHOUT R-COLORING, aə̆ , be used for this warm, generous sound.

WORDS FOR PRACTICE

1 are (sf) Bihar par spar bar=barre Babar tar catarrh guitar star r̲adar car Dakar
2 scar cigar mar Lamar sonar semin̲ar Lahr Klarr far afar shofar Lochinvar pulsar
3 czar=tsar quasar bizarre bazaar Fä-rr̲ar char jar ajar

4 Arp harp tarpaulin carp escarpment Garp Marple Tharp sharp

5 arbor harbor arbiter harbinger arbitrate parboil Barbar̲a Barbə-r̲y barb barbə-r̲ous
6 Darby=derby (British) carbon Scarbə-r̲ough garbage marble Farber

7 art heart=hart artful Hartford article artists part S̲parta Barton tart
8 start darts cart Carter garter Martin martyr sartɔ̄-r̲ial Sartr̲e Mozart chart

9 Arden harden ardor harder ardently pard pardon sparred bard=barred Bardolph tardy
10 r̲etard Dardanelles card scarred garden marred canard lard fardel sardonic shard
11 chard jarred

12 ark=arc hark Arctic Arkansas parking sparks bark Barker Berkeley (British) Tarquin
13 dark carcass mark r̲emarkable narcotic lark Farquahar sark shark charcoal

14 argot Argos argosy argue argument argal ArGYLL=ArGYLE bargain target cargo
15 gargoyle Margar̲et largo Fargo jargon

16 arm harm armə̄-r̲y harmony armə̄-r̲er armless harmless Parma barm ptarmigan dharma
17 karma Carmen garment marmot marm alarm farm varmint charm Charmian Jarman

WORDS FOR PRACTICE, Cont.

1 Arno Arnold harness barn tarnish darn carnival carnage garnish Marnie Farnsworth
2 varnish charnel

3 Arles Arlt parle Tarleton Carl=Karl Albemarle gnarled snarls Charles
4 Arliss harlot Arlen Harley parley barley darling Carlisle garland Marley gnarling
5 snarling Farley varlet Charlotte charlatan Charlemagne Charlie

6 Hertford (England) parfait scarf Garfinkle farfetched far-flung Scharf

7 Arvin Harvard Harvey parvenue starved carve Carver scarves Garvin marvel=Marvell
8 marvelous Carnarvon larva Jarvis=Gervis

9 Arthur hearth Parthenon Bartholomew Darth Carthage Carthusian Garth Hogarth Martha

10 farther farthest farthing farthingale

11 arson parson parcel parsley parsimony Parsifal sparse Barstow Darcy Carson
12 carcinoma Garson Marcie Marson Narcissus Larson farce varsity sarcenet

13 spars bars guitars stars cars scars cigars Mars=mars seminars czars chars jars

14 harsh partial marsh Marcia=Marsha Martian marshal=martial

15 arch Hartch parched parchment starch march Larchmont

16 Argentina argent barge margin Marge-ry large ARgess sergeant=Sargent charge

WORDS FOR CLARITY OF $\alpha\breve{\partial}$ PRIOR TO Υ

✓ Reminder

Make an open, clearly defined $\alpha\breve{\partial}$ sound and begin the following syllable with a clean-cut consonant Υ . In doing so, you will avoid marring the clarity of the $\alpha\breve{\partial}$ sound with r-coloring.

NOTE: The following words employ the diphthong $\alpha\breve{\partial}$ because each derives from a root word containing that diphthong sound.

17 a-ria Ha-ri spa-rring ba-rring sta-rring ma-rring ja-rring

PHRASES FOR PRACTICE

18 Υ artfully artificial Arlene
19 Υ ardently argued architecture
20 Peter Sargent's chart of the Arctic
21 on your mark, get set, start
22 remarkably barba-rous shark
23 farther and farther from the star

24 Υ armed artists and ar-mo-rers
25 Υ Arnold's artless a-ria
26 harken to arms
27 hard-hearted harlot
28 scarves from a marvelous bazaar
29 part of a scarred carcass

SENTENCES FOR PRACTICE

1 ʔ Art thou armed, thou ardently argumentative archer?
2 ʔ Arsonists argued ardently for Argentina's architecture.
3 Park the car in the darkest part of Harvard yard.
4 Hard-hearted Charles snarled and barked at Arthur.
5 Hark! Hark! The me-́rry-hearted lark!
6 Guard those arms with all your heart, sergeant.
7 Park the ark a bit farther, next to the argosy.
8 To arms, to arms, you harmless ar-mo̊ᵊ-rers!
9 Sergeant Clark started toward the garden, then charged toward the barn.
10 Such a charming garment, darling, but (what a bizarre scarf!
11 Mark me, Prince Charles, Margaret will be the star of the carnival.
12 Her parcel harbored jars and jars of a marvelous facial varnish from Elizabeth Arden.
13 Pardon me, King Arthur, for the carnage and the carcasses of the martyrs.
14 The Argentinian farmer's largess has been the marvel of the March carnival.
15 Martha's bazaar has started, but she drives a hard bargain.
16 Karl Marx hosted a large garden party near Marble Arch.
17 The starlet, the tart, and the harlot hardened their tarnished hearts.
18 Look for a large star to be the harbinger of remarkable harmony.

COMPARISON OF THE PURE VOWEL SOUND *a:* WITH THE DIPHTHONG SOUND *aɐ̆*

a:	*aɐ̆*		*a:*	*aɐ̆*		*a:*	*aɐ̆*
19 pa	— par		25 Mahdi	— Mardi Gras		31 father	— farther
20 spa	— spar		26 alms	— arms		32 Bach	— bark
21 MAma	— marmalade		27 almond	— Armand		33 Chicago	— cargo
22 hu-rrah	— Fa-rrar		28 balmy	— barmy		34 Mako	— Marco
23 Baden	— pardon		29 Bali	— barley		35 Masha	— Marsha=Marcia
24 Mikado	— Ricardo		30 lava	— larva		36 macho	— march

	/ɪə̆/	/ɛə̆/	/ʊə̆/	/ɔə̆/	/ɑə̆/	/aɪə̆/	/aʊə̆/
1*	ear	air=ere=heir=e'er	Ur (Ger)	oar=ore	are (sf)	ire	our=hour
2	hear	hair=hare	Hou-ri	whore=hoar	harm	hire=higher	Howar
3*	peer=pier	pear=pair=pare	poor	pore=pour	par	pyre	power
4*	bier=beer	bear=bare	boor=Boer	bore=boar	bar	byre=buyer	bower
5	tier=tear	tear (rip)	tour	tore=Tor	tar	tire=Tyre	tower
6	deer=dear	dare	dour	door	radar	dire	dower
7	Kier=kir	care	Coors	core=corps	car	-----	cower
8	geared	Ga-ry	gourd	gored	guard	-----	Gower
9*	mere	mare=mayor	moor=Moore	more	mar	mire=Meyer	-----
10	near	ne'er	Noor	nor (sf)	sonar	-----	Izenour
11	leer=Lear	lair	velour	lore	Lahr	lyre=liar	lour=lower (frown)
12	fear	fare=fair	Cavour	four=fore	far	fire	devour
13	sheer=shear	share	sure	shore	shard	shire	shower
14	rear	rare	Ruhr	roar	Fa-rrar	Ryerson	rower (disturber)
15*	year	Yare	your=you're	yore	yar	-----	-----
16	cheer	chair	premature	chore	char	-----	-----
17	ee-rie=E-rie	ai-ry=ae-rie	U-ri	oa-rring	a-ria (also ɑ:)	I-ra (also aɪ̆)	-----

* These lines contain words that when spoken WITHOUT R-COLORING have no tip-of-the-tongue involvement. The entire line should be spoken with the tip of your tongue relaxed behind your lower front teeth. This elimination of r-coloring will keep your sound open and forward.

SENTENCES FOR COMPARISON OF THE DIPHTHONGS AND TRIPHTHONGS OF "R"

1 The sharp sheer cliffs along the shore will surely get a fair share of the shire's showers.

2 It appears that this poor pair isn't up to par, so transport them out of the empire, Powers.

3 Mr. Bower, the boor, bore some beer from the bar to the bear in the byre.

4 The lord from Lourdes leered and loured in his lair, strumming a large lyre.

5 Would Kier care to uncork a Coors in his car, while the choir cowers in the corner?

6 The tired old tar took a detour toward the tower and, through his tears, stared at the sea.

7 I hear Howard Hardy hired a hairless whore to play a Hou-ri.

8 We admire Mayor Lamar merely for mowing more moors.

9 The dour dear is in dire need of a dower, but she dares not tell her ado-ring darling.

SENTENCES FOR CLARITY OF ɔ: ɒ AND ɑ: PRIOR TO r

10 We're po-ring over an o-rato-rical a-ria.

11 How can he be pou-ring po-rridge while spa-rring?

12 He's bo-ring me with his bo-rrowings and ba-rrings.

13 We attended a fo-rum in a fo-reign fo-rest fa-raway from home.

14 The To-ries were to-rrid when ta-rring the roads.

15 The ado-rable Do-ris and Do-rothy are sta-rry-eyed.

16 Sno-ring No-rris was ma-rring the a-ria.

17 She was soa-ring with so-rrow over the cza-rist resting place.

18 Who-ring was a ho-rror to Mata Ha-ri.

19 The flo-ra and fauna in Flo-rida are ja-rring.

20 Sco-ring with a co-rrespondent can be emotionally sca-rring.

◆ THE TRIPHTHONG AND RISING DIPHTHONG SOUNDS◆

SOUNDS SOMETIMES NECESSARY FOR USE IN VERSE

The Triphthong Sounds

h*ire*=h*igher*   aĭə̆

fl*ower*=fl*ow'r*=fl*our*   aŭə̆

The Rising Diphthong Sounds

TEd*ious*   ĭə

(When the word is pronounced in two
syllables: "TE-d*ious*.")

INfl*ue*nce   ŭə

(When the word is pronounced in two
syllables: "IN-fl*ue*nce.")

◆ THE TRIPHTHONG SOUNDS ◆
AS IN "hire" AND   as in "flower"

Represented by the spellings:

    hire=higher   byre=buyer   dire=dyer   lyre=liar

Represented by the spellings:

    flower=flow'r=flour   our=hour=Auer

A triphthong sound is one in which three vowel sounds are blended so closely that they are used and perceived as a single phonetic unit consisting of ONE syllable.

Words such as "hire" and "flower" are commonly pronounced in two syllables, with a diphthong in one syllable and the weak neutral vowel sound ə as in "surprise" in the next syllable:

    hi-re=high-er aĭ ə   flow-er=flou-r aŭ ə

However, when the rhythm of a line in verse demands that these two-syllable sequences be elided into one syllable, the three vowel sounds are blended into triphthong sounds, each representing one syllable. The small curve indicating the weaker elements is placed over the second and third elements of each triphthong sound, since those are less prominent than the first:

    hire=higher aĭə̆   flower=flow'r=flour aŭə̆

Because they are comprised of three sounds, the triphthong sounds of Spoken English are in and of themselves rather long in duration; however, they are ALWAYS transcribed without length-dots.

As for all the vowel and diphthong sounds associated with the letter "r" in the spelling of a word, the two triphthong sounds have TWO standards of pronunciation in North American speech:

aĭə̆ aŭə̆ WITHOUT R-COLORING: The tip of your tongue is relaxed behind your lower front teeth. The sound is free and forward.

aĭɚ̆ aŭɚ̆ WITH R-COLORING: The tip of your tongue is tensed up and over, the body of your tongue is retracted. The sound is tense and back.

Because of the forward, released vocal energy that comes from keeping the tip of your tongue free of tension, it is recommended that in singing and in Good Speech in classic texts the standard WITHOUT R-COLORING, aĭə̆ and aŭə̆ , be used.

In ordinary conversation and when speaking prose texts, the ONLY word in Spoken English that must be spoken with a triphthong sound is the unstressed Weak Form of "our," which consists of one sound only, the triphthong aŭə̆ .

The words for practice on page 187 are often spoken in one syllable when used in verse. In ALL other cases (conversation, prose texts and verse passages that do not require a triphthong sound) the same words are to be pronounced in a TWO-syllable sequence, WITHOUT a triphthong.

WORDS FOR PRACTICE

1 ire hire=higher pyre empire inspire perspire expire conspire byre=buyer=Byer

2 tire=Tyre=tier (one who ties) attire retired Stiers dire=dyer mire=Meyer=Myer

3 admire lyre=liar fire sire desire shire Ryerson prior=Pryor briar=brier

4 Dreyer=dryer crier=Cryer fryer=friar wire choir=quire inquire=enquire require

5 MacGuire gyre

WORDS FOR CLARITY OF aɪə PRIOR TO

✓ *Reminder* ————————————————————————————————

Make an open, clearly defined aɪə sound and begin the following syllable with a clean-cut consonant r̩ . In doing so, you will avoid marring the clarity of the aɪə sound with r-coloring.

6 hi-ring inspi-ring perspi-ring expi-ring ti-ring reti-ring admi-rer admi-ring

7 fie-ry fi-ring desi-ring prio-ry fria-ry wi-ring in-QUI-ring in-QUI-ry=en-QUI-ry

8 in-QUI-rer=en-QUI-rer requi-ring gy-ring

Since the triphthong sounds occur ONLY in verse, the following practice examples are taken from verse passages of Shakespeare's *A Midsummer Night's Dream*. You will find that in each example the word under consideration has a triphthong sound so that the line of verse will have the ten syllables required in iambic pentameter.

9 desires	Therefore, fair Hermia, question your desires,	dɪˈzaɪəz	I.i.69
10 fire	And by that fire (which) burned the Carthage queen	faɪə	I.i.176
11 quire	And then the whole quire hold their hips and laugh,	kwaɪə	II.i.56
12 fiery	But I might see young Cupid's fie-ry shaft	faɪərɪ ə	II.i.164
13 briers	For briers and thorns at their appa-rel snatch;	braɪəz	III.ii.29
14 conspired	Have you conspired, have you with these contrived	kənˈspaɪəd	III.ii.199
15 desires	My legs can keep no pace with my desires.	dɪˈzaɪəz	III.ii.445

WORDS FOR PRACTICE

1 our=hour=Auer Howar Eisenhower power powerful powerless bower=Bauer tower dower
2 cower scour Gower Izenour lour=lower (v; look threatening) Clower glower
3 flour=flower devour sour shower

WORDS FOR CLARITY OF aʊ̆ə̆ PRIOR TO r̩

✓ Reminder ───────────────────────────────────

Make an open, clearly defined aʊ̆ə̆ sound and begin the following syllable with a clean-cut consonant r̩ . In doing so, you will avoid marring the clarity of the aʊ̆ə̆ sound with r-coloring.

4 powe-ring empowe-ring towe-ring cowe-ring scou-ring flowe-ry flowe-ring

5 lou-ring=lowe-ring (adj: threatening; frowning) devou-ring showe-ring

Again, since the triphthong sounds occur ONLY in verse, the following examples are taken from *A Midsummer Night's Dream*. In each example the word under consideration has a triphthong sound so that the line of verse will have the ten syllables required in iambic pentameter.

6	power	I know not by what power I am made bold,	I.i.61
7	showers	So he dissolved, and show'rs of oaths did melt.	I.i.251
8	our	But with thy brawls thou hast disturbed our sport.	II.i.88
9	flowers	Lulled in these flowers with dances and delight;	II.i.259
10	bower	Near to her close and consecrated bower,	
	hour	While she was in her dull and sleeping hour,	III.ii.7-8
11	flow'ry	Come, sit thee down upon this flow'-ry bed,	IV.i.1

As stated above, the ONLY word in North American speech that must be pronounced as a triphthong sound in conversation and when speaking prose passages is the Weak Form of the word "our." This Weak Form is used when the word is unimportant to the meaning of its context.

12 If these are the best days of our lives, then I'd like to see the worst days of our lives.
13 This is our last chance to get our act together.
14 On Sundays our hours are noon to five.
15 Let's pack up our books, our clothes, our dishes, and our pots and pans.

The strong form of "our" is not a triphthong, but rather is spoken in two syllables:
16 These aren't yours. These are ours!

◆ THE RISING DIPHTHONG SOUNDS ◆
ɪ̆ə AS IN "ted*ious*" AND ʊ̆ə as in "infl*ue*nce"

Words such as "tedious" and "influence" are commonly pronounced using sequences of two distinct vowel sounds, which form TWO distinct, UNstressed SYLLABLES:

TE-d*i-ous* *ˈtʰiːdɪəs*   IN-fl*u*-ence *ˈɪnfluəns*

However, when the rhythm of a line in verse demands that such two-syllable sequences be elided into ONE syllable, the two vowel sounds are blended smoothly together to form new diphthongs:

TE-d*ious* *ˈtʰiːdɪ̆əs*   IN-fl*ue*nce *ˈɪnflŭəns*

What makes these diphthongs "new" and unique (not to mention distinct from ɪə as in "h*ere*" and ʊə as in "p*oor*") is that the first element is weak and the second element more prominent. In phonetic transcription the small curve placed over the weak FIRST element indicates a RISING DIPHTHONG because there is rise in either its prominence or sonority.

In Spoken English, the two rising diphthong sounds occur ONLY as required in verse; and since they are ALWAYS in unstressed syllables, their use in performance is not essential.

The rising diphthong sounds bear a certain resemblance to the consonant-vowel combinations jə and wə. These two combinations make the key words sound something like "TEED-yuss" and "IN-flwunss," respectively. In North American speech, these two pronunciations should be avoided, but are appropriate in certain kinds of British English.

In the following lines from Shakespeare's *A Midsummer Night's Dream*, you will find that each sample word contains a rising diphthong sound which assures that the line of verse has the required ten syllables of iambic pentameter.

THE RISING DIPHTHONG ɪ̆ə

1	earthlier	*ˈɜːθlɪ̆ə* But EARTH-lier happy is the <u>r</u>ose distilled	I.i.78
2	beauteous	*ˈbjuːtɪ̆əs* I am beloved of BEAU-teous Hermia.	I.i.106
3	merrier	*ˈmerɪ̆ə* A ME-rrier hour was never wasted there.	II.i.58

NOTE: In this line "hour" must be pronounced as the triphthong sound: *ˈaʊ̆ə* .

4	Indian	*ˈɪndɪ̆ən* And in the spiced IN-dian air, by night,	II.i.126

NOTE: In this line "spiced" must be pronounced in two syllables: *ˈspʰaɪsɪd* .

5	Athenian	*əˈθiːnɪ̆ən* A sweet A-THE-nian lady is in love.	II.i.265
6	Hermia	*ˈhɜːmɪ̆ə* Content with HER-mia? No! I do <u>r</u>epent	
	tedious	*ˈtʰiːdɪ̆əs* The TE-dious minutes I with her have spent.	II.ii.112-13
7	worthier	*ˈwɜːðɪ̆ə* And <u>r</u>eason says you are the WOR-thier maid.	II.ii.117

THE RISING DIPHTHONG ĭə , Cont.

1	courteous	ˈkɜːˈtʰĭəɹ Be kind and COUR-teous to this gentleman.	III.i.163
2	injurious Hermia	ɪnˈdʒʊ̆əˌɹĭəɹ ˈhɜːmĭə In-JU-rious HER-mia! most ungrateful maid!	III.ii.198

THE RISING DIPHTHONG ŭə

3		ə Such sepa-ration as may well be said	
	virtuous	ˈvɜːˈtʃŭəɹ Becomes a VIR-tuous bachelor and a maid,	II.ii.58-59

NOTE: The word "bachelor" must be pronounced in two syllables: "bach'lor."

4	virtuous	ˈvɜːˈtʃŭəɹ Whose liquor hath this VIR-tuous property,	III.ii.384
5		The skies, the fountains, every region near	
	mutual	ˈmjuːˈtʃŭəl Seemed all one MU-tual cry. I never heard	
		So musical a discord, such sweet thunder.	IV.i.119-21
6	usual	ˈjuːˈʒŭəl Where is our U-sual manager of mirth?	V.i.38

It is interesting to note that frequently there are places in verse where words containing a two-syllable sequence of ĭə do NOT have to be elided into a one-syllable rising diphthong sound in order to make ten syllables in the line. This happens frequently when such a word is the last one in a line of verse. Here are a few examples from *A Midsummer Night's Dream*, where words are spoken in verse just as they are in conversation and in prose texts.

7		Full of vexation come I, with complaint	
	Hermia	ˈhɜːˈmĭˌə Against my child, my daughter HER-mi-a.	I.i.23-24
8	worthier	ˈwɜːˈðĭˌə The other must be held the WOR-thi-er.	I.i.57
9	India	ˈɪnˌdĭə Come from the farthest steppe of IN-di-a,	II.i.70
10	Demetrius	dɪˈmiːˈtĭˌɹĭəɹ Then stir De-ME-trius up with bitter wrong;	
	(2 ways)	dɪˈmiːˈtĭˌɹĭˌəɹ And sometime rail thou like De-ME-tri-us.	III.ii.378-79

CHAPTER FOUR

THE CONSONANT SOUNDS

p	**p**ay
b	**b**ay
t	**t**an
d	**D**an
k	**c**on
g	**g**one

STOP-PLOSIVE CONSONANT SOUNDS

Stop-plosive consonant sounds are made with the articulators either stopping the breath stream and then exploding it or stopping the air and holding it. The breath used to produce stop-plosives may be voiceless (vs), which means that there is no vibration of the vocal folds and that the sound is whispered or breathed; or the breath may be voiced (vd), which means that there is vibration of the vocal folds.

Cognates

A cognate is a pair of consonant sounds produced in the SAME PLACE of articulation and in the SAME MANNER of articulation, one of the pair voiced (vd) and the other voiceless (vs). In Spoken English there are six stop-plosives or three pairs of cognates.

The stop-plosive cognates are *p* & *b* , *t* & *d* and *k* & *g*

The stop-plosive consonant sounds are made in the following PLACES OF ARTICULATION:

Place I	(BILABIAL)	The two lips articulate against each other:

p   *b*

(vs) **p**ay ca**p**er ca**p**e   (vd) **b**ay may**b**e A**b**e

Place IV-A	(ALVEOLAR)	The tip of the tongue touches the gum ridge directly behind the upper front teeth:

t   *d*

(vs) **t**an ra**tt**y ha**t**   (vd) **D**an ca**dd**y ha**d**

Place VI	(VELAR)	The back of the tongue articulates against the soft palate:

k   *g*

(vs) **c**on lo**ck**ing ho**ck**   (vd) **g**one lo**gg**er ho**g**

When a stop-plosive is followed by a vowel, diphthong sound or by silence, the breath is quickly released: you are using the PLOSIVE. There is movement of the articulators that can be seen, heard and felt:

p^h	t^h	k^h	*b*	*d*	*g*
pea	**t**oe	**k**ey	**b**ay	**d**ie	**g**o
lea**p**	oa**t**	e**k**e	A**b**e	hi**d**e	ho**g**

When a stop-plosive is followed by another consonant sound, either within the same word or in the next word of a phrase, the plosive is unreleased: you are using the STOP ONLY. The stop-plosive can be seen, heard and felt in relation to the consonant sound that follows it in the same word or the following word:

$p_,$	$t_,$	$k_,$	*b*	*d*	*g*
ca**p**ture	foo**t**ball	lo**ck**jaw	ri**bb**ed	be**d**time	e**gg**shell
dro**p** by	I though**t** so	than**k** God	e**bb** tide	a goo**d** time	bi**g** deal

The Voiceless Stop-Plosives

The voiceless stop plosives can be ASPIRATED or UNASPIRATED.

◆ ASPIRATION is marked by a small ^{h} to show that the air is RELEASED or EXPLODED.

Aspiration is used in three situations:

	p^h	t^h	k^h
— Before a vowel sound	pea	tomb	can
— Before a diphthong sound	pie	tame	coy
— Before a silence (or pause)	soap	mate	oink

These same consonants are LIGHTLY ASPIRATED:

	p^h	t^h	k^h
— Between two vowel sounds	reaper	hitter	seeker
	drop it	right away	peek over

◆ UNASPIRATION is marked by a small , to show that the air is held, or NOT released.

The air is held only before another consonant sound:

	$p_,$	$t_,$	$k_,$
— In the same word	apt	hits	clay
— In the following word	sap flows	get down	look good

Accurate articulation of aspirated and unaspirated stop-plosives is essential for distinct utterance and clarity of meaning. Omission of an aspirated plosive before a vowel, diphthong or pause sounds sloppy and obscures meaning. Inclusion of an aspirated plosive before another consonant, where it should be unaspirated, sounds self-conscious and pedantic.

The Voiced Stop-Plosives

The voiced stop plosives are not governed by the terms aspirated and unaspirated.

There are no special diacritical marks for noting release or non-release of these consonant sounds.

Accurate articulation of the voiced stop-plosives is essential for intelligibility and audibility in connected speech.

When b , d and g are followed by another consonant sound in the same word or the next word, the articulators maintain position, sustaining the vibration until the next consonant sound occurs:

b		d		g	
hobble	robbed	goodness	redbird	bigness	logbook
rob them	Bob bowed	a good day	red barn	big girl	log cabin

Nasal Plosion

Nasal plosion, which is also called implosion, occurs when a stop-plosive is followed by a nasal consonant that is made in the same place of articulation as the stop-plosive. Since the position of the articulators does not change between the unreleased stop and the nasal, the articulation is carried out by the action of the soft palate, which relaxes to release the breath stream through the nose:

p, m	bm	t, n	dn
topmost	subma-rine	beatnik	madness
		* beaten	* madden
		* patent	* wouldn't
stop me	Bob moved	great need	bad news

There is partial nasal plosion or implosion in sequences between two consonants that are NOT made in the same place of articulation:

hypnotic	hobnob	Puttman	bedmate
top notes	Bob knelt	get moving	good move

However, since these plosions are only partial, the terms nasal plosion and implosion are used in this textbook only for the sequences p, m bm t, n dn

Lateral Plosion

Lateral plosion occurs when $t,$ and d are followed by the lateral consonant l . Since the tip of the tongue remains firmly touching the gum ridge when going from the unreleased $t,$ or d to the consonant l , the articulation occurs as the sides of the tongue swiftly come down and in for l :

t, l	$d l$
softly	broadly
Atlantic	badlands
* battle	* needle

There is partial lateral plosion in sequences of consonants NOT made in the same place of articulation:

haply	jobless	reckless	England
ripe lemon	Bob left	rock ly-rics	beg leave
* ripple	* hobble	* pickle	* eagle

However, since the plosion is only partial, in this textbook the term lateral plosion will be used only for the sequences t, l and $d l$.

---

* These words contain the syllabic consonants n or l , each of which ends with an unstressed syllable containing no vowel sound. The consonant n or l has taken the place of a vowel sound in forming the weak syllable and is therefore called a syllabic consonant.

◆ THE CONSONANT SOUNDS ◆
p AS IN "pay" AND b AS IN "bay"

THE PLACE I VOICELESS BILABIAL STOP-PLOSIVE CONSONANT SOUND: p **as in "pay."**

Represented by the spellings:

Peter ri**pp**le hiccou**gh**

THE PLACE I VOICED BILABIAL STOP-PLOSIVE CONSONANT SOUND: b **as in "bay."**

Represented by the spellings:

be bu**bb**le tu**be**

Relax your lower jaw and allow the tip of your tongue to rest behind your lower teeth. Close your lips firmly against each other to stop the breath stream and then quickly release the lips to create p and b . There is NO VIBRATION of the vocal folds to produce the voiceless p , while there IS VIBRATION of the vocal folds to produce the voiced b .

The breath may be quickly exploded (this is called aspirated or released) or it may be held (this is known as unaspirated or unreleased).

✔ *Reminder* ─────────────────────────────────

The terms aspirated and unaspirated apply only to the voiceless stop-plosives.

The voiceless consonant p is aspirated p^h before:

	p^h	p^h
— A vowel sound	pea	dr**o**p in
— A diphthong sound	pay	drop out
— A pause or silence	ri̲p	Have a nice tri̲p!

The voiceless consonant p is unaspirated $p_,$ before:

	$p_,$	$p_,$	$p_,$
— A consonant sound in the same word	play	laps=lapse	leapfrog
— A consonant sound in the following word	clap for	dr̲op dead	top ten

In final position, the voiced consonant b must be carefully articulated in order to achieve accuracy and understandability without sounding pedantic. Be especially mindful of b at the end of a phrase, as in "I've a bro̲ken ri̲b."

◆ For good articulation keep your lips together for a fraction of a second, while the compressed air comes easily through your lips. This process is called an on-glide.

◆ Avoid adding an off-glide to a final b . NEVER SAY: "bro̲ken ri̲b-uh" b^∂

◆ Avoid substituting p for final b . SAY: "bro̲ken ri̲b" NOT: "bro̲ken ri̲p"

◆ When b is followed by another voiced consonant sound in the same word or the following word, the voiced stop-plosive sound is held, and the vibrated breath is released on the following consonant sound, as in:

bd	bd
ri̲bbed	My ri̲b doesn't hurt.

WORDS FOR PRACTICE

Initial *p*

1 pea pick pet pat pass purr palaver pun pool pull poetic Paul pot
2 palm pay pie poise pole powder peer=pier pear=pare=pair poor pore=pour
3 par pyre power

Medial *p*

4 keeping typical Eppy lapping chirping suppose supper looping supe-rior[2]
5 opalescent hoppity gaping wiping open cowpoke airport corpo-ral Harper

Final *p*

6 heap hip pep lap grasp chirp dollop up loop pop cape wipe rope Thorpe carp

Initial *b*

7 beat bit bet bat bath burr ba-rometer but boot beauty bullet Bohemia
8 balk bog balm bay buy=by boy=buoy bow=beau bow=bough beer=bier
9 bear=bare boor bore=boar bar buyers=Byers bower=Bauer

Medial *b*

10 fibber anybody rabbit cupboard about above dubious robber neighbor
11 Khyber sober cowboy airborn morbid arbor harbor firebird

Final *b*

12 plebe bib rib ebb deb cab Mab curb Herb tub rub boob tube daub Bob
13 job Abe babe scribe jibe globe robe orb barb

PAIRS OF WORDS FOR COMPARISON OF *p* WITH *b*

Initial		Medial		Final	
14a pea	— bee=Bea	14b reaper	— Reba	14c peep	— plebe
15a pit	— bit	15b lippy	— Libby	15c rip	— rib
16a pet	— bet	16b distemper	— September	16c rep	— Reb
17a pat	— bat	17b dapper	— dabber	17c tap	— tab
18a path	— bath	18b -----	-----	18c -----	-----
19a purr	— burr	19b disperse	— disburse	19c burp	— curb
20a putt	— butt=but (sf)	20b crumple	— grumble	20c sup	— sub
21a pooh	— boo	21b grouper	— Gruber	21c loop	— lube[2]
22a pulley	— bully	22b -----	-----	22c -----	— -----
23a Paul=pall	— bawl=ball	23b -----	-----	23c -----	— -----
24a pod	— body	24b topper	— bobber	24c bop	— Bob
25a palm	— balm	25b papa	— Ali Baba	25c -----	— -----
26a pay	— bay	26b maple	— Mabel	26c gape	— Gabe
27a pie	— bye=by=buy	27b viper	— Tiber	27c type	— vibe
28a poise	— boys=buoys	28b -----	-----	28c -----	-----
29a Poe	— beau=bow	29b opal	— global	29c rope	— robe
30a pout	— bout	30b cowpoke	— cowboy	30c -----	-----

PAIRS OF WORDS FOR COMPARISON OF p WITH b, Cont.

Initial		Medial		Final	
1a pier=peer	— beer=bier	1b ----	----	1c -----	-----
2a pear=pair	— bear=bare	2b airport	— airborn	2c -----	-----
3a poor	— boor	3b -----	-----	3c -----	-----
4a pore=pour	— bore=boar	4b torpid	— morbid	4c Thorpe	— orb
5a par	— bar	5b Harper	— harbor	5c sharp	— barb
6a pyre	— Byer=buyer	6b -----	-----	6c -----	-----
7a power	— bower	7b -----	-----	7c -----	-----

WORDS FOR PRACTICE USING A *LIGHTLY* ASPIRATED p^h BETWEEN TWO VOWEL SOUNDS, WHERE THE SECOND VOWEL SOUND IS IN AN UNSTRESSED SYLLABLE

8 peeper peeping dipper dipping leper clapper clapping developing

9 trouper trouping hopper hopping Taper=tapir taping typist typing groper groping

10 weepy dippy peppy sappy slurpy puppy droopy sloppy draper dopey

EXERCISES FOR DISTINGUISHING BETWEEN ASPIRATED p^h AND UNASPIRATED p,

p^h	p^h	p,		p^h	p^h	p,
11 leap	leap up	leapfrog	19 sap	sapid	sapling
12 lip	lipid	lip service	20 lap	lapping	lapse=laps
13 lip	lippitude	Lipton	21 hap	happy	apt
14 pep	pepper	peptalk	22 flap	flapper	flapped
15 lap	lappet	lapdog	23 loop	loopie	looplight
16 lop	lop-eared	lopsided	24 Pope	Pope Urban	Pope Paul
17 top	topper	top dog	25 ripe	ripe o-range	ripe peach
18 pop	popover	popcorn	26 gallop	gallop apace	Gallup Poll

27 Drop practicing and drop by. You must drop over!

28 Top price for the top bench? On top of the fee?

29 Keep pace and keep beats to keep on time.

30 Book your trip to Tripoli at Triptix—a top agency.

31 Weep plaintively and weep bitterly, but weep openly.

SENTENCES FOR PRACTICE USING SAME-CONSONANT BLENDS

✓ Reminder

Maintain the contact of your lips during the following same-consonant blend sequences. Clarity of enunciation is achieved by a fresh impulse of energy that begins the second word of the sequence.

32 Stop pay-ing such cheap prices for soup plates.

33 Keep peace and stop picking on Papp, Pam.

34 Rob built the club beds for Abe Benson.

35 Bob bought a scrub bucket to rub beer onto the cab bottom.

SENTENCES FOR PRACTICE USING COGNATE BLENDS

✓ *Reminder* ——————————————————————————

Maintain the contact of your lips during the following cognate blend sequences. Clarity of enunciation is achieved by the change from voiced to voiceless, or voiceless to voiced, and by a fresh impulse of energy that begins the second word in the sequence.

1 Bob paid the mob plenty to curb powerful sub patrols.
2 Rub places deep below the top bark.

WORDS FOR PRACTICE USING CONSONANT COMBINATIONS

✓ *Reminder* ——————————————————————————

Combine the stop-plosive with the lateral consonant sound so that there is NO VOWEL SOUND after the stop. Do not say $p\breve{ə}l$-.

pl- 3 plea plead pleat plinth pleasant plack=plaque plan plant plaster plunge
4 plume plu-ral applaud plot plaza play ply ploy explode plow

-pl 5 steeple stipple apple purple crumple scruple
(See pages 250-251, Syllabic l .)

✓ *Reminder* ——————————————————————————

Carry your voice through each vibrated consonant ending without adding an offglide.

-pld 6 peopled stippled dappled sampled scrupled toppled stapled

-plz 7 peoples tipples apples samples purples couples quadruples popples maples
8 disciples opals Marple's

✓ *Reminder* ——————————————————————————

Blend pr- and spr-.

9 preach print pretzel prattle prance producer prune prawn prod prong pray price
10 spree sprint spread sprat spruce sprawl sprain spry sprout

✓ *Reminder* ——————————————————————————

Keep the following consonant clusters crisp and clean.

-pt 11 leaped sipped stepped except apt napped chirped excerpt supped co-rrupt
12 looped opt hopped aped typed hoped warped carped

-pts 13 manuscripts transcripts accepts adapts co-rrupts inte-rrupts bankrupts

-ps 14 leaps lips peps raps stoops shops shapes pipes slopes corpse sharps

-mpt 15 tempt attempt contempt exempt jumped stamped cramped pumped prompt

-lp 16 whelp help scalp pulp gulp

-$pən$ 17 cheapen happen ripen open sharpen
-$pənd$ 18 deepened happened ripened opened sharpened
-$pənz$ 19 deepens happens ripens opens sharpens

✓ *Reminder* ———————————————————————————————

> **Combine the stop-plosive with the lateral consonant sound so that there is NO VOWEL SOUND after the stop. Do not say** *bəl-*.

bl-   1   bleat blink blend blab blur blunt blue blot blah blame blight blow
         2   blea-ry Blair Bloor blarney

-bl̩   3   feeble nibble scribble pebble babble burble constable bubble ruble cobble
         4   ho-rrible sable Bible foible noble marble

-bl̩d   5   enfeebled nibbled pebbled babbled troubled gobbled cabled libeled

-bl̩z   6   enfeebles scribbles gabbles eatables rubles gobbles fables Bibles

✓ *Reminder* ———————————————————————————————

> **Blend** *br-* . **Do not say** *bər-* .

         7   breed brick breath brag branch brother Brussels brewed=brood brook
         8   brochure brawl bronze bray bride broil brogue brow Brearley

✓ *Reminder* ———————————————————————————————

> **Carry your voice through each vibrated consonant ending without adding an off-glide.**

-bd   9   fibbed ebbed nabbed curbed grubbed cubed daubed bobbed barbed

-bz   10   plebes fibs webs cabs verbs subs cubes daubs babes tribes globes

SENTENCES FOR PRACTICE USING p^h , p, AND b

11   Pick a peck of pitted peaches to pack with the pickled pears, Patty.
12   Pass a piece of pecan pie to Peter, if you please!
13   Purchase a papaya, a peck of potatoes and a package of pickles.
14   Pop open a packet of potpou-rri for positive pampe-ring.
15   Perturbed people anticipate panic. Do they appreciate peace?
16   Bad-mouth Baldwin and ban him from the ballot.
17   Abide by basics! Behave!
18   Make a bid for betterment with a bona fide bonus.
19   Bad habits abound backstage.
20   It's taboo to babble rubbish.
21   Hiccoughs are supposedly typical of gasping speakers.
22   Shopkeepers keep books to keep accu-rate accounts.
23   Keep the rabbits apart from the ripe bananas.
24   Don't bang on your neighbor's cupboard.
25   Steep mountain slopes stopped my stepmother's trips.
26   You little fibber! You expect me to believe your fibs?

✓ *Reminder* ———————————————————————————————

> **Blend** p,l- **and** *bl*- **in the following sentences. Combine the stop-plosive with the lateral consonant sound so that there is NO VOWEL SOUND after the stop. Do not say** $pəl$- **or** *bəl*- .

27   Please! Applaud the playwright's plots.
28   Place an appealing plaque next to the purple plaster planter.
29   Mabel was able to sell maple sy-rup and apples.

SENTENCES FOR PRACTICE USING p^h , p_i AND b , Cont.

1 Blame the blu-rring of the blending on the bleach.
2 Bless that blond's blatant blunders!
3 Black blisters blemish Blair's blush.
4 Global opals are improbable.
5 Nibble on vegetables and gobble other eatables.
6 Scrabble's impossible on this table.
7 Sample the dappled apple blossoms near the steeples.
8 People applaud disciplined principles.
9 Will fables from the Bible still apply?

SENTENCES FOR PRACTICE BLENDING $p_i r$- AND br-

10 Practice prayer and proper praises.
11 Proper production of this piece will cost a pretty precious price!
12 Precisely what pranks are you prepared to present?
13 Bruce played the brute in *Bright Broadway*.
14 Bring brie and a brochette from the brasse-rie.
15 Briefly break to break bread.
16 Prepare a spread of sprats and sprouts for the pretzels.
17 Prone to prancing? Pay the price of a sprain!
18 Bring some British brandy to my brother in Brussels.
19 The breeze broke her beautiful but brittle brooch.

SENTENCES FOR PRACTICE USING $-p_i s$ AND $-bz$ IN FINAL POSITION

✔ *Reminder* —

Keep the following voiceless consonant endings crisp and clean. Carry your voice through each final vibrated ending without adding an off-glide.

20 We supped on chips and dip and ribs.
21 Perhaps a few scraps will help the troops in their jobs.
22 We gasped at the mishaps on the slopes.
23 The shop ships heaps of tulips and other bulbs.
24 Nabbing cabs causes hubbub in the suburbs.
25 Scribes from the tribes babble pa-rables.

SENTENCES FOR PRACTICE USING NASAL PLOSIONS $p_i m$ and $b_i m$

✔ *Reminder* —

Nasal plosion occurs when a stop-plosive is followed by a nasal consonant sound that is made in the same place of articulation as the stop-plosive.

26 Mr. Chapman is the topman on the topmost topmast. $'t^h p p, m \ni s t^h$
27 Bob moved too soon after the subma-rine submerged.

◆ THE CONSONANT SOUNDS ◆
t AS IN "*t*an" AND d AS IN "*D*an"

THE PLACE IV-A VOICELESS ALVEOLAR STOP-PLOSIVE CONSONANT SOUND: t as in "*t*an."

Represented by the spellings:

    *t*en   bi*tt*er   wipe*d*   *Th*ames   *pt*omaine   dou*bt*   li*ght*

THE PLACE IV-A VOICED ALVEOLAR STOP-PLOSIVE CONSONANT SOUND: d as in "*D*an."

Represented by the spellings:

    *d*o   a*dd*   feare*d*

Relax your lower jaw and open your mouth slightly. Raise the tip of your tongue and press it firmly and deftly to your upper gum ridge, DIRECTLY in back of your upper front teeth. Quickly drop the tip of your tongue from the gum ridge as the breath is expelled. The tongue is the active articulator during the production of the t and d so avoid any involvement of your lower jaw. There is NO VIBRATION of the vocal folds to produce the voiceless t . There IS VIBRATION of the vocal folds during the production of the voiced d .

Be sure to use the tip of your tongue rather than the blade of your tongue (the sides of your tongue will be touching the sides of your upper teeth and gums.) BE SURE THAT THE RELEASE OCCURS STRAIGHT DOWN, rather than in a slide toward your upper front teeth.

The breath may be quickly exploded (aspirated or released) or it may be held (unaspirated or unreleased).

✓*Reminder* ───

           The terms aspirated and unaspirated apply only to the voiceless stop-plosives.

A well-spoken t^h is direct, clean and dry. Avoid a sliding, splashy, overly aspirated sound.

The voiceless consonant t is one of the most frequently used consonant sounds in Spoken English. This sound is aspirated t^h before:

	t^h	t^h
— A vowel sound	tea	eat eggs
— A diphthong sound	time	eat ice
— A pause or silence	right	Yes, he's right!

The voiceless consonant t is unaspirated $t_,$ before:

	$t_,$	$t_,$	$t_,$
— A consonant sound in the same word	tray	hits	hotdog
— A consonant sound in the following word	that rail	dirt bike	best time

In final position, the voiced consonant d must be carefully articulated in order to achieve accuracy and understandability without sounding pedantic. Be especially mindful of d at the end of a phrase, as in "That's what I said!"

◆ For good articulation maintain the contact of your tongue-tip and gum ridge for a second, while the compressed air easily passes through the articulators. This process is called an on-glide.

◆ Avoid adding an off-glide to a final d . NEVER SAY: "I said-uh" $d^ə$

◆ Avoid substituting t for final d . SAY: "I said" NOT: "I set"

◆ When d is followed by another voiced consonant sound in the same word or the following word, the voiced stop-plosive sound is held and the vibrated breath is released on the following consonant sound, as in:

$$\underset{\smile}{d\,\eth} \qquad \underset{\smile}{d\,\upsilon}$$

I said that's a good voice.

When t or d is followed by θ or $\eth$, either within a word or in the next word of a phrase, it becomes DENTALIZED, that is, made with the tip of the tongue touching the back of the upper front teeth. The IPA diacritical mark for showing dentalization of a sound is placed directly underneath the phonetic letter. This mark may be thought of as a little tooth sign underneath the letter:

$$\underset{n}{t}\,\theta \qquad\qquad \underset{\underset{n}{\smile}}{t\,\eth} \qquad\qquad\qquad \underset{n}{d}\,\theta \qquad\qquad \underset{\smile}{d\,\eth}$$

eighth   ate there   hundredth   read those

In Good Speech, dentalization occurs only when t , d , n or l is followed by θ or $\eth$.

WORDS FOR PRACTICE

Initial t

1 tee=tea tease team=teem teal tip 'tis till Tim Ted ten tell tap tag tan
2 task term terse taboo tuck ton tough tool too=two=to (sf) took taught
3 tot Todd toggle Ptolemy Tanya Tay tame tale=tail tie=Ty=Thai
4 time=thyme tide=tied toys toil toe=tow tone toad toll tout town
5 tier=tear tear tour tore tar tire tower

Medial t

✓ *Reminder*
_____

Use a LIGHTLY aspirated t^h between two vowel sounds when the second vowel sound is in an unstressed syllable.

6 heating meeting cheater sitting admitting bitter betting wetting
7 setter matting patting batter casting fasting plaster blurting hurting
8 alerting atom putting (golf) cutting shutter shooting hooting booted putting
9 autumn rotting potting totter hating relating later sighting fighting
10 writer loiter doting floating coated shouter porter garter

Final t

11 sleet hit slipped nipped clipped wept debt met at apt pat cast
12 fast mast hurt avert shirt rut cut mutt looped trouped recruit
13 cute astute thought bought fought rot hot clot ate=eight
14 wiped swiped striped height=Hite adroit hoit=Hoyt moped (v) coped
15 about shout spout sauerkraut abort part

Initial d

16 deep deem deed deal dip dim din dill dish debt dead dell Des
17 dad damn=dam damage daft dervish derma dirndl dirt Duluth Dakota
18 duck does dull Duffy dumb do doodle doom dew=due domain
19 daughter daw dot dog Donna Dada day daze die=dye dime dial doily
20 dough=doe dote dome doubt down dowdy dear=deer dare dour door
21 darling dire dower

WORDS FOR PRACTICE, Cont.

Medial *d*

1 conceded heeded needed seeded bidding kidding skidding cheddar
2 Hedda ladder saddest verdict murder budding muddy <u>r</u>udder moody
3 modest bodice fodder <u>RADA</u> fading wading wader tidings hider <u>r</u>ider
4 avoiding odor louder c<u>r</u>owded howdy chowder

Final *d*

5 deed <u>r</u>ead=<u>r</u>eed seed speed heed ag<u>r</u>eed Mead=mede lead did bid
6 Cyd=Sid kid <u>r</u>ed bed lead=led Med head mad pad bad=bade sad shad
7 had curd bird third ballad thud mud cud wooed shooed food mood
8 wood should hood thawed odd Todd pod sod <u>r</u>od aid paid <u>r</u>aid
9 maid=made b<u>r</u>ide lied Lloyd Boyd Floyd avoid <u>r</u>oad=<u>r</u>owed abode code
10 toad=towed showed hoed allowed affeared cared shared pared=paired
11 dared moored toured assured accord lord afford scored <u>r</u>oared sparred
12 marred barred=bard inspired flower'd

PAIRS OF WORDS FOR PRACTICING *t* IN INITIAL AND FINAL POSITION

Front Vowels		Mid Vowels		Back Vowels		Diphthongs	
13 team	meet	18 turn	hurt	23 tool	loot	27 tame	mate
14 till	lit	19 terse	shirt	24 took	put	28 time	might
15 tell	let	20 Tacoma	abbot	25 tall	Laughton	29 toy	doit
16 tă-<u>rry</u>	răt	21 tŭ-<u>rret</u>	<u>r</u>ut	26 Tom	Mott	30 toe	oat
17 tăsk	ăsked	22 tuck	cut			31 town	out

PAIRS OF WORDS FOR PRACTICING *d* IN INITIAL AND FINAL POSITION

Front Vowels		Mid Vowels		Back Vowels		Diphthongs	
32 deem	mead	37 dirt	deterred	40 doom	mood	44 dame	made=maid
33 dim	mid	38 dumb	mud				
34 dell	led	39 Duluth	salad	41 daw	awed	45 die=dye	I'd
35 damn	mad			42 dot	Todd	46 doily	Lloyd
36 dănce	commănd			43 Da	ah'ed	47 doe=dough	owed=ode
						48 Dowd	downed
						49 dear	eared
						50 dare	aired
						51 dwarf	ford
						52 dark	card

PAIRS OF WORDS FOR COMPARISON OF t WITH d

	Initial		Medial		Final	
1a	teen	— dean	1b heating	— heeding	1c beat	— bead
2a	till	— dill	2b bitter	— bidder	2c sit	— Sid
3a	tents	— dents	3b <u>r</u>enting	— <u>r</u>ending	3c set	— said
4a	tan	— Dan	4b fatten	— McFadden	4c hat	— had (sf)
5a	tăft	— dăft	5b planted	— commănded	5c craft	— calved
6a	terse	— durst	6b hurting	— herding	6c hurt	— heard
7a	tummy	— dummy	7b Sutton	— sudden	7c cut	— cud
8a	to (sf)	— do (sf)	8b b<u>r</u>uited	— b<u>r</u>ooded	8c <u>r</u>oot	— <u>r</u>ude
9a	taunt	— daunt	9b slaughter	— Lawder	9c avaunt	— fawned
10a	togs	— dogs	10b totter	— dodder	10c tot	— Todd
11a	Tahoe	— Dada	11b sonata	— Ensenada	11c -----	-----
12a	tame	— dame	12b <u>r</u>ating	— <u>r</u>aiding	12c pate	— paid
13a	tile	— di-al	13b <u>w</u>riting	— <u>r</u>iding	13c bite	— abide
14a	toil	— Doyle	14b loiter	— avoider	14c Voight	— void
15a	tote	— dote	15b total	— yodel	15c goat	— goad
16a	tear=tier	— dear=deer	16b Weirton	— <u>R</u>eardon	16c -----	-----
17a	tear	— dare	17b Erté	— Airedale	17c -----	-----
18a	tour	— dour	18b -----	-----	18c -----	-----
19a	tore	— door	19b courting	— <u>r</u>ecording	19c abort	— aboard
20a	tar	— dark	20b hearty	— hardy	20c heart=hart	— hard
21a	tire	— dire	21b -----	-----	21c -----	-----
22a	tower	— dower	22b -----	-----	22c -----	-----

EXERCISES FOR DISTINGUISHING BETWEEN ASPIRATED t^h AND UNASPIRATED $t_,$

	t^h	t^h	$t_,$		t^h	t^h	$t_,$
23	heat	heat up	heatst<u>r</u>oke	33	boot	bootie	bootleg
24	beat	Beattie	beatnik	34	foot	footage	football
25	seat	seating	Seton	35	hot	hotter	hotdog
26	sweet	sweeter	t<u>r</u>ee	36	shot	Shotover	shotgun
27	hit	hitting	hits	37	but	butter	butler
28	pit	pitiful	pitman	38	note	notable	notebook
29	mat	matinée	matt<u>r</u>ess	39	<u>w</u>rite	<u>w</u>rite-up	<u>r</u>iteless

	t^h	t^h	$t_,$		t^h	t^h	$t_,$
30	get	get on	get tired	40	sit	sit on	sit down
31	hot	hot ale	hot tea	41	get	get off	get down
32	quit	quit eating	quit talking	42	let	let up	let go

SENTENCES USING ASPIRATED t^h AND UNASPIRATED t,

1 Get off your high horse and get down to earth!
2 The pitiful pit bull was put into the pits.
3 The hotshot shot off his shotgun.
4 Notice this and notate it in your notebook.
5 Get on with it before you get tired.
6 I thought so, too. Have you thought it over?
7 The plot thickens as it unfolds.
8 Quit arguing. And will you quit complaining?

SENTENCES FOR PRACTICE USING SAME-CONSONANT BLENDS

9 Hit Ted with some hot tips from the "Top Ten."
10 Have some hot tea at Bonwit Teller and then meet Tom before you get too tired.
11 You bad dog. You hid dad's red drawers.
12 I heard Don found Donna sitting on the ground draw-ing an old dead duck!

PRACTICE USING COGNATE BLENDS

13 Had Tessie read Tales before she had told Thomas?
14 I intend to find Todd a recognized teacher of good tennis.

PAIRS OF WORDS FOR DISTINGUISHING BETWEEN THE VOICELESS t AND VOICED d

Medial		Medial		Medial	
15a pita	— Aida	15b eater	— cedar	15c beetle	— beadle
16a kitty	— kiddy	16b bitter	— bidder	16c piteous	— hideous
17a metal	— medal	17b letter	— leaded	17c etiquette	— editor
18a atom	— Adam	18b latter	— ladder	18c hatter	— adder
19a girtle	— girdle	19b hurtle	— hurdle	19c hurting	— herding
20a shutter	— shudder	20b utter	— udder	20c mutter	— muddy
21a futile	— feudal	21b neuter	— nudist	21c tutor	— Tudor
22a putting	— pudding	22b footed	— hooded	22c -----	-----
23a plotted	— plodding	23b hotter	— plodder	23c otter	— oddity
24a waiting	— wading	24b fated	— faded	24c Haiti	— Hades
25a writer	— rider	25b title	— tidal	25c cited	— sided
26a voter	— odor	26b coating	— goading	26c Otis	— pagodas
27a doubter	— louder	27b routing	— rowdy	27c pouter	— powder

WORDS FOR PRACTICE WITH A *LIGHTLY* ASPIRATED t^h BETWEEN TWO VOWEL SOUNDS

28 ability cha-rity pitiful beauty beautiful dutiful chastity hearty satisfy
29 visibility Co-retta satisfying attitude gratitude autumn batte-ry flatte-ry
30 catacomb Vatican

ASPIRATE THE t^h SOUND IN THESE WORDS. DO NOT GLOTTALIZE!

31 matinée mutiny mutinous mutineer scrutiny scrutinize continent continuity
32 maintenance acquaintance appurtenance mountain fountain sentence retina
33 retinue countenance repentant Brittany gelatinous Quentin Lenten
34 pertinent impertinent patina wanton wantonly

WORDS FOR COMPARISON OF VOICELESS WITH VOICED ENDINGS

t	d		t,	dz
1a feet	— feed		1b heats	— heeds
2a bit	— bid		2b bits	— bids
3a debt	— dead		3b debts	— dreads
4a cat	— cad		4b cats	— cads
5a hurt	— herd=heard		5b hurts	— herds
6a mutt	— mud		6b butts	— buds
7a boot	— booed		7b brutes	— broods
8a bought	— bawd		8b salts	— scalds
9a rot	— rod		9b plots	— plods
10a late	— laid		10b fates	— fades
11a light	— lied		11b rights	— rides
12a note	— node		12b totes	— toads

WORDS FOR PRACTICE USING CONSONANT COMBINATIONS

Initial t,

✓ *Reminder*

Blend t,r- and t,w- . Do not say $t\hat{ə}$r- or $t\hat{ə}$w- .

13 tree trip tread trap traduce truculent true trawl trot tray try Troy
14 trophy trout

15 tweak twit twig twixt twinkle twelve twirl twain twine

Medial t,

✓ *Reminder*

Observe the unaspirated t, in the following combinations.

- t, 16 treats sits gest=Getz bats hurts concerts huts boots puts thoughts pots
17 fates fights doits goats shouts courts carts

- p, t, 18 Egypt's scripts adapts excerpts co-rrupts

- ft, 19 lifts gifts shifts thefts crafts shafts drafts=draughts grafts rafts wafts tufts
20 lofts Croft's

- nt, 21 mints cents pants slants punts haunts wants paints pints joints accounts

- lt, 22 tilts Celts pelts cults adults faults colts bolts moults=molts

- st, 23 feasts beasts mists fists nests quests fasts blasts bursts thirsts lusts
24 thrusts boosts roosts holocausts frosts costs pastes bastes heists foists
25 joists boasts toasts ousts jousts (See also pages 276-277.)

- k, t, 26 addicts edicts depicts expects di-rects sects affects pacts facts enacts
27 attracts contracts conducts

- t, θ 28 fifth eighth sixth twelfth   - t, θ fifths eighths sixths twelfths

- ηk, t, 29 instincts precincts adjuncts

$\begin{array}{c}t\\d\end{array}$

WORDS FOR PRACTICE USING SYLLABIC $ț,l̦$ AND $ț,n̦$

✓ *Reminder* ───

A SYLLABIC $l̦$ or $n̦$ takes the place of a vowel in forming certain UNstressed SYLLABLES, usually at the ends of words.

$-ț,l̦$ 1 beetle little br<u>i</u>ttle spittle hospital mettle=metal kettle battle Myrtle
  2 hurtle scuttle <u>r</u>ebuttal bottle thr<u>o</u>ttle chortle startle McCartle

$-ț,n̦$ 3 beaten bitten smitten thr<u>ea</u>ten fatten batten Burton mutton Laughton
  4 cotton <u>r</u>otten Caton lighten br<u>i</u>ghten tighten=Titan Morton hearten Spartan

Final t

✓ *Reminder* ───

Keep the following consonant clusters crisp and clean.

$-p,t^h$ 5 heaped nipped wept apt slurped cupped cŏ-<u>rr</u>upt grouped stopped
  6 shaped wiped eloped harped

$-ft^h$ 7 leafed lift deft wăft surfed <u>r</u>oughed <u>r</u>oofed oft chafed scarfed

$-nt^h$ 8 dint pent scant căn't burnt tr<u>u</u>ant blunt haunt font paint pint joint
  9 won't=wont don't count aren't

$-lt^h$ 10 built welt shalt exult fault bolt Arlt

$-st^h$ 11 East list best thirst August bust boost fr<u>o</u>st paste iced hoist host
  12 Faust pierced forced mar'st

$-lp,t^h$ 13 (whe̸lped) yelped helped scalped gulped

$-lft^h$ 14 delft gulfed engulfed <u>r</u>olfed golfed

$-mst^h$ 15 doom'st form'st alarm'st charm'st

$-nst^h$ 16 minced fenced advănced Ernst balanced shun'st flounced

$-lk,t^h$ 17 milked bilked bulked skulked

$-skt^h$ 18 (wh)sked fr<u>i</u>sked ăsked măsked tusked husked

$-\eta k,t^h$ 19 inked pinked banked thanked

$-nțʃt^h$ 20 pinched dr<u>e</u>nched <u>r</u>anched bunched launched

WORDS FOR PRACTICE USING CONSONANT COMBINATIONS WITH d

Initial d

✓ *Reminder* ───

Blend $d\underline{r}-$. Do not say $d\underline{ə}\underline{r}-$.

$d\underline{r}-$ 21 dr<u>ea</u>m drip drill dr<u>ea</u>d‿ dr<u>a</u>m drăft dr<u>u</u>m dr<u>oo</u>l dr<u>aw</u> dr<u>o</u>p dr<u>a</u>ma dr<u>a</u>pe
  22 dr<u>y</u> dr<u>o</u>ne dr<u>ow</u>sy dre̸ä-ry Drŭ-ry

WORDS FOR PRACTICE USING CONSONANT COMBINATIONS, Cont.

Medial d

$-d \lrcorner t^h$ 1 needst midst amidst didst couldst shouldst wouldst

$-d\theta \atop n$ 2 width br̲eadth hundr̲edth thousandth (See pages 267-268 $d \atop n$.)

$-d\theta \lrcorner \atop n$ 3 widths br̲eadths hundr̲edths thousandths

$-\ell:dz$ 4 wields builds worlds eme-r̲a̲lds $\overset{\ell dz}{}$ cuckolds scalds colds holds molds

$-n:dz$ 5 fiends winds ends lands dema̲nds almo nd z nds ponds finds hounds

Final d

✓ *Reminder* —

Carry your voice through each vibrated consonant ending without adding an off-glide.

$-bd$ 6 fibbed ebbed stabbed curbed r̲ubbed daubed sobbed absorbed garbed

$-m:d$ 7 beamed skimmed stemmed damned termed dr̲ummed doomed bombed named
8 timed foamed clowned warmed armed

$-vd$ 9 achieved lived curved observed loved pr̲oved dissolved waved a̲-r̲rived

$-ðd$ 10 sheathed soothed bathed wr̲ithed loathed mouthed

$-n:d$ 11 leaned pinned mend sand dema̲nd burned sunned mooned dawned pond
12 pained pined joined moaned found

$-\ell:d$ 13 peeled build welled furled qua̲-r̲reled dulled fooled bald wailed wild
14 boiled scold scowled gnarled

$-zd$ 15 eased fizzed buzzed used caused r̲aised pr̲ized dozed poised
16 pr̲oposed housed .

$-gd$ 17 leagued r̲igged begged bagged dr̲ugged hugged bogged hogged

$-\eta:d$ 18 winged str̲inged twanged banged longed pr̲olonged thr̲onged

WORDS FOR PRACTICE USING SYLLABIC $d\ell \atop ,$ AND $dn \atop ,$

✓ *Reminder* —

Syllabic ℓ or n takes the place of a vowel in forming certain UNstressed SYLLABLES usually at the ends of words. (See pages 250 and 239.)

$-d\ell \atop ,$ 19 needle fiddle peddle paddle girdle puddle poodle waddle ladle
20 bridal=br̲idle idle=idyll=idol fardel

$-d\ell z \atop ,$ 21 (wh)eedles r̲iddles meddles=medals paddles hurdles huddles noodles
22 caudels models br̲idles

$-dn \atop ,$ 23 Eden r̲idden deaden madden burden wooden sodden laden widen
24 hoiden=hoyden Louden warden garden

WORDS FOR PRACTICE USING SYLLABIC $d\ell$ AND $d\eta$, Cont.

$-d\eta t^h$ 1 needn't didn't pedant hadn't student wouldn't shouldn't
2 couldn't strident ardent

$-d\eta z$ 3 deadens gladdens burdens widens Haydn's Jordan's Arden's

SENTENCES FOR PRACTICE USING t^h , t, AND d

✓ *Reminder*

A well-spoken t^h is direct, clean and dry. Avoid a sliding, splashy, overly aspirated sound.

4 Lady Teazle teases and tantalizes Sir Peter.
5 Tommy and Tammy met Tilly for tea.
6 Tom tiptoed to town.
7 The torn tattered tent dropped.
8 The ten tiny timid tortoises are tame.
9 At the Thames tunnel, take a right.
10 Tom took a bite.
11 The tart tasted a trifle too tannic.
12 It takes time to untangle twenty-two tutus.
13 Tanya got tickets for tou-rists.
14 Put the tip of your tongue on the teeth.

15 Tea for two and two for tea.
16 Tippecanoe and Tyler, too.
17 A tentative ty-rant tried it.
18 Tia will eat tofu at 8:02 AM.
19 It's that teenage titan of te-rror.
20 Tina tied a tiny timepiece to her toga.
21 Teach the teeming teens to tell time.
22 Tell the tennis team to stop teasing Tom.
23 Tina's tight-fitting togs entice me.
24 The Tudor Tuna Institute raised its tuition.
   (See pages 116 and 310 ju: , Liquid U.)

25 Did Dean dare the deacon to debate the deed?
26 Discuss the disturbing data with a dedicated individual like Ed.
27 Demonstrate devotion through good deeds.
28 Dr. Eader detected dental decay under Dad's dentures.
29 Dismiss the delegates and redistribute their duties.
30 Decadent displays of devotion proved disturbing.
31 Brad was adamant about badge-ring his dad.
32 Bid a fond good-bye to friends abroad.
33 "Good riddance to bad rubbish," reads the old adage.
34 Reduce the new students' tuto-rials. (See pages 310-311, Liquid U.)
35 I'll bet you've had your hopes up! (See pages 328-333 $t\eta j$ dj .)

SENTENCES FOR PRACTICE USING t^h IN MEDIAL POSITION

✓ *Reminder*

Use a LIGHTLY aspirated t^h between two vowel sounds.

36 Get out! Get in! Get away!
37 Put it on the cutting table, Peter.
38 She's sitting at the foot of the desert.
39 Just a bit of lettuce and twenty potatoes.
40 I've written Pat a better letter about the matter.
41 It's our duty to beautify this city.

42 Put a bit of butter into the batter.
43 I'm writing a letter to the editor.
44 Patti's ditty was totally satisfy-ing.
45 I'll write a letter at a later date.
46 He's waiting to meet a better tutor.
47 It's a piteous sight, Mr. Keating.

SENTENCES FOR PRACTICE USING t^h IN MEDIAL POSITION, Cont.

✓ *Reminder* ——
In the following words, be sure to aspirate the t^h sound. Do not glottalize.

1 Is it a matinée of *Mutiny on the Bounty*?
2 From this mountain we can scrutinize the whole beautiful continent.
3 Don't be impertinent, Mr. Benton, or you'll be sentenced for an unrepentant attitude.

SENTENCES FOR PRACTICE USING d IN MEDIAL AND FINAL POSITION

4 Lead on! Lead in! Lead astray!
5 The wording of the ballad was absurdly odd.
6 Deepening meditation expanded his mind.
7 Do you need this odd width of board today?
8 Doubts deeply disturbed Addie.
9 Admit your addiction to adversity and drama.
10 He grumbled but he listened and reasoned.

SENTENCES FOR PRACTICE USING t, l AND dl (See pages 250-251, Syllabic l .)

✓ *Reminder* ——
A syllabic l may take the place of a vowel in forming an UNstressed SYLLABLE, usually at the end of a word.

11 Use that metal ladle to serve the noodle soup.
12 Take the shuttle to a cattle call, Myrtle.
13 The Beatles battled the heavy metal title-holders.
14 It's futile to settle on these battlements.
15 The cattle were startled a little bit.
16 It'll entice you to a little fertile plot.
17 Use a little metal kettle to curdle the milk.
18 Pedal through the puddles with a little caution.
19 Coddle the noodles when you handle them. They're brittle.
20 I'd like to throttle that poodle!

SENTENCES FOR PRACTICE USING t, n AND dn (See pages 239-240, Nasal Plosion.)

✓ *Reminder* ——
Nasal plosion occurs when a stop-plosive is followed by a nasal consonant that is made in the same place of articulation as the stop-plosive.

21 I've written an important letter. $ɪm'pɔɔt,nt^h$
22 Lighten that rotten cotton, Gené-ral Patton.
23 You've forgotten to fatten my marten.
24 He'll get nothing to sweeten, Sutton.
25 It was a potent and blatant mutant.
26 Jordan's wardens approved of the pardon.
27 Adam loved Eve in the Garden of Eden.
28 Fondness gladdens and hatred hardens the heart.
29 Ogden staged the London maidens to be outside the cauldron.

SENTENCES FOR PRACTICE USING t, n AND $d n$, Cont.

1 The gardens in Princeton and Boston rivaled those of Hampton Court.
2 She-ridan's tendon suddenly tightened.
3 He didn't even need to try. Wouldn't you agree?   (See pages 239-240 $d n$ $d n t^h$.)

SENTENCES FOR PRACTICE USING t, r- AND $d r$-

4 Retreat to the tree trunk, Trina.
5 We've been tripping to Trenton and To-ronto.
6 The traitor trapped me into committing treason.
7 Truman's treatment was truly tragic.
8 Try to trace the treasure to the tree trunk.
9 Will the tropical troops ever reach a truce?
10 Drape the drab dressing gown on the Dresden doll.
11 Dramatize the dragon in a dream-like draw-ing.
12 Drink a dram of dragon-wort and a drop of draught.
13 A dressy dress and coat rolled into one is a "droat."

SENTENCES FOR PRACTICE USING CONSONANT COMBINATIONS

14 Egypt boasts of feasts.
15 Who conducts *The Fifth* tonight? $f_1 f t_1 \theta$
16 Rehearsals commenced on the twelfth.
17 Best to adjust or you could go nuts!
18 List the best haunts on the East Coast.
19 She grasped the masked host!
20 Ms. Dench was drenched before the boat was launched.
21 He's disturbed and needs friends.
22 It caused raised eyebrows!
23 David resented feeling threatened and imprisoned.
24 We find our gardens lighten burdens.
25 You didn't know those wooden tiers couldn't work.   (See pages 239-240 $d n$ $d n t^h$.)

SENTENCES FOR PRACTICE USING $d n$ AND $d n$

26 He would know it's wooden, wouldn't he?
27 Good news! Gooden couldn't make it!
28 It saddened me. Hadn't you heard too?
29 Haddon had nightmares, hadn't he?
30 You should know, puddin' head, that you shouldn't do that!
31 Didney's kidney is hidden. Didn't you hear?
32 Dan can knead knees, but Sneaden needn't bother.
33 They were brewed 'n' served to prudent students.
34 We're rid now of the one who's ridden. Good riddance!

SENTENCES FOR PRACTICE USING t, d AND dz IN FINAL POSITION

✓ Reminder ——————————————————
Keep the following voiceless consonant endings crisp and clean.
1 The tou-rists' tickets limit visits to the President's monuments.
2 Psychothe-rapists offer insights to patients du-ring treatment.
3 Impressionists and Expressionists paid their respects at the recent exhibition.
4 Do these supermarkets permit shipments of walnuts?

✓ Reminder ——————————————————
Carry your voice through each vibrated consonant ending without adding an off-glide.
5 Weekends in orchards and vineyards sound grand!
6 Will hundreds of hardwood floorboards expand?
7 Diamonds and eme-ralds adorned her hands!
8 She demands they send postcards from the Islands.

DENTALIZED $t,$ AND d

In Spoken English, the alveolar consonant sounds t and d are usually made with the tip of the tongue touching the gum ridge directly BEHIND the upper front teeth. However, when one of the sounds is followed by θ or $\eth$, either within a word or in the next word of a phrase, it becomes DENTALIZED and is made with the tip of the tongue touching the back of the upper front teeth.

The IPA mark indicating dentalization of a sound is placed directly underneath the phonetic letter. This mark may be thought of as a little tooth sign underneath the letter:

$$t, \qquad d \qquad n \qquad l$$

(See pages 267-268.)

In Good Speech, dentalization occurs ONLY when these four consonant sounds are followed by θ or $\eth$ in the same word or the following word.

DENTALIZATION OF $t,$ AND d WITHIN A WORD

9 fifth $'fift,\theta$ sixth $'sik,st,\theta$ eighth $'eit,\theta$ twelfth $'twelft,\theta$
10 breadth width hundredth thousandth

SENTENCES FOR PRACTICE USING $t,$ AND d

11 It was his eighth and last theme on ancient Thebes.
12 I'll bet Thelma got thirsty after the sixth rebuttal.

13 I hate that we met them in that bar . . . one of the worst there is.
14 Let them get themselves dressed. That's why we've kept these clothes.

15 Had Thurston, the cad, tho-roughly thought out this theo-ry?
16 Bad things can happen du-ring mad thinking.

17 It's sad, though, that they almost had their day.
18 I would that they had themselves more organized.

19 God, that's the worst thing they could have had them do for that Thanksgiving.
20 I hate things such as bad theater, fat thighs, old thongs, and the habit those old thanes have of using red threads to mend things.

THE STOP-PLOSIVE CONSONANTS / 213

◆ THE CONSONANT SOUNDS ◆
k AS IN "con" AND g AS IN "gone"

THE PLACE VI VOICELESS VELAR STOP-PLOSIVE CONSONANT SOUND: k as in "con."

Represented by the spellings:

Kate **c**at **ch**ara**c**ter **q**uilt expe**c**t che**ck** pla**que**=pla**ck**

THE PLACE VI VOICED VELAR STOP-PLOSIVE CONSONANT SOUND: g as in "gone."

Represented by the spellings:

get e**gg** e**x**haust **gh**ost

Relax your lower jaw, open your mouth slightly and allow the tip of your tongue to rest behind your lower teeth. Raise the BACK of your tongue toward the raised soft palate to stop the breath stream, then quickly drop the back of your tongue away from your soft palate as the breath is expelled. There is NO VIBRATION of the vocal folds during the production of the voiceless k . There IS VIBRATION of the vocal folds during the production of the voiced g .

The breath may be quickly exploded (aspirated or released) or the air may be held (unaspirated or unreleased).

✓ *Reminder* ————————————————————————

The terms aspirated and unaspirated apply only to the voiceless stop-plosive sounds.

The voiceless consonant k is aspirated k^h before:

	k^h	k^h
— A vowel sound	key	Lake Eden
— A diphthong sound	kite	look out
— A pause or silence	ache	I have an ache.

The voiceless consonant k is unaspirated $k_,$ before:

	$k_,$	$k_,$	$k_,$
— A consonant sound in the same word	clay	backs	picture
— A consonant sound in the following word	pack <u>r</u>at	sick child	<u>r</u>ock pile

In final position, the voiced consonant g must be carefully articulated in order to achieve accuracy and understandability without sounding pedantic. Be especially mindful of g at the end of a phrase, as in "That's my bag."

◆ For good articulation maintain the contact of the back of your tongue with the soft palate for a second, while the compressed air easily passes through the articulators. This process is called an on-glide.

◆ Avoid adding an off-glide to a final g . NEVER SAY: "my bag-uh" $g^ə$

◆ Avoid substituting k for final g . SAY: "my bag" NOT: "my bak"

◆ When g is followed by another voiced consonant sound in the same word or in the following word, the voiced stop-plosive sound is held and the vibrated breath is released on the following consonant sound, as in:

gd ba**gg**ed $\underline{gd}$ I'll put my bag down here.

WORDS FOR PRACTICE

Initial k

k^h- 1 keep kin kept can curd cã-ress cup coo cook coerce caw cod

2 Khan cape chaos kind coy coal cow Kier care Coors core car cower

Medial k

-k^h- 3 tweaking licking wreckage lackey lurker looker booker occult occur

4 walker rocky raking liking ochre account porker darkest

-k,s- 5 exhibition execute sex exile[2] Texas exorcist eccentric exit[2]

6 excellent accident flaccid accent irksome oxen occident sharks

-k,$\int$- 7 diction election action Berkshires luxu-ry[2] suction function auction

Final k

-k^h 8 beak pick peck pack shirk luck fluke forsook brook walk sock lake

9 tyke oak broke pork hark

Initial g

g- 10 geese give get gap gãsp girl galore gum goose good gall=Gaul got

11 gay guy Goya go Goucher gear Gã-ry gourd gore guard Gower

Medial g

-g- 12 eaglet igloo begging agate magnetic ergo aghast suggest rugged Uganda

13 flogging ague yoga organ argot bargain

-gz- 14 exist exam example exact exhibit exempt exit[2] exile[2] luxu-ry[2] 'lʌgzərɪ

15 luxŭ-rious lʌg'zurɪəs

Final g

16 league fatigue big twig fig beg Meg leg bag drag sag berg=burgh

17 bug lug shrug tug jug hug fugue fog log bog dog Hague brogue

PAIRS OF WORDS FOR COMPARISON OF k WITH g

Initial		Medial		Final	
18a keys	— geezer	18b Meeker	— meager= meagre	18c leak=leek	— league
19a kilt	— guilt	19b Ricka	— rigger	19c tick	— dig
20a kept	— get	20b wrecker	— reggae	20c heck	— egg
21a cram	— gram	21b wracking	— ragging	21c back	— bag
22a clãss	— grãss	22b -----	-----	22c -----	-----
23a curl	— girl	23b worker	— burger	23c Burke	— burg
24a calo-ric	— galore	24b accost	— aghãst	24c -----	-----
25a cut	— gut	25b tucking	— tugging	25c buck	— bug
26a coon	— goon	26b palooka	— beluga	26c Dubuque	— a fugue
27a could	— good	27b bookie	— boogie	27c -----	-----
28a cod	— God	28b locking	— logging	28c dock	— dog
29a Kava	— guava	29b -----	-----	29c -----	-----

PAIRS OF WORDS FOR COMPARISON OF *k* WITH *g*, Cont.

Initial		Medial		Final	
1a cave	— gave	1b Aiken	—Fagin	1c ache	— Hague
2a Kyle	— guile	2b biker	— tiger	2c -----	-----
3a coin	— groin	3b troika	— Sheboygan	3c -----	-----
4a coat	— goat	4b Okie	— hoagy	4c broke	— brogue
5a crouch	— grouch	5b -----	-----	5c -----	-----
6a Kier	— gear	6b -----	-----	6c -----	-----
7a Cǎ-ry	— Gǎ-ry	7b -----	-----	7c -----	-----
8a Coors	— gourd	8b -----	-----	8c -----	-----
9a core	— gore	9b porky	— Porgy	9c pork	— Borg
10a card	— guard	10b Marco	— Margo	10c -----	-----

WORDS FOR PRACTICE USING A *LIGHTLY* ASPIRATED k^h BETWEEN TWO VOWEL SOUNDS, WHERE THE SECOND VOWEL SOUND IS IN AN UNSTRESSED SYLLABLE

11 seeker seeking leaky picker picking wrecker Becky packer packing tobacco

12 tacky lurking looking rookie locker locking rocky raking rakish joker joking

EXERCISES FOR COMPARING ASPIRATED k^h WITH UNASPIRATED $k_,$

k^h	k^h	$k_,$		k^h	k^h	$k_,$
13 pick	pickax	picture	21 hack	hacking	hacked
14 lock	locker	lockjaw	22 track	trackage	trackless
15 pick	picket	picnic	23 hack	hack it	hack cab
16 back	backache	backstrap	24 look	look out	look closely
17 arc	arcade	arctic	25 Jack	Jack N.	Jack Kenny
18 heck	Hecate	heckler	26 week	weekend	week day
19 knack	academe	acne	27 hick	hiccough	hick town
20 lack	lackey	lax=lacks	28 look	look up	look good

EXERCISES FOR DISTINGUISHING BETWEEN ASPIRATED k^h AND UNASPIRATED $k_,$

29 Look closely from the lookout nook.

30 Who could collect the trash from dark alleys on dark nights?

31 Work up to a workless weekend ăfter work-filled weekdays.

32 Could you stage a rock opera in a rock garden?

33 Can we cook chick peas with the chicken at the cookout in Cook County?

SENTENCES FOR PRACTICE USING SAME-CONSONANT BLENDS

✓ *Reminder*

Maintain the contact of the back of your tongue with the soft palate during the following same-consonant blend sequences. Clarity of enunciation is achieved by a fresh impulse of energy that begins the second word of each sequence.

34 Walk carefully or you'll kick cobbles onto those black cases of corn.

35 Look closely at the slick courtyard, Jack Kenny, before you park cars in it.

36 I beg God to give that big girl a major-league gallĕ-ry.

SENTENCES FOR PRACTICE USING COGNATE BLENDS

✓ *Reminder* —————————————————————————————————

Maintain the contact of the back of your tongue with the soft palate during the following cognate blend sequences. Clarity of enunciation is achieved by the change from voiced to voiceless or voiceless to voiced and by a fresh impulse of energy that begins the second word in each sequence.

1 Under a big coat he wore a dog collar into the log cabin.
2 Make Guy take Gay to the track gate in a big car.

PAIRS OF WORDS FOR COMPARISON OF k, s WITH gz

k, s	gz	k, s	gz	k, s	gz
3 "x"	— eggs	8 except	— exempt	13 exhale	— exhaust
4 execute	— executive	9 exarch	— exact	14 exhibition	— exhibitive
5 exhibition	— exhibit	10 excuse	— executo-ry	15 extrude	— exude
6 exCERPT (v)	— exert	11 exegetic	— exempt	16 Texas	— exact
7 elixir	— Alexander	12 exercise	— exert	17 exile[2]	— exile[2]

SENTENCES FOR PRACTICE USING CONTRASTING SOUNDS

18 The Texas eggs are, without exception, carefully examined.
19 Exert yourself when you exercise, even though exertion is exhausting.
20 Brandy Alexanders are magical elixirs!
21 Quickly execute your exercises. Inhale and exhale to relieve exhaustion.
22 Examine each excuse before you see the executive from Texas.

WORDS FOR PRACTICE USING CONSONANT COMBINATIONS

Initial k

✓ *Reminder* —————————————————————————————————

Blend the stop-plosive and the consonant in the following combinations.

k, w - 23 queen quit question quack quaff quirk qua-rrel quite quoits quote queer

k, l - 24 cleave click cleft clan class clerk clung clew=clue claw cloth clay
25 climb cloy clove cloud clear Clare McClure Clark=clerk (Brit)

k, r - 26 cream crisp crept crab craft crush crude crook crawl cross crane cry
27 Croydon crow crowd

Medial k

✓ *Reminder* —————————————————————————————————

Observe the unaspirated   in the following combinations.

- k, w - 28 bequeath acquit aquatic disqualify acquaint disquiet requite require

- k, t - 29 shrieked licked connect exact worked rebuked cooked gawked locked
30 ached   liked soaked parked

- k, t - 31 cha-racter pectin actor conductor doctor

WORDS FOR PRACTICE USING CONSONANT COMBINATIONS, Cont.

−*k,s* 1 creaks=creeks hicks=Hix checks=cheques=Czechs tacks=tax works ducks
2 crooks hawks rocks aches Ike's oaks forks Marx=marks larks

−*k,t,s* 3 conflicts subjects acts products instructs conducts

−*sk,s* 4 (wh)isks risks desks ásks básks tusks husks

−*sk,t* 5 (wh)isked frisked másked básked musked

−*ŋk,t* 6 inked pinked blinked banked flanked

−*ŋk,t/ə* 7 juncture puncture tincture

−*ŋk,s* 8 inks blinks banks flanks hunks drunks honks Bronx

−*k̂ən* 9 weaken chicken slacken awaken liken=lichen harken

−*k̂ənd* 10 weakened quickened blackened awakened likened darkened

−*k̂ənz* 11 weakens quickens blackens wakens likens tokens harkens

−*k,l* 12 pickle freckle cackle circle classical buckle local McCorkle sparkle

−*k,ld* 13 tickled heckled cackled circled buckled sparkled

−*k,lz* 14 tickles speckles tackles circles spectacles buckles

Final *k*

−*lk* 15 ilk milk silk elk talc bulk sulk skulk hulk

−*ŋk* 16 ink wink drink bank thank monk sunk drunk trunk honk

Initial *g*

✓ *Reminder* ───────────────────────────────────────

Blend *gl*- **and** *gr*- .

gl- 17 glee glib glad glánce glutton gloomy glȯ-ry gloss glaze glide glow glower

gr- 18 green grit Greta grapple grásp grub gruff group groggy gray grime
19 groin groan growl Grier

Medial *g*

−*g*- 20 regal rigged rigging Rigoletto begged begging nagged nagging navigation
21 hugged logged

−*gz*- 22 exhibit exist exempt exact exert exude exhaust auxiliá-ry

✓ *Reminder* ───────────────────────────────────────

Syllabic *l* **takes the place of a vowel in forming certain** UN**stressed** SYLLABLES, **usually at the ends of words. (See pages 250-251.)**

−*gl* 23 eagle giggle haggle bugle joggle juggle gargle argol=argal

−*gld* 24 giggled haggled bedraggled burgled struggled boggled gargled

WORDS FOR PRACTICE USING CONSONANT COMBINATIONS, Cont.

$-g\ell z$ 1 eagles beagles giggles juggles bugles joggles gargles

$-\eta g\ell d$ 2 mingled shingled angled dangled <u>wr</u>angled bungled

✓ *Reminder*

Carry your voice through each vibrated ending without adding an off-glide.

$-g z$ 3 leagues fatigues digs figs eggs begs <u>dr</u>egs bags <u>dr</u>ags sags mugs bugs
4 fugues bogs dogs catalogs=catalogues <u>Cr</u>aig's Hague's=Haig's <u>r</u>ogues Vogue's

SENTENCES FOR PRACTICE USING k AND g

5 Keep the cod cool until you cook it in this cást-metal cooker.
6 Can you keep cool with kith and kin?
7 Kelly could connect with kinematics.
8 Lock the key to the cash bank in the back corner.
9 Look, <u>Br</u>ooks, stick the backpacks in the keel.

10 Gag the gurgling gargoyle in the gallè-<u>ry</u>, garçon!
11 The galliard invokes <u>gr</u>ace and gallant<u>ry</u>.
12 A golden goose gives big eggs.
13 Getting cable into the gable was a big tásk.

14 The luxú-<u>ry</u>² of the auxiliá-<u>ry</u> guild was engaging.
15 Pick ché-<u>rries</u> for the actual picture, please.
16 Legg's on Lexington Avenue is elegant and has an excellent selection.
17 Could you collect the checks at the chess club this week?
18 <u>R</u>icka fixes an excellent egg bisque with black figs.
19 Mr. Fuchs has invoked a fugue.

SENTENCES FOR PRACTICE USING k, s AND $g z$ IN FINAL POSITION

✓ *Reminder*

Keep the following voiceless consonant endings crisp and clean.

20 Thanks to the networks for the skin flicks.
21 It looks like setbacks in the talks will occur.
22 She seeks parks in the Adí-<u>r</u>ondacks or the Ozarks.
23 Will banks overlook mistakes in checkbooks?

✓ *Reminder*

Carry your voice through each voiced consonant ending without adding an off-glide.

24 Are these hot hogs or hot dogs?
25 Who jogs in wooden clogs?
26 Could you <u>br</u>ing bags of <u>r</u>ags and some mugs?
27 Jet lag's a d<u>r</u>ag!

SENTENCES FOR PRACTICE USING SIMILAR CONSONANT COMBINATIONS

✓ *Reminder* ————————————————————————————————————

Observe the DIFFERENCES between *k,s* , *k,t* **and** *k,t,s* .

1 The flax, in fact, was fleckless.
2 Fax the facts across to the Atlantic faction.
3 He expects to inspect the specs di-rectly.
4 You've risked your wrists!
5 The Texas texts are effective for the next sects.
6 FLEX reflects product perfection.
7 Dix's predictions were ridiculous!
8 "Has Saks axed Max?" asked Mack.

$t\int$ *ch*in

$dз$ *g*in

AFFRICATES

The affricates are part of the plosive family of sounds. An affricate is a combination of a stop-plosive and a fricative that have blended together to make one sound. An affricate is articulated as a stop that is then followed by a release into a fricative sound; however, the blend of consonants is heard and felt as ONE SOUND.

There is one pair of cognates in Spoken English that is created in this way. Cognates are two consonant sounds related by being produced in the SAME PLACE of articulation, in the SAME MANNER of articulation, with one of the pair VOICELESS (vs) and the other VOICED (vd).

The affricate consonant sounds are made in the following places of articulation:

PLACE IV-A (ALVEOLAR) The tip of the tongue touches the upper gum ridge:

blended into

PLACE IV-B (ALVEOLAR) The tip of the tongue points toward the gum ridge; it does NOT touch the middle of the upper gum ridge:

$t\int$

(vs)   **ch**in   lee**ch**es   ba**tch**

$d\zeta$

(vd)   **g**in   le**g**ion   ba**dg**e

◆ THE AFFRICATE CONSONANTS ◆
$t_{,}\int$ AS IN "*ch*in" AND $d_{\mathfrak{Z}}$ AS IN "*g*in"

THE PLACE IV-A VOICELESS AFFRICATE CONSONANT SOUND: $t_{,}\int$ **as in "*ch*in."**

Represented by the spellings:

*ch*eese *c*ello ki*tch*en na*t*ure

THE PLACE IV-A VOICED AFFRICATE CONSONANT SOUND: $d_{\mathfrak{Z}}$ **as in "*g*in."**

Represented by the spellings:

*J*une *g*entlemen sol*d*ier *j*u*dg*e reli*g*ion exa*gg*erate

Allow your lower jaw to hang relaxed so that your upper and lower teeth practically touch. Blend the tip-of-the-tongue stop-plosive with the fricative so that the individual identity of both sounds is lost and one single new sound is heard.

Avoid using these two affricate sounds when speaking $t_{,\mathbf{j}}$ and $d_{\mathbf{j}}$ combinations. Use a cleanly articulated combination of a stop-plosive and the consonant j . (See page 308 for details and page 312, numbers 21-28.)

$t_{,\mathbf{j}}$	$t_{,\mathbf{j}}$	$t_{,\mathbf{j}}$
SAY: can't you	SAY: won't you	SAY: don't you
NOT: "can chew"	NOT: "won chew"	NOT: "don chew"
$d_{\mathbf{j}}$	$d_{\mathbf{j}}$	$d_{\mathbf{j}}$
SAY: could you	SAY: would you	SAY: did you
NOT: "could jōō"	NOT: "would jōō"	NOT: "did jōō"

WORDS FOR PRACTICE

Initial $t_{,}\int$

$t_{,}\int -$

1 cheat cheese chit chin chess check=cheque chat chap chȧnt chȧnce
2 church chirp chuck chubby chew choose chalk chaw chop chocolate
3 cha cha chain chase chime chide choice chose choke chow chowder
4 cheer chair chore chart

Medial $t_{,}\int$

$-nt_{,}\int t^{\iota}$ 5 inched pinched <u>wr</u>enched <u>r</u>anched lunched hunched bunched launched

$-t_{,}\int t^{\iota}$ 6 bleached <u>pr</u>eached pitched ditched etched sketched hatched thatched
7 perched besmirched clutched watched botched scorched arched

$-k_{,}t_{,}\int u-$ 8 actual factual actually $'\mathbf{æ}k_{,}t_{,}\int u\partial l$ $'\mathbf{æ}k_{,}t_{,}\int u\partial l\iota$

$-t_{,}\int\partial$ 9 culture vulture <u>r</u>apture butcher feature picture lite-<u>r</u>ature

$-k_{,}t_{,}\int\partial$ 10 fracture st<u>r</u>ucture tincture lecture <u>r</u>upture

$t_{,}\int$

$-\mathbf{s}t_{,}\int-$ 11 Christian question suggestion celestial bestial gesture tempestuous
12 gesture Sebastian pasture posture

$-k_{,}\mathbf{s}t_{,}\int\partial$ 13 mixture fixture texture

WORDS FOR PRACTICE, Cont.

Final t͡ʃ

✓*Reminder*
Keep the voiceless affricate t͡ʃ in final position crisp and clean.

-t͡ʃ
1 each breech=breach rich pitch fetch wretch stretch batch thatch catch
2 hatch search birch crutch touch Dutch scotch aitch broach=brooch
3 pouch torch arch starch march

Initial d͡ʒ

d͡ʒ-
4 Jean Jesus jiffy gyp Jeff gem Jack germ jerk Japan jump judge June
5 juice jaw Josh jolly Jay Jane gibe joy Joyce Jo=Joe jowl jeer ju-ry
6 George jargon

Medial d͡ʒ

-d͡ʒ-
7 region legion frigid rigid rejoiced Bridget fragile exagge-rate urgent
8 budget judged Eugene fugitive dodges aging raging gorgeous marginal
9 injunction grandeur

-n:d͡ʒd 10 fringed hinged avenged sponged changed ranged lounged

Final d͡ʒ

✓*Reminder*
Carry your voice through each final consonant ending without adding an off-glide.

-d͡ʒ
11 liege bridge ridge ledge hedge badge Madge urge merge surge huge
12 lodge Dodge age rage oblige Doge gouge gorge forge barge Marge

-n:d͡ʒ 13 Inge hinge singe avenge revenge sponge plunge range strange lounge
-l:d͡ʒ 14 bilge bulge indulge divulge

EXERCISES FOR COMPARING t͡s , dz , t͡ʃ ,AND d͡ʒ

t͡s	dz	t͡ʃ	d͡ʒ
15a eats	15b seeds	15c each	15d siege
16a Ritz	16b rids	16c rich	16d ridge
17a Rhett's	17b reds	17c wretch	17d dredge
18a cats	18b cads	18c catch	18d cadge
19a Bert's	19b birds	19c birch	19d Burge
20a mutts	20b muds	20c much	20d smudge
21a plots	21b plods	21c blotch	21d lodge
22a eights	22b aids	22c aitch	22d age
23a forts	23b fords	23c porch	23d forge
24a coats	24b codes	24c coach	24d cogent

SENTENCES FOR PRACTICE USING SAME-CONSONANT BLENDS

✓ *Reminder*

> Your articulators WILL move slightly during the following same-consonant blend sequences. Articulate swiftly and efficiently.

1 Which child chose to pitch che-rries into the Dutch chocolate?
2 Switch chairs as each check is delivered.
3 My liege, just don't judge George for his somewhat savage joy.
4 Oblige Jean with a huge juice and some po-rridge, Jessie.

SENTENCE FOR PRACTICE USING COGNATE BLENDS

✓ *Reminder*

> Your articulators WILL move slightly during the following cognate blend sequences. Articulate swiftly and efficiently.

5 My liege, choose not the large chicken nor the strange Chinese o-range chowder.

WORDS FOR COMPARISON OF $t\!\!\int$, d_3 **AND** $\int$
Initial

$t\!\!\int$	d_3	$\int$
6a cheek	6b jeep	6c chic
7a cheese	7b "jeez"	7c she's
8a chin	8b gin	8c shin
9a chill	9b Jill	9c shill
10a Chet	10b jet	10c Shetland
11a che-rry	11b Je-rry	11c she-rry
12a chapel	12b Japanese	12c chape-rone
13a chant	13b -----	13c shan't
14a church	14b jerk	14c shirk
15a Chuck	15b juxtapose	15c shuck
16a choose	16b Jews	16c shoes
17a chaw	17b jaw	17c Shaw
18a chop	18b Joplin	18c shop
19a cha cha	19b java	19c shah
20a chain	20b Jane	20c Shane
21a chives	21b jives=gyves	21c shies
22a choice	22b Joyce	22c -----
23a chose	23b Joe's	23c shows
24a chow	24b jounce	24c shower
25a cheer	25b jeer	25c sheer=shear
26a chair	26b -----	26c share
27a premature	27b ju-ry	27c sure
28a chore	28b George	28c shore
29a char	29b jar	29c charlatan

WORDS FOR COMPARISON OF $t,\int$ **,** $d\zeta$ **AND** $\int$ **, Cont.**

Final

$t,\int$	$d\zeta$	$\int$
1a leach	1b liege	1c leash
2a ditch	2b adage	2c dish
3a etch	3b edge	3c crèche
4a match	4b Madge	4c mash
5a search	5b surge	5c Hirsch
6a lunch	6b lunge	6c lush
7a smooch	7b Scrooge	7c ruche
8a butch	8b noodge	8c bush
9a botch	9b lodge	9c bosh
10a aitch	10b age	10c -----
11a coach	11b doge	11c gauche
12a porch	12b gorge	12c Porsche
13a march	13b Marge	13c marsh

SENTENCES FOR PRACTICE USING $t,\int$ **IN INITIAL, MEDIAL AND FINAL POSITION**

14 Are the chowder, cheese and chocolate on the cheque? Please check.
15 Make a choice to che-rish challenges.
16 Cheap chains kept the chickens in check.
17 Chop these choice chives before you chill them with the chick peas.
18 "Chat with Cheeta," chided Chester to Che-rry.

19 Did you choose to charcoal broil the cheeseburgers on a hibachi?
20 Actually, achievements are a mixture of questions and rapture.
21 The lite-rature featured pictures of the etchings.
22 The actual information was factual.

23 Can we search a-round the arch for my watch in the pitch black?
24 The sun scorched and bleached long stretches of the benches.
25 We pitched our tent, found our perch and then watched the chicks.
26 Charlie's a cinch to help out in a pinch.

SENTENCES FOR PRACTICE USING $d\zeta$ **IN INITIAL, MEDIAL AND FINAL POSITION**

27 Give the juice to Josh, the jelly to Jane and the jargon to George.
28 Jeannie's jumpy about germs.
29 Joe just jabbed Jasper? Surely you jest!
30 Jonathan justified the journey to Jordan with jocosity.
31 Does jogging jostle and jiggle your jaw?

32 The Jacobean drama divulged judgements and injunctions through jests and jibes.
33 Jot down your messages about your budget in the margins of your journal.
34 Don't you badger the lodger into gorging on po-rridge.
35 Take the plunge! Indulge your urges and imagination.

SENTENCES FOR PRACTICE USING $dʒ$ IN INITIAL, MEDIAL AND FINAL POSITION, Cont.

1 That huge o-range looks strange, Marge.
2 Oblige me and meet on the bridge and not in the lounge.
3 Call it revenge, but I urge you to discharge that liege.

SENTENCES FOR COMPARISON OF $t,ʃ$ WITH $dʒ$

4 Who chose Joe over Che-rry and Je-rry to congratulate the graduates? $kˆən 'græt,ʃə leitˋ$
5 Jello on my cello! I'll choke you for that joke!
6 It's your choice, Joyce. But you'd be a chump not to jump at this chance.

7 Re-do the edging a-round the etching, then note it in the ledger for Mr. Boetcher.
8 Three merchants are merging. They're rejoicing on Orchard Street.

9 Burn your breeches on the bridges? Will you also burn several batches of badges?
10 I've a hunch we'll lunge into Inge right after lunch.

SENTENCES FOR COMPARISON OF $t,ʃ$, $dʒ$ AND $ʃ$

11 Chug a jug of java before you cha cha with the Shah.
12 I visited the chapel in Japan with a chape-rone.
13 Only a jerk would shirk his duty at the church!
14 Does Je-rry always take his she-rry with a che-rry?
15 Chet wants to take his shetland on the jet?
16 Give Ge-rald his fair share of the chair.
17 Chow down on the chowder before you jounce in the shower.
18 I got chucked on the chin and the shin. I need gin!

19 That dish has a sharp edge, Mr. Leach.
20 Dropping your aitches at your age sounds old-maidish.
21 Coolidge's pooch seemed ghoulish.
22 I've a clear image of the spinach dish.
23 I finished the reSEARCH in a surge, a gigantic flou-rish!
24 The wretch went over the edge in Bangladesh.
25 Hush up, you Dutchman; keep on with the drudge-ry.
26 In my imagination, I saw the dishwasher in the ditch.
27 Oh hush! Is nurtu-ring always an emergency with you?

m **m**y

n **n**o=**kn**ow

$ŋ$ si**ng**

NASAL CONTINUANT CONSONANT SOUNDS

Nasal continuant consonants are the ONLY sounds in Spoken English that are made with the soft palate in a relaxed and lowered position. All other consonant sounds, and every vowel and diphthong sound in Spoken English, are made with the soft palate in a raised or lifted position. The lowered position for the three nasal continuant consonant sounds allows the vibrated breath to exit through and resonate in the nasal passages.

Good nasal resonance of the three nasal continuants m , n and η is an essential element of the whole resonating system. These sonorous and musically rich consonants are needed to promote beautiful and balanced resonance in the voice. Both m and n rank among the ten most frequently used consonants in Spoken English.

The three voiced nasal continuant consonant sounds do not have voiceless cognates or partners in Spoken English.

It is crucial that the lower jaw and tongue be relaxed during the production of these three sounds, even though the tip of the tongue is raised for n , the back raised for η and the lips are touching for m . Unnecessary tension in ANY of the articulators will impede vibration and reduce the fullness of these sounds.

The nasal continuant consonant sounds are made in the following places of articulation:

Place I	(BILABIAL)	The two lips articulate against each other:		
m	(vd)	**my**	swi**mm**ing	hy**mn**

Place IV-A	(ALVEOLAR)	The tip of the tongue touches the gum ridge directly behind the upper front teeth:		
n	(vd)	**kn**ow=**n**o	fi**n**al	bo**n**e

Place VI	(VELAR)	The back of the tongue articulates against the soft palate:		
η	(vd)	-----	si**n**k	si**ng**

η does not occur in initial position in Spoken English.

Nasal Plosion

Nasal plosion, sometimes called implosion, occurs when a stop-plosive is followed by a nasal consonant and the nasal is made in the same place of articulation as the stop-plosive. Since the position of the articulators does not change between the unaspirated stop and the nasal, the articulation is carried out by the action of the soft palate, which relaxes to release the breath stream through the nose:

p m	*b m*	*t, n*	*d n*
topmost	subma-rine	beatnik	madness
		* beaten	* madden
		* patent	* wouldn't
stop me	Bob moved	great need	bad news

* Each of these four words, which end with an unstressed syllable that lacks a vowel sound, contains the syllabic consonant n . The consonant n , which has taken the place of a vowel sound in forming the weak syllable, is called a SYLLABIC CONSONANT.

There is partial nasal plosion or implosion in sequences between two consonants that are NOT made in the same place of articulation:

p,n	bn	t,m	dm	k,m	gm
hypnotic	hobnob	Pittman	bedmate	<u>R</u>ickman	pi<u>g</u>ment
top notes	Bob knelt	get moving	good move	picnic	dignity

However, since these implosions are only partial, the terms nasal plosion and implosion are used in this textbook only for the sequences: p,m bm t,n dn

In Spoken English the consonants m and n may be syllabic in such words as:

$'æn\theta m$	$'rI\eth m$	$'he\ roŭizm$	$'blɒsm$	$'p,rIzm$	$'spæzm$
anthem	<u>rh</u>ythm	he-<u>r</u>oism	blossom	prism	spasm

$'fæʃn$	$'hi:\eth n$	$'ɒrəzn$	$'meIʌn$	$'p,rIzn$	$'ʌvn$
fashion	heathen	o-<u>r</u>ison	mason	prison	oven

The nasal continuants m , n and η , like all continuants in Spoken English, are subject to lengthening. Consonant sounds are notated ONLY short or long; there is no half-long. These three consonant sounds are LONG when they are found in the LAST syllable of a word, provided that is a STRESSED syllable:

— Before another voiced consonant: $'k,raĭm:z$ $'el:m:z$ $'fren:d$ $bi'lɒŋ:z$

                                     c<u>r</u>imes   elms   f<u>r</u>iend   belongs

— The last sound of a word when it comes after one of the short vowel sounds:

                                 $kən'dem:$ $'men:$ $bi'lɒŋ:$

                                 condemn   men   belong

THE PLACE I VOICED BILABIAL NASAL CONTINUANT CONSONANT SOUND: m **as in "me."**

Represented by the spellings:

me su**mm**er hy**mn** to**mb** phle**gm** pa**lm** Ba**n**ff

This consonant sound does not have a voiceless partner in Spoken English.

Bring your lips gently together. Allow your lower jaw to hang relaxed and your tongue to be released on the floor of your mouth, with the tip gently resting behind the lower front teeth. Your SOFT PALATE IS LOWERED, and the vibrated breath resonates within the nasal passages. The resonance and vibration of m is also felt on the lips. Unnecessary tension in the region of the soft palate or the nostrils will produce an undesirably metallic and constricted sound.

A well-produced m is sonorous and musical; it promotes beautiful and balanced resonance of your voice, and melody and richness of your speech.

When m is in final position of a word before a pause, allow your lips to remain in contact with each other until you have finished the breath, to avoid adding an off-glide. For instance, with the word "hum," say "hummm," not "hum-uh." $m^{ə}$

This consonant may be syllabic, m ; it may take the place of a weak vowel in certain unstressed, and often final, syllables, as in "rhythm."

✓*Reminder* ─────────────────────────────────────

> **Nasal plosion occurs when a stop-plosive is followed by a nasal consonant, and the nasal is made in the same place of articulation as the stop-plosive, as in "topmost."**

WORDS FOR PRACTICE

Initial m

m -
1 me meet=mete=meat mean Minnie men many mention man mandate master
2 mask mermaid Merv mercy murder murmur murmu-rer money mull moon
3 mood mute maw maul=mall memo-rial mop mom monsoon mamma may
4 my moi-e-ty moist Moe=mow moan mound mere mare=mayor moor
5 more mar mire

Medial m

- m -
6 schemer timber chimney member lemon lemming Thames (England) ˈtʰemːz bamboo
7 firmer summer roomer=rumor maiming diamond foaming former harmony

Final m

✓*Reminder* ─────────────────────────────────────

> **Carry your voice through each vibrated consonant ending without adding an off-glide.**

- m
8 beam team=teem deem theme gleam seem=seam scheme ream stream cream
9 Tim dim se-raphim Kim Jim=gym rim him=hymn (wh)m slim scrim prim

10 phlegm gem them (sf) hem stem condemn

11 Pam BAM tam damn=dam cam gam ram ham ma'am lamb sham Sam swam

12 perm term derm germ firm squirm worm

WORDS FOR PRACTICE, Cont.

Final m

1 album atom Adam wisdom hokum aluminum² column some (wf)
2 fŏ-rum Dŭ-rham Peachum

3 bum dumb come gum thumb numb sum=some (sf) rum

4 boom tomb doom loom room=rheum zoom whom

5 spume costume legume Hume illume² fume consume exhume

6 bomb Tom mom

7 palm balm calm psalm (These words are spoken with no l sound.) Vietnam

8 aim tame dame came game maim=Mame same lame shame

9 I'm time=thyme dime climb crime chime lime mime

10 dome comb foam loam gnome=Nome roam=Rome

11 storm dorm norm form warm swarm

12 charm harm swarm farm alarm

WORDS FOR COMPARISON OF b **WITH** m **FOR AWARENESS OF NASAL RESONANCE**

Initial		Medial		Final	
13a be	— me	13b Reba	— reamer	13c glebe	— gleam
14a bean	— mean	14b Thebes	— themes	14c Antibes	— team
15a bit	— mitt	15b dibber	— dimmer	15c rib	— rim
16a bet	— met	16b Deb's	— Thames	16c deb	— condemn
17a bat	— mat	17b crabbing	— cramming	17c crab	— cram
18a bad	— mad	18b rabble	— ramble	18c dab	— dam=damn
19a batch	— match	19b jabbing	— jamming	19c cab	— cam
20a burr	— myrrh	20b Durban	— derma	20c disturb	— term
21a bud	— mud	21b dubbing	— dummy	21c rub	— rum
22a buck	— muck	22b Bubba	— bummer	22c hub	— hum
23a butter	— mutter	23b tubby	— tummy	23c tub	— tum
24a butte	— mute	24b tuber	— tumor	24c tube	— costume
25a boo	— moo	25b booboo	— muu-muu	25c rube	— room
26a bawd	— Maud	26b -----	-----	26c -----	-----
27a bawl	— maul	27b -----	-----	27c -----	-----
28a Bob	— mob	28b Bobby	— mommy	28c Bob	— bomb

WORDS FOR COMPARISON OF *b* **WITH** *m* **, Cont.**

Initial		Medial		Final	
1a bay	— may	1b Abie	— aiming	1c babe	— blame
2a buy=by	— my	2b briber	— rimer=rhymer	2c jibe	— chime
3a boist	— moist	3b foible	— Pacoima	3c -----	-----
4a bode	— mode	4b phobia	— foamier	4c lobe	— loam
5a bound	— mound	5b -----	-----	5c -----	-----
6a beer=bier	— mere	6b -----	-----	6c -----	-----
7a bare=bear	— mare	7b airborn	— Palermo	7c -----	-----
8a boor	— moor	8b -----	-----	8c -----	-----
9a bore=boar	— more	9b Forbes	— forms	9c orb	— form
10a bar	— mar	10b Farber	— farmer	10c barb	— harm

CONSONANT COMBINATIONS

-mpʰ 11 imp limp primp hemp camp champ clamp scamp lump hump plump pomp
12 swamp

-mp,s 13 imps scrimps blimps glimpse hemps Kemps amps lamps revamps slumps
14 chumps jumps rumps stomps romps chomps

-mp,tʰ 15 skimped attempt contempt camped vamped bumped slumped prompt romped

-mf 16 lymph nymph Banff amphitheater triumph galumph

-mfs 17 lymphs nymphs Banff's triumphs galumphs

✔ *Reminder*

Carry your voice through each vibrated consonant ending without adding an off-glide.

-m:d 18 deemed esteemed trimmed skimmed condemned hemmed jammed
19 diagrammed squirmed termed hummed strummed doomed resumed bombed
20 famed flamed chimed rhymed foamed roamed reformed performed harmed armed

-m:z 21 deems schemes dreams creams limbs hymns gems hems hams jams exams
22 terms thumbs comes crumbs drums booms glooms plumes assumes psalms
23 qualms claims climbs limes chimes homes roams forms storms arms alarms

-l:m 24 film elm helm overwhelm realm

-lm:z 25 films elms helms overwhelms realms

-lm:d 26 filmed overwhelmed

-tʰəm 27 atom phantom symptom custom bottom accustom

-dəm 28 random Adam macadam wisdom Wyndham madam=madame

-ləm 29 column bedlam emblem problem McCallum solemn slalom

WORDS FOR PRACTICE USING SYLLABIC 𝓂̦

✓ *Reminder*

Syllabic 𝓂̦ takes the place of a vowel in forming certain UNstressed SYLLABLES, usually at the ends of words.

-θ𝓂̦ 1 anthem

-ð𝓂̦ 2 rhythm fathom loga-rithm

-s𝓂̦ 3 blossom balsam transom ransom flotsam jetsam hansom=handsome Epsom

-z𝓂̦ 4 bosom spasm truism he-roism atheism manne-rism Buddhism Judaism Methodism

5 malapropism Catholicism criticism witticism baptism patriotism prism chasm

6 enthusiasm sarcasm barba-rism journalism egotism idealism spasm

WORDS FOR PRACTICE USING NASAL PLOSION

✓ *Reminder*

Nasal plosion occurs when a stop-plosive is followed by a nasal consonant and the nasal is made in the same place of articulation as the stop-plosive.

-p̦𝓂- 7 topmost topmast topman stepmother

-b̦𝓂- 8 submit submerge subma-rine cabman

SENTENCES FOR PRACTICE USING SAME-CONSONANT BLENDS

✓ *Reminder*

Maintain the contact of your lips during the following same-consonant blend sequences. Clarity of enunciation is achieved by a fresh impulse of energy that begins the second word of the sequence.

9 Pam mentioned the exam might be in the AM, Monday.
10 How many dim moments made up Sam Mann's home movies?
11 The tram moved like warm molasses up the calm mountainside.
12 Come, Mimi, climb mountains and swim many streams.
13 Some mention of a firm mandate made Tom murmur.

SENTENCES FOR PRACTICE

14 Mamma may meet me in Miami by moonlight.
15 Do you mean for me to mind the many miming maniacs?
16 He's scheming for an undreamed-of sum.
17 Remember my mommy and her dreams of home.
18 Moisture makes the magnolias bloom in the me-rry month of May.
19 The hymns and psalms are calming.
20 Much mischief was made by many men into much mise-ry.
21 The Ame-rican Ambassador marched in a magnificent uniform.
22 Steam the plump shrimps and warm the molasses.
23 A glimpse of the nymph's triumphs prompted alarms.

SENTENCES FOR PRACTICE, Cont.

 1 She deemed it necessa-ry to come to terms with the reforms.
 2 The programs affirmed calm and were welcomed.
 3 Eames assumes the exams will overwhelm him!
 4 Can you fathom more rhythm for the anthem?
 5 The random atoms seemed to make phantom symptoms.
 6 Enthusiasm flamed her metabolism and slimmed her frame.
 7 Are you accustomed to criticism? Does sarcasm overwhelm you?
 8 Removing the emblem along the column was a problem.

SENTENCES FOR PRACTICE USING NASAL PLOSIONS p, m AND b m

 9 It was of the utmost importance for me to stop my submissiveness.
10 I hope moving was the topmost prio-rity to Mr. Liebman.
11 Was it a figment of my imagination, or did Bob make a submission this morning?
12 Club members must submit moneys to Bob Murphy.
13 The subma-rine will submerge at the right moment.
14 Club Med will help stop me from isolating myself.

THE PLACE IV-A VOICED ALVEOLAR NASAL CONTINUANT CONSONANT SOUND: *n* as in *"no."*

Represented by the spellings:

     *no=kno*w=*N*oh   ru*nn*ing   **m***n*emo*n*ic   **p***n*eumo*n*ia

     *gn*ome=*N*ome   rei*gn*=rai*n*=rei*n*

Allow your lower jaw to hang relaxed, and your soft palate to be RELAXED AND LOWERED; the tip of your tongue should touch the gum ridge directly behind your upper front teeth. The vibrated breath resonates within the nasal passages and is also felt where the tongue-tip touches the gum ridge.

When *n* is in final position of a word before a pause, maintain contact between the articulators until you have finished the breath, to avoid adding an off-glide. For instance, with the word "<u>r</u>un," say "<u>r</u>unnn," not "<u>r</u>un-uh." *n*ᵊ

This consonant is syllabic — *n̩* — when it takes the place of a weak vowel in an unstressed, and often final, syllable, as in "<u>wr</u>itten." (See page 208, numbers 3-4.)

✔*Reminder* ——————————————————————————————

> Nasal plosion occurs when a stop-plosive is followed by a nasal consonant and the nasal is made in the same place of articulation as the stop-plosive, as in "midnight." (See page 211, numbers 21-29 and page 212 numbers 1-3 and 26-34.)

WORDS FOR PRACTICE

Initial *n*

n –

1 knee need=knead kneel=Neal=Neil neat=neet Nimes Nim nimble knit net
2 Ned neck Neff never Nash=gnash Nancy nap gnat knack nă-<u>rr</u>ow năsty
3 nerve Napoleon nurse numb nun=none null noŭ-<u>r</u>ish noodle noose
4 new=knew Nobel notô-<u>r</u>ious gnaw not knowledge anon nay knave knives
5 Nile noise know=no=Noh now near ne'er nă-<u>r</u>y normal gnarled

Medial *n*

6 sinner penny Benny Annie Shanley Werner money sooner bonny
7 waning (wh)ining owning c<u>r</u>owning announce aŭnt plănt advănce ănswer

Final *n*

✔*Reminder* ——————————————————————————————

> Carry your voice through each vibrated consonant ending without adding an off glide.

– *n*

8 e'en=ean bean fourteen Dean keen mean seen sheen se-<u>r</u>éne
9 pin bin=been tin din kin fin sin shin (wh)im win chin gin
10 pen ben ten den men Len fen then (wh)en yen
11 Ann=Anne pan ban tan Dan can (sf) began man Nan fan van than (sf)
12 earn=urn burn turn=tern Kern fern Lucerne learn Ahearn churn

Final *n*

13 open turban Lenten London omen Lennon Ellen Quinlan he-<u>r</u>ŏn
14 pun bun ton done=dun gun Munn none=nun fun sun=son Hun won=one
15 pawn dawn lawn fawn=faun d<u>r</u>awn Shawn
16 upon anon wan swan shone (British)
17 Kahn

WORDS FOR PRACTICE, Cont.

1 pane=pain bane ta'en Dane cane gain main inane lane chain Jane
2 fain vane=vain Thane sane insane rain=reign=rein
3 pine tine dine thine sign=sine shine Rhine (wh)ne wine
4 Assiniboine coin Des Moines loin purloin join
5 own bone tone cone moan=mown known phone sewn=sown shone (American)
6 town down gown brown drown crown
7 porn born torn adorn corn acorn morn Lorne forlorn thorn warn
8 barn darn yarn

WORDS FOR COMPARISON OF d WITH n FOR AWARENESS OF NASAL RESONANCE

9a	Dee	— knee	9b	needy	— keening	9c	seed	— seen
10a	dill	— nil	10b	kidder	— sinner	10c	lid	— Lynn
11a	dead	— Ned	11b	ready	— Rennie	11c	dead	— den
12a	Dan	— Nan	12b	haddie	— handy	12c	Brad	— bran
13a	daft	— nasty	13b	-----	-----	13c	-----	-----
14a	Dirk	— nerd	14b	wordy	— Ernie	14c	curd	— Kern
15a	dub	— nub	15b	rudder	— runner	15c	dud	— done=dun
16a	doodle	— noodle	16b	Rudy	— Rooney	16c	booed	— boon
17a	daw	— gnaw	17b	audit	— awning	17c	laud	— lawn
18a	dot	— not	18b	toddy	— tonic	18c	Todd	— crouton
19a	day	— nay=neigh	19b	raiding	— raining=reigning	19c	paid	— pain=pane
20a	die=dye	— nigh	20b	Dido	— Dinah	20c	lied	— line
21a	doit	— noise	21b	avoiding	— adjoining	21c	Lloyd	— loin
22a	doe=dough	— no=know=Noh	22b	Rhoda	— Rona	22c	load	— loan=lone
23a	dow	— now	23b	dowdy	— downy	23c	endowed	— down
24a	deer=dear	— near	24b	-----	-----	24c	-----	-----
25a	dare	— ne'er	25b	-----	-----	25c	Baird	— bairn
26a	door	— nor (sf)	26b	ordain	— ornate	26c	bored=board	— born
27a	dark	— narcotic	27b	hardest	— harness	27c	card	— darn

DENTALIZED $\underset{\text{\tiny n}}{n}$

In Spoken English, the alveolar consonant sounds t , d , n and ℓ are usuall
made with the tip of the tongue touching the gum ridge directly BEHIND the upper front teeth. However, when one of the sounds is followed by θ or $\eth$, either within a word or in the next word
of a phrase, it becomes dentalized, or made with the tip of the tongue touching the back of the
upper front teeth.

The IPA diacritical mark for dentalization of a sound is placed directly underneath the phonetic
letter. This mark may be thought of as a little tooth sign underneath the letter:

$$\underset{\text{\tiny n}}{t},\qquad \underset{\text{\tiny n}}{d}\qquad \underset{\text{\tiny n}}{n}\qquad \underset{\text{\tiny n}}{\ell}\qquad\qquad\qquad \text{(See pages 267-268.)}$$

In Good Speech, dentalization occurs ONLY when these four sounds are followed by θ or $\eth$.

WORDS FOR PRACTICE USING DENTALIZED $\underset{\text{\tiny n}}{n}$ BEFORE θ

1 hyacinth Co-rinth laby-rinth month seventh ninth tenth eleventh sixteenth

2 anthem Pentheus pantheon panther Anthony Samantha lycanthropy plinth

3 hyacinths Co-rinths months fifteenths thirteenths eighteenths billionths

4 thousandth $-\underset{\text{\tiny n}}{n}\underset{\text{\tiny n}}{d}\theta$ thousandths $-\underset{\text{\tiny n}}{n}\underset{\text{\tiny n}}{d}\theta s$

CONSONANT COMBINATIONS

$-ns$ 5 since tense finance roMANCE enhance dance advanced prance once sconce
6 ounce

$-n\text{:}z$ 7 means pins pens pans earns puns moons yawns swans pains wines
8 owns crowns yarns

$-nt^h$ 9 mint meant ant aunt burnt vehement hunt haunt want paint pint
10 won't=wont point mount

$-nt,s$ 11 hints repents ants grants hunts fonts taints pints points counts

$-n\text{:}d$ 12 weaned wind mend send sand demand earned sunned mooned yawned
13 pond stained rained=reigned pined bind owned moaned pound a-round
14 found abound

$-n\text{:}dz$ 15 fiends winds ends lands demands funds wounds bonds grinds grounds

$-nt,\int$ 16 inch wrench ranch branch lunch launch

$-nt,\int t^h$ 17 pinched wrenched ranched branched launched munched

$-n\text{:}dʒd$ 18 hinged binged cringed avenged sponged lunged changed a-rranged

$-n\ell$ 19 venal annal panel funnel spinal final tonal

$-p^hən$ 20 deepen happen dampen Aspen misshapen ripen open reopen sharpen

$-bən$ 21 ribbon Lisbon Eban bourbon Reuben carbon

$-k^hən$ 22 weaken chicken blacken drunken awaken liken broken darken

$-gən$ 23 Regan wagon Volkswagen flagon ptarmigan Reagan

WORDS FOR PRACTICE USING SYLLABIC *n̩*

✓ *Reminder* ——————————————————————————————————

Syllabic *n̩* takes the place of a vowel in forming certain UNstressed SYLLABLES, usually at the ends of words.

-fn̩   1   stiffen   McGiffen   deafen   <u>r</u>oughen   toughen   often

-vn̩   2   even   uneven   Steven=Stephen   forgiven   st<u>r</u>iven   heaven   eleven   leaven   <u>r</u>aven (v)

        3   oven   p<u>r</u>oven   haven   <u>r</u>aven (n)   unshaven   enliven   Beethoven   interwoven

-sn̩   4   Gleason   decent   listen   delicatessen   Anderson   loosen   mason   Carson

-zn̩   5   <u>r</u>eason   p<u>r</u>ison   <u>r</u>isen   c<u>r</u>imson   courtesan   citizen   ô-<u>r</u>ison   dozen   cousin

        6   blazon   poison   chosen

-ʃn̩   7   addition   mission   action   <u>r</u>eaction   <u>tr</u>action   satisfaction   intə-<u>r</u>action

        8   invention   convention   mention   scansion   expansion

-ʒn̩   9   adhesion   version   aversion   invasion   persuasion   Asian   e-<u>r</u>osion   co-<u>rr</u>osion

-tʃn̩   10   kitchen   G<u>r</u>etchen   Patchen   luncheon   escutcheon   <u>tr</u>uncheon

-dʒn̩   11   collagen   ni<u>tr</u>ogen   oxygen   carcinogen   est<u>r</u>ogen   pathogen   Imogen

-dʒn̩-   12   <u>r</u>egent   <u>r</u>egency   agent   cogent

WORDS FOR PRACTICE USING NASAL PLOSIONS *t̚, n̩* AND *dn̩*

-t̚, n̩   13   Eaton=Eton   <u>wr</u>itten   mitten   smitten   th<u>r</u>eaten   fatten   Staten   flatten   Burton

        14   mutant   forgotten   cotton   <u>r</u>otten   Satan   blatant   lighten   heighten   potent

        15   potency   important   importance   hearten

-t̚, n̩-   16   beatnik   witness   Etna   wet-nurse (v)   Putney   chutney   b<u>r</u>ightness

-dn̩   17   Eden   c<u>r</u>edent   needn't   bidden   didn't   <u>r</u>idden   <u>r</u>iddance   pedant   gladden

        18   hadn't   sadden   burden   p<u>r</u>udent   student   wooden   wouldn't   couldn't   shouldn't

        19   b<u>r</u>oaden   maiden   Haydn   D<u>r</u>yden   olden   golden   <u>r</u>odent   garden   harden   ardent

-dn̩-   20   midnight   blandness   fondness   kindness   blindness   <u>r</u>oundness

        21   sadness   madness   good-natured   goodness

SENTENCES FOR PRACTICE

22   Nana's neighbo<u>r</u>s need knives for noodles.

23   Nancy has a notô:-<u>r</u>ious knack for announcements.

24   Never kneel near the Nile.

25   It's the fourteenth <u>r</u>ainy June night.

26   None of the nuns shunned <u>Rh</u>ine wine.

27   The mæ-<u>r</u>athon ə-<u>r</u>ound the pond was the main event.

28   The dænce enhænced and advænced their <u>r</u>oMANCE.

29   Heinz owns the g<u>r</u>ound ə-<u>r</u>ound the pond.

30   The winds sent the sand th<u>r</u>ough the pines.

SENTENCES FOR PRACTICE, Cont.

1 He moans *when* the nurse attends his wounds.
2 Each inch of the br*a*nch was wrenched to the ground.
3 A change in the hinge can rea-rrange the window pane.
4 Will the Aspen Open Tournament really happen?
5 Reuben found a hand-blown gl*a*ss ribbon at SteuBEN.
6 Even Steven was unshaven before eleven.
7 Can Gleason dine at Carson's Delicatessen?
8 The Volkswagen's traction's a fine bargain.
9 We gleaned with satisfaction many things from this version of the action.
10 Gretchen's luncheon contained no carcinogens.

SENTENCES FOR PRACTICE USING DENTALIZED *n* WITH θ AND ð

11 Hyacinths can be found a-round the fifteenth or eighteenth of June.
12 They'll win things *when* they intone the Panther anthem.
13 Joan thinks that the seventh or the sixteenth will be fine then.
14 Anthony, Samantha and Dan thought the town thief had been caught.

PRACTICE USING THE NASAL PLOSIONS *dn* AND *dn*

15 He found no notes of kindness.
16 The strident wind never stops.
17 Rodney is an important student.
18 He did no turns. He didn't try.   (See page 212 *dnt*ʰ.)
19 Didn't the band need Ned?
20 The wooden ones wouldn't do.
21 I dem*a*nd nothing but sudden fondness.
22 We need nine, but you needn't hu-rry.
23 You needn't get garden rodents, Gordon.
24 It's hidden now, as if you didn't know.
25 I didn't widen the wooden door. I couldn't!
26 The pedant got a tanned nose at Arden's.
27 Her sudden blindness saddened no one but the students.
28 "Goodness, it's midnight madness," he intoned good-naturedly.
29 Her fondness for grandness hadn't diminished.

SENTENCES FOR PRACTICE USING SAME-CONSONANT BLENDS

30 It had nine knees, ten noses and eleven nails.
31 Soon no one knew that Dawn needed to sin nightly.
32 Can Nancy nail the broken needles into the wooden knobs?

THE PLACE VI VOICED VELAR NASAL CONTINUANT CONSONANT SOUND: η as in "si*ng*"

Represented by the spellings:

so**ng**   thi**n**k   to**ngue**

This consonant sound occurs ONLY in medial and final position.

Allow your lower jaw to hang relaxed, your soft palate to be relaxed and LOWERED and your tongue to be released on the floor of your mouth. Raise the back of your tongue as for the sounds of k and g ; maintain contact between the back of your tongue and the lowered soft palate, while the vibrated air resonates through your nasal passages and is emitted through your nose.

When η is in final position of a word before a pause, allow the articulators to remain in contact with each other until you have finished the breath; avoid adding an off-glide. For instance, with the word "sing," say "sing," not "sing-uh." Remember that the "g" in "sing" is spoken as part of the sound. Avoid adding the sound that is known as a hard "g"; do not say "sing-guh." *sɪŋgə*

All words that end with the spelling "ng" utilize the consonant η as the final sound. These include:

— Words with the "-ing" suffix:

r̲ing r̲inging clang clanging thr̲ong thr̲onging nothing farthing being

— MOST words with the suffixes "-er," "-ster," "-ly," and "-ful":

r̲inger=wr̲inger gangster kingly wr̲ongful

The combination of ηg is spoken when:

— The comparative or superlative degree is added to adjectives such as:

long, str̲ong and young;

long + "er" is *ˈlɒŋgə*   long + "est" is *ˈlɒŋgɪst*

— Certain suffixes are added to a root word ending in "ng":

pr̲olong + "ate" is *pɪroˈlɒŋgeɪt*

diphthong + "al" is *ˈdɪfθɒŋgl*

— "ng" is medial in the root part of the word:

ηg

England English single finger language warmonger

In Spoken English, the spelling "ng" may also represent these pronunciations:

nːdʒ
r̲ange

ndʒ
inge̲st

WORDS FOR PRACTICE

Final η

✔ *Reminder* ────────────────────────────────

Carry your voice through each vibrated consonant ending without adding an off glide.

-η:

1 ping bing ming wing thing ding pang bang r̲ang me̊-r̲ingue hå-r̲angue

2 bung among tongue flung clung lung sung young hung Kong pong

3 bong thong tong dong long w̲rong str̲ong thr̲ong song gong

Medial η

-eŋθ 4 length str̲ength

NOTE: AVOID SAYING ʹle̱nθ and ʹst̠,re̱nθ

-η:d 5 winged r̲inged str̲inged hanged clanged twanged longed belonged

6 w̲ronged pr̲onged thr̲onged

-η:z 7 wings things r̲ings=w̲rings spr̲ings sings kings pangs fangs gangs hangs

8 bungs tongues lungs longs songs w̲rongs pr̲ongs thongs

-ηkʰ 9 ink link pink blink clink br̲ink dr̲ink shr̲ink bank dank hank lank r̲ank

10 blank clank cr̲ank shr̲ank punk shr̲unk tr̲unk spunk Lincoln banquet

11 anchor r̲ancor banker tanker ankle uncle donkey inked winked blinked

12 r̲anked cr̲anked planked flanked thanked

-ηk,s 13 inks sinks blinks dr̲inks shr̲inks thinks banks blanks cr̲anks monks tr̲unks

-ηk,t,s 14 instincts pr̲ecincts adjuncts

-ηk,tʃə 15 juncture puncture acupuncture conjuncture tincture

-ηk,ʃ- 16 anxious function compunction unctious

Final η

✔ *Reminder* ────────────────────────────────

Do not tense and nasalize the / in -ıη endings.

-ıη

17 Ming seeming beaming teeming dr̲eaming gleaming scheming

18 tr̲imming squirming humming coming dr̲umming dooming calming

19 aiming taming timing miming climbing homing r̲oaming charming

20 meaning sinning winning tanning manning earning turning burning cunning

21 mooning dawning fawning r̲aining=r̲eining r̲emaining gaining pining mining

22 joining owning moaning Downing cr̲owning dr̲owning warning ironing

WORDS FOR PRACTICE WITH THE COMBINATION -η-

✔ *Reminder* ────────────────────────────────

Do not insert a g sound in any of these words.

23 hanger=hangar singer singing gingham Birmingham Binghamton Cunningham

24 br̲inging clinging stinging str̲inging swinging Langham banging clanging

25 twanging longing belonging thr̲onging

WORDS FOR PRACTICE WITH THE COMBINATION ŋg

✓ *Reminder* ———————————————————————————————

Speak all of these words with g .

1 angular triangular rectangular singular England English dangle jangle
2 mangle spangle strangle tangle jingle mingle shingle single bungle angry
3 hungry anguish distinguish extinguish language linguist stronger strongest
4 longer longest younger youngest

COMPARE: – ŋk – ankle   tinkle   anchor   rankle   banker

–ŋg– angle   tingle   anger   wrangle   Bangor

–ŋgld 5 mingled tingled singled shingled jingled angled mangled tangled
6 dangled wrangled spangled bungled

PHRASES AND SHORT SENTENCES FOR PRACTICE USING ŋ FOLLOWED BY A VOWEL OR DIPHTHONG

✓ *Reminder* ———————————————————————————————

Speak all of these phrases without inserting an intrusive g .

7 Bring awning along.
8 Sing on Long Island.
9 The singers are humming.
10 looking at gingham
11 The singer sang of young love.
12 Rising early is becoming a drag.
13 the strong arm of Mr. Cunningham
14 A warning is a strong thing.
15 Anxious Uncle Bing is dreaming of roaming in Hong Kong.
16 Swimming is calming and slimming.
17 Scheming is seemingly cunning.
18 The length of Len's song was all wrong!
19 The King of Hong Kong offered something else.

20 seeing everything in Birmingham
21 going out to the hangar
22 banging away at hanging a picture
23 I'm longing to throw mē-ringue at King Otto.
24 Walking along is bringing us down.
25 swinging among a throng of young adults
26 King Edward sang a long ā:-ria on Long Island.
27 King Kong is alarming us.

SENTENCES FOR PRACTICE USING ŋ AND ŋg

28 Mr. Langham's a distinguished English linguist.
29 Those spangles nearly strangled that singer.
30 King Kong and Bing Crosby will sing a jingle for the King of England in the spring.
31 At length, his strength became singularly distinguished.
32 The bell hung at too much of an angle to jangle.
33 Don't mingle with the youngest singer from Birmingham.
34 Speaking as the youngest, I think your language is becoming angry-sounding.

SENTENCES FOR COMPARISON OF /n **WITH** /ŋ

1 If you talk in r̲hyme inside, are you talking or r̲hyming, Ms. Morningside?
2 I thought you said to "walk in" if I was walking by!
3 I'm dr̲opping the idea of a dr̲op-in this holiday.
4 That dr̲ess shop in the mall offers gr̲eat shopping.
5 Being thin was her thing!

SENTENCES FOR COMPARISON OF ŋk **WITH** ŋg

6 Is that a bangle fr̲om your banker in Bangor I see anchored to your ankle?
7 The rancor of my uncle r̲ankles the family. He wr̲angles over everything.
8 The new-fangled, tr̲iangular glȁss chimes tinkle and tingle. I had no inkling they'd jingle so!

SENTENCES FOR PRACTICE USING ŋk, s

9 Mr. Minx uses his instincts with linguistic distinction.
10 He thinks acupuncture shr̲inks swelling in his lȁ-r̲ynx.
11 That dr̲awing, *The Pink Sphinx*, r̲anks among distinguished inks.

ℓ **l**aw

THE LATERAL CONSONANT

There is only one lateral consonant sound in Spoken English. This voiced consonant sound which does not have a voiceless partner or cognate in Spoken English, is created by the tip of the tongue touching the gum ridge just in back of the upper front teeth. The body of the tongue is broad and flat, and air is emitted OVER THE SIDES of the tongue, or laterally.

All ℓ sounds are to be kept forward and clearly resonated. It is imperative that the vibration of this sound be felt at the gum ridge by the tip of the tongue, NEVER with the back of the tongue and the soft palate. There are many different, equally correct ℓ sounds, their quality depending on their positions in words and the sounds surrounding them.

In Good Speech a BRIGHTER ℓ is used when it is adjacent to front vowel sounds, and a DARKER ℓ is used when adjacent to back vowel sounds and when followed by another consonant sound. Also, ℓ sounds in initial positions will be brighter, while those in final positions will be darker.

The consonant ℓ is one of the ten most frequently used consonant sounds in Spoken English and its lyrical, liquid quality contributes greatly to the overall resonance and tone of your vocal projection.

In Spoken English the alveolar consonant ℓ is usually made with the tip of the tongue touching the gum ridge directly BEHIND the upper front teeth.

Place IV-A (ALVEOLAR)   The tip of the tongue touches the gum ridge:

$$\ell$$

(vd)   law   si**ll**y   ta**ll**

However, when ℓ is followed by θ or $\eth$, either within a word or in the next word of a phrase, it becomes dentalized, or made with the tip of the tongue touching the back of the upper front teeth. The IPA diacritical mark for dentalization of a sound is placed directly underneath the phonetic letter. This mark may be thought of as a little tooth sign underneath the letter:

wealth $'wo\underset{\sqcap}{\ell}\theta$ Tell them. $'t\hat{e}\underset{\sqcap}{\ell}\colon \eth\partial m$

In Good Speech, dentalization occurs ONLY when t , d , n , or ℓ is followed by θ or $\eth$.

Lateral Plosion

Lateral plosion occurs when the consonant t, or d is followed by the consonant ℓ and is exploded, or released, over the sides of the tongue. The tip of the tongue remains in touch with the alveolar ridge: $\underline{t_\sqcup \ell}$ $t_,\ell$ $\underline{d\ell}$ $d\ell$
                                 softly   rattle   badlands   riddle

Lengths

The consonant ℓ , like all continuants in Spoken English, is subject to lengthening. Consonant sounds are notated only long and short; there is no half-long. An ℓ is long when it is in the LAST SYLLABLE of a word, if that syllable is a stressed syllable:

— Before another voiced consonant sound:

$d\iota'fa\ddot{\imath}\cdot\ell\colon d$ $'e\ell\colon m\colon z$
defiled   elms

— The last sound of a word when preceded by one of the short vowel sounds:

$'f\upsilon\ell\colon$
full

NOTE: ℓ IS SHORT IN ALL OTHER INSTANCES.

THE PLACE IV-A VOICED ALVELOAR LATERAL CONTINUANT CONSONANT SOUND: ℓ **as in "*l*aw"**

Represented by the spellings:

*l*ap a*ll*

This consonant sound does not have a voiceless partner or cognate in Spoken English.

Relax the jaw, open the mouth and broaden the tongue, raising its tip to the gum ridge behind the upper front teeth without touching the teeth. Let air pass over the sides of the tongue in a voiced sound, keeping the tongue relaxed and forward for a clear, liquid sound. DO NOT TENSE THE BACK OF THE TONGUE; because that would give the sound a thick quality.

When ℓ is in final position in a word before a pause, maintain contact between the articulators until you have finished the breath, to avoid adding an off-glide. For instance, with the word "feel," say "feelll," not "feel-uh." ℓ^∂

WORDS FOR PRACTICE

Initial ℓ

$\ell-$

1 leap lick let lack l$\overset{a}{a}$st learn lurk Laconda luck lull loop loom look
2 loquacious law lock llama lay lie=lye Lloyd low loud Lear=leer lair
3 Lourdes lore Lahr lyre=liar lower (frown)

Medial ℓ

$-\ell-$

4 pee-ling fee-ling dea-ling knee-ling sea-ling stea-ling
5 Bi-lly Wi-lly di-lly ni-lly si-lly t<u>r</u>i-lling ki-lling bi-lling
6 Li-ly abi-lity E-laine phi-losophy
7 be-lly embe-llish <u>r</u>e-lish Ke-lly
8 fa-llow va-lley Ta-lly Sa-lly sha-llow Ca-liban
9 (wh)r-ling hur-ling cur-ling unfur-ling pear-lish gir-lish Mer-lin
10 c<u>r</u>u-e-lly tow-e-ling di-a-ling
11 cu-lling mu-lling lu-llaby
12 foo-lish ghou-lish poo-ling <u>r</u>u-ling Doo-ley t<u>r</u>u-ly
13 pu-lling pu-lley bu-lly fu-lly woo-llen woo-lly
14 fa-lling appa-lling c<u>r</u>aw-ling d<u>r</u>aw-ling <u>R</u>a-leigh
15 Hai-ley dai-ly fai-ling sai-ling jai-lor sai-lor
16 pi-ling fi-ling ti-ling di-late begui-ling
17 fo-li-age <u>r</u>o-lling bow-ling ho-ly=who-lly low-ly po-lling cajo-ling

WORDS FOR PRACTICE

✓ *Reminder*

Smoothly and efficiently connect each vowel and diphthong sound to final ℓ . Do not say $\underset{\smile}{'i:}\;\partial\ell$ **in two syllables.**

Final ℓ

$-\ell$

18 eel meal kneel peal=peel Beale teal deal keel feel we'll=weal (wh)eel
19 he'll=heel congeal conceal <u>r</u>eel

20 ill mill nill pill bill till dill kill gill fill will chill Jill

ℓ

WORDS FOR PRACTICE, Cont.

1 El Mel Nell pell bell tell dell gell fell well fareWELL yell hell

2 Al pal Temescal Dal Cal gal Val

3 earl Merle pearl Berle curl girl unfurl hurl churl

✓ *Reminder* ——————————————————————————————————

Do not add a superfluous consonant w **or** j **at the beginning of the second syllable in the words on lines 4 and 5.**

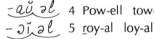

4 Pow-ell tow-el trow-el vow-el bow-el vi-al di-al tri-al jew-el cru-el

5 roy-al loy-al

6 lull Tull dull cull gull mull null skull hull Stull

7 pool cool fool school stool mule Yule=you'll tool ghoul rule

8 pull full wool bull

9 Paul=pall all=awl ball=bawl tall call Gaul=gall hall=haul Saul scrawl
10 mall=maul fall

11 doll moll noll loll alcohol Sol

12 ale=ail pail=pale bail=bale tail=tale dale Kael=kale Gail=gale mail=male
13 hail=hale vail=vale they'll sale=sail shale rail Braille trail jail=gaol whale
14 wail quail Yale

Final ℓ

COMPARE: $e\ell$: 15 bell   tell   fell   hell   shell   yell

            $e\cdot r\cdot \ell$ 16 bail=bale tail=tale fail   hail=hale shale   Yale

17 aisle=I'll=isle pile bile tile guile mile Nile file vile rile while

18 oil boil toil Doyle coil gargoyle turmoil foil soil

19 pole=poll bowl=boll toll dole coal=Cole goal mole foal sole=soul=Seoul
20 roll=role troll droll hole=whole

21 owl cowl howl fowl=foul jowl

22 parle Carl gnarl snarl

EXERCISES FOR COMPARING A LONG VOWEL OR DIPHTHONG FOLLOWED BY ℓ
IN ONE SYLLABLE, AND THE SAME OR SIMILAR VOWEL OR DIPHTHONG FOLLOWED BY -əℓ
IN TWO SYLLABLES

✓ *Reminder*

Do not add a superfluous consonant *w* **or** *j* **at the beginning of the second syllable.**

1	howl	— How-ell	7	Stole	— Sto-well
2	fowl	— Pow-ell	8	rile	— tri-al
3	vile	— vi-al	9	foil	— loy-al
4	cowl	— Cow-ell	10	soil	— roy-al
5	Jule	— jew-el	11	Carl	— co-ral
6	Yule	— Ew-ell	12	cajole	— Jo-el

PHRASES FOR PRACTICE USING *lj* COMBINATION (See page 311.)

13 Italian William   15 a million Italians   17 the Auxilia-ry's cotillion
14 peculiar failure   16 a valuable medallion   18 a billion tatterdemalions

WORDS FOR PRACTICE USING ʌℓ

19 Ulster cull culture gull gulf gulp vulture mull tumult exult result pulp consult
20 consultant annulment culpable cult ebullient culminate gulp bulb adult adulte-ry
21 pulse repulsive compulsive impulsive revulsion ulcer sulk bulge divulge indulge
22 gulch bulk gully Tully Culligan

CONSONANT COMBINATIONS

-ℓpʰ   23 whelp help scalp pulp gulp whelps whelped scalps gulps gulped

-ℓ:m   24 film elm helm overwhelm realm films filmed overwhelms overwhelmed

-ℓf   25 sylph sylphs self himself herself itself elf shelf gulf engulfed wolf

-ℓ:v   26 twelve delve valve dissolve involve resolve solve dissolves dissolved

-ℓtʰ   27 built wilt guilt=gilt lilt shalt adult tumult salt fault bolt colt dolt

-ℓ:d   28 field revealed build builds grilled held beheld whirled world worlds
        29 curled hurled unfurled eme-rald culled fooled scald bawled=bald wailed
        30 spoiled threshold bold cold gold behold snarled gnarled

-ℓs   31 else pulse impulse repulse false

-ℓ:z   32 eels peels=peals pills bills wills bells cools school's pearls pails piles
        33 poles Charles

-ℓk   34 ilk milk silk elk bulk hulk milks milked silks

-ℓtʃ   35 filch belch Welch squelch gulch mulch

ℓ

WORDS FOR PRACTICE USING LATERAL PLOSION IN WHICH THE CONSONANTS t_i AND d ARE FOLLOWED BY ℓ. (See pages 211, numbers 11-20.)

✓ *Reminder* ──────────────────────

Do not use a glottal stop in place of the unaspirated t_i **in the following words:**

SAY: sweetly ˈswiˑt̬ˌlɪ   NOT: ˈswiˑʔlɪ

$t_i\ell$ 1 sweetly discreetly   swiftly instantly ghăstly lăstly overtly
2 perfectly justly hotly motley lightly brightly tightly nightly=nitely
3 witless sightless Maitland Caitlin

$d\ell$ 4 badly madly sadly broadly badlands hardly
5 needless headless wordless godless mindless soundlessly

WORDS FOR PRACTICE USING SYLLABIC ℓ

✓ *Reminder* ──────────────────────

Syllabic ℓ **takes the place of a vowel in forming certain UNstressed SYLLABLES, usually at the ends of words.**

$-p_ˌ\ell$ 6 people steeple triple apple ample sămple exămple purple topple

$-b\ell$ 7 feeble possible hŏrrible in-to-lĕ-ra-ble culpable trouble able

$-t_ˌ\ell$ 8 beetle little ⓦhittle brittle mettle=metal nettle settle settlement battle
9 battlements cattle fertile shuttle scuttle hostel=hostile chortle startle

$-d\ell$ 10 needle riddle meddle=medal saddle noodle hurdle idle=idol=idyll bridle=bridal

$-k_ˌ\ell$ 11 pickle trickle freckle tackle circle classical ŏracle sparkle

$-g\ell$ 12 eagle giggle strangle struggle juggle jungle bugle gargle

$-m\ell$ 13 minimal enamel mammal animal pommel primal

$-n\ell$ 14 venal annals panel channel runnel final spinal tonal

$-f\ell$ 15 gleeful baffle awful lawful offal hateful delightful doubtful

$-v\ell$ 16 evil drivel revel travel removal novel revival

$-\theta\ell$ 17 lethal ethyl=Ethel Athol brothel

$-s\ell$ 18 ⓦhistle epistle thistle bristle vessel wrestle vassal căstle

$-z\ell$ 19 weasle drizzle chisel embezzle damsel dazzle puzzle refusal nasal

$-\int\ell$ 20 special nuptial spatial palatial Marshall=martial

$-r\ell$ 21 vĭ-rile stē-rile bărrel mackĕ-rel funĕ-ral chŏ-ral aʊ-ral=ɔː-ral flɔː-ral cɔː-ral
22 mŏ-ral quă-rrel nostril April vĭ-ral rŭ-ral² mŭ-ral²

WORDS FOR PRACTICE USING SYLLABIC ℓ , Cont.

REPEAT APPROPRIATE WORDS IN WORDS FOR PRACTICE USING SYLLABIC ℓ ON PREVIOUS PAGE ADDING d AND z :

$-p_{,}\ell d$	peopled	steepled	tripled	sampled
$-p_{,}\ell z$	peoples	steeples	triples	samples

PHRASES AND SHORT SENTENCES FOR PRACTICE USING ℓ

1 a little old lady
2 Little by little they'll leave.
3 Feel the keel as you kneel.
4 Bill will kill for a dill pickle.
5 Willy the silly hillbilly feels Philly's too chilly.
6 Tell Mel to go to hell!
7 The bells will peal in Louisville.
8 a Lily Langtry look-alike
9 Hal had a pal in Temescal, California.
10 *Talley's Folly* had a lot of belly laughs.
11 Who'll put coolant in the pool?
12 Pull the pulpit toward the bull.
13 Wally Holly liked a lot of alcohol.
14 Shirley and Earle hurled down the pearls.
15 whirled round the world
16 The laughing little girl had a curl.
17 eleven benevolent elephants
18 Elaine the lovable was elated.
19 Ms. Stull was a culture vulture.
20 *The Seagull* starred Mr. Siegal.
21 the tumult of those gulls on the gulf
22 The adulte-ry resulted in an annulment.
23 Indulge the impulsive cult!
24 Culligan was ebullient in Ulster
25 Don't sulk, you repulsive culprit.
26 All hail the unsailable sailors!
27 The teller loved Elizabeth Taylor.
28 Mel mailed it to Mailor.
29 Hell left him hale and hearty.
30 Amy Pel looked paler and paler.
31 Elliot was an alien at Yale.
32 The delicate delegate was Delilah.
33 miles and miles of smiles
34 I'll go down the aisle with Kyle.

35 The vile vi-al fell into the Nile.
36 Tell Tyler to file it while he waits.
37 Try a little smile at the tri-al.
38 Lloyd was loy-al to roy-al-ty.
39 toil and toil in the soil
40 double double toil and trouble
41 Foley entered the fold like a bolt.
42 all the molten golden notes
43 Behold the old gold in the hold.
44 Do it highly and holily.
45 Howl like an owl in a cowl.
46 a sparkling Long Island lake
47 Lily was willingly wild.
48 cool and cold in the hold
49 the lascivious pleasing of a lute
50 lolling on a lewd love-bed
51 Lady Lucy licked a lollipop.
52 Elated Lilliputians hurled the poles.
53 He helped himself to the elf's shelf.
54 Hello to that mellow fellow in L.A.
55 Willy, will you fill it with ethyl?
56 Put on the metal kettle.
57 the little people in Alpha
58 Alvin Ailey held a cattle call audition.
59 Whittle a whistle and a rattle.
60 The ru-ral fune-ral was immo-ral.
61 Evil Knievel read a dreadful novel.
62 a li-te-ra-lly classical pickle
63 Lily's philosophical ability was lovely.
64 Mumble an example from the Bible.
65 Culligan was culling calla lilies.
66 Lillian was lonesome for Caliban.
67 Lucid Lucy was ludicrously late.
68 Lay a lullaby on the lunatic.

PHRASES AND SHORT SENTENCES FOR PRACTICE USING ℓ , Cont.

1 a little world of hills and fields

2 Will anyone else like to waltz?

3 Hallelujah! Lily's little child Niles!
4 Lillian Langley lolled on a lily pad.
5 It'll be cold enough to chill your liver.
6 An idle mind is the devil's tool.

7 Paul Bunyan was ebullient.

8 All the Molson Golden is cold.
9 There's a sale on sailor suits at Gail's.

10 Alvin Ailey, Hayley Mills and Grace Paley—they'll all hail the railroad.

11 The gnarled Karl Marx snarled at Prince Charles.

12 How sweetly and politely they behave.
13 Exactly. It was an overtly beastly night.
14 Softly, softly, it's only partly ghastly.
15 Will you please pass the plate of lemons and limes to Peter?

16 Will D.W. Kassalow call Eileen, or will Eileen have to call him?

17 Does little Miss Kelly believe in Santa Claus?
18 Sally feels turmoil is avoidable.

When ℓ is followed by θ or ð , either within a word or in the next word of a phrase, it becomes DENTALIZED, or made with the tip of the tongue touching the back of the upper front teeth. The IPA diacritical mark for dentalization of a sound is placed directly underneath the phonetic letter. This mark may be thought of as a little tooth sign underneath the letter:

t̪   d̪   n̪   l̪   (See pages 267-268.)

In Good Speech, dentalization occurs ONLY when any of these four consonant sounds is followed by θ or ð in the same word or the following word.

DENTALIZATION OF l̪ WITHIN A WORD

19 wealth ˈwɛl̪θ   20 health ˈhɛl̪θ   21 stealth ˈstɛl̪θ   22 filth ˈfɪl̪θ

DENTALIZATION OF l̪ WITHIN A PHRASE

23 sell things   24 tell Theo   25 sell those   26 tell them

SENTENCES FOR PRACTICE USING DENTALIZED l̪

27 Tell healthy Thelma that we'll thaw the eel.
28 Mel thought he'd sell this filth for millions!
29 My pal thinks you'll throw the bale there stealthily.
30 I feel that Al and Dale Thurston didn't tell those lies!

SENTENCES FOR PRACTICE USING SAME-CONSONANT BLENDS

✔ Reminder ——————————————————————

Maintain the contact of the tip of your tongue and gum ridge during the following same-consonant blend sequences. Clarity of enunciation is achieved by a fresh impulse of energy that begins the second word of the sequence.

31 Bill Leeds will let the whole lot of them tell lies.

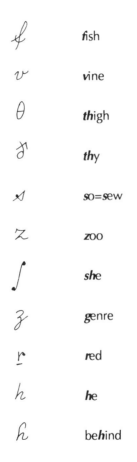	**f**ish
	vine
	thigh
	thy
	so=**s**ew
	zoo
	she
	genre
	red
	he
	be**h**ind

THE FRICATIVES

Fricative consonant sounds are made with the articulators partially obstructing the flow of breath. The air, voiced or voiceless, is forced through a narrow opening and creates turbulence and a friction-like sound.

The breath used to produce fricative consonants may be voiceless (vs) (no vibration of the vocal folds) or voiced (vd) (with vibration of the vocal folds). The vibration of the voiced sounds will be immediately felt when you place the tips of your fingers at the front of your larynx, or Adam's apple, while producing them.

In Spoken English, there are eleven consonant sounds created when the breath is impeded in this manner, and within these sounds are five pairs of cognates. COGNATES are two consonant sounds related by being produced in the SAME PLACE of articulation, in the SAME MANNER of articulation, with one of the pair VOICELESS (vs) and the other VOICED (vd).

The fricative cognates are   *f* & *v*   *θ* & *ð*   *s* & *z*   *ʃ* & *ʒ*   *h* & *ɦ*

The voiced consonant **r** does not have a voiceless partner, or cognate, in Spoken English.

The fricative sounds are made in the following places of articulation:

Place II	**(LABIO-DENTAL)**	The lower lip articulates against the edge of the upper front teeth:

f

(vs) fi**sh**   o**ff**ice   ca**lf**   *v* (vd) **v**ine   li**v**es   lo**v**e

Place III	**(DENTAL)**	The tip of the tongue articulates against the edge of the upper front teeth:

θ

(vs) **th**igh   e**th**er   tee**th**   *ð* (vd) **th**y   ei**th**er   tee**the**

The fricative sounds made in Places IV-B-1 and IV-B-2 are collectively known as SIBILANTS. The voiceless sibilants are known as HISSES, and the voiced sibilants are known as BUZZES.

Place IV-B	**(ALVEOLAR)**	The tip of the tongue points toward the gum ridge, but does NOT touch:
(1)	(POST-DENTAL)	The extreme front of the upper gums or teeth;

s

(vs) **s**o=**s**ew   ra**c**ed   ta**x**   *z* (vd) **z**oo   di**ss**olve   love**s**

(2)	(PALATO-ALVEOLAR)	The middle of the upper gums;

ʃ

(vs) **sh**in   o**ce**an   ba**sh**   *ʒ* (vd) **g**enre   le**s**ion   bei**ge**

(3)	(POST-ALVEOLAR)	The extreme back of the upper gums;

r

(vs) -----   -----   -----   *r* (vd) **r**ed   ·p**r**ay   so-**rr**y   (ginge**r**-ale)

Place VII   **(GLOTTAL)**   In the larynx:

h

(vs) **h**e   mis**h**ap   -----   (vd)   -----   be**h**ind   -----

h does not occur in final position in Spoken English.

$\hbar$ does not occur in initial or final position in Spoken English.

Accurate articulation of all fricative consonants is essential for understandability and satisfactory communication of the ideas and emotional values of words. All fricative consonants in final positions must be ended without any hint of an off-glide.

THE PLACE II VOICELESS LABIO-DENTAL FRICATIVE CONTINUANT: _f_ **as in** "fish."

Represented by the spellings:

fist   **ph**onetics   cu**ff**   tou**gh**   ca**lf**

THE PLACE II VOICED LABIO-DENTAL FRICATIVE CONTINUANT: _v_ **as in** "vine."

Represented by the spellings:

voice   o**f**   Ste**ph**en=Ste**v**en

Allow your lower jaw to hang relaxed and the tip of your tongue to touch the back of your lower teeth. Press your lower lip to the edges of your upper teeth, so that the breath will be forced out between the teeth and lower lip.

The voiceless consonant sound _f_ suggests a lightness and gives a delicacy to the word spoken. Do not waste your breath by trying to force out a tense, protracted sound.

_f_ is always sounded for the "v" in the phrase "have to" when it means "must":

$$'h\,æ\,f\,t\,ə$$
I have to go now.

The voiced consonant sound _v_ is characterized by a vibrating friction that is necessary to create a smooth, rich sound. Accurate articulation of this sound is central to understandability and contributes to the overall energy of your voice and speech. Pay particular attention to _v_ at the end of a phrase, as in "He's got a lot to give."

When _v_ is in final position of a word before a pause, maintain contact between your articulators until you have finished the breath. Premature movement of your articulators creates an extraneous vowel sound, or off-glide, after the consonant. For instance, with the word "give,"

SAY: "givvv" $'g\,ı\,v{:}$ NOT: "giv-uh" $'g\,ı\,v^{ə}$

◆ Avoid substituting _f_ for final _v_ . NEVER SAY "giff" for "give."

◆ Avoid dropping _v_ when another consonant follows. SAY: "five cents" NOT: "fi cents"

WORDS FOR PRACTICE

Initial _f_

1 feed feet=feat fit Phil=fill fed fad fa̱st fur=fir phonetic fun fool few
2 full foment fall fob father phase fight foil foe phone phobia fowl=foul
3 fear fare=fair four=fore=for (sf) far fire

Medial _f_

4 r̲eefer difficult deafen daffy chaffinch r̲a̱fter surfer camouflage suffer
5 pr̲oofing hoofer offender awful offer chafing wifely loafing tearful careful
6 morphine scarfed direful

Final _f_

7 beef tiff deaf gaff ha̱lf turf tough r̲oof cough safe life coif loaf howff
8 endomorph scarf

Initial _v_

9 veal visit vest vat va̱st verve vali̱se vulture voodoo view vault volume
10 vale vice void vote vow veer va̠ry vortex varnish

WORDS FOR PRACTICE, Cont.

Medial 𝓋

1 evil livid seven lavish slovenly groovy slave̘-ry rival oval marvel=Marvell

2 every beverage average sovereign

Final 𝓋

✓*Reminder* ───

Carry your voice through each final vibrated consonant ending without adding an off-glide.

3 Eve heave peeve grieve we've=weave sheave Steve sleeve thieve naive

4 achieve receive preconceive misconceive perceive Tel Aviv recitative

5 give forgive live (v) sieve olive plaintive captive abrasive

6 have (sf)

7 halve ′h a 𝓋 salve ′s a 𝓋 calve ′kᴸ a 𝓋

8 curve Merv=Merve nerve swerve serve observe conserve deserve preserve

9 of (wf)

10 above dove love shove glove ladylove foxglove

11 move you've groove remove approve improve reprove disapprove

12 of (sf)

13 pave brave Dave cave gave save shave behave wave

14 dive chive jive live (adj) alive five revive thrive survive beehive

15 cove Jove rove mauve stove grove

EXERCISES THAT DISTINGUISH BETWEEN ℓ AND 𝓋

✓*Reminder* ───

The words with final ℓ are shorter than the words with final 𝓋 .

	Initial			Medial			Final	
16a	fees	— "V'"s	16b	beefy	— peavey	16c	sheaf	— sheave
17a	feel	— veal	17b	leafing	— leaving	17c	grief	— grieve
18a	fix	— vixen	18b	sniffle	— snivel	18c	bailiff	— live
19a	fit	— vitriol	19b	affinity	— divinity	19c	belief	— believe
20a	fender	— vendor	20b	heifer	— ever	20c	shelf	— shelve
21a	fat	— vat	21b	raffish	— ravish	21c	gaff	— have (sf)
22a	famish	— vanish	22b	Africa	— avid	22c	have to (must)	— have (sf)
23a	fa̘st	— va̘st	23b	ha̘lfway	— ha̘lving	23c	ca̘lf	— ca̘lve
24a	fervor	— verve	24b	PERfume	— purview	24c	serf=surf	— serve
25a	fa̘-rrago	— vi-rago	25b	affirm	— avert	25c	-----	-----
26a	fulminate	— vulpine	26b	bluffer	— plover	26c	a buff	— above
27a	food	— voodoo	27b	proofing	— proving	27c	roof	— groove
28a	few	— view	28b	euphony	— uvula	28c	-----	-----
29a	feud	— viewed	29b	-----	-----	29c	-----	-----
30a	faun=fawn	— Vaughan	30b	-----	-----	30c	-----	-----
31a	folly	— volley	31b	offish	— Ovid	31c	off	— of (sf)

EXERCISES THAT DISTINGUISH BETWEEN f AND v , Cont.

	Initial			Medial			Final	
1a	feign=fane	— vane=vein	1b	Sheaffer	— shaver	1c	safe	— save
2a	face	— vase[3]	2b	safer	— saver	2c	waif	— wave
3a	fie	— vie	3b	rifle	— rival	3c	life	— alive
4a	foist	— voice	4b	joyful	— oi vey	4c	-----	-----
5a	focal	— vocal	5b	woeful	— oval	5c	oaf	— mauve
6a	foe	— vote	6b	Sophie	— soviet	6c	loaf	— clove
7a	fear	— veer	7b	-----	-----	7c	-----	-----
8a	fai-ry	— va-ry	8b	-----	-----	8c	-----	-----
9a	forceps	— vortex	9b	orphan	— Orville	9c	dwarf	— wharve
10a	farley	— varlet	10b	Garfield	— Garvey	10c	scarf	— carve
11a	fire us	— vi-rus	11b	-----	-----	11c	-----	-----

WORDS FOR PRACTICE USING DOUBLE CONSONANT ENDINGS

12a	a chief's — $f\!s$		12b	achieves — vz
13a	reefs		13b	Reeves
14a	Jeff's		14b	Bev's
15a	shelf's		15b	shelves
16a	calf's		16b	calves
17a	proofs		17b	proves
18a	wolf's		18b	wolves
19a	safes		19b	saves
20a	oafs		20b	cloves
21a	dwarf's		21b	dwarves

WORDS FOR COMPARISON OF p WITH f

	Initial			Medial			Final	
22a	pea	— fee	22b	tipi	— beefy	22c	leap	— leaf
23a	peat	— feet	23b	leaping	— leafing	23c	keep	— O'Keefe
24a	pill	— fill	24b	sippet	— syphilis	24c	tip	— tiff
25a	pell	— fell	25b	depend	— defend	25c	Shep	— chef
26a	pat	— fat	26b	tapioca	— taffy	26c	gap	— gaff
27a	past	— fast	27b	hasping	— half-done	27c	gasp	— calf
28a	purr	— fur=fir	28b	usurped	— you surfed	28c	usurp	— serf=surf
29a	pursed	— first	29b	chirping	— surfing	29c	Earp	— Murph
30a	pun	— fun	30b	puppy	— puffy	30c	cup	— cuff
31a	pool	— fool	31b	droopy	— roofing	31c	loop	— aloof
32a	pew=Pugh	— few	32b	-----	-----	32c	-----	-----
33a	put	— foot	33b	whoopee	— hoofing	33c	-----	-----
34a	pall=Paul	— fall	34b	pauper	— awful	34c	-----	-----
35a	pond	— fond	35b	copy	— coffee	35c	cop	— cough

WORDS FOR COMPARISON OF p WITH f , Cont.

	Initial			Medial			Final	
1a	pay	— fey=Fay	1b	shaping	— chafing	1c	chape	— shape
2a	pie	— fie	2b	stipel	— stifle	2c	stripe	— strife
3a	poi	— Foy	3b	-----	-----	3c	-----	-----
4a	pone	— phone	4b	soapy	— Sophie	4c	ope	— oaf
5a	pound	— found	5b	-----	-----	5c	-----	-----
6a	peer=pier	— fear	6b	-----	-----	6c	-----	-----
7a	pair=pare= pear	— fair=fare	7b	airport	— airfoil	7c	-----	-----
8a	pore=pour	— four= fore=for (sf)	8b	porpoise	— porphy-ry	8c	warp	— wharf
9a	par	— far	9b	harpoon	— HARfleur	9c	scarp	— scarf
10a	pyre	— fire	10b	diaper	— direful	10c	-----	-----

EXERCISE FOR COMPARING w WITH v (See page 306 for further drills.)

	Front Vowels			Mid Vowels			Back Vowels	
11	we	— "V"	16	worse	— verse	18	wooed	— voodoo
12	Winnie	— Vinnie	17	wicker	— vicar	19	wail	— vale=veil
13	west	— vest				20	wile	— Weill=vile
14	wending	— vending				21	wea-ry	— vee-ring
15	wacky	— vacuum				22	wa-ry	— va-ry

WORDS FOR COMPARISON OF b WITH v

	Initial			Medial			Final	
23a	bee="B"	— "V"	23b	Evan	— ebon=Eben	23c	plebe	— leave
24a	bean	— Venus	24b	ability	— civility	24c	lib	— live (v)
25a	biddy	— video	25b	dribble	— drivel	25c	glib	— give
26a	be-rry=bu-ry	— ve-ry	26b	Lebanon	— leavening	26c	celeb	— Lev
27a	ban	— van	27b	gabble	— gavel	27c	rehab	— have (sf)
28a	burble	— verbal	28b	Thurber	— server	28c	curb	— curve
29a	bulk	— vulcan	29b	cupboard	— cover	29c	bub	— above
30a	boo	— voodoo	30b	ruble	— removal	30c	rube	— prove
31a	butte	— viewed	31b	rebuke	— review= revue	31c	cube	— you've
32a	bane=Bain	— vain=vein	32b	fable	— Favel	32c	Gabe	— fave
33a	buy=by=bye	— vie	33b	libel	— lively	33c	tribe	— strive
34a	Boyd	— void	34b	Hoibey	— oi vey	34c	-----	-----
35a	boat	— vote	35b	lobes	— loaves	35c	robe	— rove
36a	bow-el	— vow-el	36b	-----	-----	36c	-----	-----
37a	beer	— veer	37b	-----	-----	37c	-----	-----
38a	bea-ring	— va-ry	38b	-----	-----	38c	-----	-----
39a	barley	— Varley	39b	marble	— marvel	39c	barb	— carve
40a	barn	— varnish	40b	harbored	— Harvard	40c	-----	-----

WORDS FOR PRACTICE USING CONSONANT COMBINATIONS

fl –　1　flee flit fling flimsy fleck phlegm flap flag flăsk flirt flamingo
　　　2　flutter flue=flew flaw flaunt floss flame fly fli-er flow
　　　3　float flout flounder fleer flare Fluor floor flour=flower

–fl　4　gleeful sniffle <u>f</u>retful <u>r</u>affle hurtful shuffle <u>r</u>ueful lawful <u>wr</u>ongful
　　　5　waffle <u>g</u>rateful <u>f</u>rightful joyful woeful doubtful careful harmful

fr –　6　<u>f</u>ree <u>f</u>reak <u>f</u>reeze <u>f</u>rill Phrygia <u>f</u>riction <u>f</u>ringe <u>f</u>ritter <u>f</u>ret French <u>f</u>reckle
　　　7　<u>f</u>raction <u>f</u>ragile <u>f</u>ragment Frănce <u>f</u>rontier <u>f</u>ruit <u>f</u>rugal <u>f</u>raught <u>f</u>rock <u>f</u>rost
　　　8　<u>f</u>ray <u>f</u>reight <u>f</u>ry <u>f</u>right <u>f</u>ro <u>f</u>rozen <u>f</u>rounce <u>f</u>rowner <u>f</u>riar

fju: –　9　few fewer fewest fuse feud <u>r</u>efuse <u>r</u>efute <u>r</u>efuge confuse fuchsia fume
　　　10　fumigate fugue confute

– mf　11　lymph nymph <u>t</u>riumph

– lf　12　sylph elf self shelf gulf Beowulf wolf <u>R</u>olf

sf –　13　sphinx sphere sphe͡-rical

– fs　14　thief's sheaf's grief's beliefs chiefs sniffs skiffs (wh)ffs she͡-riffs turfs
　　　15　Murph's muffs bluffs cuffs snuffs stuffs <u>p</u>roofs <u>r</u>oofs hoofs doffs
　　　16　scoffs oafs

– ftʰ　17　leafed lift <u>r</u>ift gift <u>d</u>rift <u>thr</u>ift theft deft left be-<u>r</u>eft heft wăft drăft shăft
　　　18　crăft grăft witchcrăft lăughed stăffed surfed Luft tuft cuffed scuffed
　　　19　oft loft soft aloft <u>c</u>roft

✔ *Reminder* ─────────────────────────────────────

Use an unaspirated *t,* **in the consonant clusters in 20-22. (See page 202.)**

– ft, s　20　lifts sifts gifts <u>d</u>rifts shifts lefts clefts thefts wăfts <u>r</u>ăfts shăfts grăfts
　　　21　lofts crofts

– ft, θ　22　fifth　　　　fifths　　　twelfth　　　twelfths　　(See page 213 *t,* .)

– lftʰ　23　Delft engulfed golfed

– lfs　24　sylphs elf's gulfs wolfs

✔ *Reminder* ─────────────────────────────────────

The consonant *n* **is syllabic when it takes the place of a weak vowel in an UN-stressed SYLLABLE. (See page 239.)**

– fn　25　stiffen deafen baffin muffin toughen <u>r</u>oughen often soften coffin hyphen

– fnd　26　stiffened toughened <u>r</u>oughened softened

– fnz　27　stiffens toughens <u>r</u>oughens softens hyphens

WORDS FOR PRACTICE USING CONSONANT COMBINATIONS, Cont.

✔ *Reminder* ─────────────────────────────────────

The consonant ℓ is syllabic when it takes the place of a weak vowel in an UN-stressed SYLLABLE. (See pages 250-251.)

-fld   1   baffled   raffled   muffled   ruffled   shuffled   snuffled   rifled   trifled   stifled

-flz   2   baffles   raffles   muffles   ruffles   scuffles   shuffles   snuffles   rifles   trifles   stifles

✔ *Reminder* ─────────────────────────────────────

Carry your voice through each final vibrated consonant ending without adding an off-glide.

-l:v   3   delve   twelve   valve   solve   absolve   evolve   dissolve   involve   resolve

-vd   4   grieved   believed   conceived   achieved   received   reprieved   relieved   lived
      5   sieved   outlived   curved   swerved   loved   shoved   moved   proved   raved
      6   braved   paved   waved   a-rrived   deprived   carved   starved

-l:vd   7   shelved   absolved   devolved   dissolved   involved   resolved   revolved

-vz   8   heaves   weaves   believes   conceives   olives   gives   relatives   executives
      9   locomotives   missives   captives   forgives   halves   serves   curves   nerves
     10   observes   doves   moves   proves   disapproves   caves   slaves   paves   survives
     11   drives   hives   loaves   roves   (wharves)   carves   scarves

-l:vz   12   elves   delves   selves   shelves   valves   wolves   solves   absolves   involves   resolves

-vn   13   even   Stephen=Steven   driven   leaven   heaven   oven   haven   raven (n)   maven
     14   craven   enliven   woven

-vnz   15   evens   heavens   elevens   sevens   ovens   ravens (n)   cravens   havens   enlivens

-vl   16   festival   shrivel   drivel   swivel   snivel   bevel   level   revel   dishevel   travel
     17   gavel   gravel   grovel   hovel   shovel   novel   marvel=Marvell   carvel

-vld   18   driveled   shriveled   sniveled   swiveled   beveled   disheveled   leveled   reveled
     19   raveled   traveled   shoveled   groveled   marveled

-vlz   20   snivels   drivels   festivals   levels   revels   travels   gavels   intervals   shovels
     21   approvals   removals   novels   marvels

SENTENCES FOR PRACTICE USING f

22   Fight fairly! Fight face to face.
23   A few fast-food facilities are fashionable.
24   Five familiar farces are favored by festivals.
25   You fool! Can't you forgo a mouthful of fudge and fruit?
26   Are the festivities to benefit the chauFFEURS on Friday?
27   Do you feel you face difficulties with laughter?
28   "Hang tough," say the youthful fighters.
29   Acting aloof is a turnoff to the staff, Daphne.
30   Be truthful to yourself and faithful to your beliefs.
31   Fear led him to fireproof the bookshelf and burglar-proof the roof.

SENTENCES FOR PRACTICE USING

1. Did you vacation in Venice, Vegas or Vermont?
2. Are vitamins vital for vigor?
3. The evil rival craved a victo-ry.
4. Does verbena relieve vascula-rity?
5. Did you have to read the rave reviews for *To Have and Have Not?*
6. Did Bev observe the move?

SENTENCES FOR PRACTICE USING ℓ AND 𝓋

7. If you forget and forgive you'll feel relieved.
8. Vicious developers deprived family and friends of vacancies.
9. Investments in Vegas are fearfully frivolous.
10. If you don't behave you'll have to leave.
11. Vim and Vigor offers fish, veal and vegeta-rian fare.

✓*Reminder*

Keep the voiceless consonant endings crisp and clean. Carry your voice through each vibrated consonant ending without adding an off-glide.

12. You'll have to hire someone to read the proofs. That proves your point.
13. Only oafs would eat cloves of raw garlic.
14. Bev's staying at Jeff's house tonight?
15. Did the serf serve the loaves to the oafs?

SENTENCES FOR COMPARISON OF 𝓋 WITH 𝓌 (See pages 306-307.)

16. You'll wait in vain for Wayne.
17. Who served the volleyball over the wall?
18. The verbiage was ve-ry wea-ring on Vernon.
19. Vinnie and Winnie will weed the vineyard on Wednesday.

SENTENCES FOR COMPARISON OF ℓ , 𝓋 AND 𝓌

20. The first version wasn't fun.
21. That's a fine vintage wine.
22. The first verse wasn't my favorite one.
23. Waterford Valley is famous for vacationing.
24. I fear that driving in reverse is the worst!
25. Did you fix the wicker chair for the vicar?

SENTENCES FOR COMPARISON OF 𝓋 WITH 𝒷

26. That old biddy watches videos all day. She won't venture from that bench!
27. Put that verse in your burse! I'm tired of your verbal burble.
28. Was Bain waiting in vain for the plebe to leave?
29. Favel's fable imbued a few neighbors with knave-ry.
30. We took a vow on the bow of the boat to vote for Eben and not Evan. 'e ʰrən

SENTENCES FOR COMPARISON OF f WITH v

1 Keep O'Keefe away from the defendant. He's too dependent.
2 Pay Fay for the fine pine. They're better than par by far.
3 Have some coffee while I copy this menu for the chef, Shep.
4 Paul's fond of the pond in the fall. A leaf makes him leap for joy!

SENTENCES USING CONSONANT COMBINATIONS

5 Flappers often flaunt their flippancy.
6 It's doubtful that the raffle is lawful. Is it wrongful?
7 To be frugal, freeze the fragments of French-fried fritters.
8 Use a few fuchsias to fumigate the fuse room.
9 I put *Beowulf* back on the shelf myself.
10 Is there a sphere of light on the sphinx near the sphe-rical fountain?
11 The she-riffs' rustproof handcuffs were foolproof.
12 The craft gift gave a lift to Luft.
13 Shafts of light flooded the lofts on the left.
14 Was this figure divided by one-fifth or two-fifths? $'fɪƒt,θ$
15 The selfish elf's figure is sylph-like.
16 The twelfth's fine for me. Do you prefer the twelfth? $'t,welƒt,θ$
17 I often soften the muffins for Stephano.
18 The ruffles muffled the shuffles and scuffles.
19 Did you find that the review of the revue had an odd viewpoint?
20 Try some solvent on the twelve valves of the Volvo.
21 The executives resolved to invest in shelves that revolve.
22 Even Stephen was enlivened by the eleven ravens.
23 The seven craven ravens have vanished into the raven haven.
24 Let's travel to the festival to marvel at the novel ventures.
25 Level anyone who grovels and snivels for approval.

SENTENCES FOR PRACTICE USING SAME-CONSONANT BLENDS

✓ *Reminder* ————————————————————————————————

> **Maintain the contact of your articulators during same-consonant blend sequences. Clarity of enunciation is achieved by a fresh impulse of energy that begins the second word of the sequence.**

26 The chief foe was half fish and half fowl.
27 The roof felt safe from life, famine and tough fortune.

SENTENCE FOR PRACTICE USING COGNATE BLENDS

✓ *Reminder* ————————————————————————————————

> **Maintain the contact of your articulators during the following cognate blend sequences. Clarity of enunciation is achieved by a change from voiced to voiceless, or voiceless to voiced, and by a fresh impulse of energy that begins the second word in the sequence.**

28 Live fish cannot live freely with excessive frost on their native feeding grounds.

◆ THE CONSONANT SOUNDS ◆
θ AS IN "*th*igh" AND $\eth$ AS IN "*th*y"

THE PLACE III VOICELESS DENTAL FRICATIVE CONTINUANT: θ as in "*th*igh."

Represented by the spellings:

*th*in Ma*tt*hew

The PLACE III VOICED DENTAL FRICATIVE CONTINUANT: $\eth$ as in "*th*y."

Represented by the spellings:

*th*e ba*th*e

Relax your lower jaw and raise the tip of your tongue against the biting edge of your upper front teeth. Your soft palate is raised, and the sides of your tongue are in contact with your upper molars. Keep the rim of your tongue broad and flattened; the breath is directed through the narrow passage between the tip of your tongue and your upper teeth.

Strive to articulate θ and $\eth$ cleanly in ALL consonant combinations and clusters, and be sure to carry your voice through final consonant endings involving $\eth$.

When $\eth$ is in final position of a word before a pause, maintain contact between your articulators until you have finished the breath. Premature movement of your articulators creates an extraneous vowel sound, or off-glide, after the consonant. For instance, with the word "breathe,"

SAY: "breathe" $'br i:\eth$ NOT: "breathe-uh" $'br i:\eth^\ni$.

◆ Avoid substituting θ for final $\eth$. NEVER SAY "breeth" for "breathe."

WORDS FOR PRACTICE

Initial θ

1 theme thieves thief thesis theo-rem theocracy theosophy theism theo-ry
2 theater=theatre Thea thick thicket think thimble thistle the-rapy thespian
3 theft thatch thank Thapsia third thirst thirty thermal Thurston thermos
4 thud thug thumb thump thunder tho-rough thrust through Thule
5 thu-rible thaw thought thong throng throttle thane thigh thousand thorn

Medial θ

6 ether Heathrow lethal Lethe Ethan Elizabethan Lithuania lethargic
7 dithy-ramb pithy lithography Ithaca a-rithmetic Ethel lethargy healthy
8 Gethsemane method athletic catheter pathological bathday mirthful
9 birthday earthly earthy pathetic cathedral nothing anything something
10 truthful youthful Othello author brothel Gothic frothing faithful
11 pathos bathos atheism python southward mouthpiece mouthful northwest
12 orthodox Martha Arthur Parthenon McCarthy

Final θ

13 teeth sheath heath beneath underneath myth sith pith Edith monolith
14 Elizabeth Me-redith tallith sixtieth fortieth Beth Macbeth death Seth=saith
15 breath hath math path bath earth Perth birth=berth dearth girth mirth
16 firth worth Sabbath Plymouth mammoth Monmouth doth uncouth booth
17 sooth truth vermouth tooth Ruth sleuth youth Goth moth cloth sloth
18 broth froth troth (American) oath both loth=loath (adj; unwilling) troth (British)
19 mouth south north forth Darth Garth hearth

WORDS FOR PRACTICE, Cont.

Initial ð

1 thee these this then thence them themselves than that thus they
2 thy thine though=tho' those thou their=there=they're therefore thereof
3 thereafter therein

Medial ð

4 teething breathing either² neither² dither Mithers smithy thither
5 stithy slither blithe-ring hither (wh)ither wither without within tether
6 nether Netherlands feather heather (wh)ether weather gather Mather
7 slather blather lather rather burthen² murther² further worthy other
8 t'other mother another Sutherland southern=Sothern Sotheby's Southwark
9 brother smoother bother Rotherhithe father bathing either² neither²
10 tithing blithely loathing (n; hating) clothing clothier farthing farther

Final ð

✔ *Reminder* ───

Carry your voice through each vibrated consonant ending without adding an off-glide.

11 teethe seethe breathe with soothe smoothe lathe bathe swathe tithe
12 lithe Blythe=blithe Rotherhithe writhe loathe (v; to hate) unclothe clothe

COMPARE: θ 13	teeth	breath	heath	bath	worth	youth	booth
ð 14	teethe	breathe	heathen	bathe	worthy	youths	booths
θ 15	cloth	south	mouth (n)	north			
ð 16	clothing	southern	mouth (v)	northern			

DISTINGUISH 17	seethe	breathe	with	soothe	tithe	ð
BETWEEN: 18	seize	breeze	Wiz	Sue's	ties	z
ð 19	clothe	unclothe	writhe	lathe		
z 20	close	oppose	rise	laze=lays		

WORDS FOR COMPARISON OF θ WITH ð

Initial		Medial		Final	
21a theme	— thee	21b Ethan	— either²	21c teeth	— teethe
22a thin	— this	22b a-rithmetic	— rhythm	22c pith	— with
23a theft	— then	23b lethargy	— leathe-ry	23c -----	-----
24a thatch	— that	24b catheter	— gather	24c -----	-----
25a -----	-----	25b wrathful	— rather	25c bath	— bathe
26a thud	— the	26b Cuthbert	— t'other	26c -----	-----
27a thane	— they	27b pathos	— bathing	27c -----	-----
28a thigh	— thy	28b python	— tithing	28c -----	-----
29a Thole	— though	29b oath's	— oaths	29c loath (adj)	— loathe (v)
30a thousand	— thou	30b mouthful	— mouthing	30c mouth (n)	— mouth (v)

EXERCISES FOR COMPARING SIMILAR CONSONANT SOUNDS

	Initial			Final	
	θ	tʰ		θ	tʰ
1a	theme	— team=teem	1b	heath	— heat
2a	thesis	— teases	2b	sheath	— sheet
3a	thin	— tin	3b	pith	— pit
4a	thé-rapy	— té-rrapin	4b	Beth	— bet
5a	Thacke-ry	— tacky	5b	hath	— hat
6a	thermal	— terminal	6b	birth=berth	— Burt=Bert
7a	thirst	— terse	7b	earth	— hurt
8a	thumb	— tummy	8b	doth	— tut
9a	thews	— Tuesday	9b	sooth	— toot
10a	thought	— taught=taut	10c	-----	-----
11a	thong	— tong	11b	Roth	— rot
12a	thane	— ta'en	12b	faith	— fate
13a	thigh	— tie=Ty=Thai	13b	-----	-----
14a	thymus	— thyme=time	14b	-----	-----
15a	thole	— toll	15b	oath	— oat
16a	thousand	— Towson	16b	mouth	— out
17a	theo-ry	— tea-ry	17b	-----	— -----
18a	thorn	— torn	18b	north	— snort
19a	Tharp	— tarp (tarpaulin)	19b	hearth	— heart

	Initial			Final	
	ð	d		ð	d
20a	thee	— "D"	20b	wreathe	— read=Reed=rede
21a	these	— "D'"s	21b	breathe	— breed
22a	this	— dish	22b	with	— squid
23a	then	— den	23b	-----	-----
24a	thence	— dense	24b	-----	-----
25a	that	— datchet	25b	-----	-----
26a	thus	— dust	26b	-----	-----
27a	-----	-----	27b	soothe	— sued[2]
28a	-----	-----	28b	smooth	— mood
29a	they	— day	29b	lathe	— laid
30a	thy	— dye=die	30b	blithe=Blythe	— applied
31a	though=tho'	— dough=doe	31b	loathe	— load=lode
32a	thou	— Dow	32b	mouth (v)	— bowed (nodded)
33a	there	— dare	33b	-----	-----

CONSONANT COMBINATIONS

$\theta\underline{r}-$ 1 three thrift thrill thriller threat thread thresh thrash thrush
2 threw=thru=through=thro' thrall throb throng throstle throttle Thrace
3 thrice thrive throat throne throve throaty

$\theta w-$ 4 thwack thwaite thwart

✔ *Reminder*

Carry your voice through each vibrated consonant ending without adding an off-glide.

$-\delta z$ 5 teethes sheathes wreathes breathes bathes soothes youths moths
6 tithes writhes scythes oaths loathes clothes mouths

COMPARE: $-\delta z$ 7 teethes soothe breathes bathes tithes clothes
$-z$ 8 tease Sue's= breeze bays ties close (v)
Sioux's
$-d$ 9 teed sued breed bayed tied=tide glowed

$-\delta d$ 10 teethed sheathed wreathed breathed seethed soothed bathed tithed clothed
11 loathed mouthed

CONSONANT CLUSTERS

$-\theta s$ 12 Edith's heaths Smith's myths breaths deaths depths earth's youths growths

$-m\theta s$ 13 warmth warmth's

$-p_,\theta$ 14 depth depths

$-e\eta\theta$ 15 length strength lengths strengths

$-e\eta\theta nd$ 16 lengthened strengthened

$-e\eta\theta nz$ 17 lengthens strengthens

$-l f t_,\theta$ 18 twelfth twelfth's

WORDS USING DENTALIZATION OF $t_,$, $d_,$, $n_,$ AND $l_,$

✔ *Reminder*

Remember that in Good Speech, these four alveolar consonant sounds are dentalized only when they are followed by θ or δ in the same word or the following word.

19 fifth $'f_,if_t,\theta$ sixth $'s_,ik_,s_t,\theta$ eighth $'eit,\theta$ twelfth $'t_,wel f t,\theta$

$-d_,\theta$ 20 breadth width hundredth thousandth

$-n_,\theta$ 21 ninth tenth eleventh thirteenth fourteenth fifteenth sixteenth seventeenth
22 eighteenth nineteenth millionth billionth trillionth enthrall enthusiasm
23 enthrone plinth Co-rinth hyacinth Cynthia labÿ-rinth menthol Anthony
24 anthem anthology anthropology panther Pantheon lycanthropy Samantha
25 Grantham unthinking Gunther month

WORDS USING DENTALIZATION OF t , d , n AND l , Cont.

–lθ 1 filth health healthy wealth wealthy stealth stealthy Althea

2 Waltham (Massachusetts)

–lð– 3 although

PHRASES USING DENTALIZATION OF t , d , n AND l

$t\,θ$	$d\,θ$	$n\,θ$	$l\,θ$
4 want things	8 good thoughts	12 green thumb	16 feel thirst
5 meat thaws	9 red thermos	13 one thousand	17 Bill Thatcher

$t\,ð$	$d\,ð$	$n\,ð$	$l\,ð$
6 meet them	10 read the paper	14 win this	18 well then
7 get thee gone	11 would they	15 on the nose	19 all the same

SENTENCES FOR PRACTICE USING DENTALIZED t , d , n AND l

20 The warmth helped the hyacinths of Co-rinth to blossom in the ninth month.

21 Samantha's rapid growth in the seventh, tenth and eleventh months of this year was met with enthusiasm by the anthropology faculty.

22 Gunther drank to health and wealth at the *Twelfth Night* celebration.

23 The depth of the laby-rinth exceeded its width and breadth.

24 I've thought that again for the hundredth or thousandth time.

25 I don't think he got things right, Theodore.

26 You didn't thank that thin man for his *Henry the Fifth*?

27 He met them late the other night, the cad.

28 "Get thee to the vet, thou rat!" they cried.

29 We heard things like loud thuds along the width and breadth of the red throne.

30 Do you think Samantha had thought she'd thrive as a mad theo-rist?

31 Would that they could put their weapons down.

32 I've had this planned this time: we hand them a thousand, then read them the riot act.

33 Last Thursday the sound that a-rrested them was that of distant thunder.

34 You wanted them, you bought them, you cooked them, now you eat them!

35 Well then, what will they tell the health inspector?

36 Until this gets well-thickened, peel thin strips of well-thawed veal, Theo.

SENTENCES FOR PRACTICE USING $θ$

37 Ether is neither thin nor thick.

38 Is theology as the-rapeutic as it is thoughtful?

39 Tho-roughly think through any theo-ry before you say thanks for it.

40 Is he both slothful and uncouth?

41 Save your theatrics for the theater, Ethel!

42 Beth strayed from the path of truth this month.

43 Will Kenneth and Me-redith serve vermouth at their "fiftieth"?

44 Which theater is featu-ring *Twelfth Night* by that Elizabethan author?

SENTENCES FOR PRACTICE USING ð

✓ *Reminder* —————————————————————————————

> **Carry your voice through each vibrated consonant ending without adding an off-glide.**

1   Unclothe your body to let it breathe while you sunbathe.
2   The mother further studied breathing, and so did the father.
3   There are those who are always there for me.
4   Don't gather any more feathers if it's too much bother.
5   Keep breathing although you're writhing in pain.

SENTENCES FOR PRACTICE USING θ AND ð

6   The theme is weak and, therefore, this theater piece is without worth.
7   I'll run another bath and then bathe your little brother.
8   Be truthful! Did you maintain all your oaths or just one oath?
9   He's seething with loathing yet says nothing about anything.   wɪð
10 Cutting a tooth? Use this teething ring to soothe her teeth ridge.
11 We're both loth (adj; loath) to loathe te-rry cloth clothing.

SENTENCES FOR COMPARISON OF t WITH θ

12 Ty's thigh was torn by the thorns in the thicket.
13 I thought I taught tacky Thacke-ry to throw away the thin tin.
14 Thanks for the tanks. I brought the broth in them.
15 This thick ticket is tied to my thigh.
16 I'll bet Beth will tell all to Thelma.
17 I root less for one who's ruthless.
18 Matt, math class requires more thinking than a-rithmetic.

SENTENCES FOR COMPARISON OF d WITH ð

19 He laid the lathe in the dust and then he lay down in the den.
20 This dish will hold enough warmth for the dough, though.
21 Are those does? I know that they're deer.
22 They remember the day the Dow dropped by thousands.

SENTENCES FOR COMPARISON OF t, r-WITH θr –

23 It's true that the throughway is covered with thousands of thread-like treads.
24 Throw that trash into the trasher that's over there by the three trees.
25 I trust this is the thrust of the thrilling trilogy?
26 Is Ruth Reed from Bay-reuth really truthful through and through?   ˈbaɪ rɔɪtʰ
27 Did Tracey threaten to throw away her trophy?

SENTENCES FOR COMPARISON OF ð WITH z

28 I'm enthused about zoos. Zoos soothe Sue's nerves.   ɪn ˈθjuːzd
29 I said yes, though Zoe was opposed to being unclothed at the close of day.
30 The wizard appeared to wither in the wet weather.
31 You're close enough to close the clothes closet door.
32 "Breathe with ease. It's soothing," says Susan.

SENTENCES FOR PRACTICE USING SAME-CONSONANT BLENDS

✓ Reminder ——————————————————————————————

Maintain the contact of your tongue and the bottom of your upper front teeth during the following same-consonant blend sequences. Clarity of enunciation is achieved by a fresh impulse of energy that begins the second word of the sequence.

1 My breath thickened as I trod a päth through the south thicket.

2 Beth thought to teach the youth things about health theo-ries.

3 Hath theology given thee both thoughts worth thinking and a faith?

4 So! This month Thelma will give birth, thank goodness!

5 Breathe there? I'd loathe that!

6 Unclothe those babies when you bathe them.

7 Breathe the air and mouth these vows with thine own lithe lips.   wɪð

8 I loathe this city where they won't clothe the poor and soothe their so-rrows.

SENTENCES FOR PRACTICE USING COGNATE BLENDS

✓ Reminder ——————————————————————————————

Maintain contact between your tongue and the bottom of your upper front teeth during the following cognate blend sequences. Clarity of enunciation is achieved by the change from voiced to voiceless, or voiceless to voiced, and by a fresh impulse of energy that begins the second word of each sequence.

9 The truth then? I loathe things!

10 To smooth things over, bathe thrice daily, breathe thrillingly and sheathe thoughts of revenge.

◆ THE CONSONANT SOUNDS ◆
ᔆ AS IN "so" AND ƶ AS IN "zoo"

THE PLACE IV-B VOICELESS SIBILANT POST-DENTAL FRICATIVE CONTINUANT : ᔆ as in "so."

Represented by the spellings:

see   **ps**ycho   **sch**ism   **c**ent=**sc**ent   mi**c**e   a**x**   mi**ss**   pi**zz**a

THE PLACE IV-B VOICED SIBILANT POST-DENTAL FRICATIVE CONTINUANT : ƶ as in "zoo."

Represented by the spellings:

zebra   **x**ylophone   di**s**aster   hi**s**   no**s**e   bu**zz**   e**x**am

Keep your teeth close together, and the body of your tongue grooved, with the tip free and pointing toward the gum ridge (the sides of your tongue may or may not touch the sides of your upper teeth). It is possible to produce these sounds with the tongue behind the bottom teeth, but the sound will probably be overly sibilant.

The voiceless sound ᔆ is short and sharp, and the vibrated sound ƶ is energized and buzzed. There are many deviations from the correct sound; all are called LISPS.

REQUIREMENTS FOR GOOD SIBILANTS

- ◆ The teeth should be almost closed, as when biting, but should not actually touch
- ◆ The tip of the tongue should be raised high toward the gum ridge, BUT SHOULD NOT TOUCH IT
- ◆ The lips should be slightly spread, as in the i: position of "L**ee**"
- ◆ A very thin column of air should be directed down the middle of the tongue toward the teeth and gum ridge and should be swiftly emitted
- ◆ BE SURE THAT:
  - — The tip of the tongue is raised and free.
  - — A thin swift column of air is directed toward the gum ridge.

OBSERVE THE RULE OF USAGE FOR "S" PLURALS AND POSSESSIVES:

— If the sound preceding the final "s" is voiceless the "s" is spoken as ᔆ .

p,ᔆ   f,ᔆ   θᔆ   t,ᔆ   k,ᔆ
sips   (wh)ffs   math's   hats   likes

— If the sound preceding the final "s" is voiced, the "s" is spoken as ƶ .

b·z   vƶ   ðz   dz   /ƶ   /ƶ   gƶ   /ƶ
fibs   gives   bathes   cads   <u>r</u>ouges   judges   <u>r</u>ags   passes

LEARNING TO SEE, FEEL AND HEAR THE SOUNDS IN A NEW WAY

- ◆ Use your imagination to "see" the sound as you wish to "say" it.
  - — The phonetic letters ᔆ and ƶ will help you to visualize the consonant sounds that they represent.
- ◆ Establish new physical behavior.
- ◆ Listen to speakers who consistently use good sibilants in their speech.

EXERCISES FOR FINDING THE POSITION OF THE ARTICULATORS FOR *l* AND *z*

The sounds of *l* and *z* are made with the tip of your tongue POINTING TOWARD, BUT NO TOUCHING, the gum ridge directly behind the upper front teeth.

Use the following consonant sequences to

— Increase your awareness of the tip of your tongue in relation to your gum ridge;

— Strengthen and make flexible the tip of your tongue.

1	n	n	n	l	l	l		n	l	n	l	nee	lee nee lee	repeat
2	n	d	d	l	d	d		n	d	n	d	nee	dee nee dee	repeat
3	n	t	t	n	t	t		n	t	n	t	nee	tee nee tee	repeat
4	n	d	t	n	d	t		n	d	n	t	nee	dee nee tee	repeat

Hold the position of an unaspirated *t,* for a moment, as indicated by "...." IMAGINE *l* befor you say it.

Front Vowels	**Mid Vowels**	**Diphthongs**
5 neat...seat	9 inert...Cert	13 night...sight
6 knit...sit	10 nut...Sutter	
7 net...set		
8 gnat...sat	**Back Vowels**	
	11 naught...sought	
	12 not...sot	

Notice the position of the tip of your tongue when you say *n* . IMAGINE *l* before you say it.

Front Vowels	**Mid Vowels**	**Diphthongs**
14 Eugene...seen	18 earn...sir	23 Jane...sane
15 gin...sin	19 hun...sun	24 nine...sign
16 Jen...sent		25 Joan...sewn
17 Jan...sand	**Back Vowels**	26 clown...sound
	20 June...soon	
	21 lawn...saw	
	22 upon...sop	

Maintain the position for *l* after you have finished the sound. IMAGINE *l* before you say it.

Front Vowels	**Mid Vowels**	**Diphthongs**
27 kneel...seal	31 hull...sulk	33 nail...sail
28 nil...sill		34 oil...soil
29 Nell...sell	**Back Vowels**	35 dole...soul
30 Al...Sal	32 all...Saul	

Increase your awareness of the tip of your tongue as you articulate the following series of words. Notice the AMOUNT of energy at the tip of your tongue during each initial sound.

	l	*n*	*d*	*tʰ*	*z*	*ʃ*
1	Lee	knee	Dee	tea	"Z"	see
2	lip	nip	dip	tip	zip	sip
3	lap	nap	dapper	tap	zap	sap
4	Lew=Lou	gnu	do	too=two	zoo	Sioux
5	law	gnaw	daw	taw	-----	saw
6	lot	not	dot	tot	-----	sot
7	lay	nay	day	Tay	Zane	say
8	lie	nigh	die	Ty	Zion	sigh

EXERCISES FOR PRACTICE RELATING THE POSITION OF *t* TO *ʃ*

t, ʃtʰ	*ʃ*		*t, ʃtʰ*	*ʃ*		*t, ʃtʰ*	*ʃ*
9 teat...steam	seem=seam	14 hurt...stir	sir	18 tate...state	say
10 teat...steep	seep	15 Tut...stuck	suck	19 tight...sty	sigh
11 tilt...stilt	sill			20 hoit...Tolstoy	soy
12 tête...Stella	cellar	16 toot...stoop	soup	21 tote...stow	so
13 tat...stat	sat	17 tot...stop	sop		
				22 teared...steer	seer
				23 torte...Storch	sort
				24 tart...start	Sartre

25 Steam seeped through the seams it seems.
26 I can still stir, sir.
27 I'll bet Stella went into the cellar.
28 Stack the sacks of sand by Stan.
29 The stones will be sold on the stoop.

30 Don't put that stool on the stoop too soon.
31 I stayed to say the sty made me sigh.
32 That stŏ-ry of Storch was sort of mean.
33 The starlet started trouble for Sartre.
34 Who stopped the stŏ-ry entitled "Soa-ring"?

t, ʃ	*t,ʃ*		*t, ʃ*	*t,ʃ*		*t, ʃ*	*t,ʃ*
35 heat...s	heats	39 hurt...s	hurts	43 bait...s	baits
36 hit...s	hits	40 hut...s	huts	44 bite...s	bites
37 bet...s	bets			45 doit...s	doits
38 bat...s	bats	41 hoot...s	hoots	46 boat...s	boats
		42 rot...s	rots	47 bout...s	bouts

48 Will the heat stay in the neat sheets all night, Sy?
49 Can Kit start Sarni on hot meats yet, Sandy?
50 I bet Stan lost bets. Did he bet on the Mets?
51 Hear the fat cats meowing for "Chits" tidbits!
52 Don't hurt Bert's feelings about desserts.
53 Light Bites are great spots for light snacks.

EXERCISES FOR PRACTICE RELATING THE POSITION OF *t* **TO** *ɹ* **, Cont.**

	tʰ	*t,ɹ*	*ɹ*	*ɹtʰ*		*tʰ*	*t,ɹ*	*ɹ*	*ɹtʰ*
1	peat	Pete's	piece	pieced	6	loot	loots	loose	loosed
2	mit	mits	miss	mist=missed	7	lot	lots	loss	lost
3	met	Met's	mess	messed					
4	hurt	hurts	hearse	rehearsed	8	pate	pates	pace	paced
5	mutt	mutts	muss	must	9	right	rights	rice	iced

10 A lot of Lot's loss was lost time.
11 That's right! Wright's rice needs to be iced.
12 I hate my mate's face (when) spaced out.
13 But, if the mutts make a muss they must go!
14 Bert's hurt. Get the nurse first!
15 I bet Bess that we'll miss the final dress at the Met.
16 Admit that your debts are a mess!

	nt,ɹ	*nɹ*	*nɹɪz*		*nt,ɹ*	*nɹ*	*nɹɪz*
17	mints	mince	minces	20	cents	sense	senses
18	prints	prince	princes	21	dents	dense	condenses
19	Quint's	quince	Quincey's	22	chants	chance	chances

23 Wasting cents makes no sense.
24 Mint tea and mince pie? Or mint tea and quince pie?
25 This turn of events convinced me of Providence.
26 Commence with expense but dispense with preTENSE.

	l	*ɹl*	*ɹl*	*ɹ*		*l*	*ɹl*	*ɹl*	*ɹ*
27	panel	Hansel	slack	sack	30	tunnel	tinsel	slit	sit
28	fennel	pencil	slender	sender	31	tonal	tonsil	slog	soggy
29	tunnel	utensil	slay	say	32	comical	council	slough	sow

33 The tunnel tinsel needs to be slit so we can sit.
34 The annals of Hansel Slackman sacrificed since-rity for sensationalism.
35 See this pencil? Slip it to Sis.
36 It was comical that the council slept through that session.

PAIRS OF WORDS FOR COMPARISON OF ʃ WITH ʒ

Initial		Medial		Final	
1a see	— "Z"	1b policing	— pleasing	1c obese	— bees
2a seen	— Zeno	2b piecing	— appeasing	2c peace	— appease
3a seep	— zebra	3b deceased	— diseased	3c niece	— knees
4a sit	— zit	4b whist	— whizzed	4c hiss	— his
5a sith	— zither	5b kisser	— gizzard	5c miss	— Ms.
6a send	— Zen	6b pressing	— president	6c "S"	— Des
7a sand	— Zan	7b passel	— Basil=basil	7c ass	— as (sf)
8a sap	— zap	8b tassel	— dazzle	8c Cass	— jazz
9a Serkin	— zircon	9b mercy	— Mersey	9c curse	— curs
10a circus	— Xerxes	10b thirsty	— Thursday	10c purse	— purrs
11a Serbian	— Zerbe	11b absurd	— observe	11c immerse	— demurs
12a Sioux	— zoo	12b abusive	— amusing	12c use (n)	— use (v)
13a so-rrow	— Zo-rro	13b crossbow	— Crosby	13c boss	— Boz
14a sane	— Zane	14b Macy	— Maisie	14c pace	— pays
15a sakes	— Zakes	15b lacey	— lazy	15c base	— bays
16a Sadie	— zany	16b basis	— braises	16c race	— rays=raise
17a savior	— Xavier	17b faces	— phases	17c place	— plays
18a sigh	— xylophone	18b enticing	— appetizing	18c entice	— ties
19a psycho	— zygote	19b pricing	— prizing	19c mice	— surmise
20a soya	— Zoya	20b noisome	— noisy	20c rejoice	— joys
21a so	— Zoe	21b post	— posed	21c dose	— doze
22a sa-ri	— Czar	22b pasta	— Mazda	22c Haas	— spas

Final — Front Vowels

ʃ	ʒ
23 Patrice	— trees
24 Matisse	— tease
25 lease	— Lee's=leas
26 fleece	— fleas
27 decrease	— decrees
28 Reese	— Ma-rie's
29 miss	— Ms.

Final — Back Vowels

ʃ	ʒ
34 goose	— McGoo's
35 moose	— moos
36 loose	— lose
37 Russe	— ruse=rues
38 juice	— Jews
39 Bruce	— brews=bruise
40 puce	— pews=Pugh's
41 deuce	— dues
42 sauce	— saws

Final

(vs)		(vd)	
	ʃ		ʒ
49 repeats		— impedes	
50 defeats		— feeds	
51 pleats		— pleads	
52 bets		— beds	
53 plaits		— plaids	
54 mates		— maids	
55 fates		— fades	
56 false		— falls	
57 chumps		— chums	
58 lamps		— lambs	
59 grates		— grades	
60 leaks		— leagues	
61 sax		— sags	
62 oath's		— oaths	
63 knife's		— knives	
64 limps		— limbs	
65 humps		— hums	
66 cramps		— crams	
67 sinks		— sings	

Mid Vowels

ʃ	ʒ
30 purpose	— Sherpas
31 Dorcas	— orca's
32 bus	— buzz
33 fuss	— fuzz

Diphthongs

ʃ	ʒ
43 nice	— denies
44 rice	— rise
45 spice	— spies, despise
46 voice	— envoys
47 douse	— endows
48 house (n)	— house (v)

The following three groups of exercises are designed to promote an economically-spoken *s* sound when it is in combination with the three voiceless stop-plosive consonant sounds *p* , and *k* .

SENTENCES FOR PRACTICE USING *st* ENDINGS

NOTE: Do not linger and waste breath on the *s* sound. Aim for the *t* sound at the end of the word.

1 The best and brightest live in the West.
2 The fastest and most honest live in the East.
3 He kissed her first, but lost her at the last.
4 That chest will cost you most of the last paycheck.
5 Thrust that crust into the dust if you must.
6 Dost thou hoist thy crest amongst us?

In the following combinations *st, s* , *sp, s* and *sk, s*, do not linger on the first *s* sound. Aim for the unaspirated plosive and hold its position for a split second, then proceed to the very short *s* sound that begins the following word. ZAP to the plosive, CHECK OFF the second *s* .

ZAP-CHECK PRACTICE SENTENCES

7 The first song was from *West Side Sto-ry*.
8 Last Saturday Steve made a fast search for the lost songs.
9 The last sound she heard was the mast snapping.
10 He made the first score with a fast serve to the lowest seed.
11 Forgetting the past seemed the best solution.
12 My the-rapist says that my analyst stopped listening du-ring my last session.
13 Tonight's guest star is the best singer in East Sweden, Mr. August Strindberg.

14 His lisp certainly isn't a crisp sound.
15 Grasp something or clasp someone's hand if you feel unsteady.
16 Unclasp such a tight collar. You'll gasp surely!

17 May I ask something about the task set for me?
18 Did the Basque say that the bisque seemed to be burnt?
19 Ask Sam to (wh)isk Susan away from the Romanesque sculpture.

In the following combinations of *st, s* , *sp, s* and *sk, s* , linger slightly on the first *s* sound, then swiftly articulate the plosive with the second sound as if they were one affricate sound. SWING on the first *s* , then CHOP it off with the "ts," "ps" or "ks." At conversational speed, these words will have a syncopated rhythm.

SWING-CHOP PRACTICE SENTENCES

20 The guests behaved like beasts at the feasts.
21 The tests of strength were made with fists.
22 The priests made boasts and jests du-ring the toasts.
23 The case of the physicists conTRASTS with that of the analysts.
24 It ingests the pot roasts and then tastes the rest of the beast's repast.
25 She detests the pests, as do her guests of all castes.

SWING-CHOP PRACTICE SENTENCES, Cont.

1 These wasps leave wisps on the cups of the clasps.
2 The clasps seem fragile. Use hasps instead of the clasps.

3 Set Mrs. Fiske's disks on the desks next to the masks.
4 Removing husks and tusks from the masks involves taking risks.

SENTENCES FOR COMPARISON OF ◁ WITH ℤ

5 Please lease Lee's freezer to Lisa Gleason for a reasonable fee.
6 My blessings upon thee, and I absolve thee of the sins of thy resolutely dissolute life.
7 Dissatisfied with cities, he's dissolved his business practices and has settled in Azusa.
8 What is existence for Jasper, the jazz person from Curzon Street?
9 Since Che's chastisement, he hasn't faced up to the noises of his "voices."
10 The consensus is that at these prices she deserves prizes that dazzle the senses.
11 Croesus decrees that unless the diseased crazies cease he will seize the deceased Caesar.
12 Hasn't the has-been husband hassled his kissing cousin just as he pleases?
13 It's the in's and out's of these incidents that depress the present peasant president.
14 My niece's sneezes are the reasons for diseases, as Reese sees it.

CONSONANT CONTRASTS TO STABILIZE THE SOUNDS OF ◁ AND ℤ

You should be able to see the tip of your tongue articulating against the bottom of your upper front teeth for θ , and your tongue should disappear behind your upper front teeth when articulating ◁ . Now close your eyes and produce θ several times, then ◁ several times. IMAGINE each sound before you say it.

	Initial			Final	
	θ	◁		θ	◁
15a	theme	— seem=seam	15b	wreath	— Reese
16a	thick	— sick	16b	myth	— miss
17a	thing	— sing	17b	Beth	— Bess
18a	thank	— sank	18b	math	— mass
19a	-----	-----	19b	path	— pass
20a	third	— sir	20b	worth	— worse
21a	thuds	— suds	21b	doth	— bus
22a	thew	— sue	22b	vermouth	— moose
23a	thought	— sought	23b	-----	-----
24a	thong	— song	24b	moth	— moss

CONSONANT CONTRASTS TO STABILIZE THE SOUNDS OF θ **AND** z **, Cont.**

	Initial		**Final**	
	θ	s		θ	s

Initial θ	s	Final θ	s
1a thane	— sane	1b wraith	— race
2a thigh	— sigh	2b Forsyth	— precise
3a thole	— soul=sole=Seoul	3b growth	— gross
4a theo-ry	— Si-ri	4b south	— souse

Initial, Medial ð   z   **Final** ð   z

Initial, Medial ð	z	Final ð	z
5a thee	— "Z"	5b teethe	— tease
6a wither	— quizzer	6b with	— wiz
7a then	— Zen	7b -----	-----
8a than (sf)	— Zan	8b -----	-----
9a brother	— buzzer	9b -----	-----
10a bathing	— Basingstoke	10b bathe	— bays
11a tithing	— appetizing	11b writhes	— rise
12a though	— Zoe	12b oaths	— owes
13a clothing	— closing	13b loathes	— lows

Close your eyes and produce ʃ several times and s several times. IMAGINE each sound before you say it.

Initial ʃ	s	Medial ʃ	s	Final ʃ	s
14a she	— see	14b machine	— Massine	14c leash	— lease
15a shin	— sin	15b leashes	— leases	15c Cornish	— cornice
16a Shick	— sick	16b fished	— fist	16c tarnish	— harness
17a shell	— sell=cell	17b precious	— presses	17c Tesh	— Tess
18a shuttle	— subtle	18b gushing	— Gussie	18c mush	— muss
19a shoe	— Sioux	19b Aleutian	— loosen	19c ruche	— Russe
20a shook	— soot	20b pusher	— Wooster	20c push	— puss
21a Shaw	— saw	21b caution	— Lawson	21c -----	-----
22a shod	— sod	22b washed	— wast	22c bosh	— boss
23a Shea	— say	23b Hypatia	— pacer	23c -----	-----
24a shy	— sigh	24b Fleischer	— splicer	24c -----	-----
25a show	— so	25b lotion	— docent	25c gauche	— dose
26a shore	— sore=soar	26b Portia	— porcelain	26c Porsche[2]	— remorse
27a Arsham	— arson	27b partially	— parsley	27c harsh	— farce
28a shower	— sour	28b -----	-----	28c -----	-----

SENTENCES FOR COMPARISON OF CONSONANT SOUNDS s θ z ð

1 A sane thane?
2 What's the theo-ry, Si-ri?
3 Is that Bes or Beth?
4 Look at the mouth on that mouse!
5 The truth seems of no use to the youth.
6 That Matisse sets my teeth on edge!
7 Register my niece in the suite underneath you.
8 Hit the buzzer, brother.
9 See *The Wiz* with all stars!
10 I saw Shaw thank the chauFFEUR.
11 May I lease a leash?
12 Show the Cornish cornice to Zsa Zsa.
13 Send a porcelain of Portia to the Shah.
14 Russell casually confessed at confession.
15 Treasure shipments of pe-rishables from Pa-ris.
16 His decision was decisive.
17 Is this rash from raspbe-rries as red as rouge?
18 Caution Lawson that we're close to a closure.
19 I missed the allusion to the Aleutian Islands.
20 She sought thoughts along this theme, it seems.
21 No truce, in truth, preceded the intrusion.
22 Cass received cash from the catastrophe.
23 Eat fresh fish with partially fresh parsley.
24 Shun the sun. Shade your face from its rays.

WORDS FOR PRACTICE

Initial s

s –
25 see sit set sat sample sir Samoa such soothe suit^2 soot saw song
26 psalm say sigh soy sew sow sear Sa-rah sore sark sire sour

sp-
27 speed spill spell span spur spaghetti spud spoon spook spew Spokane
28 spawn spot spay spy spoil spoke spout spear spare spoor spore spar spire

sm-
29 Smee smith smell smash smirk smug smooth small smock smile . smote
30 smear smart

sw-
31 sweet swizzle sweat swam swerve swung swoon swan suave sway swine
32 Swoyer swear swore

sf-
33 sphinx sphe-rical sphere

st-
34 steel still step stack stir stability stuck stooge stew stood stall
35 stock stay sty stole stout steer stare=stair store star Stiers

sn-
36 sneeze snip snell snap Snerd snuggle snooze snooky snob snake snide
37 snow snout sneer snare snore snarl

sl-
38 sleeve slim sled slam slander slur Slavonia slough (shed skin)
39 slew=slough (mud hole) Slovenia slaughter slot Slav slay sly slow
40 slough (marsh)

sk-
41 scheme skill sketch scan scourge scuff school skewer scald scoff
42 skate sky scope scowl scare score scar scour

spl-
43 spleen split splendid splash splurge splutter splayed splice

spr-
44 spree sprig spread sprang sprung spruce sprawl sprocket spray sprite sprout

str-
45 stream strict stress strand strategic struck strudel strook straw strong
46 stray strike stroy strove Stroud

skw-
47 squeeze squib squelch squirm squall squab Squeers square squire

WORDS FOR PRACTICE, Cont.

Initial ʂ

ʂk,r-   1 scream script scrap scruff screw scrawl scrod scrape scribe scroll
       2 scrounge

Medial ʂ

- ʂ -   3 leasing kissing lesson lassie pặssing nursing aside fussy looser Osi-rĭs
       4 awesome tossing racing dicing voicing closer (adj) grousing piercing
       5 forcing larceny tiresome

-ʂp,t^h   6 lisped gặsped rặsped grặsped clặsped cusped

✓ *Reminder* ————————————————————————

> SWING on the first ʂ , then CHOP it off with the "ps," "ts" or ks." (See pages 276-277.)

-ʂp,ʂ   7 lisps wisps crisps asps gasps rasps clasps grasps hasps cusps wasps

-ʂt,ʂ   8 beasts priests mists lists fists cysts insists wrists pests bests detests
       9 guests nests vests rests behests quests chests jests blặsts cặsts fặsts
      10 lặsts mặsts repặsts Hearst's firsts bursts dursts thirsts busts gusts musts
      11 lusts rusts crusts thrusts boosts exhausts costs pastes bastes tastes wastes
      12 heists foists hoists posts boasts toasts coasts ghosts roasts hosts jousts

-ʂk,ʂ   13 bisques disks Fisk's risks (wh)sks desks grotesques casques cặsks ặsks
      14 bặsks tặsks mặsks=mặsques musks Rusk's husks tusks

✓ *Reminder* ————————————————————————

> Syllabic 𝑛 or ℓ takes the place of a vowel in forming certain UNstressed SYLLA-BLES usually at the end of a word.

-ʂnz   15 listens christens glistens lessons fặstens worsens loosens hastens chastens
      16 bisons Tyson's bosuns=boatswains Pierson's coarsens Orson's Carson's

-ʂℓz   17 (wh)stles bristles thistles nestles vessels vassals hassles tassels
      18 cặstles rehearsals bustles hustles apostles jostles morsels parcels

-dʂt^h   19 needst midst didst standst couldst shouldst wouldst
      20 call'dst form'dst arm'dst alarm'dst

-ʂtʃ   21 Christian mixture fixture question suggestion texture celestial
      22 bestial gesture tempestuous Sebastian pặsture posture

Final ʂ

✓ *Reminder* ————————————————————————

> Keep final ʂ brief. Strive for efficient articulation and management of your breath.

-ʂ   23 lease miss mess lass pặss purse porpoise pus loose use (n) sauce loss
      24 ace ice voice close (adj) mouse pierce bourse horse sparse

-p,ʂ   25 leaps lips reps wraps chirps gallops cups hoops hops apes types hopes
      26 harps

WORDS FOR PRACTICE, Cont.

Final ʃ

−*lp,ʃ* 1 yelps (wh)elps helps alps scalps gulps

−*mp,ʃ* 2 limps chimps scrimps shrimps wimps Kemp's camps stamps ramps vamps

3 lamps champs humps chumps pumps stumps rumps jumps Gump's chomps

−*ʃp,ʃ* 4 lisps wisps crisps asps rạsps clạsps grạsps hạsps cusps wasps

−*fʃ* 5 thief's (wh)iffs chefs lạughs turfs huffs roofs hoofs chafes strifes loafs scarfs

−*mfʃ* 6 nymphs lymphs Banff's triumphs galumphs

−*lfʃ* 7 sylphs elf's shelf's self's Ralph's gulfs wolf's golfs

−*θʃ* 8 teeth's myths deaths pạth's berths=births Sabbaths Ruth's broths

9 Forsyth's growths fourths depths

−*d̯θʃ* 10 widths hundredths breadths thousandths

−*n̯θʃ* 11 Cǒ-rinth's hyacinths plinths labỷ-rinths tenths months ninths

−*l̯θʃ* 12 healths wealth's stealth's

−*t̯,θʃ* 13 fifths sixths eighths

✓ *Reminder* ──

Observe the unaspirated stop-plosives in the following combinations.

−*t,ʃ* 14 heats bits bets bats hurts spigots huts boots puts thoughts cots

15 bites Voit's boats bouts ports parts

COMPARE: −*p,ʃ* 16 gyps	Scripps	temps	upsets	lapse	chirps
−*p,t,ʃ* 17 Egypt's	scripts	attempts	accepts	adapts	excerpts
−*p,ʃ* 18 tops	romps	Krupps			
−*p,t,ʃ* 19 adopts	prompts	cǒ-rrupts			

−*ŋk,ʃ* 20 thinks drinks sinks jinx thanks tanks cranks punks monks honks Bronx

COMPARE: −*ŋk,ʃ* 21 stinks	sinks	junks	
−*ŋk,t,ʃ* 22 instincts	precincts	adjuncts	

−*ft,ʃ* 23 lifts gifts sifts shifts drifts lefts thefts clefts shạfts crạfts

24 drạfts=drạughts grạfts rạfts wạfts tufts lofts Croft's

COMPARE: −*lt,ʃ* 25 pelts	faults	catapults	consults	results
−*lʃ* 26 else	false	pulse	repulse	convulse
−*lt,ʃ* 27 cults	adults			
−*lʃ* 28 Hulce	Dulcie			

WORDS FOR PRACTICE, Cont.

COMPARE: $-nt,Ȿ$ 1 mints prints cents tents dents pants

$-nⱾ$ 2 mince prince sense tense dense expanse

$-nt,Ȿ$ 3 chănts confidănts

$-nⱾ$ 4 chănce dănce

$-Ⱥt,Ȿ$ 5 beasts cysts rests măsts firsts lusts boosts exhausts costs wastes

$-k,Ȿ$ 6 lurks bă-rracks dukes crooks hawks docks aches bikes yoicks oaks

COMPARE: $-k,Ȿ$ 7 Dick's = Dix picks specks wrecks sex

$-k,t,Ȿ$ 8 edicts addicts depicts expects di-rects sects

$-k,Ȿ$ 9 ax packs fax tracks snacks ducks

$-k,t,Ȿ$ 10 acts pacts facts contracts enacts ducts

$-lk,Ȿ$ 11 milks silks elks Belk's talcs bulks sulks skulks

$-Ⱥk,Ȿ$ 12 bisques desks casques ăsks husks

Initial ⱬ

$ⱬ-$ 13 zee zebra zenith zeal zinc zest zephyr zircon zirconium zoo zounds[2]

14 Zeus zoology zoological zany xylophone zone czar

Medial ⱬ

$-ⱬ-$ 15 freezing business busy Lisbon dazzle hazzard frazzle deserve

16 dozen buzzard cousin music closet lazy rises noises ozone

$-ⱬd$ 17 eased (wh)zzed jazzed abused paused buzzed crazed prized housed

✓ *Reminder* ——————————————————————————————

Syllabic m , n and l take the place of a weak vowel in certain UNstressed SYLLABLES.

$-ⱬm$ 18 atheism criticism witticism prism spasm chasm enthusiasm hĕ-roism barbă-rism

$-ⱬn$ 19 reason season citizen prison resin hŏ-rizon dozen blazon brazen poison

20 crimson

$-ⱬl$ 21 easel weasel fizzle grizzle embezzle dazzle pĕ-rusal bamboozle nasal

22 Hazel reprisal disposal că-rousal

Final ⱬ

✓ *Reminder* ——————————————————————————————

Carry your voice through each final vibrated consonant without adding an off-glide

$-ⱬ$ 23 appease fizz says as (sf) burrs furs does (sf) fuzz whose=who's Oz was (sf)

24 lays rise noise nose ă-rouse fears pairs tours oars cars fires

25 flowers=flow'rs=flours

$-bⱬ$ 26 fibs ebbs cabs curbs rubs tubes daubs cobs Abe's gibes robes orbs garbs

$-m:ⱬ$ 27 deems limbs gems hams worms comes looms palms aims times homes

28 forms arms

WORDS FOR PRACTICE, Cont.

$-vz$ 1   weaves gives moves h^aalves curves loves grooves behaves hives groves

$-ðz$ 2   sheathes wreaths b^aaths smoothes bathes writhes scythes clothes loathes

$-dz$ 3   beads bids beds lads words buds woods lauds gods aids sides avoids

        4   odes crowds

$-n:z$ 5   beans bins dens cans yearns buns spoons yawns dons panes=pains

        6   pines loins owns downs mourns=morns barns=Barnes

$-l:z$ 7   (whⓔels) feels peels bills fills bells yells pals gals hurls pearls gulls hulls

        8   fools tools pulls wools halls crawls dolls lolls pales=pails tails=tales

        9   isles=aisles styles boils toils bowls rolls=roles fowls=fouls cowls

$-gz$ 10   leagues digs eggs bags burghs jugs bogs hogs Hague's vogues

$-ŋ:z$ 11   things rings kings pangs gangs hangs lungs tongues wrongs throngs

       12   songs belongs

$-l:bz$ 13   bulbs De Kalb's albs

$-l:m:z$ 14   films elms realms ove(rwh)elms Helms

       15   elves delves selves shelves valves wolves absolves dissolves involves resolves

$-n:dz$ 16   fiends winds ends bands lands hands dem^aands comm^aands funds

       17   wounds bonds ponds finds binds abounds astounds

✓ *Reminder* _____

Syllabic $l̩$ and $n̩$ take the place of a weak vowel in certain UNstressed SYLLABLES. (See pages 250 and 239.)

Carry your voice through each vibrated consonant ending without adding an off-glide.

$-p̩lz$ 18   peoples ripples cripples apples grapples s^aamples ex^aamples purples

       19   disciples couples topples maples

$-blz$ 20   enfeebles scribbles pebbles babbles sociables bubbles troubles rubles

       21   gobbles fables tables Bibles foibles nobles marbles

$-mlz$ 22   animals mammals camels Friml's pommels

$-nlz$ 23   annals panels runnels channels funnels tunnels

$-fn̩z$ 24   stiffens toughens softens hyphens orphans

$-flz$ 25   baffles raffles muffles shuffles snuffles rifles trifles stifles

$-θlz$ 26   Ethel's Bethel's Athol's brothels

$-eŋθn̩z$ 27   strengthens lengthens

WORDS FOR PRACTICE, Cont.

–ðn̩z 1 heathens Sneathen's

–vn̩z 2 evens elevens sevens ovens ravens havens enlivens

–vl̩z 3 snivels levels travels removals novels rivals ovals marvels

–dl̩z 4 needles riddles meddles saddles curdles muddles noodles waddles bridles

–sn̩z 5 listens glistens fastens persons loosens hastens chastens=Chasen's moistens
6 Towson's Pierson's Orson's parsons

–sl̩z 7 epistles (wh)istles thistles nestles vessels vassals castles bustles hustles apostles

–zn̩z 8 reasons seasons citizens prisons cousins dozens raisins poisons

–zl̩z 9 weasels embezzles frazzles dazzles puzzles muzzles bamboozles

–k,l̩z 10 pickles freckles circles mi-racles buckles cycles snorkels sparkles

–tʃn̩z 11 kitchens Mitchens escutcheons luncheons

–dʒn̩z 12 Weejuns pigeons widgeons surgeons sturgeons dudgeons dungeons
13 bludgeons Cajun's

–tʃl̩z 14 Mitchell's satchels Rachel's Vachel's

✓ Reminder ──

> **Nasal plosion occurs when a stop-plosive is followed by a nasal consonant and the nasal is made in the same place of articulation as the stop-plosive. (See pages 239-240.)**

–t,n̩z 15 sweetens threatens fattens buttons lightens shortens heartens

–dn̩z 16 Edens reddens saddens burdens guerdons Gordon's gardens

SENTENCES FOR PRACTICE USING s IN INITIAL POSITION

1 See Cy's secretā-ry Sandy.
2 Sue saw the soft sā-ri on Sunday.
3 Oh sir, such a safe sigh you've sounded.
4 The soil will be sown for the sow.
5 A seer said that Sā-rah will sell some sardines.
6 Slip me a sip of cider.
7 Did you spot the spill on the sill?
8 That smooth smell will sell.
9 Swift swimmers will swoon soon.
10 Is that a sphinx on the sphere, Si-ri?
11 Stack the sacks of newly-stocked socks.
12 Set the snare for the snake near the snowdrift.
13 A sled needs a slippē-ry slope to really sail.
14 That's a skillful sketch of the sky, Cy.
15 This display of splendor is a splurge of spending.
16 "A spray of spruce sprigs," I'd say.
17 Stress and strain will obstruct your sanity! (See page 279, numbers 45-46 st,r-.)
18 This is secured by seven straps and several strings.
19 It seems the streamers constricted anything of consequence.
20 Squeeze the squab while you sob.
21 Scrap the script. It's sappy.
22 Sitting through the lesson is no loss to Mr. Hoss.

SENTENCES FOR PRACTICE USING s IN MEDIAL POSITION

23 You sent that lassie out of the house, you louse?
24 The passing of Flossie is a loss to the boss, but he'll toss it off.
25 This nice dressing is for the hearts of lettuce salad.
26 Say thrice: Mr. Messing's a blessing, Mr. Messing's a blessing, Mr. Messing's a blessing!
27 This mess on the dresser is distressing, if you get my message.
28 Whisk some whiskey into the bisques while the egg whites are stiff.
29 Who listens to Tyson's lessons? Does Jessie or Bessie?
30 Sew the thistles onto the tassels before the rehearsal's ended.
31 This question is also a mixture of suggestions.
32 This is a Christian question, with elements both celestial and bestial. 'bes.t.fl

SENTENCES FOR PRACTICE USING s IN FINAL POSITION

33 Pass the nice grapes while we listen to tapes of the Pope's address.
34 Will Scripps publish the scripts or just clips of hits?
35 Do gulps serve as helps in the Alps?
36 Gumps never scrimps on shrimps for the camps.
37 Will the temps make attempts to finish the scripts from Scripps?
38 Wisps of wiste-ria attracted wasps.
39 Hats off to him who accepts upsets!
40 Toss me the shē-riff's handcuffs!

SENTENCES FOR PRACTICE USING ᴣ IN FINAL POSITION

1 The nymphs were triumphs at Banff's summer theater. 'ʤ æ m fs

2 I see the force of myths.

3 Hyacinths blossomed in the widths and breadths of both laby-rinths.

4 This piece looks at hurts and broken hearts.

5 Pour your drinks into the sinks. Thanks!

6 The crafts at Crofts' make great gifts.

7 Falsehoods are faults even in adults, Dulcie.

8 You're too tense to dance, Chance.

9 Could you mince the mints?

10 Since when do you mince the quince for the quince pie?

11 Wasting cents makes little sense.

12 A chance roMANCE enhanced my trip to France.

13 This impulse proved false.

14 Are hawks, ducks and larks affected by the ice?

15 Put the beasts through the tests at all costs.

16 I expect to see Dick's edicts to the addicts.

17 Did you fax the facts regarding the contracts and the sound tracks to Max?

SENTENCES FOR PRACTICE USING ᴢ IN INITIAL, MEDIAL AND FINAL POSITION

✓ Reminder

Carry your voice through each vibrated consonant ending without adding an off-glide.

18 His zebra from Zululand shows zest and zeal for the zithers and zoos.

19 Are the zones in Lisbon organized in ZIP codes?

20 The business is hazardous to his health. It frazzles his nerves.

21 Whose topaz stones and jazzy furs and things are those?

22 His music includes jazz on the xylophone.

23 He behaves as though dazed and crazed. Who advised him to be so used and abused?

24 Who decides which pesticides have acceptable phosphides?

25 Who provides guides for the rides through the Tyneside countryside?

26 I have some skepticism for anyone who shows enthusiasm for criticism of his manne-risms.

27 It seems that there are times when rhymes and reasons coincide.

28 The biggest reason for delay-ing the season was that several dozen of the citizens were in prisons.

29 Put a dozen beans in the bins and the cans next to the spoons.

30 Hazel dazzled all her pals with the pearls she embezzled.

31 Lots of wheels and tools were at his disposal.

32 How many pubs and nightclubs cater to snobs in the suburbs?

33 These are the jobs: changing light bulbs; cleaning cobwebs from the bathtubs; and cooking the crabs.

34 Adam's diagrams show the beams, the platforms and the zig-zag co-rridors of the rooms.

35 Despite the acclaims, I'd say these items have problems.

36 The sleeves and scarves were disposed of by the executives.

37 The resolves they made for themselves were disastrous.

38 It grieves me to see the thieves bring in the sheaves.

SENTENCES FOR PRACTICE USING $\cancel{z}$ IN INITIAL, MEDIAL AND FINAL POSITION, Cont.

1 This medication relieves most headache pains.
2 Will you wash the bedclothes and underclothes when you wash the other clothes?
3 Change your clothes after you close the door.   (See page 267, numbers 7-8.)
4 Will you build sheaths with keys to hold the wreaths?
5 The crowds are on all sides of the woods.
6 Put the eggs in the bags and put the jugs and mugs in the closet.

SENTENCES FOR PRACTICE USING $\cancel{z}$ IN INITIAL, MEDIAL AND FINAL POSITIONS, Cont.

✔ *Reminder*

Carry your voice through each vibrated consonant ending without adding an off-glide.

7 Things like gangs can be reasons for killings.
8 Meg's hogs are in leagues unto themselves.
9 De Kalbs' bulbs are displayed "On Sale for Two Shillings."
10 *Desire Under the Elms* overwhelms Helmsley.
11 Designate a time to make some resolves amongst yourselves.
12 Some couples brought samples of apples, and others brought cuttings from the maples in their orchards.
13 Living on a few rubles troubles the constables.
14 The animals, including the camels, were featured in the panel's annals.
15 Serve the muffins after the butter softens.
16 It baffles me that they serve waffles and trifles at the raffles.
17 Ethel's expe-rience strengthens Bethels' faith. Faith lengthens life.
18 That enlivens me! It evens the score with those heathens.
19 I like novels in which the he-roine levels her rivals and travels a-round the world to see its marvels.
20 This both brightens and lightens the colors.
21 Patton's buttons are gluttons' buttons.
22 These troubles and burdens destroy Eden's se-renity.
23 Add the noodles before the milk curdles.
24 The dew moistens the grass and glistens in the dawn.
25 Are there good reasons for rea-rranging this season's shows?
26 The vassals hauled water in vessels to the castles.
27 Did the apostles write all the epistles?
28 The citizens brought dozens of boxes of raisins to their cousins in the prisons.
29 These puzzles frazzle my nerves.
30 This sauce thickens and then darkens in color as it cooks.
31 Natu-ral cycles flow easily in circles and bring about mi-racles.
32 Bring Rachel's satchels into Mitchens' kitchen, please.

SENTENCES FOR PRACTICE USING SAME-CONSONANT BLENDS

✓ *Reminder*

Maintain the position of your tongue during the following same-consonant blend sequences. Clarity of enunciation is achieved by a fresh impulse of energy that begins the second word of the sequence.

1 This same Miss Sally will meet us soon at the bus stop.

2 Her lips smiled at this snide, crass salesman.

3 Please, Zeus, his zoo will raise zebras zealously.   'zj u:ʑ

4 These are hers, Xenia, and those xylophones Zeke's.

SENTENCES FOR PRACTICE USING COGNATE BLENDS

✓ *Reminder*

Maintain the position of your tongue during the following cognate blend sequences. Clarity of enunciation is achieved by a change from voiced to voiceless, or voiceless to voiced, and by a fresh impulse of energy that begins the second word of the sequence.

5 Tis so! The wise senators will raise six bronze statues soon.

6 He's saved his sala-ry for his summer vacation.

THE PLACE IV-B VOICELESS PALATO-ALVEOLAR FRICATIVE CONTINUANT : ʃ **as in *"she."***

Represented by the spellings:

ᵴ*h*out ᵴure o*c*ean ma*ch*ine an*x*ious permi*ss*ion

con*sc*ious mo*t*ion *sch*napps

THE PLACE IV-B VOICED PALATO-ALVEOLAR FRICATIVE CONTINUANT : ʒ **as in *"genre."***

Represented by the spellings:

*Zs*a *Zs*a négligé mira*g*e a*z*ure trea*s*ure bi*j*ou

Relax your lower jaw and raise the tip and blade of your tongue toward the back part of the gum ridge without touching it. The sides of the tongue should touch the sides of your upper teeth, and the front of your tongue should be arched. Direct the breath over the tip of the tongue in a narrow stream, but do not allow any air to escape over the sides of your tongue. Your lips should remain neutral and relaxed. Use your breath economically to produce a gentle, cleanly articulated ʃ, and a warm, richly buzzed ʒ.

(See pages 225-226 for comparison of tʃ , dʒ and ʃ .)

WORDS FOR PRACTICE

Initial ʃ

ʃ—

1 she sheen she'll sheaf sheep sheath sheathe ship shin shift shell
2 chef shadow shack shall (sf) sham shank shad shag shăn't shirk shirt
3 chagrin shun shut shoe shoot should'st sugar shook should (sf) Shaw
4 shawl shop shot shock shave shame Shay=Shea shake shy
5 shine show shoal shout sheer share sure shore sharp shire shower

ʃr—

6 shriek shrill shred shrank shrew shrive shrove shroud

Medial ʃ

—ʃ—

7 vicious anxious precious ocean associate conscience machine sexual
8 sunshine seashore pressure fissure=fisher assure pressure unsure Russia
9 tissue issue appreciate negotiate fascist

—ʃ l̦

10 essential influential credential tŏ-rrential inconsequential
11 expé-riential existential palatial spatial racial partial martial=marshal nuptial

—ʃt ᴸ

12 unleashed fished refreshed mashed smashed brushed rushed pushed washed

—ʃn̦

13 admission commission recognition condition fashion legation vacation
14 Russian action faction attraction reaction Haitian patient Thracian

Final ʃ

—ʃ

15 leash wish relish flesh sash cash bush wash knavish gauche moŏ-rish
16 harsh

Initial ʒ

ʒ—

17 Gigi jardinière genre Genet Zsa Zsa gendarme

∫ ʒ

WORDS FOR PRACTICE, Cont.

Medial ʒ

-ʒ-
1 bijou seizure leisure visual pleasure treasure azure usual
2 usu-rer casual
3 regime glazier explosion vision illusion[2] persuasion envision intrusion
4 Hoosier Asia Persia collusion[2] freesia aphasia euthanasia abrasion lesion
5 oziers Brezhnev occasion allusion[2] Andalusian[2] Frazier

Final ʒ

✔ *Reminder* ——————————————————————————————————————

Carry your voice through each vibrated consonant ending without adding an off-glide.

-ʒ
6 prestige rouge ga-rage massage mi-rage camouflage corsage espionage
7 badinage beige cortege ba-rrage Vosges ménage

SENTENCES FOR PRACTICE USING ∫

8 Should the shipments of shampoo be shelved?
9 She'll shop for shirts, shoes and shoelaces for the nuptial bash. *'nʌpʃḷ*
10 Surely shocking fashions aren't stylish?
11 Shred the shrunken shrubs with the machine.
12 I wish to shun all shrill shrieks.
13 Will swordfish and shellfish mix with succotash?
14 Rush the Spanish rosebush to the pa-rish!
15 Surely she'll say, "That's rubbish!"
16 Will you mention that this special lotion is for facials?
17 Don't you wish this was an official vacation?
18 The pa-rish in Pa-ris is near the ocean.
19 I've seen a machine that presses with less pressure.
20 Replenish the stash of hash.
21 Can't you shout your change of heart? (See page 312 *tʃ* .)
22 Won't you share a chair?
23 Don't you shoot your chickens?

SENTENCES FOR PRACTICE USING ʒ

24 Genet treasured the jardiniere?
25 Zsa Zsa made all decisions for the gendarme.
26 This casual negligé is a vision of persuasion.
27 This regime is occasionally a pleasure.
28 It's an unusual ménage.
29 The explosion may camouflage the invasion.
30 Is this an entou-rage or a mi-rage?
31 Wear a lot of rouge when you wear this beige negligé.
32 Did your jardinière come from Germany? (See page 312 *dʒ* .)

SENTENCES FOR COMPARISON OF ∫ **WITH** ʒ

1 Buy-ing rouge is my passion.
2 Is living under a delusion an act of dilution?
3 Could a glazier cut zig-zags in this glacier?
4 His revision was in good condition.
5 I envision my rash as a mi-rage.
6 Decisive actions are decisions.
7 Is there sufficient conclusive evidence for the conclusion?
8 Persuasive conversation makes for friendly persuasion.
9 Any advice to ensure safe vision?

SENTENCES FOR PRACTICE USING SAME-CONSONANT BLENDS

✔ *Reminder*
> **Maintain the position of your articulators during the following same-consonant blend sequences. Clarity of enunciation is achieved by a fresh impulse of energy that begins the second word of the sequence.**

10 To wash shelves, push sugar over them with a harsh shaking motion.

11 I wish she'd wash shirts to diminish shabbiness.

12 Fresh shallots should accompany fresh shellfish.

13 Have a massage, Gigi, or read something from the espionage genre.

14 Your corsage, Zsa Zsa, is in the beige jardinière.

SENTENCE FOR PRACTICE USING COGNATE BLENDS

✔ *Reminder*
> **Maintain the position of your articulators during the following cognate blend sequence. Clarity of enunciation is achieved by the change from voiced to voiceless, or voiceless to voiced, and by a fresh impulse of energy that begins the second word of the sequence.**

15 The entou-rage should wear the usual beige shoes, camouflage shirts and rouge shawls.

◆ THE CONSONANT SOUND AS IN "red" ◆

THE PLACE IV-B VOICED POST-ALVEOLAR FRICATIVE CONTINUANT : *r* as in "red."*

The consonant r has no voiceless partner, or cognate, in Spoken English.

Represented by the spellings:

right=write=Wright=rite   tarry   rheumatism

✓ *Reminder* —————————————————————————————

Throughout the exercises in this text the consonant sound *r* is noted by a line beneath the "r" in the spelling of a word as well as beneath the phonetic letter *r* . Any "r" not so underlined is to be spoken as a vowel, diphthong or triphthong sound of "r."

Return the surprise singers' cup.   Dear, they're sure the roar's far away.

Relax your jaw; raise, or groove, the front of your tongue to a place behind the gum ridge; keep the tip free, pointing toward (but not touching) the extreme back of your upper gums; and curl the tip back slightly as the sound is made. The breath (voiced) passes over the tip of the tongue, causing friction between the tongue and the gum ridge, and produces a strong murmuring sound.

Do not let tension cause the sound to revert to *ɝ* , and do not let the sound take on a buzz like *ʒ* .

Approximate position of tongue
for consonant *r*

Tip-of-tongue touches the gum ridge for *d* and points toward the gum ridge for *r* .

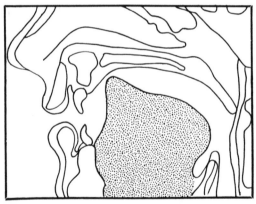

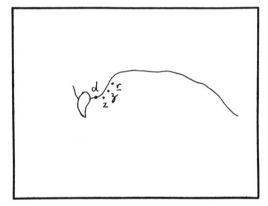

PRACTICE: a   dddddddzzzzzzzeeeeeee   *dz:i:*

b   dddddddzhzhzhzheeeeeee   *dʒ:i:*

c   dddddddrrrrrrreeeee   *dr:i:*

d   rrrrrrrrrrrrreeeeeeee   *ri:*

e   rrrrrrrrrrrrrrrrrrrrr   *r:*

Also avoid the trilled or rolled "r" that can be created if the tongue is allowed to flap as the vibrated breath passes over its tip. This trilled or rolled "r" is never used in North American speech, not even in classic texts.

* The correct phonetic letter for this consonant sound as assigned by the IPA is an upside down letter "r" *ɹ* . However *r* appears right-side-up in the majority of texts on Spoken English, and will so appear in this textbook.

Pronounce the consonant *r* only if it is followed by a vowel or diphthong sound.

This occurs in four positions:

1   At the beginning of a word:

> ring=<u>wr</u>ing   <u>rh</u>yme

2   In consonant combinations, where *r* is preceded by another consonant and followed by a vowel or diphthong sound:

> p<u>r</u>ay   sp<u>r</u>ing   t<u>r</u>ees   st<u>r</u>ing   c<u>r</u>ook   sc<u>r</u>eam   F<u>r</u>ench-f<u>r</u>ied   th<u>r</u>ee   sh<u>r</u>edded
>
> b<u>r</u>eak   d<u>r</u>eam   g<u>r</u>een

3   Between two vowel sounds:

> mi-<u>r</u>acle   he<u>-rr</u>ing

✓ *Reminder*

> **Be sure that you pronounce the first vowel sound with great purity and follow it with a clean-cut, definite consonant r . Do not give that first vowel r-coloring and then eliminate the true consonant r . (See page 89.)**
>
> **SAY: mi-<u>r</u>acle   NOT: mere a cle   SAY: he<u>-rr</u>ing   NOT: hair ing**

4   In phrases that contain a linking "r," there is optional usage when a word ends with a vowel or diphthong of "r" and the next word in the same phrase begins with a vowel sound. Say the usual vowel or diphthong that ends the first word and then link a consonant *r* onto the vowel that begins the next word.*

SAY: fire chief   BUT: fi<u>r</u>e engine

---

* In *Everyman's English Pronouncing Dictionary*, by Daniel Jones, an asterisk (*) is placed at the end of all words that are capable of taking this linking r . In *A Pronouncing Dictionary of American English*, by John S. Kenyon and Thomas A. Knott, these words are marked by (r.

WORDS FOR PRACTICE USING r IN INITIAL POSITION

1 ream reap reed=read=rede wreath reel regal reach regis reason

2 rip written rid rim rink wring=ring receive receipt reply remorse remove

3 wreck Reginald red=read render rest restau-rant register wretched reggae

4 rap=wrap rabbit rat radish ram ran rang ravish ravening rabble ratchet

5 rasp raft wrath rascal rather raspbe-rries raspiness

6 rum run rung=wrung rug rut rough

7 rue rude rule room rune roof route=root rumor=roomer Ruth ruminate

8 rook

9 robust roMANCE romantic rotation Romania Rochelle

10 raw wrought raucous

11 rot rock wrong Rhonda Rothschild rotten robber

12 rays=raise race rain=rein=reign rate rail Rachel rage radiate

13 rice rhyme=rime rhymer Rhine ripe right=rite=write=Wright rifle

14 row=roe roam=Rome roan rose=rows rode=road wrote=rote rotate
15 roll=role rope robe

16 row rowdy round rout rouse
17 rear rare ru-ral roar

PHRASES FOR PRACTICE

Initial r

18 red riding hood	24 rude Ruth	30 recreate a role	36 Rogue River
19 red Rolls Royce	25 Red Ryder	31 rah! rah! rah!	37 rowdy rhymes
20 rough river	26 red rover	32 the rain it raineth	38 raise the roof
21 read reams	27 Ralph Roister	33 rock 'n' roll riff	39 ru-ral route
22 a rich, rare reward	28 round and round	34 rotten wrapper	40 raucous roMANCE
23 wretched rascal	29 read 'n' write	35 rose-red wreath	41 really real

PHRASES FOR PRACTICE USING r IN CONSONANT COMBINATIONS PRECEDED BY A
CONSONANT AND FOLLOWED BY A VOWEL OR DIPHTHONG SOUND

1 previous president	preach in print	pretty primrose	practice praises
2 prayers prevail	provide proof	predictable pranks	profound progress
3 approved principles	appreciate pranks	prayed for a raid	Roman promo price
4 breathe briefly	brick bridges	brown brushes	a brave brigade
5 a brawling brother	British brandy	brittle brushes	brew broth
6 abbreviate the brief	break bread	the bridge's ridge	red bread
7 French-fried fritters	freezing freshmen	franchised in France	fruit from France
8 freshly frozen fruit	frugal friar	Friday fish fry	frequently frantic
9 Fred read	afraid of freedom	fried on rye	French wrench
10 through and through	three thrills	throaty thrush	he thrusts thrice
11 through the throat	threaten the throne	thread throughout	threepenny thrills
12 rush the thrushes	thrash with rashes	wrong throngs	through with rue
13 trip to Troy	trick or treat	train tracks	Troy will triumph
14 trapped in a tree trunk	a tryst in Trenton	tragic trilogy	tried and true
15 a country retreat	Trafalgar traditions	a Rio trio	contribute ribs
16 drinking drills	dread the draft	drea-ry drama	dreadful drought
17 a drastic drive	dresser drawer	droop and drool	Dru-ry Lane drama
18 address drugs	bedraggled drummer	drains of rain	driveway rivals
19 shrunk, shrank	a shrill shrew	a shrouded shrink	shrunken shrubbe-ry
20 short-shrifted shrink	shrill shrieks	rub the shrubs	rude and shrewd
21 crazy credit	creepy creatures	cru-el crew-el	crippled criminal
22 accredited cryptology	crucial cross-stitch	crave raves	crumbs and rum
23 greet a greedy grocer	grow great grapes	grim and gruesome	grow gratefully
24 regressive groups	aggressively grouchy	grope for the rope	round the ground
25 a spree in Sprague	a sprig of spruce	spray the sprite	a spry osprey
26 springtime spree	spread the sprouts	rays from sprays	Springfield rings
27 a streaking stripper	streaky striped	straight stripes	strangled by stress
28 wrapped with straps	a strange range	astride rides	rest if stressed
29 stretch out stress	strewn strings	structured stress	astral strain
30 a strong construction	strictly abstract	obstructed street	abstract strip
31 scrap the scrim	scribbled manuscript	scrubby scratches	screeching scream
32 describe scruples	scrub and rub	discreet of Rita	reach a screech

r

SENTENCES FOR PRACTICE USING r

1 Reeves reaches for reams of reeking reels.
2 Rude Ruth's rooms were roofed by the Rule's rooster.
3 Is rawhide wrought with raw wrought iron?   ˈɑ̆ˌ ə n
4 Hŭ-rrah! Rahway's gă-rage is a mi-rage.
5 A rough raging river ran through the ru͡ə-ral country retreat.

SENTENCES FOR PRACTICE USING r IN CONSONANT COMBINATIONS

6 The previous priests preached in a preening manner.
7 Prove to Prudence that prunes have been approved for Proust.
8 Prawns provoked praise from the pragmatists in Pravda.

9 Brooding Brutus bruised the brute with a broom.
10 What brought on the broad, raucous brawls?
11 Brunches of bread and brandy were bracing.

12 Retrieve the trees from the "Trick-or-Treat Trio."
13 True, she truly tried to reach a truce with the troops.
14 Trampling on the treasured trestle a-roused trauma.

15 Dreamily, she dreamed a dream of Dreeson.
16 The drooping Druid drew a drooling draw-ing.
17 Draft an address for Dromio to read to the dreaded Adrenalin Council.

18 Can creepy cream creep into the creek?

19 The greedy Greek agrees to greet Mr. Green with grease.
20 Griselda expressed her gratitude with regrettable grammar.

21 Can the freaks be set free before they freeze?
22 Mr. Frew was frugal with fruit.
23 Frivolous friendships frankly frightened Frieda.

24 Thro' thick and thro' thin the threesome thought that three and three makes thirty-three.
25 Three thrifty Thracians were in the enthralling throes of a thrilling throng.

26 The shrieking shrew was shrewd in Shrewsbu-ry and Shreveport.
27 Shroud the shrine at Schrafft's from the shrapnel.

28 Spruce up for a spree.
29 Spray the sprigs with a sprinkle of Sprite.

30 "Screaming and screeching will screw up your voice," said the inscrutable Scrooge.
31 Scramble and scrape the scraps onto the scrimpy screens.

32 Restrictions reduced stress and strife.
33 We strove to construct strong astral abstractions.
34 Let's strike Bess Strong from the list straight away.

SENTENCES FOR PRACTICE USING r IN CONSONANT COMBINATIONS, Cont.

1 Your strategy for reducing stress includes restricting strawbé-rry jam and straw wine?

2 Restrain the street people from obstructing the street cars.

3 The shrew misconstrued the instructions.

4 Did the shah shriek on Reet Street?

5 Streams of streaking pedestrians strewed sheets of real German strudel onto the streets.

EXERCISES USING CONSONANT COMPARISIONS TO ESTABLISH ACCURATE ARTICULATION OF THE CONSONANT r

6 Is Ron's gá-rage rented?   — ʒ r —

7 This is the espionage rate.

8 Was that mi-rage real?

9 The massage relaxed me.

10 Make the corsage red.

11 You cán't camouflage rage.

12 Their badinage revived me.

13 The bá-rrage wreaked havoc on the cortege rows.

14 His genre was Realism?

15 Has Genet at his zenith been reSEARCHED?

16 Rick resented the *La Cage* rehearsal room.

17 Lee's decision restored his prestige.

18 The mission's revision was a rightly-reached decision.

19 Zsa Zsa endured a bá-rrage of gauche rhymes.

20 Too little leisure, as usual, for Judge Reed.

21 Will Frazier go to Asia with Roger and Rita?

22 Did zeal drive Rita to finish her massage-rest regime?

23 The imagery of the beverage's savagery was just average.

ZHRAH ZHRAH EXERCISE FOR r

24 There was a rich Shah

25   known as Zhrah Zhrah   ˈʒraː ʒra

26 Who má-rried a Czech

27   known as Zsa Zsa.   ˈʒaː ʒa

28 He was crude but romantic,

29   a little pedantic

30 She was ragged and faded,

31   a little bit jaded

32 But better together than both be alone

33 For better or worse they both became known

34   As the rich Shah and his Missus, Zsa Zsa Zhrah Zhrah!

WORDS FOR PRACTICE USING THE FRONT VOWELS WITH ⌣r–
(See page 87 for additional drills.)

I r	e r	ɛə̆ r	æ r
1 e-rase	E-ric	ai-ry=ae-rie	a-rid
2 py-rrhic	pe-rish	pa-ring	pa-rish
3 be-rate	bu-ry=be-rry	bea-ring=ba-ring	Ba-rrie=Ba-rry
4 ty-ranny	te-rrible	tea-rable	ta-rry
5 di-rect	De-rry	dai-ry	Da-rrow
6 Ki-rin	Ke-rry	ca-ring	Ca-rry
7 mi-rror	me-rry	Ma-ry	ma-rrow
8 mi-racle	Ame-rica	Ma-rian	Ma-rilyn
9 ly-ric	cele-rity	hila-rious	hila-rity
10 vi-rile	ve-ry	va-ry	Va-rro
11 si-rrah	se-renade	Sa-rah	Sa-racen
12 he-roic	he-rring	hai-ry	Ha-rry
13 spi-rit	Spe-rry	spa-ring	spa-rrow

SENTENCES FOR PRACTICE USING ⌣r–
14 My race e-rased resistance.
15 Dye wrecks for di-rect reasons.
16 The rate of the rent was be-rating.
17 The wrens se-renade at rest.
18 I bet Rick and E-ric rip reams of red tape.
19 Are there paired rings of pa-rings?
20 That row of spa-rrows is rowdy.
21 Can you get rid of the a-rid Rhine wine?

WORDS FOR PRACTICE USING THE MID VOWELS WITH ⌣r–
(See page 110 for additional drills.)

3: r	ə r	ʌ r
22 bu-rry	drape-ry	bu-rrow
23 fu-rry	suffe-rer	fu-rrow
24 cu-rrish	conque-ror	cou-rage
25 sti-rring	su-rrender	Su-rrey
26 (wh)-rring	wande-rer	wo-rry
27 my-rrhic	summa-ry	Mu-rray

SENTENCES FOR PRACTICE USING ⌣r–
28 Is it right to bu-rrow in the bu-rriest drape-ries?
29 Get rid of the fu-rry suffe-rer in the fu-rrow.
30 (Wh)ere is it writ, "Wo-rry about the (wh)-rring wande-rer?"
31 To the ridge! The cu-rrish conque-ror's cou-rage needs cu-rry!
32 Rica sent my-rrhic wreaths to Tamo-ra and Mu-rray.
33 She made rings by sti-rring with the Su-rrey sti-rrer.

WORDS FOR PRACTICE USING THE LAST THREE BACK VOWELS WITH _r–_

ɔː r	ɒ r	aː r
1 au-ricle	o-racle	a-ria
2 Lau-ra	lo-rry	La-ra
3 cho-rus	Co-rin	ca-rabao
4 Mau-reen	mo-rals	Ma-ra
5 o-rally	o-range	a-ria
6 pou-ring ɔə̆	po-rridge	spa-rring aə̆
7 bo-ring ɔə̆	bo-rrow	ba-rring aə̆
8 sto-ry	to-rrid	sta-rring aə̆

SENTENCES FOR PRACTICE USING _r–_

9 Mr. Rickle was an o-racle to Lau-ra and La-ra.
10 The rusty cho-rus sang to Co-rin's ca-rabao. ˌkʰaː rə ˈbra·oŭ
11 Rally for Ma-ra's mo-rals, Mau-reen.
12 Is it really an o-rally o-range a-ria?
13 Ringo, try pou-ring the po-rridge while spa-rring.
14 Rahway was hit by a ba-rrage of bo-ring bo-rrowings and ba-rrings.
15 Reese roared over the sto-ries of the to-rrid ta-rrings.

WORDS FOR PRACTICE USING THE FIVE ALWAYS-SHORT DIPHTHONGS OF "R" FOLLOWED BY THE CONSONANT r

ɪə̆ r	ɛə̆ r	juə̆ r	ɔə̆ r	aə̆ r
16 pee-ring	pa-ring	pu-rity	pou-ring	spa-rring
17 dea-rie	da-ring	endu-ring	ado-ring	guita-rist
18 fea-ring	fai-ry	fu-ry	fo-rearm	fa-raway

SENTENCES FOR PRACTICE USING _r–_

19 Get rid of appea-rances of impu-rities.
20 Rinse the pa-rings before pou-ring a-round the roast.
21 Oh, dea-rie. Your romantic da-ring is ado-rably en-during. ɪnˈdjuə̆ rɪŋ
22 It's ridiculous, but I'm fea-ring the fu-ry of your fo-rearm.
23 Run away to fai-ryland. It's in fa-raway Rahway.

**PHRASES AND SENTENCES FOR PRACTICE USING THE LINKING *r*

1 a pair of shoes
2 fear of forgetting
3 tear a page
4 stir a cup of coffee
5 steer a course
6 brother-in-law
7 (where are you
8 there is and there isn't
9 The door is left ajar each morning.
10 My fear is that care is far away.
11 There is no way to bear all costs.
12 No further ideas are included.
13 I want to hear about your Far East trip.
14 The flo-rist rented the floor of a brownstone.
15 Sti-rring without a sti-rrer is absurd.

**SENTENCES FOR PRACTICE USING A *LIGHTLY* ARTICULATED LINKING *r*

NOTE: Avoid putting so much energy into the consonant *r* that a new word is formed and the original meaning is obscured.

16 It resembles their anchor. (NOT: their rancor)
17 Can you recite a more honest reason for each? (NOT: for reach)
18 Review the four interviews with the four abbots. (NOT: four rabbits)
19 Her expé-rience with her ex was regrettable. (NOT: her Rex)

USE THE CORRECT LINKING *r* . DO NOT ADD AN INTRUSIVE "R"

(See pages 101-102, and Review Practice to Eliminate Intrusive "R.")

20 The idea ended before it started.
21 China is finer on lace cloths.
22 These ado-rable rings are at India Antiques?
23 There are a great number of registrations for the Plaza opening.
24 I saw all the runners before it was over.
25 *The Ca-rolina* is the ocean liner on the right.
26 Rita and Reba are a-rranging the dinner in China in October.

◆ THE CONSONANT SOUNDS ◆
h AS IN "*he*" AND $ɦ$ AS IN "be*h*ind"

THE PLACE VII VOICELESS GLOTTAL FRICATIVE CONSONANT : h as in "*he*."

Represented by the spellings:

*h*e w*h*o mis*h*ap

THE PLACE VII VOICED GLOTTAL FRICATIVE CONSONANT : $ɦ$ as in "be*h*ind."

Represented by the spellings:

be*h*ind O*h*io Je*h*ovah

Phoneticians disagree as to how, and how often, the voiced glottal fricative consonant $ɦ$ is used by speakers of English, and many texts do not include this sound when examining consonant sounds of Spoken English. However, a few texts do include the voiced $ɦ$ because it is used in accents. It is important for you to know that the voiced $ɦ$ occurs only between two voiced sounds. The production of $ɦ$ is easy; it occurs automatically because of the surrounding voiced sounds. Words including $ɦ$ are used in the sentences for practice at the end of this section.

✓ *Reminder* —————————————————————————————

The vs h and vd $ɦ$ NEVER occur in final position.

The vd $ɦ$ ONLY occurs between two voiced sounds.

Allow your lower jaw to hang relaxed and let the tip of your tongue rest behind your lower teeth. Emit a puff of breath through the mouth. This sound is also known as an aspirate because it is pronounced with an emission of breath through the positions of the vowel or diphthong sound that always follows it. It is an uninterrupted flow of air and is essentially a voiceless vowel sound.

h is OMITTED:

— In SOME compound words where "h" begins the second syllable:

-p⁀ɚd -rɪd -ŋɚm -tɚm -ʃoŭld -rɚm
shepherd fo-rehead gingham Chatham threshold Du-rham

— In SOME words that begin with the spelling "ex":

ɪgˈzɔ- ɪgˈzɪ- ɪgˈzoǎ- ɪgˈzɪ-
exhaust exhibit exhort exhilă-rate

— In SOME words that begin with an "h" in the spelling of the word:

ˈɝ·b ˈɛǎ ˈaŭɚ ˈɒnɚ ˈɒnɪst⁀
herb heir hour honor honest

— In VERY CASUAL UTTERANCE, when the weak forms of the pronouns "he," "her," "him," "his," or "hers" directly follow a preposition, verb or noun:

Just hand it to him gently. = Just hand it to 'im gently.

No, I don't know her. = No, I don't know 'er.

That's the book her mother gave her. = That's the book 'er mother gave 'er.

Where have all the people gone? = Where 'ave all the people gone?

h / h

WORDS FOR PRACTICE

Initial h

h-

1 he heap heat heed heaved hit hitch hill hick him heck helpless
2 heavy health hedge hat happy ham hack HÁ-rassed Hamlet handy
3 hã-rrowing hálf her heard=herd hearse hurt husband hungry hundred
4 hú-rry who whose hoofs hookey hoofer hall Hawes hó-rror hó-rrible
5 holiday Hollywood hale=hail Haye's=hay's=haze hazy hasty Hamish hike
6 height=Hite highway wholly hopeless how hounds house here=hear
7 hair=hare hoú-ri whore=hoar heart=hart higher=hire

hju:-

8 hue=hew=Hugh Hughes=Hewes hewn Hume hubris Huguenot human
9 humanity huge hugeous hugeously humane humanism humanitá-rian
10 humanize humanly humanoid humate humé-ral humic humid humidity
11 humidor humiliate humility humor=humour humó-ral humó-resque
12 humó-rist humorless humó-rous=humé-rus Houston (Texas) Hugo Hubert

COMPARE: ju: 13 you=ewe Youmans Euston you go

hju: 14 hue=hew=Hugh human's Houston (Texas) Hugo

SENTENCES FOR PRACTICE

15 Heave the heathens onto the heaths in a heap.
16 His histrionics seem to hinder his happiness.
17 He had high hopes to have happiness despite the HÁ-rassment.
18 Há-rry heard Herbie, the héi-ress Helen's husband, say they inhé-rited their Hartford House.
19 "Huzza, huzza," hé-ralded happy Há-rry after he'd handled the highway hazards. hʊ'za:
20 Herb's herbs helped to heal the headache he had across his fó-rehead. fɔrɪd
21 The shepherds hú-rried their herds to the high hill.
22 Whose huge ewe and hyena are halting the highway traffic?
23 Hazel had hundreds of happy holidays in Hollywood!
24 Help! I hate heights and feel hopeless here!
25 Honey, just be an honest and honó-rable husband.
26 Will Howard be here within the hour?
27 I'll hand this to you, Hugh, and then you go to Hugo.
28 Send hálf on behálf of the apprehensive inhabitants of Ohio.
29 Is the mahogany highboy too high to be placed behind the mohair sofa?
30 Perhaps it's best for your head to look ahead ráther than look behind.
31 How was her behavior at rehearsals, anyhow?
32 New habits and new behavior are exhibited áfter a stay at a rehabilitation center.
33 Mr. Euston from Houston is happiest when he's high in the Himalayas.

◆ **THE GLIDE CONSONANTS** ◆

$\mathcal{M}$ **wh**ich

$\mathcal{w}$ **w**itch

$\mathcal{j}$ **y**ou=ewe

◆ INFORMATION ABOUT THE GLIDE CONSONANTS ◆

GLIDES

Glides are the only consonant sounds in Spoken English that are produced without interruption or detouring of the breath stream; they have a vowel-like quality and therefore are known as semi-vowels. The articulators glide, or move swiftly, from one position to another during the production of the consonant/semi-vowel to the position of the vowel or diphthong sound that follows it. In Spoken English glides are always followed by a vowel or diphthong sound.

There is a total of three sounds in Spoken English that are created in this manner, and two of these sounds form a pair of cognates. Cognates are two consonant sounds related by being produced in the SAME PLACE OF ARTICULATION, in the SAME MANNER OF ARTICULATION, with one of the pair VOICELESS (vs) and the other VOICED (vd).

The glide consonant cognates are ʍ and w .

The consonant j does not have a voiceless partner in Spoken English

The glide consonant sounds are made in the following places of articulation:

Place I **(BILABIAL)** The two lips articulate against each other:

ʍ			w		
(vs) ***wh***ich	any***wh***ere	-----	(vd) ***w***itch	q***u***it	-----

Place V **(PALATAL)** The front of the tongue articulates against the front of the hard palate:

j		
(vd) ***y***ou=ewe	m***u***se Son***y***a	-----

ʍ , w and j do not occur in final position in Spoken English.

◆ THE CONSONANT SOUNDS ◆
$\mathcal{M}$ AS IN "*wh*ich" AND $\mathcal{W}$ AS IN "*w*itch"

THE PLACE I VOICELESS BILABIAL CONSONANT GLIDE: $\mathcal{M}$ **as in "*wh*ich."**

Represented ONLY by the spelling "wh" as in:

(**wh**)eel   any(**wh**)ere

✓ *Reminder*
_____

The spelling "wh" is circled in the text to denote $\mathcal{M}$.

THE PLACE I VOICED BILABIAL CONSONANT GLIDE: $\mathcal{W}$ **as in "*w*itch."**

Represented by the spellings:

we   **w**ow   lang**u**age   q**u**een   **o**ne   San **J**uan

The voiceless $\mathcal{M}$ and voiced $\mathcal{W}$ NEVER occur in final position.

Relax your lower jaw and allow the tip of your tongue to rest behind your lower teeth. Round your lips and arch the back of your tongue as in the position for the vowel sound $u:$. Your rounded lips swiftly move to a following vowel position as the breath stream passes through them. $\mathcal{M}$ and $\mathcal{W}$ are ALWAYS followed by a vowel or diphthong sound in Spoken English, and both sounds are vowel-like in that there is little or no friction during their production.

✓ *Reminder*
_____

A glide means that the articulators move from one position to another during the creation of the sound. There is no friction during the production of $\mathcal{W}$ **, and minute friction during the production of** $\mathcal{M}$.

The voiceless consonant $\mathcal{M}$ should be used in most words with "wh" in the spelling of the word; however, the following words spelled with "wh" are spoken with the sound h :

who   whom   whose   whole   wholly   whore   whooping

WORDS FOR PRACTICE USING $\mathcal{W}$

$\mathcal{W}-$ 1 weed wit wet wag were word worst won=one woo wood worsted wall

2 was wallah way wise wove wow we're=weir wear=ware wore=war wire

$d\mathcal{W}-$ 3 dwindle dwell dwelt dwarf

$s\mathcal{W}-$ 4 sweep sweet=suite swift swim Swiss sweat swell swam swirl swoon swat

5 sway suede=swayed assuage swine swollen swear swore swarthy swarm

$t,\mathcal{W}-$ 6 tweezer between betwixt twenty 'twere 'twirl 'twas twain Twyla twilight

$k,\mathcal{W}-$ 7 queen quit question quack quirk qu$\overset{a}{a}$ff qua-$\overset{v}{rr}$el qualm quiet queer

8 equal misquote acquiescence aquatic acquire acquaint acquit

$sk,\mathcal{W}-$ 9 squeak squeal squeeze squib squint squelch squi-$\overset{3:}{rr}$el squall squab squash

10 square squire

SENTENCES FOR PRACTICE USING $\mathcal{W}$

11 It's wise to wear warm worsted woolens du$\overset{\upsilon\breve{o}}{-}$ring winters in Worcester. $^{\prime}w\upsilon st^{h}\partial$

12 The waiter's work was worst in warm weather.

13 Wanda wooed Wally into a Wednesday wedding.

SENTENCES FOR PRACTICE USING *W*, Cont.

1 We'll wait at the Waverly for that wild and wonderful woman.
2 Would a queen swim in a swamp?
3 A quarter for a quart gives me qualms about squande-ring wages.
4 Squelch all questions with this quintessential quotation.
5 Stop quibbling and we'll acquire the quo-rum.
6 Acquittance was required by the acquaintance.

EXERCISES FOR COMPARING Ɱ WITH *W*

Front Vowels		Mid Vowels		Diphthongs	
7 wheat	— weed	20 whir	— were	23 whey	— way=weigh
8 wheel	— we'll	21 whirred	— word	24 whales	— Wales=wails
9 which	— witch			25 whale	— wail
10 Whig	— wig			26 why	— Y
11 whist	— wist	**Back Vowel**		27 while	— wile
12 whit	— wit	22 what	— watt=wot	28 white	— wight
13 whither	— wither				
14 whether	— weather				
15 whelp	— wealth			**Diphthongs of "R"**	
16 whe-rry	— wa-ry			29 where	— wear=ware
17 when	— wend				
18 whet	— wet				
19 whack	— WAC, wacky				

EXERCISES FOR COMPARING Ɱ OR *W* WITH *V*

Front Vowels		Mid Vowels		Diphthongs	
30 we	— V	40 worse	— verse	44 whale	— vale=veil
31 wean	— venal			45 wane	— vane=vein
32 we'll	— veal			46 Y	— vie
33 wicket	— victim			47 while	— vile
34 whim	— vim	**Back Vowels**		48 whine	— vine
35 Willy	— villa	41 woo	— voodoo	49 won't	— vote
36 wet	— vet	42 Walt	— vault	50 wow	— vow
37 when	— venom	43 Wanda	— Vonda	**Diphthongs of "R"**	
38 whelp	— velvet			51 weird	— veered
39 wedge	— vegeta-rian			52 wa-ry	— va-ry
				53 wore	— vortex

SENTENCES FOR PRACTICE USING Ɱ AND *W*

54 Why not, Watson? Which one?
55 When do we leave?
56 What's up? What's that? Who are you?
57 Where do we go?
58 Why, what would you?
59 Why wait for Mr. White?

SENTENCES FOR PRACTICE USING ⁀m AND w , Cont.

1 Whither wander you?
2 Why are you whining about wining and dining?
3 When shall we whistle?
4 Tell me why I wheeze at the Y.
5 Well, let's go somewhere, anywhere!
6 We don't know why, when or where.
7 I know what you want.
8 The wheels of fate are wẖ:-rring wildly.
9 Wherefore should I weep?
10 The whimpe̊-ring whale wandered.
11 What, will you whisper?
12 Whitman caught a whopping whiting.
13 Which witch is the wicked witch?
14 The whales of Wales wailed wantonly.
15 The words of Whistler overwhelm me.
16 Why is the white line winding?
17 The winds whipped up the whitecaps.
18 What wild and whirling words!
19 We'll wheel the wheat into Weed.
20 Meanwhile, the wildebeest whinnied.
21 Why dost thou whet thy knife?
22 This whatnot is not what I wanted.
23 Let's while away the time with whiskey.
24 "Whigs everywhere," whispered Whistler.
25 Who gave the wacky lady a whack?
26 Whoa! Is that a wholly new holy white wine?
27 We'll wheel the whetstone near the wet wheat and weeds.

SENTENCES FOR PRACTICE USING w AND v

28 Vic, quick!
29 The wine is divine.
30 That verse is worse!
31 Wade evaded the inevitable.
32 We've a "V" in this weave.
33 We were wisely advised about Western investments.
34 Is it wise to vie for a wicked victo̊-ry?
35 It's weird to have veered so far from the villa.
36 When are Wanda, Juan and Mr. Vaughan å-rriving in Venice?
37 Why whine about wines from these vines?
38 Are the whales near Wales in a vale?

◆ THE CONSONANT SOUND *j* AS IN "you" ◆

THE PLACE VI VOICED PALATAL CONSONANT GLIDE: *j* as in "you."

Represented by the spellings:

*y*es Will*i*am *u*se n*ew*=kn*ew* bea*u*ty *J*ugoslavia=*Y*ugoslavia

Allow your lower jaw to hang in a relaxed way and let the tip of your tongue rest behind your lower front teeth. Arch the FRONT of your tongue high toward the hard palate as in the position for the highest front vowel sound *i:* . As you begin to produce voice, quickly withdraw the tongue, letting the voice continue and keeping your tongue tip behind the lower front teeth. Avoid unnecessary tongue tension. This sound is vowel-like in that there is no friction during its production.

This consonant sound is ALWAYS followed by a vowel or diphthong sound, and it NEVER occurs in the final position in Spoken English.

This consonant sound joins with the highest BACK vowel sound to create *ju:* —commonly known as "Long U" or "Liquid U." This combination is appropriately used in words following the sounds of *t*, , *d* and *n* ; optional usage after the sounds *l* and *ʃ* . (See page 116.)

tune *'t͡ju:n* duke *'dju·kʰ* new *'nju:*

lewd² *'lju:d* or *'lu:d* suit² *'sju·tʰ* or *'su·tʰ*

j MUST BE cleanly articulated when preceded by the consonant sounds *t* , *d* , *l* *ʃ* , and *z* .

SAY: cán't you *t͡j* NOT: "can chew" NEVER GLOTTALIZE "can ʔ you"

SAY: did you *d͡j* NOT: "did joo" or "did ja"

SAY: will you *l͡j* NOT: "wioh you"

SAY: miss you *ʃ͡j* NOT: "mishoo"

SAY: as you *z͡j* NOT: "azhoo"

WORDS FOR PRACTICE

Initial *j*

1 ye yield yean yeast Yiddish yet yell yellow yelping yesterday Yellowstone
2 yam yak yearn young yuppy you=ewe youth yule use unit unite
3 yawn yonder yon
4 yea yowl year your yore yard Yardley

Medial *j*

5 Sonja Vanya Kenya Tanya Bunyan=bunion=bunyon Runyon canyon
6 churchyard vineyard schoolyard brickyard farmyard barnyard
7 minion pinion opinion dominion companion union reunion communion

l͡j {
8 million scallion rapscallion medallion Italian batallion hellion rebellion
9 billion jillion trillion zillion quadrillion vermilion cotillion
10 civilian pavilion Williams Hilliard
}
11 Bjorn fjord

WORDS FOR COMPARISON OF INITIAL *j* WITH *dʒ*

	Front Vowels			Back Vowels	
	j	*dʒ*		*j*	*dʒ*
1	ye	— gee	12	you	— Jew
2	yip	— jip=gyp	13	Yule=you'll	— Jules
3	yes	— jest	14	use (n)	— juice
4	yet	— jet	15	yaw	— jaw
5	yell	— jell=gel	16	yacht	— jot
6	yellow	— Jello	17	yon	— John
7	yam	— jam			
8	yak	— Jack		**Diphthongs**	
			18	Yale	— jail=gaol
	Mid Vowels		19	yoke	— joke
9	yearning	— journey	20	yowl	— jowl
10	yerk	— jerk			
11	young	— junk	21	year	— jeer
			22	you're=your	— abjure
			23	yard	— jarred

WORDS FOR COMPARISON OF MEDIAL *j* WITH *dʒ*

	Front Vowels			Back Vowels	
24	reunion	— rejuvenate	31	ocula.	— lockjaw
25	Binion	— bingeing			
26	Kenya[2]	— engine			
27	companion	— banjo			
28	Dracula	— tragic			

Mid Vowels

29	Ursula ˈɝːʃjʊlə	— urgent
30	a yuppie	— adjust

SENTENCES FOR COMPARISON OF *j* WITH *dʒ*

32 That yokel! That joker! You know, Juno!!

33 I like jam on my yam, have much use for juice, but I hate yellow Jello!

34 I'll spend the Yule with Jules on his yacht. A reunion will rejuvenate me.

35 My companion Angie plays the banjo. So does Tanya.

36 It's urgent, Ursula. I'm yearning to adjourn.

37 Yes, Jess! I say send that Yale man to jail.

38 Is the jet set at the fjord in Jordan yet?

WORDS FOR COMPARISON OF $u{:}$ WITH $ju{:}$

1 ooze	— use (v)	12 Dooley	— duly	22 loot	— lute[2]
2 who	— hue= hew=Hugh	13 coo	— cue	23 loom	— luminous
3 Pooh	— pew=Pugh	14 cool	— reticule	24 loob	— lewd[2]
4 bamboo	— imbue	15 goo	— ague	25 snood	— nude
5 boot	— Butte	16 goose	— argues	26 Foo	— few
6 booty	— beauty	17 moo	— mew	27 food	— feud
7 cartoon	— costume	18 moos	— mews= muse	28 voodoo	— view dew
8 two's	— Tuesday	19 noose	— news	29 Sioux	— sue[2]
9 do	— dew=due	20 loo	— lieu	30 souter (cobbler)	— suitor
10 Doobie	— dubious	21 zoom	— presume		
11 Doon	— dune				

CONSONANT COMBINATIONS USING $ju{:}$ AND $j\upsilon$

31 puny impugn pule puling computer
32 beauty abuse Buchanan imbue bugle bucolic butane rebuke abusive
33 Beaufort (South Carolina) Buford
34 muse music musical museum mute permute mutate mutilate mutage mutine
35 mutiny mutual amuse immune commune communication amused immutable
36 few fu-el fugal=fugle fugacious fugitive fugue fugist futile fuse
37 confuse refuse infuse refute confusion Confucius
38 view viewer viewpoint review=revue preview overview
39 enthuse enthused enthusiasm enthusiastic Thucydides Bethune Matthew
40 cued=queued cute acute accuse cuticle acutangular cube Cuba cubic
41 culina-ry reticule incu-rable
42 argue argute argutely ague legume
43 hew=hue=Hugh human humor=humour humanity humid humic humiliate humility
44 skew askew skewer excuse

WORDS FOR PRACTICE USING $ju{:}$ FOLLOWING $t,$, d OR n

45 tune tuber tuberculosis tumor tumult costume Tudor attitude latitude
46 gratitude longitude beatitude servitude turpitude opportunity tulip Tuesday
47 studious Stewart=Stuart stupid institute tutor stew steward tube tuba
48 tuna tubular tuition Tulane tumid tumescence tunic Tunisia turpitude obtuse Tuba

49 duke duty dutiful dew=due subdue residue adieu dude dune duplicate deuce
50 introduce deduce reproduce du-al=du-el duet duly Dumain duality ducal duo
51 duplex duplicity Deute-ronomy

52 new=knew news newspaper Newbe-rry Newark New York Newport Newman
53 newsreel Newton renew avenue renewal nude minute (small) nutrition nutriment
54 neuter nuisance REvenue reVENue (often in verse) neutral nuance ingenuity nuclear
55 nucleus nume-ral nume-rous nume-rology enume-rate nume-rate nume-rical annuity retinue

OPTIONAL USAGE OF *ju:*. CHOOSE *ju:* OR *u:* AFTER *s* OR *l*

1 suit sue ensue super superlative supe-rintendent supine assume consume
2 consumer suicide supreme sucrose suda-ry suet suitable suitability suitor
3 (ALSO: *zju:* resume presume Zeus exube-rant exube-rance exude)

4 lewd lute lucid lieu lieutenant aluminum allude delude ABsolute
5 REsolute DIssolute salute illuminate Lucifer lunar lunatic ludicrous
6 allusion illuso-ry volume lucrative lubricate Lucerne lucidity Lucrece

WORDS FOR PRACTICE USING *ju* IN UNSTRESSED SYLLABLES

7 reputation deputy copulate popular ambulance occupy incubator calculate masculine
8 truculent o-racular Dracula spectacular particular oculist mi-raculous
9 articulate innoculate innocuous argument regular jugular communist
10 arduous peninsula annual valuable Ursula

WORDS FOR PRACTICE USING *juə*

11 pu-rity Pu-ritan fu-ry endu-ring endu-rance lu-rid mu-ral Mu-riel du-rable du-ring
12 secu-rity fu-rious obscu-rity cu-rious cu-riosity procu-rer U-ranus matu-rity du-ration
13 neu-ritis neu-ral thu-rible Thu-ringia

✓ *Reminder* ———————————————————————————————

The *ju:* combination NEVER follows certain consonants.

assure	ə'ʃuə	azure	'æʒə	rude	'ru:d
woo	'wu:	chew	't,ʃu:	June	'dʒu:n
slew	'slu:	blue	'blu:	plume	'p,lu:m
flue=flew	'flu:	clue	'k,lu:	glue	'glu:

The following exercises are designed to refine the production of *lj*. Refer to pages 246-252 for production of the consonant *l*. Engage the tip of your tongue against the gum ridge in the production of *l* before the consonant *j*. Practice the following combinations for clear articulation of *lj*.

		n:j		*l:j*	
14	minion	minnnnnnnnnnnn-yun	——————>	millllllllllllll-yun	million
15	onion	onnnnnnnnnnnn-yun	——————>	mullllllllllllll-yun	mullion
16	canyon	cannnnnnnnnnnn-yun	——————>	scallllllllllllll-yun	scallion
17	win ya	winnnnnnnnnnnn-ya	——————>	Willllllllllllll-yum	William
18	petunia	petunnnnnnnnnnn-ya	——————>	pecullllllllllllll-yar	peculiar
19	Bunyan	bunnnnnnnnnnnn-yun	——————>	billllllllllllll-yun	billion
20	-----	brinnnnnnnnnnnn-yun	——————>	brilllllllllllll-yunt	brilliant

REPEAT THE FOLLOWING PHRASES THREE TIMES AS QUICKLY AND EFFICIENTLY AS POSSIBLE.

21 will you William   22 brilliant Italian William   23 value Julia's millions

PHRASES FOR PRACTICE USING *l j*

1 will you William
2 brilliant Italian William
3 the Italian stallion
4 a million millions
5 rebellious Ophelia
6 I'll tell you
7 the battalion won't fail you
8 familia-rize Emilia
9 a million trillion scallions
10 Celia is a failure
11 I'll sell you scallions
12 a peculiar Julia
13 I'll mail you a million
14 a familiar civilian
15 hail you at the billiard pavilion
16 Solyony and Salie-ri
17 alienate Molière
18 feel your filial value

REPEAT THE FOLLOWING PHRASES THREE TIMES AS QUICKLY AS POSSIBLE

19 can't you won't you don't you William
20 did you could you would you William

SENTENCES FOR COMPARISON OF *t, j* WITH *t, ʃ* AND *d j* WITH *dʒ*

21 I can chew. Why can't you?
22 Vote yes for chess . . . or can't you choose?
23 Can't you chant? Can't you hit your notes?
24 Won't you check? I want you to, Chuck.
25 Take charge, why don't you!
26 Did you juice the o-ranges?
27 Did you hide your journal?
28 Would you just wait, Jean?

SHORT PHRASES AND SENTENCES FOR REFINING THE ARTICULATION OF *s j* AND *z j*

29 Address your envelopes.
30 this you know
31 I'll miss you.
32 I want to kiss you, Shelly.
33 It's your fault, Monsieur. *mə 'sjɜ:*
34 *As You Like It*
35 'tis your turn
36 I'll buzz you.
37 I'll not tease you, by Jesu. *'dʒ i: z ju*
38 Miss Universe, a Jesuit, was Ms. Utah.

DIALOGUE FOR REFINING THE ARTICULATION OF *t j , d j* AND *l j*

39 X: Did you find yourself a film?
40 Y: Yes. A brilliant Italian film.
41 X: Won't you tell me the title?
42 Y: You bet your life I'll tell you: *Ophelia's Millions.* (*Pause.*) Didn't you hear me?
43 X: I heard you, but you must know that I'm familiar with *Ophelia's Millions.*
44 Y: When did you see it?
45 X: A billion years ago. When I was a civilian.
46 Y: Didn't you like it?
47 X: A failure. A peculiar failure.
48 Y: A peculiar but brilliant failure, don't you think?
49 X: Why did you like it?
50 Y: I asked you first.
51 X: I've told you. Why won't you tell me what you liked about it?
52 Y: Why don't you mind your own business?
53 X: Why don't you admit you're wrong?
54 Y: Couldn't you just cut the cackle and conclude?

◆ ADDITIONAL ARTICULATION EXERCISES ◆

REVIEW FOR ACCURATE ARTICULATION OF SINGLE, DOUBLE AND TRIPLE CONSONANT TONE ENDINGS OF WORDS

✓ *Reminder* ——————————————————————————————

Carry your voice through each final, vibrated PLOSIVE ending without adding an off-glide.

–b   1 plebe nib Deb Mab Herb tub boob tube daub job Abe tribe lobe
       2 orb barb

–d   3 deed did bed mad bird ballad thud mood could thawed odd paid
       4 ride code allowed affeared shared moored accord marred inspired flower'd

–g   5 league fig Meg drag burg=burgh lug fugue log vague vogue

✓ *Reminder* ——————————————————————————————

When *b* , *d* or *g* is followed by another consonant sound in the same word or the next word, your articulators maintain their positions, sustaining vibration until the next sound occurs.

–bz   6 plebes ribs ebbs dabs herbs rubs boobs cubes cobs babes bribes robes
       7 orbs barbs

–dz   8 heeds rids Ed's cads thirds spuds moods woods pods spades abides
       9 modes clouds

–gz 10 leagues digs eggs rags burgh's hugs fugue's dogs Hague's rogues

–bd 11 fibbed ebbed gabbed curbed snubbed daubed bobbed jibed robed
       12 orbed garbed

–gd 13 rigged begged sagged tugged hogged

✓ *Reminder* ——————————————————————————————

Carry your voice through each vibrated AFFRICATE ending without adding an off-glide.

–dʒ 14 liege siege bridge ledge urge budge Scrooge lodge age Doge
       15 George large

–dʒd 16 besieged bridged edged urged judged lodged raged obliged gouged
       17 forged charged

✓ *Reminder* ——————————————————————————————

Carry your voice through each NASAL CONTINUANT in final position without adding an off-glide.

–m   18 beam dim gem ham worm column come doom calm fame
       19 time=thyme home dorm charm

–n   20 keen din wren ban earn Roman bun June dawn Don Kahn
       21 fain=feign pine coin own down bairn bourn morn=mourn barn

–ŋ   22 be-ing wing woo-ing saw-ing bang tongue wrong

REVIEW FOR ACCURATE ARTICULATION OF SINGLE, DOUBLE AND TRIPLE CONSONANT TONE ENDINGS OF WORDS, Cont.

✓ *Reminder* ───

The nasal continuant consonants are subject to lengthening and are spoken long when they are in final stressed syllables before another voiced consonant.

$-m{:}z$ 1 dreams limbs gems lambs worms comes rooms bombs calms tames
   2 *Times* homes warms harms

$-n{:}z$ 3 preens begins lens tans learns buns moons tunes lawns dons pains
   4 pines Poins tones towns Cairns adorns barns=Barnes

$-\eta{:}z$ 5 things pangs throngs

$-m{:}d$ 6 deemed rimmed condemned damned firmed hummed loomed consumed [2]
   7 bombed calmed aimed timed roamed formed harmed

$-n{:}d$ 8 leaned pinned mend banned burned shunned wound tuned dawned
   9 bond waned pined joined intoned wound adorned darned

$-\eta{:}d$ 10 ringed banged tongued longed belonged

✓ *Reminder* ───

Carry your voice through each vibrated FRICATIVE ending without adding an off-glide.

$-v$ 11 Eve live have curve love prove save strive drove carve

$-\eth$ 12 seethe with soothe bathe tithe unclothe mouth (v)

$-z$ 13 ease his says as hers dramas does ooze laws Oz days eyes boys
  14 rose allows fears shares assures shores cars

$-\mathsf{3}$ 15 prestige rouge ga-rage mi-rage camouflage corsage badinage beige
  16 ba-rrage ménage

$-vz$ 17 reprieves gives curves loves moves wolves saves dives

$-\eth z$ 18 breathes soothes bathes tithes clothes mouths (v and plural)

$-vd$ 19 grieved lived served loved moved saved a-rrived

$-\eth d$ 20 seethed soothed bathed tithed loathed mouthed

$-zd$ 21 eased whizzed buzzed refused raised=razed prized dozed housed

✓ *Reminder* ───

Carry your voice through each vibrated LATERAL ending without adding an off-glide.

$-l$ 22 eel ill bell Cal Earle hull who'll pull all doll ale=ail I'll=isle=aisle
  23 oil toll fowl

REVIEW FOR ACCURATE ARTICULATION OF SINGLE, DOUBLE AND TRIPLE CONSONANT TONE ENDINGS OF WORDS, Cont.

The lateral consonant is subject to lengthening and is spoken long when it is in final stressed syllables followed by another voiced consonant.

−l:z 1   seals   bills   tells   Sal's   curls   skulls   pools   pulls

          2   enthralls   dolls   pales=pails   tiles   toils   poles=polls=Poles   jowls   Charles

−l:d 3   peeled   killed   spelled   co-rralled   hurled   lulled   ruled   pulled

          4   scrawled   lolled   hailed   piled   toiled   told   scowled   gnarled

−n:$d$$_3$$d$ 5   cringed   fringed   hinged   binged   singed   avenged   revenged

          6   lounged   changed   a-rranged

−n:dz 7   fiends   bends   mends   attends   lends   hands   bands   brands   funds

          8   wounds   bonds   grinds   hounds   abounds   zounds[2]

−l:m:z 9   films   elms   helms   realms   overwhelms   Wilhelm's

REVIEW FOR DENTALIZATION OF CONSONANTS t, , d , n AND l

The alveolar consonant sounds t , d , n and l are dentalized when they are followed by θ or δ in the same word or the following word. This means that these four consonant sounds are made with the tip of the tongue touching the back of the upper front teeth.

1   Let those who ran thirteen miles reveal their secrets for healthful living!

2   Let's drink to good health and great wealth each day of this month!

3   Wait there until the fifteenth unless you feel that there's a better plan, Theodore.

4   I should think you'd thank me for stopping this mad thinking.

5   I'll bet that the eighth theo-ry will threaten Brad Thurston.

6   It's too bad there are several things that must wait 'til next month's meeting.

7   The width and breadth of the project makes me feel the depth of my commitment there.

8   Our hyacinths should bloom by the sixth of this month.

9   The sixth man thought that he'd thrown the ball there.

10   Tell Theo for the thousandth time that this filth must be cleaned up by the tenth.

REVIEW FOR SAME-CONSONANT BLENDS

✓ *Reminder*

Maintain the contact of your articulators during same-consonant blend sequences. Clarity of enunciation is achieved by a fresh impulse of energy that begins the second word of the sequence.

p, p

1 Stop paying such cheap prices for soup plates.

2 Keep peace and stop picking on Papp, Pam.

b, b

3 Rob built the club beds for Abe Benson.

4 Bob brought a scrub bucket to rub beer onto the cab bottom.

t, t

5 Hit Ted with some hot tips from the Top Ten.

6 Have some hot tea at Bonwit Teller and then meet Tom before you get too tired.

d, d

7 You bad dog. You hid Dad's drawers.

8 I heard Don found Donna sitting on the ground draw-ing an old dead duck.

k, k

9 Walk carefully or you'll kick cobbles onto those black cases of corn.

10 Look closely at the slick courtyard, Jack Kenny, before you park cars in it.

g, g

11 I beg God to give that big girl a major-league galle-ry.

12 Drag Ga-ry in to have a vague glimpse of the bag girl.

m, m

13 Pam mentioned the exam might be in the AM, Monday.

14 How many dim moments made up Sam Mann's home movies?

n, n

15 It had nine knees, ten noses and eleven nails.

16 Can Nancy nail the broken needles into the wooden knobs?

l, l

17 Bill Leeds will let the whole lot of them tell lies.

18 We'll lull LulaBelle and the Colonel with a swell little lullaby.

f, f

19 The chief foe was half fish and half fowl.

20 The roof felt safe from life, famine and tough fortune.

v, v

21 Live vigo-rously, grieve vengefully and love vivaciously.

22 I've voted for five vain and half-alive villains.

θ, θ

23 My breath thickened as I trod a path through the south thicket.

24 Beth thought to teach the youth things about health theo-ries.

ð, ð

25 Breathe there? I'd loathe that!

26 Unclothe those babies when you bathe them.

s, s

27 This same Miss Sally will meet us at the bus stop.

28 Her lips smiled at this snide, crass salesman.

z, z

29 Please, Zeus, his zoo will raise zebras zealously.

30 These are hers, Xenia, and those xylophones Zeke's.

ʃ, ʃ

31 To wash shelves, push sugar over them with a harsh shaking motion.

REVIEW FOR SAME-CONSONANT BLENDS, Cont.

1 Fresh shallots should accompany fresh shellfish.

2 Have a massage, Gigi, or read something from the espionage genre.

3 Your corsage, Zsa Zsa, is in the beige jardinière.

✔ *Reminder* ───

Your articulators will move slightly in same-consonant blend sequences involving the affricates. This slight movement should be swift and efficient.

4 Which child chose to pitch che-rries into the Dutch chocolate?

5 Switch chairs as each check is delivered.

6 My liege, just don't judge George for his somewhat savage joy.

7 Oblige Jean with a huge juice and some po-rridge, Jessie.

REVIEW FOR COGNATE BLENDS

✔ *Reminder* ──

Cognates are two consonant sounds related by being produced in the SAME PLACE OF ARTICULATION, one of the pair VOICED (VD) and the other VOICELESS (VS).

Maintain the positions of your articulators during the following cognate blend sequences. Clarity of enunciation is achieved by the change from voiced to voiceless, or voiceless to voiced, and by a fresh impulse of energy that begins the second word of the sequence.

b p   1 Bob paid the mob plenty to curb powerful sub patrols.

2 Rub places deep below the top bark.

d t   3 Had Tessie read *Tales* before she had told Thomas?

4 I intend to find Todd a recognized teacher of good tennis.

g k   5 Under a big coat he wore a dog collar to the log cabin.

6 Make Guy take Gay to the track gate in a big car.

v f   7 Live fish CAnnot live freely with excessive frost on their native feeding grounds.

             θ ð

ð θ   8 The truth then? I loathe things!

9 To smooth things over, bathe thrice daily, breathe thrillingly and sheathe thoughts of revenge.

z s   10 'Tis so! The wise senators will raise six bronze statues soon.

11 He's saved his sală-ry for his summer vacation.

             ᴜ

ʒ ʃ   12 The entou-rage should wear the usual beige shoes, camouflage shirts and rouge shawls.

✔ *Reminder* ──

Your articulators will move slightly during cognate blend sequences involving the affricates. This slight movement should be swift and efficient.

                                                            ᴘ

dʒ tʃ   13 My liege, choose not the large chicken nor the strange Chinese o-range chowder.

ACCURATE ARTICULATION OF THE CONSONANT *l*

Lillian Di Roselli

1   Italian Lillian Di Roselli had several medallions, valued at many millions

2   of dollars. The legalities of dealing with Lilly's pearls and eme-ralds

3   were capably handled by Lil's lawyer, Leonard L. Lansing. Lansing felt that

4   the logical solution to holding such valuables in the household was a

5   wall safe, one especially built to baffle the most resourceful thief or

6   criminal.

7   Lilly was a wild and lascivious soul and divulged the nume-rical

8   details of her millions to one and all. Not surprisingly, her jew-els were   'dʒuəlz

9   stolen! Clever Leonard L. Lansing held several insu-rance policies to

10 cover such calamities.

11   Lillian felt the burgla-ry was essentially a blessing! She revealed that

12 she had always felt a little peculiar about the eme-ralds and pearls and eagerly

13 set out to replace the jew-el-ry with other gems. Now Italian Lillian Di

14 Roselli sparkles with sprinkles of new lovely glimme-ring stones and smiles a

15 peculiarly whimsical smile as she exclaims, "After all, *diamonds* are a

16 girl's best friend."

ARTICULATION OF THE CONSONANT *s*

✓ *Reminder*

Clarity of enunciation of the consonants *s* and *z* is achieved through accurate positioning of the articulators and efficient management of the breath.

Observe the rule of usage for "s" plurals and possessives:

— If the sound preceding the final "s" is voiceless, the "s" is spoken as *s*

-*t, s*	-*t, s*	-*p, s*
swimsuits	jests	ship's

— If the sound preceding the final "s" is voiced, the "s" is spoken as *z*

-*l:z*	-*i:z*	-*l:z*
seashells	fleas	Sal's

My Sister Sally's Seashell Shop

1   My sister Sally has a shop by the seashore (wh)ch sells seashells, sandals,

2 swimsuits, statione-ry, soap, soda, snacks, and other such sundries. At first,

3 the shop's name was simply "Sally's Seashell Shop." Sally started the shop six

4 seasons ago and concentrated on a selection of seashells to satisfy the most discriminating

5 seashell shopper. Certainly, seashells of va-rious sizes and nume-rous shapes

6 and colors were sold by the score. Hence, the name "Sally's Seashell Shop."

7   Subsequent to the seashell shop's inception, business expanded, and it seemed

8 that Sally needed to stay abreast of the situation and at least update the shop's sign.

9 The shop's sign still said "Sally's Seashell Shop," the several words painted on a seashell.

10 Several strangers suggested to Sally that "Sally's Seashell Shop" was misleading since

11 so many sundries were being sold, and to say that Sally's shop was a seashell shop

12 seemed to some severely simplistic.

13   Sally saw the possibility of seven, separate seashell signs, each announcing a

14 sundry such as "Sandals," "Swimsuits," "Statione-ry," "Soap," "Soda," "Snacks,"

15   and "Sundries." Alas, seven seashell signs seemed silly!

16   So Sally sought a new shop sign to suggest the sundries without naming each one.

17 Seconda-rily, Sally had always been sensitive to the jests about "Sally selling

18 seashells by the seashore," so this seemd a perfect time to replace the

19 "Sally's Seashell Shop" sign with one that simply says "Sal's Gen'ral Store."

ACCURATE ARTICULATION OF THE CONSONANT   z

Zachariah

1 Zacha-̄riah is a zealot for zoological concerns.   ˌzoʊ ə ˈlɒdʒək̩l̩

2 He studies zoos from Zu-rich to Brazil.   ˈzjʊ͝ə rɪkʰ

3 His recent zoographical endeavors are so zany   ˌzoʊ ə ˈgræɟək̩l̩

4 that Zach's friends believe he is ve-̄ry ill! As

5 his conversation zig-zags from zephyrs to Zo-rillas   zo ˈrɪl əz

6 his eyes are glazed: Zacha-̄riah seems a zombie.

7 His passions reach a zenith as he describes his favorite zebra,

8 whose name is Zanzibar, and a Ziphius simply known as Tombie.   ˈzɪɟɪ əʌ

9 Meals are another example of Zach's zaniness. He feeds

10 on zucchini, olives, hay and zwieback baked with cheese.   ˈt̩ʌwiːˌbɑ·kʰ

11 He wears a zoot suit stitched of leather, trimmed with furs.

12 And his voice! Sometimes he growls, sometimes he purrs.

13 He loves zoometry, zoography and praises zoothe-̄rapy.   zo ˈɒmətˌrɪ
                                              zo ˈɒgrəfɪ

14 He reads *Zen and the Art of Zoolotry*,   ˌzoʊ ə ˈθe rəpˠɪ
                                        zo ˈɒlətˌrɪ

15 and other such guides to idolatry,

16 and says of himself, "I'm just that kind of guy!"

17 So zooanthropic Zacha-̄riah moves from zoo to zoo to zoo,   ˌzoʊ ən̩ ˈθrɒpˠɪkʰ

18 and adamantly declares that in the end

19 it's a zoo zoo and a zibet and a zebu that're his friends,   ˈzɪbɪtʰ

20 and with but a zircon in his pocket and a zloty in his purse,   ˈziːbju
                                             ˈzɜ·kɒ̆n

21 he's satisfied to be the celebrated subject of this verse!   ˈzlɒtʰɪ

The following lyrics from two operas by W.S. Gilbert and Arthur Sullivan provide a workout for your entire voice and speech mechanism. The rapid-fire delivery of these patter songs requires economical management of your breath and efficient coordination of your breath and articulators; therefore, plan your inhalations so that you have sufficient breath to maintain vocal energy through the end of each phrase. It is also essential to maintain clarity of sense as well as clarity of enunciation.

Isolate troublesome combinations and refine the physical movement required to speak these words. When you are comfortable making these sounds, put the words back into the phrase or sentence. Work for precision of articulation within the framework of the overall rhythm of the piece before endeavoring to zip along at top speed. Work with patience and persistence.

You may find it useful to listen to a recording of "The Major-General Song," in order to find the rhythm and stress of certain syllables. Once you have mastered the basic articulation challenges of these lyrics, you may wish to use the music that accompanies them to refine your delivery.

The Major-General Song
from *The Pirates of Penzance*   *pɛ̆n ˈzænz*
by W.S. Gilbert and Arthur Sullivan

Major-General:

1 I am the vĕ-ry model of a modern Major-Gene-ral;   *ˈdʒɛ nə rəl* ⁻ʳˡ

2 I've information ve-ge-ta-ble, animal, and minĕ-ral:

3 I know the kings of England, and I quote the fights histŏ-rical,

4 From Mă-rathon to Waterloo, in order categŏ-rical.

5 I'm vĕ-ry well acquainted, too, with matters mathematical;

6 I understand equations, both the simple and quadrătical;

7 About bi-no-mĭăl The-ŏ-rem I'm teeming with a lot o' news,   *ˈθiː ə rem*

8 With many cheerful facts about the square of the hypotenuᵴe:

Chorus:

9 With many cheerful facts about the square of the hypotenuse,

10 With many cheerful facts about the square of the hypotenuse,

11 With many cheerful facts about the hypoten-potenuse.

Major-General:

12 I'm vĕ-ry good at integral and diffĕ-rential calculus;

13 I know the scientific names of beings animalculous.

14 But still, in matters ve-ge-ta-ble, animal, and minĕ-ral,

15 I am the vĕ-ry model of a modern Major-Genĕ-ral.

Chorus:

1   But still, in matters ve-ge-ta-ble, animal, and mine-ral,

2   He is the ve-ry model of a modern Major-Gene-ral!

Major-General:

3   I know our mythic histo-ry, King Arthur's, and Sir Ca-radoc's,

4   I answer hard acrostics, I've a pretty taste for Pa-radox:

5   I quote, in Elegiacs, all the crimes of Heliogabalus!   ˌhiːl jo ˈgæbələs

6   In conics I can floor peculia-rities pa-rabulous.

7   I can tell undoubted Raphaels from Ge-rard Dows and Zoffanies.   ˈdʒe raăd

8   I know the croaking cho-rus from the *Frogs* of A-ristophanes!

9   Then I can hum a fugue, of (wh)ich I've heard the music's din afore,

10 And (wh)stle all the airs from that infernal nonsense, *Pinafore*!

Chorus:

11 And (wh)stle all the airs from that infernal nonsense, *Pinafore*,

12 And (wh)stle all the airs from that infernal nonsense, *Pinafore*,

13 And (wh)stle all the airs from that infernal nonsense, *Pina-pinafore*.

Major-General:

14 Then I can write a washing bill in Babylonic cuneiform,

15 And tell you ev'ry detail of Ca-ractacus's uniform.   kʰə ˈræk, tʰəkʰəsɪz

16 In short, in matters ve-ge-ta-ble, animal, and mine-ral,

17 I am the ve-ry model of a modern Major-Gene-ral.

Chorus:

18 But still, in matters ve-ge-ta-ble, animal, and mine-ral,

19 He is the ve-ry model of a modern Major-Gene-ral!

Major-General:

1 In fact, when I know what is meant by "mamelon" and "ravelin";

2 When I can tell at sight a chassepôt rifle from a javelin;

3 When such affairs as sorties and surprises I'm more wa-ry at;

4 And when I know precisely what is meant by commissa-riat;

5 When I have learnt what progress has been made in modern gunne-ry;

6 When I know more of tactics than a novice in a nunne-ry;

7 In short, when I've a smatte-ring of elemental strategy—

8 You'll say a better Major-Gene-RAL has never sat a **gee**;

ˈmæmələn

ˈrævəlɪn

ˈʃæs p̊oŭ

ˈdʒiː

dʒe nə ˈræl (rhythm of lyric)

Chorus:

9 You'll say a better Major-Gene-RAL has never *sat* a gee,

10 You'll say a better Major-Gene-RAL has never *sat* a gee,

11 You'll say a better Major-Gene-RAL has never *sat* a, sat a gee.

Major-General:

12 For my milita-ry knowledge, tho' I'm plucky and adventu-ry,

13 Has only been brought down to the beginning of the centu-ry,

14 But still, in matters ve-ge-ta-ble, animal, and mine-ral,

15 I am the ve-ry model of a modern Major-Gene-ral.

Chorus:

16 But still, in matters ve-ge-ta-ble, animal, and mine-ral,

17 He is the ve-ry model of a modern Major-Gene-ral.

The Nightmare Song

from *Iolanthe*

by W.S. Gilbert and Arthur Sullivan

aɪ o ˈlæn̯ θɪ

1 (Wh)en you're lying awake with a dismal headACHE, and repose is

2   taboo'd by anxiety,   hed ˈeɪ̆kʰ   (for rhythm of lyric)

3 I conceive you may use any language you choose to indulge in,

4   without impropriety;

5 For your brain is on fire—the bedclothes conspire of usual slumber to   ˈjuːʒʊəl

6   plunder you:

7 First your counterpane goes, and uncovers your toes, and your sheet

8   slips demurely from under you;

9 Then the blanketing tickles—you feel like mixed pickles—so te-rribly

10   sharp is the pricking,

11 And you're hot, and you're cross, and you tumble and toss till

12   there's nothing 'twixt you and the ticking.

13 Then the bedclothes all creep to the ground in a heap, and you pick

14   'em all up in a tangle;

15 Next your pillow resigns and politely declines to remain at its usual

16   angle!

17 Well, you get some repose in the form of a doze, with hot eye-balls

18   and head ever aching,

19 But your slumbe-ring teems with such ho-rrible dreams that you'd ve-ry

20   much better be waking;

21 For you dream you are crossing the Channel, and tossing about in a

22   steamer from Ha-rwich—   ˈhærɪdʒ

23 (Wh)ich is something between a large bathing machine and a ve-ry

24   small second-class ca-rriage—

25 And you're giving a treat (penny ice and cold meat) to a party of

26   friends and relations—

27 They're a ravenous horde—and they all came on board at Sloane

28   Square and South Kensington Stations.

1 And bound on that journey you find your attorney (who started that

2   morning from Devon);

3 He's a bit undersiz'd, and you don't feel surpris'd when he tells you

4   he's only eleven.

5 Well, you're driving like mad with this singular lad (by the bye the

6   ship's now a four-wheeler),

7 And you're playing round games, and he calls you bad names when

8   you tell him that "ties pay the dealer";

9 But this you can't stand, so you throw up your hand, and you find

10   you're as cold as an icicle;

11 In your shirt and your socks (the black silk with gold clocks),

12   crossing Sal'sbu-ry Plain on a bicycle: ˈsɔːlz bə rɪ

13 And he and the crew are on bicycles too—which they've somehow

14   or other invested in—

15 And he's telling the tars all the PARticuLARS of a company he's   ˈpʰaə tʰɪ kʲjʊ ˈlaəz

16   inte-REsted in—   ɪn tʰə ˈreʃ tʰɪd (for rhythm of lyric)

17 It's a scheme of devices, to get at low prices, all goods from cough

18   mixtures to cables

19 (Which tickl'd the sailors) by treating retailers, as though they were   ri ˈtʰeɪ ləz

20   all vegeTAbles —   ve dʒə ˈtʰeɪ bɫz (for rhythm of lyric)

21 You get a good spadesman to plant a small tradesman, (first take off

22   his boots with a boot-tree),

23 And his legs will take root, and his fingers will shoot, and they'll

24   blossom and bud like a fruit-tree—

25 From the greengrocer tree you get grapes and green pea, cauliflower,   kʰɒ lɪ ˈflaʊ ə

26   pineapple, and cranbe-rries,   pʰaɪn ˈæp,ɫ

27 While the pastry-cook plant, che-rry brandy will grant, apple puffs, and

28   three-corners, and banbe-rries—

29 The shares are a penny, and ever so many are taken by Rothschild

30   and Ba-ring,

1 And just as a few a͟re allotted to you, you awake with a shudder

2   despai͟-ring— _{ɛə̆}

3 You'͟re a r͟egular w͟reck, with a c͟rick in your neck, and no wonder

4   you snore, for your head's on the floor͟, and you've needles and

5   pins f͟rom your soles to your shins, and your flesh is a-c͟reep, for

6   your left leg's asleep, and you've c͟ramp in your toes, and a fly on

7   your nose, and some fluff in your lung, and a fevě-͟rish tongue, and

8   a thirst that's intense, and a genə̆-͟ral sense that you haven't been

9   sleeping in clover;

10 But the darkness has pa͟ss'd; and it's daylight at la͟st, and the night

11   has been long—ditto, ditto my song—And thank goodness they're

12   both of them over!

ARTICULATION OF t, AND d WHEN FOLLOWED BY "YOU"

Would You—Wouldn't You
by Pierre Lefevre

1 He: Would you?

2 She: Wouldn't you?

3 He: Only if I haven't met you before.

4 She: Maybe I wouldn't want you to.

5 He: Wouldn't you?

6 She: I've just told you, maybe not.

7 He: Even if I convinced you?

8 She: Could you?

9 He: Well, I impressed you when we first met?

10 She: I think I impressed you, first.

11 He: What made you think so?

12 She: Can't you think? . . . Guess!

13 He: The way I looked at you?

14 She: No.

15 He: The way I winked at you?

16 She: Guess again.

17 He: The way I smiled at you?

18 She: (*Smiles and nods affectionately*)

19 He: I'll let you in on a secret . . . (*Whispers*) That's what I thought you were . . .

20 She: I hate you! If I thought you . . .

21 He: So! I had impressed you. And had I tried, I might have convinced you . . .

22 She: Don't you dare try now!

23 He: Try what?

24 She: To convince me! But (*She beckons to him*) could you . . . (*She whispers*)

25 He: (*Smiles, as she whispers to him*) And would you?

26 She: (*Looks away*) Wouldn't you?

27 He: (*Turns her head to him*) And could you?

28 She: Couldn't you?

ARTICULATION OF $t,$ AND d WHEN FOLLOWED BY "YOU" AND "YOUR"

Cut the Cackle and Conclude
by Pierre Lefevre

1 A: Did you slam that door?

2 B: Didn't you see me?

3 A: Would you mind not doing it again?

4 B: And would you mind your own business?

5 A: Did you say to me: "Mind your own business?"

6 B: "Mind your own business!" That's what I told you.

7 A: That's what I thought you said. Don't you dare say that again! Do you hear?

8 B: What did you say?

9 A: Don't you dare say that again.

10 B: "Do you hear."

11 A: What did you say?

12 B: "Do you hear." That's what you said. "Don't you dare say that again! DO YOU HEAR?" Didn't you?

13 A: Yes I did! And don't you dare do it again!

14 B: Do what again?

15 A: *Say* it again!

16 B: WHAT?

17 A: Don't you dare say it again.

18 B: Say what again?

19 A: (*Shouts*) "Mind your own business!"

20 B: Does it upset you?

21 A: (*Furious*) Can't you see that?

22 B: (*Angry*) Can't you see that you upset me as much as I upset you?

23 A: Must you always be told to control your infernal temper?

24 B: Must you always be told to control your mo-ralizing?

25 A: Can't you keep your cool?

26 B: Can't you cut the cackle?

27 A: Would you please not be vulgar?

28 B: Would you please get off my back?

1 A: Could you stop be-ing aggressive?

2 B: Could you stop be-ing bossy?

3 A: I won't let you call me bossy!

4 B: I won't let you call me aggressive!

5 A: Need you go on and on and on?

6 B: No, I need not! Need you?

7 A: No, I need not either!

8 B: Good. Then let's you and I cut the cackle and conclude. . . . You'll mind your own business, and I'll mind mine.

ARTICULATION OF t, , d AND l WHEN FOLLOWED BY "YOU" AND "YOUR"

Two Characters
by Pierre Lefevre

A is in the room. A knock at the door. (Pause) Another knock. (Silence) A final knock. (Boredom)

1 B: *(Bursting into the room)* Didn't you hear me? *(Pause)* Didn't you hear me? *(Pause)*

2 I've asked you, didn't you hear me knock at your door?

3 A: I heard you.

4 B: Then why wouldn't you or why couldn't you answer?

5 A: Why don't you stop shouting and I'll tell you! *(B tries to calm down.)*

6 I didn't greet you because you let your rebelliousness . . .

7 B: But you said you . . .

8 A: Will you please hold your tongue while I . . .

9 B: But you . . .

10 A: Would you shut up before I . . .

11 B: I hate you. I'm glad I hurt you.

12 A: I find your attitude useless. Couldn't you . . . Can't you . . .

13 B: Quit your bilious bo-ring . . .

14 A: Have I bored you?

15 B: Haven't you bored yourself?

16 A: Yes. Yes. Yes.

17 B: Before I met you, I had only heard about you.

18 A: Had you?

19 B: Didn't you know that your brother William introduced you to my sister Cecelia?

20 A: I thought you said your sister's name was Ophelia.

21 B: Not Ophelia . . . Cecelia. I'm sure I told you Cecelia.

22 A: Did you? And you had your news about me from this sister Cecelia?

23 B: Will you keep it a secret if I tell you?

24 A: Won't you tell me if I let your secret out universally?

25 B: Why don't you give me a straight answer?

26 A: Because you usually can't get your questions straight.

27 B: All right, I'll tell you. Cecelia says you could use a little better etiquette when

28 a friend you find arduous knocks at your door.

29 A: Don't you find your sister Cecelia peculiar?

30 B: Ve-ry.

CHAPTER FIVE

THE APPLICATION

OF WELL-SPOKEN ENGLISH

◆   **CHALLENGERS FOR THE ACTOR WITH GOOD SPEECH**   ◆

The performer wants to be easily heard and readily understood by an audience, no matter what the style of play, no matter what the role. The features of speech that you have been studying—forward placement of tone and speech sounds; clarity of tip-of-the-tongue consonants; follow-through of voice and energy in tone endings of final consonant sounds; appropriate use of strong and weak forms; the relaxed production of sound that is the basis for good projection; and other skills of speaking on stage—are required for all plays, whatever their style, whatever the period in which they are set.

However in certain plays, those often referred to as "elevated texts" or "classics," a performer must use words and language with greater agility, zest and musicality than most people do in ordinary life. The following Challengers for the Actor with Good Speech, gleaned from the speech sounds of North American English, bring a special brilliance, energy and resonance to the spoken word in the theater. These sounds are not often used in kitchen-sink drama, nor are they found in certain dialects or accents; but they are indispensable to meeting the challenge of the world repertory of plays and characters.

◆ Theater Standard _ʍ_ in words such as "what," "why," "wherefore," and "whether."

◆ Theater Standard _ju:_ following _t_ , _d_ , _n_ , _l_ , and _s_ .

◆ The vowel sound _I_ in prefixes and suffixes of words.

◆ Theater Standard _a_ in the Ask-List of words.

◆ The use of strong and weak forms in personal pronouns, prepositions, conjunctions, auxiliary verbs, and articles.

◆ Theater Standard _O_ in UNstressed SYLLABLES.

◆ The use of the two vowel, five diphthong and two triphthong sounds of "r" spoken without r-coloring or inversion.

◆ The use of the open, rounded short vowel sound _ɒ_ as in "honest."

◆ The use of the neutral vowel sound _ə_ in the second-to-last syllable of polysyllabic endings: "-ory"; "-ery"; "-ary"; and "-berry."

The examples for the Challengers are taken from William Shakespeare's comedy *Twelfth Night, or, What You Will*. A few phonetic notations are consistently used in all the quotations from the play: the device of underlining the consonant _r_ , and the use of a hyphen to delineate the syllables containing an intervocalic consonant _r_ have been employed; all Ask-List words are marked; and all words spelled with "wh" that are spoken as _ʍ_ are indicated. The Challenger under consideration in each section is also indicated. You may wish to write in the other Challengers, as well as reminders of same-consonant blends; cognate blends; accurate articulation of "you" and "your" following _t_ , _d_ , _n_ , _l_ , _s_ and _z_ ; and of course your personal speech considerations.

A thorough reading of *Twelfth Night* is recommended before you embark on the material in this section. Please note that details of punctuation may vary from one edition of the play to another, and when working on a role you may find it useful to compare texts and even look at the *First Folio* edition. You may also find it helpful to consult *Shakespeare Lexicon and Quotation Dictionary*, edited by Alexander Schmidt; *Shakespeare's Names: A Pronouncing Dictionary*, edited by Helge Kökeritz; and the *Oxford English Dictionary* (O.E.D.).

The voiceless consonant $\mathcal{M}$ should be used in most words spelled with "wh," so as not to confuse the meaning of the word. (See pages 305-307 for details of production and comparisons of $\mathcal{M}$ and w .)

COMPARE the pronunciations of the following pairs of words that utilize $\mathcal{M}$ and w :

$\mathcal{M}$	w	$\mathcal{M}$	w	$\mathcal{M}$	w
which — witch		what — watt		where — wear=ware	

✓ Reminder

Some words spelled with "wh" are spoken with the sound h .

who   whom   whose   whooping-cough   whole   wholly   whore

1   Why, would that have mended my hair?   I.iii.95

2   Why, this is the best fooling, when all is done.   II.iii.30-31

3   And thus the whirligig of time brings in his revenges.   V.i.379

COMPARE w WITH $\mathcal{M}$ IN NUMBERS 4 AND 5

4   . . . and as many lies as will lie in thy sheet
of paper, although the sheet were big enough for
the bed of Ware in England, set 'em down.   III.ii.47-49

5   Where shall I find you?   III.ii.52

6   I had a sister,
whom the blind waves and surges have devoured.
Of cha-rity, what kin are you to me?
What countryman? What name? What pa-rentage?   V.i.228-31

◆ THEATER STANDARD *ju:* FOLLOWING ◆
t , *d* , *n* , *l* , AND *ʃ*

The consonant-vowel combination *ju:* is commonly known as "Long U" and is properly used in words following the sounds of *t* , *d* , *n* , *l* , and *ʃ* ; words involving *l* and *ʃ* may be pronounced with the sound *ju:* or *u:* .

(See pages 116-118 for details of production and drill of *ju:* .)

(See page 310 for CONTRAST of *ju:* and *u:* .)

tune	*'tˌju:n*	tyōōn	duke	*'dju·kʰ*	dyōōk	new	*'nju:*	nyōō

lewd[2]	*'lju:d*	lyōōd or	*'lu:d*	lōōd
suit[2]	*'ʃju·tʰ*	syōōt or	*'ʃu·tʰ*	sōōt

'tˌju:n
1   Out o' tune, sir?   II.iii.113

'dju·kʰ
2   I'll serve this duke.   I.ii.54

'dju:
3   There lies your way, due west.   III.i.136

ə'dju:
4   And so adieu, good madam.   III.i.163

5   He does smile his face into more lines
'nju:
than is in the new map with the augmentation of the

Indies.   III.ii.78-80

'nju:z
6   How now? (Wh)at news from her?   I.i.24

✓ *Reminder* ──
Words involving *l* and *ʃ* may be pronounced with the sounds *ju:* or *u:* .

7   I was one, sir, in this interlude, *'ɪntʰəˌlju:d* or *'ɪntʰəˌlu:d*   V.i.374

8   I will believe thou hast a mind that suits   *'ʃju·tˌʃ* or *'ʃu·tˌʃ*

With this thy fair and outward cha-racter.   I.ii.50-51

9   Nay, pursue him now, lest the device take air *pʰə'ʃju:* or *pʰə'ʃu:*

and taint.   III.iv.137-38

◆ THE VOWEL SOUND / IN ◆
PREFIXES AND SUFFIXES OF WORDS

The use of the vowel sound   /   in unstressed prefixes and suffixes of words contributes to the rhythm, clarity and precision of the word and the entire phrase.

(See pages 61-63 for details and production of the vowel sound   / .)

(See pages 64-66 for a listing of prefixes and suffixes that are spoken with the vowel sound / .)

In the lines that follow, use the short sound   /   in the first syllable of the words "believe" and "belie":

(bɪ–)

Dear lad, believe it;

(bɪ–)

For they shall yet belie thy happy years

That say thou art a man.   I.iv.29-31

SAY: "bi-" <i>bɪ</i>–   NOT: "buh-"   <i>bə</i>–

NOR: "bee-"   <i>bi</i>–

NOR: "beh-"   <i>be</i>–

1   But as a madman's ẹpistles are

no gospels, so it skills not much (when) they are
dɪ
delivered.   V.i.287-89

2   (Why), let her ẹxcept befọre ẹxcepted.   I.iii.7

3   Make youṛ ẹxcusẹs wiselỵ, you were best.   I.v.30

4   I marvel your ladyship takes delight in such
æ   ɑ
a ba-rren rạscal.   I.v.82-83

5   My gentleman Cesa-rio?   V.i.183

6   Rẹceive it so.   II.ii.11

7   You throw a strange regard upon me,   V.i.212

THE VOWEL SOUND *I* IN PREFIXES AND SUFFIXES OF WORDS, Cont.

1   Thou shalt *pɪˌrɪ*present me as an eunuch to him;   I.ii.56

2   "give me this *pɪˌrɪ*pre-rogative of

        speech."   II.v.71-72

3   Sure you have some hideous matter to *dɪ*deliver,

        when the courtesý of it is so fearful.   I.v.205-06

4   Infirmity, that *dɪ*decays the wise, doth ever make the

        better fool.   I.v.75-76

5   *dɪ*Disguise, I see thou art a *ɪdˌɪ*wickedness

        *ɛə̆*Whe-rein the pregnant enemý does much.   II.ii.27-28

6   I am afraid this great lubber, the world,

        will prove a cockneý.   IV.i.14-15

7   There's moneý for thee.   IV.i.19

8   Excellentlý done, if God did all.   I.v.236

9   *ə ɪ*Leche-ry? *dɪ*I defy *ə ɪ*leche-ry.   I.v.125

10   And tell them, there thy *ɪd*fixed foot shall grow

        Till thou have audience.   I.iv.17-18

11   Be not offended, *ɪd*dear *ʃɪ a:*Cesa-rio.   IV.i.50

12   Talkést thou nothíng but of ladiés?   IV.ii.27

13   What thríftless sighs shall poor Olivia breathe?   II.ii.39

THE VOWEL SOUND *I* IN PREFIXES AND SUFFIXES OF WORDS, Cont.

1   No way but gentleness; gently, gently.   III.iv.116

2   How easy is it for the proper false
    In women's waxen hearts to set their forms!   II.ii.29-30

3   I would I had bestowed that time in the tongues that I have
    in fencing, dancing, and bear-baiting.   I.iii.90-92

4   For the rain it raineth every day.   V.i.394

5   and speaks three or four languages word
    for word without book,   I.iii.26-27

6   It shall advantage thee more than
    ever the bea-ring of letter did.   IV.ii.113-14

The vowel sound ɑ as in "ask" is called the Intermediate "A" because some perceive it as a sound in between the vowel æ as in "Ann" and the vowel ɑː as in "father."

(See pages 81-83 for an alphabetical listing of Ask-List words.)

For the Ask-List of words, use the Eastern Standard, or Intermediate "A" pronunciation in preference to the Broad "A" ɑː which is the British Standard, and in preference to the Short "A" æ , which is the general North American Standard. (See pages 79-80 for details of production and drill of ɑ .)

In the following lines compare the vowel sounds in "can," "thanks" and "answer."

✓ Reminder ———————————————————————
"Answer" is an Ask-List word and is spoken with the vowel sound ɑ .
I can no other answer make, but thanks,

And thanks, and ever thanks;   III.iii.14-15

1   By mine honor, half drunk.   I.v.116

2   What is love? 'Tis not hereafter;

     Present mirth hath present laughter;   II.iii.48-49

3   A witchcraft drew me hither.   V.i.76

4   for your opposite hath in him what

     youth, strength, skill, and wrath can furnish man

     withal.   III.iv.239-41

5   I am one

     that had rather go with sir priest than sir knight.   III.iv.275-76

6   I did send,

     After the last enchantment you did here,

     A ring in chase of you.   III.i.113-15

7   "I may command where I adore." Why, she

     may command me: I serve her; she is my lady.   II.v.125-26

1   There is no slander in an allowed fool, though

he do nothing but rail;   I.v.94-95

2   Calling my officers about me, in my

branched velvet gown;   II.v.47-48

3   He might have took his answer long ago.   I.v.264

4   There is example for't.   II.v.39

✔ *Reminder* ——————————————————————————

"Pass" may be spoken as $'p^h a \wedge$; **"passage" is only spoken as** $'p^h æ \wedge \imath dʒ$.

"Can't" may be spoken as $'k^h a n t^h$; **"can" (sf), "canst" and "cannot" are only spoken as** $'k^h æ n:$, $'k^h æ n \wedge t^h$ **and** $'k^h æ n v t^h$.

(See page 86 for more words comparing the sounds of *a* **with** *æ* .)

5   This practice hath most shrewdly passed upon thee;   V.i.354

6   for there is no

Christian that means to be saved by believing

rightly can ever believe such impossible passiges

of grossness.   III.ii.70-74

7   'Thou canst not choose but know who I
am.'   II.v.190-91

8   I cannot be so answered.   II.iv.89

◆ THE USE OF STRONG AND WEAK VOWELS ◆
IN PERSONAL PRONOUNS, PREPOSITIONS, CONJUNCTIONS, AUXILIARY VERBS, AND ARTICLES

Certain common words change pronunciation according to their importance as key idea word in Spoken English. (See pages 21-25 for details of the best usage of strong and weak forms of words

✓ *Reminder*

> The Strong Form (sf) is the one usually listed in a dictionary and is used when th word is stressed or in a strong position.
>
> The Weak Form (wf) is used when the word is unstressed, or unimportant to th main thought being conveyed. Weak Forms tend to subordinate the nonessenti words and preserve the sentence rhythm and flow of Spoken English.
>
> A speaker may change a strong form of a word to a Weak Form by employing on or all of the following devices:
>
> ◆ Taking away the stress
> ◆ Making the sounds in the weak form SHORT
> ◆ Changing to a weaker vowel
> ◆ Omitting a sound completely

1 am   'æm: (sf) What I am, and what I would, are as secret as maidenhead:

to your ears, divinity; to any other's, profanation.   I.v.216-17

2 am   əm   (wf) I am a messenger.   I.v.204

3 are   'aə   (sf) I see you what you are; you are too proud;   I.v.251
       a   (wf)

4 do   'du: (sf) You might do much.   I.v.279

5 do   du   (wf) I knew 'twas I, for many do call me fool.   II.v.82

6 must   'mʌst   (sf) Sooth, but you must.   II.iv.90

7 must   məst   (wf) By my troth, Sir Toby, you must come in

earlier a'nights   I.iii.4-5

8 would   'wʊd   (sf) I would you were as I would have you be.   III.i.144
       wəd   (wf)

9 be   'bi: (sf) Well, let it be.   I.v.299

10 be   bi   (wf) I'll be sworn thou art.   I.v.292

The vowel sound ○ is used as a pure vowel sound only in unstressed syllables of words and is usually found in the first syllable of a word. (See pages 122-124 for details of production and drill of ○ .)

✓ *Reminder* ───────────────────────────────────

> **The vowel sound ○ is NOT found at the ends of words; instead, the diphthong o ŭ is invariably used.**

1 Halloa your name to the _reverbe_rate hills   (_reverb'_rate)

And make the babbling gossip of the air

Cr_y_ out "Olivia."   I.v.277-79

2 He does obey ever_y_ point of the letter

that I d_r_opped to bet_r_ay him.   III.ii.77-78

3   If this young gentleman

Have done offense, I take the fault on me;

If you offend him, I for him defy you.   III.iv.324-26

4 He is sure possessed, madam.   III.iv.8

SUMMATION CHART FOR THE LETTER "R"
In Spoken English the following sounds are

Sound	Description	Usage
1 the consonant r	a strong murmur	must be followed by a vowel or diphthong sound
2 the strong vowel $3{:}$	a soft murmur	usually in a STRESSED syllable
3 the weak vowel ∂	a weak neutral sound "uh"	ALWAYS in an UNstressed syllable
4-8 the five diphthongs of "r" $I\breve{\partial}$ $\varepsilon\breve{\partial}$ $\upsilon\breve{\partial}$ $\mathfrak{I}\breve{\partial}$ $a\breve{\partial}$	all end with the weak, neutral, vowel sound ∂	varied
9-10 the two triphthongs of "r" $a\breve{I}\breve{\partial}$ $a\breve{\upsilon}\breve{\partial}$	both end with the weak, neutral, vowel sound ∂	varied: optional pronunciation of diphthong plus vowel in two separate syllables $a\breve{I}\,\partial$ $a\breve{\upsilon}\,\partial$

For Good Speech in classic texts and elevated texts,

SOUNDS OF "R" SPOKEN WITHOUT R-COLORING OR INVERSION ◆

(PRONOUNCED "ARE") IN THE SPELLING OF A WORD
associated with the letter "r" in the spelling of a word:

Examples		Placement of Tongue				Page
ring=wring	ˈrɪŋː	tip of tongue is POINTED UP toward				292
pray=prey	ˈpˌreˑï·	last part of gum ridge ɾ				
spi-rit	ˈspˤɪrɪtˤ					
ginger ale	ˈdʒɪndʒəɾ ˈeˑï·l					
MUR-der	ˈmɜːdə	WITHOUT	r-coloring	WITH	r-coloring	89
pre-FER	pˌrɪ ˈf3ː	3ː	tip relaxed	3ᶜː	tip tensed	
con-CUR	kˤənˈkˤ3ː		down		up and back	
MUR-der	ˈmɜːdə	WITHOUT	r-coloring	WITH	r-coloring	92
suffer	ˈsʌfə	ə	tip relaxed	əc	tip tensed	
conquer	ˈkˤɒŋkˤə		down		up and back	
here's	ˈhɪə̆z	WITHOUT	r-coloring	WITH	r-coloring	169
their	ˈðɛə̆	ə̆	tip relaxed	ə̆c	tip tensed	171
poor	ˈpˤʊə̆		down		up and back	174
ore	ˈɔə̆					177
car	ˈkˤɑə̆					180
hire	ˈhaɪ̆ə̆	WITHOUT	r-coloring	WITH	r-coloring	186
flower	ˈflaʊ̆ə̆	ə̆	tip relaxed	ə̆c	tip tensed	
			down		up and back	

speak the sounds in numbers 2 through 10 without r-coloring.

    ʊə̆ ɜ: ɜ: ʊə̆ ɜ:

1   Your servant's servant is your servant, Madam.   III.i.104

    ɑə̆ ə

2   To the gates of Tartar, thou most excellent devil

of wit.   II.v.207-08

    ʊə̆ ɜ: ə   ə ə

3   And let your fervor, like my master's, be

Placed in contempt.   I.v.288-89

    ɪə̆

4   Fear'st thou that, Antonio?   V.i.222

    ʊɜ   ɑ ɛə̆

5   But if you were the devil, you are fair.   I.v.252

    ʊə̆

6   What thriftless sighs shall poor Olivia breathe?   II.ii.39

    ʊə̆ ɔə̆

7   Your lord does know my mind; I cannot love him.   I.v.258

    ɑ ə

8   After him I love
    ɔə̆   ɔə̆
more than I love these eyes, more than my life,
    ɔə̆   ɔə̆   ɛə̆
more, by all mores, than e'er I shall love wife.   V.i.134-35

    ɜ: ɑə̆ ɑə̆

9   O, sir, I will not be so hard-hearted.   I.v.244

    ɑɪə̆

10   And my desires, like fell and cruel hounds,
    ɛə̆   ə
E'er since pursue me.   I.i.23-24

    ɔə̆

11   Away before me to sweet beds of flow'rs;
    ɑʊə̆
    ɑʊə̆
Love-thoughts lie rich when canopied with bow'rs.   I.i.41-42

◆ THE USE OF THE OPEN, ROUNDED ◆
SHORT VOWEL SOUND ɒ , AS IN "HONEST"

This vowel sound is round, open and always short. This sound tends to be distorted in various dialects and accents of Spoken English. Keep ɒ crisp and pure to maintain its characteristically sharp, tart quality.

(See pages 129-133 for details of production and drill.)

1 By my tr**ɒ**oth, the fool has an excellent

br**e**ast.
[NOTE: 'tɾɒŏθ (British)]   II.iii.19-20

2 And I (poor m**ɒ**onster) f**ɒ**ond as much **ɒ**on him;   II.ii.34

3 She did commend my yellow st**ɒ**ockings **ə**of

late, she did pr**a**ise my leg being cr**ɒ**oss-gartered;   II.v.166-67

4 I am g**ɒ**one, sir,
   And an**ɒ**on, sir,

   I'll be with you again,   IV.ii.123-25

5 How now, s**ɒ**ot?   I.v.121

✓ *Reminder* ———————————————————————————————
**The words "on," "'twas," "what," and "wasn't" use the vowel sound ɒ .
These words have no Weak Forms.**

6 If music be the food **ə**of love, play **ɒ**on,   I.i.1

7 **ɒ**On your attendance, my lord, here.   I.iv.11

8 I knew '**ɒ**twas I, for many do call me fool.   II.v.82

9 A gentleman? Wh**ɒ**at gentleman?   I.v.119

◆ THE USE OF THE NEUTRAL VOWEL SOUND ə IN ◆
SECOND-TO-LAST SYLLABLE OF POLYSYLLABIC ENDINGS "-ORY," "-ERY," "-ARY," AND "-BERRY"

Words such as "repertory," "stationery," "secretary," and "cranberry" are spoken with the weak neutral vowel sound ə in the penultimate syllable, prior to the consonant r̰ :

repertory	ˈrepʌə̆ t̆ə rɪ	RE-puh-tuh-ry
stationery	ˈsteɪʃə nə rɪ	STA-tio-nuh-ry
secretary	ˈsekˌrə t̆ə rɪ	SE-cruh-tuh-ry
cranberry	ˈkˌrænbə rɪ	CRAN-buh-ry

This is in preference to the British Standard (RP), which may drop a syllable:

repertory	ˈrepʌə tˌrɪ	RE-puh-try

and in preference to the General American Standard, which uses a diphthong sound:

repertory	ˈrepʌ̆ˌt̆ɔ̆ə rɪ	RE-per-tore-y

(See pages 99-100 for details of production and drill.)

1   Methinks sometimes I have

        no more wit than a Christian or̰ an ordina-ry man

        has.   I.iii.82-84

2   It shall be in-

        vento-ried, and every particle and utensil labeled

        to my will: I.v.248-250

One of the most exciting aspects of your speech study is the use of phonetics to develop your ear for the "music" of a text. Good writers of verse and prose employ devices such as alliteration, assonance and consonance to evoke mood and emotion; sometimes these enhance the sense of the words, sometimes they operate in counterpoint. In a good play, the dramatist gives each character a particular "voice," or mode of expression. The sounds and rhythms of a character's language tell much about the inner life and can even convey the emotional tenor of a situation. Your awareness and sensitivity to the SOUND as well as the meaning of a text are essential for a fully realized interpretation.

The "score" that you create for speech is a starting point. It equips you with the basics of pronunciation, the dramatic values of certain sounds, indicates lengths and spotlights rhythms, and it helps clarify ideas. It is there to remind you of sounds and rhythms, operative words, phrasing and inflections. The score cannot notate the subtleties of tempo, melody or other elements of interpretation that evolve during the creative exploration of a text, but it can serve as a springboard for your imagination and talent.

The introductory example for "How To Create a Score" is the poem "Tarantella," by the British writer Hilaire Belloc (1870-1953). This is an excellent poem with which to learn to create a score because the sense is clear, and the strong rhythms and vivid speech sounds are fun to speak out loud. Read the poem to yourself several times, for meaning and first impressions. Then, when you understand the overall sense of the verse, make sure that you know the meaning of every word and phrase. Look up the definitions of "tarantella," "tedding," "Pyrenees," "clapper," "hoar," "Aragon," and any other words about which you feel uncertain. When dealing with any text, but especially one that is not contemporary, it is imperative that you look up words in a reliable dictionary. Do not take them for granted! A word that signifies one thing today may have had quite a different connotation 75 or 100 or 300 years ago.

Tarantella

by Hilaire Belloc

Do you remember an Inn,
Miranda?
Do you remember an Inn?
And the tedding and the spreading
Of the straw for a bedding,
And the fleas that tease in the High Pyrenees,
And the wine that tasted of the tar?
And the cheers and the jeers of the young muleteers
(Under the vine of the dark verandah)?
Do you remember an Inn, Miranda,
Do you remember an Inn?
And the cheers and the jeers of the young muleteers
Who hadn't got a penny,
And who weren't paying any,
And the hammer at the doors and the Din?
And the Hip! Hop! Hap!
Of the clap
Of the hands to the twirl and the swirl
Of the girl gone chancing,
Glancing,
Dancing,
Backing and advancing,
Snapping of the clapper to the spin
Out and in——
And the Ting, Tong, Tang of the Guitar!
Do you remember an Inn,
Miranda?
Do you remember an Inn?

Never more;
Miranda,
Never more.
Only the high peaks hoar:
And Aragon a torrent at the door.
No sound
In the walls of the Halls where falls
The tread
Of the feet of the dead to the ground
No sound:
But the boom
Of the far Waterfall like Doom.

Score for Tarantella

u: ʊ ɪ e ˈɪn:
1 do you remember an inn

ɪ æ
2 mi-randa?

e ˈɪn:
3 do you remember an inn?

e ɪŋ ən e ɪŋ
4 and the tedding and the spreading

ə ɔ: e ɪŋ
5 of the straw for a bedding

i:z ə i:z aːɪ ɪ i:z
6 and the fleas that tease in the high py-renees pʰɪ rəˈni:z (stress third syllable for verse)

aːɪ·n ə eɪ ɪ aə
7 and the wine that tasted of the tar?

ɪəz ɪəz ʌŋ: ɪəz
8 and the cheers and the jeers of the young muleteers mjuləˈtʰɪəz

ʌ aːɪ·n aə ə æ
9 (under the vine of the dark ve-randah)?

ɪ ˈɪn: ɪ æ
10 do you remember an inn mi-randa

ɪ ˈɪn:
11 do you remember an inn?

ɪəz ɪəz ʌŋ: ɪəz
12 and the cheers and the jeers of the young muleteers (run-on line)

æ ɒ enɪ
13 who hadn't got a penny

eɪ enɪ
14 and who weren't pay-ing any ˈwɜ·ntʰ

æ ɔəz ɪn:
15 and the hammer at the doors and the din?

ɪ ɒ æ
16 and the hip! hop! hap!

ə æ
17 of the clap

ə æn:dz ɜ:l ɜ:l
18 of the hands to the twirl and the swirl

ə ɜ:l ɒn: a ɪŋ
19 of the girl gone chancing

a ɪŋ
20 glancing

a ɪŋ
21 dancing

æ ɪŋ a ɪŋ
22 backing and advancing

æ ɪŋ æ ɪn:
23 snapping of the clapper to the spin

aʊtʰ ɪn:
24 out and in——

NOTE: æ "backing" (line 22), which interrupts a cascade of a sounds (lines 19-22), would have been an even more extreme contrast to Belloc, for whom, as an Englishman, the Ask-Words are pronounced with a· .

ˈtʼɪŋˌtʼʊŋˈtʼæŋː   tʼaə̆
25 and the ting tong tang of the guitar!

ˈɪnː
26 do you remember an inn

ɪ æ
27 mi-randa?

ˈɪnː
28 do you remember an inn?

ɔə̆
29 never more;

ɪ æ
30 mi-randa

ɔə̆
31 never more.

oŭ ɪ aˑĭˑ jˑ ɔə̆
32 only the high peaks hoar:

æ ʋ ʋ ə ɔə̆   ˈæ r̲ə gʋn
33 and a-ragon a to-rrent at the door.

oˑŭˑ aˑŭˑnːd
34 no sound

ɔːl̥ːz ɔːl̥ːz ɔːl̥z
35 in the walls of the halls where falls ●—
ṇ
e
36 the tread

ə jˑ e aˑŭˑnːd
37 of the feet of the dead to the ground

oˑŭˑ aˑŭˑnːd
38 no sound:

ə uːm
39 but the boom

aə̆ ɔˑ ɔːl̥ uːm
40 of the far waterfall like doom.

GUIDELINES FOR CREATING A SCORE

The following suggestions are useful visual aids to speaking. If you retype or copy out a section of your script, or are working on a monologue, poem or piece of prose, you will find it helpful to number the lines and maintain the visual form of the lines, especially if the text is in verse. Preserve all punctuation except commas and capital letters. While commas are used to indicate phrases on the printed page, they may not indicate the best phrasing to use when speaking, and capital letters have no relationship to a word's importance or pronunciation. Underline the letter "r" in the spelling of a word if it is to be spoken as a consonant ɾ sound, and use a hyphen to delineate the syllables of a word containing an intervocalic consonant ɾ as in spi-rit, me-rry, Ma-ry, and ma-rry. Then mark the following sound and pronunciation features in your score.

◆ The Challengers for the Actor with Good Speech, if their use is appropriate;

◆ The vowel or diphthong sounds in the stressed syllables of the operative or key-idea words. As the primary tone-carriers of the English language, these sounds are used by good writers for the dramatic and musical values they bring to a text. Consonant sounds may also have dramatic values, but these qualities are usually easy to spot without phonetic letters. The practice of phonetic notations puts you in touch with the sound palette the author has used.

However, these dramatic values, which to some people comprise an "orchestra" of sound, must never be in the forefront of either your interpretation or the audience's perception of your performance;

◆ Tone endings of words. Final voiced consonants of words are useful for their dramatic qualities and essential for understandability;

◆ Length of sound. The duration of words, and the contrast between long and short sounds, are the basis for the rhythm of your character's speech;

◆ Particular speech sounds that need your special consideration;

◆ Operative words, AS NEEDED. (Since the thoughts in "Tarantella" are clear and straightforward, no operative words are marked in the sample score on page 351-352. Discussion of operative words is found on page 357, and operative words have been marked in the score of the more complex thoughts of "Sonnet LXXI," found on page 360.)

You may also find that some research is required in order to enhance your comprehension and appreciation of a text. You may want to know about the author of the text, the circumstances under which a work was written or the identity of a person named in the work. Intensive investigation is not necessary for an understanding of "Tarantella," but additional knowledge about Hilaire Belloc may lend richness to your interpretation of the poem.

For instance, it is interesting to note that Belloc traveled widely and wrote vivid descriptions of his adventures, notably of his treks through the Pyrenees Range of mountains that connect Southern France and the North of Spain. Belloc particularly loved small inns. In an essay he recalls a Basque inn where a river flowed beneath a verandah, on which he could stand and see the mountains in the distance. He describes the inn as a place of both conviviality and despair, a duality that is also present in "Tarantella."

Anyone reading the poem for the first time is bound to ask: "Who was Miranda?" As far as anyone knows, Belloc presented the original version of the poem (then titled "For Miranda") to Miranda Mackintosh, the daughter of a good friend. You as interpreter of the poem are left with the questions "What's Miranda to him, or he to Miranda . . . ?"

Belloc loved sound and rhythm. For some poems, including "Tarantella," he actually wrote and recorded melodies. Certainly the musical characteristics of the tarantella are found in the verbal music of Belloc's poem. If you are interested in hearing a tarantella, you might listen to those composed by either Frédéric Chopin or Franz Liszt, or to one of Stephen Heller's Tarantellas for piano, which have been learned by countless students, or even the one in the musical comedy *Peter Pan*.

The tarantella is a Neapolitan folk dance for one couple that is danced in 6/8 time (two beats of triplets per measure) to the accompaniment of tambourines and castanets. In some quarters, the dance was considered the only cure for the bite of the poisonous tarantula, which possibly explains why the dance gets increasingly fast, its music typically alternating between major and minor keys. These features have been translated by Belloc into the rhythms and sounds of his poem.

FINDING THE MUSIC OF THE TEXT

Note the following sound features in the score for "Tarantella" found on pages 351-352.

✓ *Reminder* ───

The example is merely ONE good way of scoring this poem.

Rhythm and Tempo

◆ Just as the dance music of the tarantella is in 6/8 time, employing beats of 2 and 3, Belloc alternates rhythms of 2 and 3 throughout the poem in order to subtly shift emphasis and flow.

(3 beats) do you remember an inn

(2 beats) chancing glancing dancing

◆ There is a steady build in tempo that reaches a peak at line 28.

◆ Just as the dance music alternates major and minor keys, Belloc gives us a "major" first stanza (lines 1-28) written in a spirit of hedonistic fun and a "minor" second stanza (lines 29-40) written in a sense of inevitable doom.

◆ Note that the fast, "major" first stanza has only single-consonant endings while the slower, "minor" second stanza has numerous double-consonant endings.

◆ Note the use of stop-plosive sounds throughout, suggesting the sounds of castanets and contributing to the velocity of the poem's first stanza.

Contrast of Rhythm

◆ Belloc uses sharp contrast of length of sounds. Note the predominantly short "diamond" and "emerald" vowel sounds I and e of lines 1-5, and the long open sounds of lines 6 and 7.

Short	Long
I remember inn Miranda	$\mathcal{O}$: straw
e tedding spreading bedding	i: fleas tease Pyrenees
$e\breve{\imath}$ tasted	$a\cdot\imath\cdot$ wine

Similarly, note the short sounds of lines 13-17 and lines 19-26 contrasted with the long sounds that interrupt in lines 18 and 19, and the long n: sounds in line 23.

Short	Long
hadn't got penny paying any	din
hammer hip hop hap clap	hands twirl swirl girl gone
chancing glancing dancing	
backing advancing	ting tong tang

In the second, "minor" stanza, the long sounds are dominant:

Short	Long
Aragon torrent	walls halls falls
tread feet dead	ground no sound boom waterfall doom

◆ Note the contrasting use of short, deft, tip-of-the-tongue consonant sounds t and d with the dramatic, rhythmic lengthening of $l:$, $n:$ and $\eta:$.

Tonality

◆ Note the contrasting closed and open sounds within a line:

5 of the straw for a bedding

6 and the fleas that tease in high Pyrenees

7 and the wine that tasted of the tar

9 under the vine of the dark verandah

32 only the high peaks hoar

33 and Aragon a torrent at the door

40 of the far waterfall like doom

Contrast of Tonality

◆ Note the contrast of FRONT vowel sounds with BACK vowel and diphthong sounds:

Front

$i:$ fleas tease feet peaks Pyrenees

I inn din spin in ting

e remember tedding spreading bedding penny any never tread

$æ$ Miranda hadn't hammer hap clap hands backing clapper tang Aragon
        verandah

a chancing dancing advancing (high wine vine) $a\cdot\breve{\imath}\cdot$

Back

$u:$ do you boom doom

$ɔ:$ straw walls halls falls waterfall (doors more door hoar)

$ɒ$ got hop gone tong Aragon torrent

$a\ddot{a}$ tar dark far guitar

$o\breve{u}\cdot$ only no

$a\cdot\breve{u}\cdot$ sound ground

You will undoubtedly note other uses of sound and rhythm in the poem. There are no rules by which your ear senses the music and poetry in language, and there certainly are no rules for making them live in performance. The score you make will alert you to the creative uses of sound and rhythm in the text and should stimulate you to a deeper understanding of its meaning.

Sonnet LXXI

by William Shakespeare

No longer mourn for me when I am dead
Than you shall hear the surly sullen bell
Give warning to the world that I am fled
From this vile world, with vilest worms to dwell.
Nay, if you read this line, remember not
The hand that writ it; for I love you so
That I in your sweet thoughts would be forgot
If thinking on me then should make you woe.
Oh if, I say, you look upon this verse
When I perhaps compounded am with clay,
Do not so much as my poor name rehearse,
But let your love even with my life decay,
    Lest the wise world should look into your moan
    And mock you with me after I am gone.

OPERATIVE WORDS AND DEGREES OF STRESS

Finding the operative words in a text depends upon the arrangement of the thoughts and then upon your interpretation of them. In any utterance, a variety of emphases is possible, and you as an individual will give unique shadings and weight to the words. But for practical purposes, when you score a text, you should only note a few degrees of emphasis; if a word is unimportant, either because it is not operative or because it is a weak form, you should not underline it.

A broken line indicates that the word has a slight degree of emphasis in the flow of thought.

A single solid line indicates an operative word, important to the sense of the thought.

Double solid lines indicate a strong operative word (in the particular scoring of "Sonnet LXXI" in this textbook, it is not necessary to note a strong emphasis).

The following sentences contain operative words. Say each phrase as you normally would and you will most likely give the emphases that are indicated:

1 Give me liberty or give me death.

2 Thou shalt not bear false witness against thy neighbor.

3 Thou shalt not steal.

4 We have nothing to fear but fear itself.

5 Frankly, Scarlett, I don't give a damn.

6 Play it again, Sam.

7 Let them eat cake.

8 Doctor Livingstone, I presume?

9 What's up, Doc?

10 Where there's a will there's a way.

11 Would you buy a used car from this man?

12 Wild horses couldn't drag it out of me!

When scoring a text, mark the operative words in pencil because different words may become operative as your interpretation changes. Remember that underlining is a tool that can help you find the meaning of a text—it is not intended to "set" the way you speak a line. With time and experience, you will need to mark only those sounds that you find particularly problematic to your speech, and just as your production of correct sounds will eventually become habitual, so your application of them to texts will become habitual, too.

Sonnet LXXI

by William Shakespeare

Shakespeare's sonnets are wonderful to read out loud because they spring from a unique personal voice and are also filled with an amazing variety of word- and sound-play, highly charged imagery and sophisticated thought. Speaking the sonnets demands depth and imagination, clarity of idea and simplicity of utterance. Creating the score for a Shakespearean sonnet will illuminate the sense of the verse, highlight the use of dramatic values in the sounds and rhythms and remind you of speech sounds and combinations that need your special attention.

Read through the entire sonnet as many times as you wish until you understand the sense of the words and phrases. To find the meanings of words that are archaic or no longer used, consult either the *Oxford English Dictionary* (O.E.D.); *Shakespeare Lexicon and Quotation Dictionary*, edited by Alexander Schmidt; or *A Shakespeare Glossary*, edited by C.T. Onions.

When you have consulted these books and used your own interpretive skills, you may then find it helpful to paraphrase clauses and sentences. But remember while you are doing this that paraphrasing must take into account ALL the clauses and phrases; a glib, generalized notion of a sentence will dilute the meaning of the text and will dull your own imaginative response to it. Paraphrasing a line of Shakespeare usually proves just how deep, precise and succinct his language is. Then, when you have paraphrased individual lines and sentences, encapsulate the meaning of the entire poem in one sentence, using your own words. It is the germ of this sentence that provides the impulse to begin the sonnet and will find completion in the couplet.

The Form of Shakespeare's Sonnets

The Shakespearean sonnet uses a rhyme scheme of *abab cdcd efef gg*. Each of these three sets of four lines is called a QUATRAIN. In some of Shakespeare's sonnets, he stated the theme in the first quatrain and then explored it in each of the subsequent ones, summarizing the resolution of the theme or ARGUMENT in the COUPLET, or final two lines. He wrote other sonnets that were essentially 12-line poems followed by a concluding couplet, and in still others he presented the theme in the first eight lines, or OCTAVE, and a distillation of the theme in the final six lines, or SESTET. "Sonnet LXXI" falls into this last category. Note that in this sonnet each quatrain (lines 1-4, 5-8, 9-12) is a complete sentence and that the couplet (lines 13 and 14) springs directly from the meaning of line 12 while at the same time completing the sense of the entire poem.

Scansion

Scansion is the analysis of the rhythmic components of verse. With one exception, Shakespeare wrote his sonnets in a meter, or rhythm, known as IAMBIC PENTAMETER. Each line of the poem is based on a rhythmic line comprised of five iambic feet. Each iambic foot has two beats or syllables, the first weak and the second strong. In other words, a line of iambic pentameter produces a pattern of unstressed and stressed syllables that sound like "ta-TUM ta-TUM ta-TUM ta-TUM ta TUM." This is traditionally written ⌣ / ⌣ / ⌣ / ⌣ /, with ⌣ above the weak syllables and / above the strong syllables. The rhythm of the thought in a line of iambic pentameter will often include a natural break or pause in the line, usually after the second or third foot. This slight pause in the line is called a caesura:

$$\overset{\smile}{\text{no}} \ \overset{/}{\text{longer}} \ \overset{\smile}{\text{mourn}} \ \overset{/}{\text{for}} \ \overset{\smile}{\text{me}} \ \overset{/}{} \qquad \overset{\smile}{\text{when}} \ \overset{/}{\text{I}} \ \overset{\smile}{\text{am}} \ \overset{/}{\text{dead}}$$

no longer mourn for me   when I am dead

Keep in mind, however, that the metrical structure of a poem provides a unifying undercurrent to the thoughts and images. The rhythm of "ta-TUM ta-TUM ta-TUM ta-TUM ta-TUM" is not meant to be reproduced mechanically and slavishly when spoken. Just as a composer may use syncopation to point up certain notes by placing them off the beat, so a poet often emphasizes a word by placing its stressed syllable on a normally weak beat of the meter.

Scansion of the verse will not only give you clues to the emphasis and phrasing of the lines, it may even suggest aspects of character and situation. However, remember that the main purpose of metrical rhythm is to impel the flow of thought and provide a measured emotional undercurrent to the meaning of the language.

Theme or argument: Let your love for me die when I die, lest the world see your sorrow and mock you because of me.

Follow the guidelines for creating a score. (See page 353.) This score illustrates ONE good way of scoring "Sonnet LXXI."

1 no longer mourn for me   when i am dead ●—

2 than you shall hear   the surly sullen bell ●—

3 give warning to the world   that i am fled

4 from this vile world   with vilest worms to dwell. ⌐

5 nay if you read this line   remember not ●—

6 the hand that writ it   for i love you so ●—

7 that i in your sweet thoughts   would be forgot

8 if thinking on me then   should make you woe. ⌐

9 oh if i say ●—   you look upon this verse

10 when i perhaps   compounded am with clay ⌐

11 do not so much as my poor name rehearse

12 but let your love   even with my life   decay

13 lest the wise world   should look into your moan

14 and mock you with me   after i am gone. ⌐

●—   the idea continues—sustained inflection

⌐   the idea finishes—falling inflection

⌐   the word is important and inflected, but the thought is not finished

Knowing now the literal sense of what you are saying, use your phonetic letters to zero in on how the sounds and lengths used by the poet invoke mood and enhance the meaning of the poem.

First Quatrain (lines 1-4):

Note Shakespeare's use of the nasal continuants, the darker ℓ sounds, the glide w, some vowel and diphthong sounds of "r," and long sounds in general to create a dark, ominous, somber mood. When saying the poem, do not play the mood or the dramatic values of the sounds; they are there as an undercurrent to evoke the funereal subject of the first sentence:

m n η	no longer mourn sullen warning worms		
ℓ	shall surly sullen bell world vile vilest dwell		
w	warning world worms dwell ($\mathcal{M}$ when)		
$з:$	surly world worms	$ə$	longer
$\mathfrak{ɔ}\breve{ə}$	mourn for warning	$ı\breve{ə}$	hear

Note alliteration of:

m	mourn for me	
s	surly sullen bell	
w	warning to the world	
v w	vile world	vilest worms to dwell

Second Quatrain (lines 5-8):

Through the use of short vowel and diphthong sounds, the bright front vowel sounds and their related diphthongs, and the lighter, more delicate tip-of-the-tongue consonant sounds in initial positions of words, particularly t and θ, Shakespeare effects an increase in speed, perhaps implying urgency or haste, a quickening of the blood. Note, too, the alliteration of:

$\underline{r}$	read remember writ
θ	thoughts thinking
$ð$	(in the unimportant words) this the that then

Third Quatrain (lines 9-12):

The quatrain begins with the strong impulse of the interjection "oh" and quickens through Shakespeare's continued use of short sounds, plosive consonants, the incisive s sounds, and the clear initial ℓ sounds:

p	upon perhaps compounded poor
k	look compounded clay decay
ℓ	look let love life
s	say this verse perhaps so rehearse

Couplet (lines13-14):

Line 13 returns to the long mournful sounds of the first quatrain, as well as the rich, dark lip-rounded sounds:

m	**m**oan **m**ock **m**e	*n*	moa**n** go**n**e
w	**w**ise **w**orld **w**ith		
u	int**o** y**o**u		
ʊ	sh**ou**ld l**oo**k	(*ʊə* y**ou**r)	
ɒ	m**o**ck g**o**ne		
o·ŭ·	m**oa**n		

Notice the use of strong and weak forms of words. Appropriate use of the strong forms of words reinforces the rhythm of the verse and the elevated style of the writing, while the use of appropriate weak forms assures an easy, unaffected flow of thought and utterance. Note, line by line, the unimportant, and therefore unemphasized, words that maintain their normal pronunciation and especially the weak forms of such unimportant words as articles, auxiliary verbs, pronouns, and connecting words. The weak form of a word is unstressed, short in length and may contain a weak vowel sound. In verse, the weak forms that eliminate a consonant sound from a word are generally not used since the missing consonant weakens the rhythm.

Strong Vowels in Unemphasized Words	**Weak Forms of Unemphasized Words**
Line	
1 no when	for me I am
2	than you shall the
3 give	to the that I am
4 this with	from to
5 if this not	you
6 it	the that for I you
7 in	that your would be
8 if one then	me should you
9 upon this	I you
10 when am with	I
11 do not so	as my
12 with	but your my
13	the should into your
14 with	and you me I am

Perhaps you will find additional or entirely different operative words and emphases in the poem, as well as other sonorities and rhythms that evoke the changing moods of the thoughts. The important thing is to delve into both the sense and the music of the text. It is the unity of thought, rhythm and sound that embodies the full meaning of the poem. From the technique of creating a score for various texts, your awareness of this unity will become heightened and second-nature, so that eventually you may not need to use a score at all to help you "hear" a text in detail.

The forthcoming selections of prose and poetry were chosen to give you a variety of styles and subjects as you continue to apply the principles of well-spoken English.

The Passionate Shepherd to His Love

by Christopher Marlowe

Come live with me and be my love,
And we will all the pleasures prove
That valleys, groves, hills, and fields,
Woods, or steepy mountain yields.

And we will sit upon the rocks,
Seeing the shepherds feed their flocks,
By shallow rivers, to whose falls
Melodious birds sing madrigals.

And I will make thee beds of roses
And a thousand fragrant posies,
A cap of flowers, and a kirtle
Embroidered all with leaves of myrtle;

A gown made of the finest wool,
Which from our pretty lambs we pull;
Fair linèd slippers for the cold,
With buckles of the purest gold;

A belt of straw and ivy buds
With coral clasps and amber studs:
And if these pleasures may thee move,
Come live with me and be my love.

The shepherd swains shall dance and sing
For thy delight each May morning:
If these delights thy mind may move,
Then live with me and be my love.

To His Son

by Sir Walter Raleigh

Three things there be that prosper all apace,
   And flourish while they are asunder far;
But on a day they meet all in a place,
   And when they meet they one another mar.

And they be these—the wood, the weed, the wag:
   The wood is that that makes the gallows tree;
The weed is that that strings the hangman's bag;
   The wag, my pretty knave, betokens thee.

Now mark, dear boy, while these assemble not,
   Green springs the tree, hemp grows, the wag is wild;
But when they meet, it makes the timber rot,
   It frets the halter, and it chokes the child.
   God bless the child.

With How Sad Steps, O Moon

by Sir Philip Sidney

With how sad steps, O moon, thou climb'st the skies,
  How silently, and with how wan a face.
  What, may it be that even in heavenly place
That busy archer his sharp arrows tries?
Sure, if that long-with-love-acquainted eyes
  Can judge of love, thou feel'st a lover's case;
  I read it in thy looks; thy languisht grace,
To me that feel the like, thy state descries.

Then, even of fellowship, O moon, tell me
  Is constant love deemed there but want of wit?
Are beauties there as proud as here they be?
  Do they above love to be loved, and yet
Those lovers scorn whom that love doth possess?
Do they call virtue there ungratefulness?

Thrice Toss These Oaken Ashes In the Air

by Thomas Campion

Thrice toss these oaken ashes in the air,
Thrice sit thou mute in this enchanted chair,
And thrice three times tie up this true love's knot,
And murmur soft, 'She will, or she will not.'

Go burn these poisonous weeds in yon blue fire,
These screech-owl's feathers and this prickling briar,
This cypress gathered at a dead man's grave,
That all thy fears and cares an end may have.

Then come, you fairies, dance with me a round!
Melt her hard heart with your melodious sound!
In vain are all the charms I can devise:
She hath an art to break them with her eyes.

To My Dear and Loving Husband

by Anne Bradstreet

If ever two were one, then surely we.
If ever man were loved by wife, then thee;
If ever wife was happy in a man,
Compare with me, ye women, if you can.
I prize thy love more than whole mines of gold,
Or all the riches that the East doth hold.
My love is such that rivers cannot quench,
Nor aught but love from thee give recompense.
Thy love is such I can no way repay;
The heavens reward thee manifold, I pray.
Then while we live, in love let's so persever,
That when we live no more we may live ever.

Jealousy

by Esther Johnson

Oh, shield me from his rage, celestial Powers!
This tyrant that embitters all my hours.
Ah! Love, you've poorly played the monarch's part:
You conquered, but you can't defend, my heart.
So blessed was I throughout thy happy reign,
I thought this monster banished from thy train;
But you would raise him to support your throne,
And now he claims your empire as his own:
Or tell me, tyrants, have you both agreed
That where one reigns the other shall succeed?

To His Coy Mistress

by Andrew Marvell

Had we but world enough, and time,
This coyness, Lady, were no crime.
We would sit down and think which way
To walk and pass our long love's day.
Thou by the Indian Ganges' side
Shouldst rubies find; I by the tide
Of Humber would complain. I would
Love you ten years before the Flood,
And you should, if you please, refuse
Till the conversion of the Jews.
My vegetable love should grow
Vaster than empires, and more slow;
An hundred years should go to praise
Thine eyes and on thy forehead gaze;
Two hundred to adore each breast,
But thirty thousand to the rest;
An age at least to every part,
And the last age should show your heart.
For, Lady, you deserve this state,
Nor would I love at lower rate.
    But at my back I always hear
Time's wingèd chariot hurrying near;
And yonder all before us lie
Deserts of vast eternity.

Thy beauty shall no more be found,
Nor, in thy marble vault, shall sound
My echoing song; then worms shall try
That long preserved virginity,
And your quaint honor turn to dust,
And into ashes all my lust:
The grave's a fine and private place,
But none, I think, do there embrace.
    Now therefore, while the youthful hue
Sits on thy skin like morning dew,
And while thy willing soul transpires
At every pore with instant fires,
Now let us sport us while we may,
And now, like amorous birds of prey,
Rather at once our time devour
Than languish in his slow-chapped power.
Let us roll all our strength and all
Our sweetness up into one ball,
And tear our pleasures with rough strife
Thorough the iron gates of life:
Thus, though we cannot make our sun
Stand still, yet we will make him run.

Beneath the Cypress Shade

by Thomas Love Peacock

I dug, beneath the cypress shade,
    What well might seem an elfin's grave;
And every pledge in earth I laid,
    That erst thy false affection gave.

I pressed them down the sod beneath;
    I placed one mossy stone above;
And twined the rose's fading wreath
    Around the sepulchre of love.

Frail as thy love, the flowers were dead,
    Ere yet the evening sun was set:
But years shall see the cypress spread,
    Immutable as my regret.

Remember Thee! Remember Thee!

by George Gordon, Lord Byron

Remember thee! remember thee!
    Till Lethe quench Life's burning stream
Remorse and Shame shall cling to thee,
    And haunt thee like a feverish dream!

Remember thee! Aye, doubt it not.
    Thy husband too shall think of thee:
By neither shalt thou be forgot,
    Thou *false* to him, thou *fiend* to me!

The Tyger

by William Blake

Tyger, Tyger, burning bright,
In the forests of the night,
What immortal hand or eye
Could frame thy fearful symmetry?

In what distant deeps or skies
Burnt the fire of thine eyes?
On what wings dare he aspire?
What the hand dare seize the fire?

And what shoulder, and what art,
Could twist the sinews of thy heart?
And when thy heart began to beat,
What dread hand? And what dread feet?

What the hammer? What the chain?
In what furnace was thy brain?
What the anvil? What dread grasp
Dare its deadly terrors clasp?

When the stars threw down their spears
And watered heaven with their tears,
Did he smile his work to see?
Did he who made the Lamb make thee?

Tyger, Tyger, burning bright,
In the forests of the night,
What immortal hand or eye
Dare frame thy fearful symmetry?

On Dullness

by Alexander Pope

Thus Dullness, the safe opiate of the mind,
The last kind refuge weary Wit can find,
Fit for all stations, and in each content,
Is satisfied, secure, and innocent.
No pains it takes, and no offence it gives:
Unfeared, unhated, undisturbed it lives.
And if each writing author's best pretence
Be but to teach the ignorant more sense,
Then Dullness was the cause they wrote before,
As 'tis at last the cause they write no more.
So Wit, which most to scorn it does pretend,
With Dullness first began, in Dullness last must end.

Lines to a Reviewer

by Percy Bysshe Shelley

Alas, good friend, what profit can you see
In hating such a hateless thing as me?
There is no sport in hate where all the rage
Is on one side: in vain would you assuage
Your frowns upon an unresisting smile,
In which not even contempt lurks to beguile
Your heart, by some faint sympathy of hate.
Oh, conquer what you cannot satiate!
For to your passion I am far more coy
Than ever yet was coldest maid or boy
In winter noon. Of your antipathy
If I am the Narcissus, you are free
To pine into a sound with hating me.

Sympathy

by Paul Laurence Dunbar

I know what the caged bird feels, alàs!
When the sun is bright on the upland slopes;
When the wind stirs soft through the springing grass,
And the river flows like a stream of glass;
When the first bird sings and the first bud opes,
And the faint perfume from its chalice steals—
I know what the caged bird feels!

I know why the caged bird beats his wing
Till its blood is red on the cruel bars;
For he must fly back to his perch and cling
When he fain would be on the bough a-swing;
And a pain still throbs in the old, old scars
And they pulse again with a keener sting—
I know why he beats his wing!

I know why the caged bird sings, ah me,
When his wing is bruised and his bosom sore,—
When he beats his bars and he would be free;
It is not a carol of joy or glee,
But a prayer that he sends from his heart's deep core,
But a plea, that upward to Heaven he flings—
I know why the caged bird sings!

A Noiseless Patient Spider

by Walt Whitman

A noiseless patient spider,
I mark'd where on a little promontory it stood isolated,
Mark'd how to explore the vacant vast surrounding,
It launch'd forth filament, filament, filament, out of itself,
Ever unreeling them, ever tirelessly speeding them.

And you O my soul where you stand,
Surrounded, detached, in measureless oceans of space,
Ceaselessly musing, venturing, throwing, seeking the spheres to
    connect them,
Till the bridge you will need be form'd, till the ductile anchor
    hold,
Till the gossamer thread you fling catch somewhere, O my soul.

Drowning Is Not So Pitiful

by Emily Dickinson

Drowning is not so pitiful
As the attempt to rise.
Three times, 'tis said, a sinking man
Comes up to face the skies,
And then declines forever
To that abhorred abode,
Where hope and he part company—
For he is grasped of God.
The Maker's cordial visage,
However good to see,
Is shunned, we must admit it,
Like an adversity.

from *The Devil's Dictionary*

by Ambrose Bierce

Fool, *n*. A person who pervades the domain of intellectual speculation and diffuses himself throu͏g͏h the channels of moral activity. He is omnific, omniform, omnipercipient, omniscient, omnipoten͏t. He it was who invented letters, printing, the railroad, the steamboat, the telegraph, the platitude and the circle of the sciences. He created patriotism and taught the nations war—founded theolo͏gy, philosophy, law, medicine and Chicago. He established monarchical and republican governmen͏t. He is from everlasting to everlasting—such as creation's dawn beheld he fooleth now. In the mor͏n͏ing of time he sang upon primitive hills, and in the noonday of existence headed the procession ͏of being. His grandmotherly hand has warmly tucked-in the set sun of civilization, and in the twili͏g͏h͏t he prepares Man's evening meal of milk-and-morality and turns down the covers of the univer͏s͏al grave. And after the rest of us shall have retired for the night of eternal oblivion he will sit up ͏to write a history of human civilization.

Looking-glass, *n*. A vitreous plane upon which to display a fleeting show for man's disillusion give͏n.

The King of Manchuria had a magic looking-glass, whereon whoso looked saw, not his o͏w͏n image, but only that of the king. A certain courtier who had long enjoyed the king's favor and w͏as thereby enriched beyond any other subject of the realm, said to the king: "Give me, I pray, t͏he wonderful mirror, so that when absent out of thine august presence I may yet do homage before t͏he visible shadow, prostrating myself night and morning in the glory of thy benign countenance, which nothing has so divine splendor, O Noonday Sun of the Universe!"

Pleased with the speech, the king commanded that the mirror be conveyed to the courtie͏r's palace; but after, having gone thither without apprisal, he found it in an apartment where w͏as naught but idle lumber. And the mirror was dimmed with dust and overlaced with cobwebs. This so angered him that he fisted it hard, shattering the glass, and was sorely hurt. Enraged all the more ͏by this mischance, he commanded that the ungrateful courtier be thrown into prison, and that the gla͏ss be repaired and taken back to his own palace; and this was done. But when the king looked aga͏in on the mirror he saw not his image as before, but only the figure of a crowned ass, having a bloo͏dy bandage on one of its hinder hooves—as the artificers and all who had looked upon it had befo͏re discerned but feared to report. Taught wisdom and charity, the king restored his courtier to liber͏ty, had the mirror set into the back of the throne and reigned many years with justice and humility; a͏nd one day when he fell asleep in death while on the throne, the whole court saw in the mirror t͏he luminous figure of an angel, which remains to this day.

from *The Devil's Dictionary*

by Ambrose Bierce

Lord, *n.* In American society, an English tourist above the state of a costermonger, as, Lord 'Aberdasher, Lord Hartisan and so forth. The traveling Briton of lesser degree is addressed as "Sir," as, Sir 'Arry Donkiboi, of 'Amstead 'Eath. The word "Lord" is sometimes used, also, as a title of the Supreme Being; but this is thought to be rather flattery than true reverence.

Miss Sallie Ann Splurge, of her own accord,
Wedded a wandering English lord—
Wedded and took him to dwell with her "paw,"
A parent who throve by the practice of Draw.
Lord Cadde I don't hesitate here to declare
Unworthy the father-in-legal care
Of that elderly sport, notwithstanding the truth
That Cadde had renounced all the follies of youth;
For, sad to relate, he'd arrived at the stage
Of existence that's marked by the vices of age.
Among them, cupidity caused him to urge
Repeated demands on the pocket of Splurge,
Till, wrecked in his fortune, that gentleman saw
Inadequate aid in the practice of Draw,
And took, as a means of augmenting his pelf,
To the business of being a lord himself.
His neat-fitting garments he wilfully shed
And sacked himself strangely in checks instead;
Denuded his chin, but retained at each ear
A whisker that looked like a blasted career.
He painted his neck an incarnadine hue
Each morning and varnished it all that he knew.
The moony monocular set in his eye
Appeared to be scanning the Sweet Bye-and-Bye.
His head was enroofed with a billycock hat,
And his low-necked shoes were aduncous and flat.
In speech he eschewed his American ways,
Denying his nose to the use of his A's
And dulling their edge till the delicate sense
Of a babe at their temper could take no offence.
His H's—'twas most inexpressibly sweet,
The patter they made as they fell at his feet!
Re-outfitted thus, Mr. Splurge without fear
Began as Lord Splurge his recouping career.
Alas, the Divinity shaping his end
Entertained other views and decided to send
His lordship in horror, despair and dismay
From the land of the nobleman's natural prey.
For, smit with his Old World ways, Lady Cadde
Fell—suffering Caesar!—in love with her dad!

from *Poems in Prose*
by Oscar Wilde

The House of Judgment

And there was silence in the House of Judgment, and the Man came naked before God.

And God opened the book of the life of the Man.

And God said to the Man, "Thy life has been evil, and thou hast shown cruelty to those wh were in need of succour, and to those who lacked help thou hast been bitter and hard of heart. Th poor called to thee and thou didst not hearken, and thine eyes were closed to the cry of My afflic ed. The inheritance of the fatherless thou didst take unto thyself, and thou didst send foxes into th vineyards of thy neighbour's field. Thou didst take the bread of the children and gave it to the dog to eat, and My lepers who lived in the marshes, and were at peace and praised me thou didst driv forth onto the highways, and out of My earth out of which I made thee thou didst spill innocer blood."

And the Man made answer and said, "Even so did I."

And again God opened the book of the life of the Man.

And God said to the Man, "Thy life hath been evil, and the beauty I have shown thou ha sought for, and the Good I have hidden thou didst pass by. The walls of thy chamber were painte with images, and from the bed of thy abominations thou didst rise up to the sound of flutes. Tho didst build seven altars to the sins I have suffered, and didst eat of the thing that may not be eate and the purple of thy raiment was broidered with the three signs of shame. Thine idols were neith of Gold nor of silver that endure, but of flesh which dieth. Thou didst stain their hair with perfum and put pomegranates in their hands. Thou didst stain their feet with saffron and spread carpets be fore them. With antimony thou didst stain their eyelids and their bodies thou didst smear wit myrrh. Thou didst bow thyself to the ground before them, and the thrones of thine idols were set i the sun. Thou didst show to the sun thy shame and to the moon thy madness."

And the Man answered and said, "Even so did I."

And a third time God opened the book of the life of the Man. And God said to the Man, "Ev hath been thy life, and with evil didst thou requite good, and with wrongdoing kindness, the hanc that fed thee thou didst wound, and the breasts that gave thee suck thou didst despise. He wh came to thee with water went away thirsting, and the outlawed men who hid thee in their tents a night thou didest betray before dawn. Thine enemy who spared thee thou didst snare in an ambush and the friend who walked with thee thou didst sell for a price, and to those who brought thee Lov thou didst ever give Lust in thy turn."

And the Man made answer and said, "Even so did I."

And God closed the book of the life of the Man, and said, "Surely I will send thee into Hel Even into Hell I will send thee."

And the Man cried out, "Thou canst not."

And God said to the Man, "Wherefore can I not send thee to Hell, and for what reason?"

"Because in Hell I have always lived," answered the Man.

And there was silence in the House of Judgment.

And after a space God spake, and said to the Man, "Seeing that I may not send thee into Hel surely I will send thee unto Heaven. Even unto Heaven will I send thee."

And the Man cried out, "Thou canst not."

And God said to the Man, "Wherefore can I not send thee unto Heaven, and for what reason?"

"Because never, and in no place, have I been able to imagine it," answered the Man.

And there was silence in the House of Judgment.

from *Alice in Wonderland*

by Lewis Carroll

Chapter IV

Alice noticed with some surprise that the pebbles were all turning into little cakes as they lay on the floor, and a bright idea came into her head. "If I eat one of these cakes," she thought, "it's sure to make some change in my size: and as it can't possibly make me larger it must make me smaller, I suppose."

So she swallowed one of the cakes, and was delighted to find that she began shrinking directly. As soon as she was small enough to get through the door, she ran out of the house, and found quite a crowd of little animals and birds waiting outside. The poor little lizard, Bill, was in the middle, being held up by two guinea-pigs, who were giving it something out of a bottle. They all made a rush at Alice the moment she appeared, but she ran off as hard as she could, and soon found herself safe in a thick wood.

"The first thing I've got to do," said Alice to herself, as she wandered about in the wood, "is to grow to my right size again; and the second thing is to find my way into that lovely garden. I think that will be the best plan."

It sounded an excellent plan, no doubt, and very neatly and simply arranged; the only difficulty was, that she had not the smallest idea how to set about it; and while she was peering about anxiously among the trees, a little sharp bark just over her head made her look up in a great hurry.

An enormous puppy was looking down at her with large round eyes, and feebly stretching out one paw, trying to touch her. "Poor little thing!" said Alice in a coaxing tone, and she tried hard to whistle to it, but she was terribly frightened all the time at the thought that it might be hungry, in which case it would be very likely to eat her up in spite of all her coaxing.

Hardly knowing what she did, she picked up a little bit of stick, and held it out to the puppy; whereupon the puppy jumped into the air off all its feet at once, with a yelp of delight, and rushed at the stick, and made believe to worry it; then Alice dodged behind a great thistle, to keep herself from being run over, and, the moment she appeared on the other side, the puppy made another rush at the stick, and tumbled head over heels in its hurry to get hold of it; then Alice, thinking it was very like having a game of play with a carthorse, and expecting every moment to be trampled under his feet, ran round the thistle again: then the puppy began a series of short charges at the stick, running a very little way forward each time and a long way back, and barking hoarsely all the while, till at last it sat down a good way off, panting, with its tongue hanging out of its mouth, and its great eyes half shut.

This seemed to Alice a good opportunity for making her escape, so she set off at once, and ran till she was quite tired and out of breath, and till the puppy's bark sounded quite faint in the distance.

"And yet what a dear little puppy it was," said Alice, as she leaned against a buttercup to rest herself, and fanned herself with one of the leaves: "I should have liked teaching it tricks very much, if—if I'd only been the right size to do it! Oh dear! I'd nearly forgotten that I've got to grow up again. Let me see—how *is* it to be managed? I suppose I ought to eat or drink something or other; but the great question is, what?"

The great question certainly was, what? Alice looked all round her at the flowers and the blades of grass, but she could not see anything that looked like the right thing to eat or drink under the circumstances. There was a large mushroom growing near her, about the same height as herself, and when she had looked under it, and on both sides of it, and behind it, it occurred to her that she might as well look and see what was on the top of it.

She stretched herself up on tiptoe, and peeped over the edge of the mushroom, and her eyes immediately met those of a large blue caterpillar, that was sitting on the top with its arms folded, quietly smoking a long hookah, and taking not the smallest notice of her or of anything else.

from *David Copperfield*

by Charles Dickens

Chapter LV

There had been a wind all day; and it was rising then, with an extraordinary great sound. In an other hour it had much increased, and the sky was more overcast, and blew hard.

But as the night advanced, the clouds closing in and densely overspreading the whole sky, then very dark, it came on to blow, harder and harder. Sweeping gusts of rain came up before this storm like showers of steel; and, at those times, when there was any shelter of trees or lee walls to be got we were fain to stop, in a sheer impossibility of continuing the struggle.

When the day broke, it blew harder and harder. I had been in Yarmouth when the seamen said it blew great guns, but I had never known the like of this, or anything approaching to it. . . .

As we struggled on, nearer and nearer to the sea, from which this mighty wind was blowing dead on shore, its force became more and more terrific. . . .

The tremendous sea itself, when I could find sufficient pause to look at it, in the agitation of the blinding wind, the flying stones and sand, and the awful noise, confounded me. As the high water walls came rolling in, and, at their highest, tumbled into surf, they looked as if the least would en gulf the town. As the receding wave swept back with a hoarse roar, it seemed to scoop out deep caves in the beach, as if its purpose were to undermine the earth. When some white-headed billow thundered on, and dashed themselves to pieces before they reached the land, every fragment of th late whole seemed possessed by the full might of its wrath, rushing to be gathered to the compos tion of another monster. Undulating hills were changed to valleys, undulating valleys (with a solitar storm-bird sometimes skimming through them) were lifted up to hills; masses of water shivered an shook the beach with a booming sound; every shape tumultuously rolled on, as soon as made, change its shape and place, and beat another shape and place away; the clouds flew fast and thic I seemed to see a rending and upheaving of all nature. . . .

In the difficulty of hearing anything but wind and waves, and in the crowd, and the unspeak ble confusion, and my first breathless efforts to stand against the weather, I was so confused that looked out to sea for the wreck, and saw nothing but the foaming heads of the great waves. A hal dressed boatman, standing next to me, pointed with his bare arm (a tattoo'd arrow on it, pointing the same direction) to the left. Then, O great Heaven, I saw it, close in upon us!

One mast was broken short off, six or eight feet from the deck, and lay over the side, entangle in a maze of sail and rigging; and all that ruin, as the ship rolled and beat—which she did without moment's pause, and with a violence quite inconceivable—beat the side as if it would stave it i Some efforts were even then being made, to cut this portion of the wreck away; for, as the shi which was broadside on, turned towards us in her rolling, I plainly descried her people at work wi axes, especially one active figure with long curling hair, conspicuous among the rest. But, a gre cry, which was audible even above the wind and water, rose from the shore at this moment; the se sweeping over the rolling wreck, made a clean breach, and carried men, spars, casks, planks, bu warks, heaps of such toys, into the boiling surge.

APPENDICES

AND

GLOSSARY

◆ PHONETIC TRANSCRIPTION ◆

The most frequently used phonetic alphabet is the International Phonetic Alphabet (IPA). The principle of the IPA is that each letter represents one speech sound and one speech sound only. Conversely, a single, distinct speech sound is represented by one phonetic letter only.

In addition to the phonetic letters, the IPA has small signs and symbols called diacritical marks, to modify the phonetic letters in various ways. The diacritical marks denote such details of spoken language as length, or duration, of sound; stress; intonation; and minute features of placement and articulation that distinguish shades of sound within the same speech sound. A compilation of diacritical marks of the IPA may be found on pages 380-383.

In the beginning, the IPA was used in two degrees of phonetic transcription: Narrow Transcription, which is detailed notation of speech sounds employing diacritical marks; and Broad Transcription, which is simplified notation of speech sounds employing a minimum of diacritical marks.

Over the years, however, the IPA has undergone modification, so that today, what was originally meant to be a standard, in practice is found in several slightly different versions. Even the established and popular pronouncing dictionaries employ differing versions of the IPA. For the student who may at some point use all the available texts, the following section offers a comparison of three versions of the IPA and also spelling approximations that are occasionally encountered.

COLUMN I: The speech sound in a key word of Spoken English.

COLUMN II: The IPA in Very Narrow Transcription. This is the transcription used in *Speak with Distinction* (SWD). It features notation of lengths, aspiration and unaspiration, syllabic consonants, the weak element of a diphthong, and other aspects of speech. The letters are used here in their script forms. Because of its precision and detail, Very Narrow Transcription is the only transcription recommended for the study of speech, dialects and accents.

COLUMN III: The IPA in Narrow Transcription. This is the version that is used commonly in the British Isles and with teachers of Received Pronunciation throughout the world. It is the version used by Daniel Jones (DJ) in *Everyman's English Pronouncing Dictionary*. It gives some details of pronunciation, but does not provide for the notation of lengths (the long vowel sounds are always marked long regardless of their actual duration in a particular word); aspiration and unaspiration; and other aspects of pronunciation. Since this version of the IPA is most familiar through its use in various British pronouncing dictionaries and textbooks, the letters shown in Column III are in their printed forms.

COLUMN IV: The IPA in Broad Transcription. This is the IPA's least detailed form, but it is used by many teachers in North America and is also used in *A Pronouncing Dictionary of American English*, by John S. Kenyon and Thomas A. Knott (K&K). Some incomplete features of Broad Transcription are, for example, its employment of a single letter for the diphthong sounds in "pa**y**" and "g**o**"; its failure to distinguish the vowel sound in "l**e**t" from the first vowel element in the diphthong sound "**ai**r"; and its notation of the r-colored diphthongs of "r" by means of the first vowel element followed by the consonant r . This version of the IPA seems to be found most often with the letters in their printed form, which is how they are shown here.

COLUMN V: A system of approximating the sounds of the language through English spellings. It is not phonetic (in spelling approximations, one sound may be represented by two letters); not very accurate; and impractical for those coming to the English language for the first time.

COMPARISON OF LETTERS USED IN VERY NARROW, NARROW, AND BROAD TRANSCRIPTION

I KEY WORD	II IPA VERY NARROW (SWD)	III IPA NARROW (Brit—DJ)	IV IPA BROAD (USA—K&K)	V SPELLING APPROXIMATIONS
1 Lee	i: i· i	i:	i	ee
2 will	ɪ	ɪ (formerly i)	ɪ	i
3 let	e	e	ɛ	e eh

(The original phonetic letter assigned to the vowel sound in "let" was e⊤ written with a low tongue modifier (⊤), while the simple e was assigned to a pure vowel that does not occur in Spoken English. However, the use of the simple letter e for the Spoken English vowel sound in "let," and the use of e·i· for the diphthong sound in "pay," are now common, though by no means universal.)

I	II	III	IV	V
4 Pat	æ	æ	æ	a
5 pass	a	Not used in RP. (ɑː is given for the Ask-Words.)	a	aa
6 stir	3: 3· 3	ɜ : (formerly ə :)	ɜ	Not used.
7 stir*	3ʳ: 3ʳ· 3ʳ	Not used in RP.	ɜʳ	er ER
8 surprise	ə	ə	ə	Not used.
9 surprise*	əʳ	Not used in RP.	ɚ	er
10 the	ə	ə	ə	uh
11. cup	ʌ	ʌ	ʌ	u
12 who	u: u· u	u:	u	oo o͞o
13 you	ju: ju· ju	ju:	ju & ɪu	yoo yo͞o
14 would	ʊ	ʊ (formerly u)	ʊ	uu o͝o
15 obey	o	əu (British "oh"; formerly ou)	o	oh

(The original phonetic letter assigned to the vowel sound in "obey" was o⊤ written with a low tongue-modifier (⊤), while the simple o was assigned to a pure vowel that does not occur in Spoken English. However, the use of the simple letter o for the Spoken English vowel sound in "obey," and the use of o·ʊ· for the diphthong sound in "go," are now common, though by no means universal.)

*With r-coloring

I KEY WORD	II VERY NARROW (SWD)	III NARROW (Brit—DJ)	IV BROAD (USA—K&K)	V SPELLING
16 all	ɔ: ɔ· ɔ	ɔ:	ɔ	aw
17 honest	ɒ	ɒ (formerly ɔ)	ɒ	o
18 fathers	ɑ: ɑ· ɑ	ɑ:	ɑ	ah
19 pay	e·ĭ· eĭ	eɪ	e	ay
20 my	a·ĭ· aĭ	aɪ	aɪ	ī igh
21 boy	ɔ·ĭ· ɔĭ	ɔɪ	ɔɪ	oy oi
22 go	o·ŭ· oŭ	ɜʊ (British "oh"; formerly ou)	o	oh
23 now	a·ŭ· aŭ	aʊ	aʊ	ow
24 here	ɪə̆	ɪə	ɪə	Not used.
25 here*	ɪə̆˞	Not used in RP.	ɪr	eer
26 their	ɛə̆	eə	ɛə	Not used.
27 their*	ɛə̆˞	Not used in RP.	ɛr	air
28 poor	ʊə̆	ʊə	ʊə	Not used.
29 poor*	ʊə̆˞	Not used in RP.	ʊr	oor
30 ore	ɔə̆	ɔ: in RP.	ɔə	Not used.
31 ore*	ɔə̆˞	Not used in RP.	ɔr	or
32 car	aə̆	ɑ: in RP.	ɑ:	Not used.
33 car*	aə̆˞	Not used in RP.	ɑr	ar ahr
34 pie	pʰ p,	p	p	p
35 buy	b	b	b	b
36 tie	tʰ t,	t	t	t
37 do	d	d	d	d

*With r-coloring

I KEY WORD	II VERY NARROW (SWD)	III NARROW (Brit—DJ)	IV BROAD (USA—K&K)	V SPELLING
38 come	kʰ k̩	k	k	k
39 go	g	g	g	g
40 my	m	m	m	m
41 no	n	n	n	n
42 sing	ŋ	ŋ	ŋ	ng
43 low	l	l	l	l
44 fish	f	f	f	f
45 vine	v	v	v	v
46 thin	θ	θ	θ	th
47 this	ð	ð	ð	<u>th</u>
48 so	s	s	s	s
49 zoo	z	z	z	z
50 shoe	ʃ	ʃ	ʃ	sh
51 pleasure	ʒ	ʒ	ʒ	zh
52 read	r̲	r	r	r
(The original letter assigned was ɹ but it is rarely used today.)				
53 he	h	h	h	h
54 behind	h	Not used.	Not used.	Not used.
55 which	ʍ	hw	hw	hw
56 witch	w	w	w	w
57 yes	j	j	j	y
58 chin	t̚ʃ	tʃ	tʃ	ch
59 gin	dʒ	ʤ	ʤ	j

◆ IPA DIACRITICAL MARKS FOR USE IN NARROW TRANSCRIPTION ◆

1 **'** at the upper left corner of a syllable indicates that it has primary (strong) stress.

OB-ject (n) 'ɒb dʒɪk̚ t̚ʰ   ob-JECT (v) əb 'dʒɛk̚ t̚ʰ

2 **ˌ** at the lower left corner of a syllable means that it has secondary (weak) stress.

CA-li-<u>FORN</u>-ia ˌk̚æləˈfɔǒnjə   con-TA-mi-<u>NA</u>-tion k̚ənˌt̚æməˈneɪ̯ʃn̩

3 Unstressed syllables (including WEAK FORMS) are left unmarked in phonetic transcription.

4 **:** Two dots to the right of a phonetic letter indicates that the sound is long.

feed 'fi:d   friends 'f<u>r</u>ɛn:dz   will 'wɪl:

5 **·** One dot to the right of a phonetic letter indicates that the sound is half-long.

feet 'fi·t̚ʰ   being 'bi·ɪŋ   burnt 'b3·nt̚ʰ

6 Sounds that are short are left unmarked in phonetic transcription.

answer 'ænsə   penny 'pʰɛnɪ   willing 'wɪlɪŋ

7 **˘** placed over an element of a diphthong sound indicates that it is the weak element.

pie 'pʰa·ɪ̆·   fear 'fɪə̆

8 **ʰ** The little "h" at the upper right corner of pʰ tʰ kʰ indicates that they are aspirated.

topic 't̚ʰɒpʰɪkʰ   picket 'pʰɪkʰɪt̚ʰ   Stop it. 'st̚ɒpʰ ɪt̚ʰ

9 **ˌ** A short vertical line at the lower right corner of p, t, k, indicates that they are unaspirated.

deflects dɪ'flɛk̚ t̚ˌs   preach 'p̚ˌri·t̚ʃ   let go 'lɛt̚ˌ 'go·ŭ·

10 **˞** A little spur attached to 3: and ə indicates that they are made with r-coloring.

3˞:   ə˞

11 **ˌ** A short vertical line directly underneath a letter indicates that the sound is a syllabic consonant sound.

prism 'p̚ˌrɪzm̩   button 'bʌt̚n̩   little 'lɪt̚l̩

12 **ₙ** A little tooth directly underneath a letter indicates that the sound is dentalized.

Get them. 'gɛt̪ ðəm width 'wɪd̪θ month 'mʌn̪θ wealth 'wɛl̪θ

13 ʔ   This is not a diacritical mark, but the phonetic letter for a glottal stop.

14 ~   A line through the letter   *l*   indicates that the sound is thick, or velarized.   *ł*

15 ~   A tilde   ~   over a phonetic letter indicates that the sound is nasalized.   *æ̃*

16 ₒ   A small circle under a phonetic letter indicates that it is devoiced or breathed.   *v̥*

17 ••   Two dots placed over a phonetic letter indicates that the sound is centralized, with the position of the tongue-arch towards the center of the mouth.   *ü*

18 ᵓ   to the right of a phonetic letter indicates that the sound has more lip-rounding.   *ɔᵓ*

19 ᶜ   to the right of a phonetic letter indicates that the sound has more lip-spreading.   *iᶜ*

20 ᵊ   A small letter   ᵊ   placed at the upper right corner of the consonant phonetic letter indicates that a little "uh" has been added to the consonant—an off-glide.

swim   *ˈswɪmᵊ* ("swim-uh")   leg   *ˈlegᵊ*   ("leg-uh")

21   TONGUE MODIFIERS, used as little arrows to the right of a phonetic letter, indicate changes in the placement of the tongue-arch:

       ⟂   tongue-arch is lower

       ⊥   tongue-arch is higher

       ⊢   tongue-arch is farther forward

       ⊣   tongue-arch is farther back

For example,   *æ*   can be produced with the tongue-arch higher than a well-open sound as in "Ann," yet not so high in tongue-arch that it becomes the vowel sound   *ɛ*   . This is transcribed as   *æ⊥*   .

If the vowel sound in "all" is swallowed and made too far back, this is transcribed as *ɔ⊢*.

◆ SOME NON-IPA SIGNS AND IDIOMS USED IN THIS TEXT ◆

1 be-ing   A hyphen indicates that care must be taken to articulate clean syllables.

2 ho-rror   A hyphen separating the vowel sound from the consonant r indicates that great care must be taken to articulate the CORRECT CLEAR VOWEL SOUND followed by a clean-cut r. The word "horror" should be pronounced "ho-rror" rather than "whore-er."

3 ⌣⌣   A wavy line shows the division of syllables in phonetic transcription.

4 I'm mad   This is a reminder to use a same-consonant blend: $a \breve{\imath} m \; {}^{\prime}m \ae d$

5 'tis so   This is a reminder to use a cognate blend: $t \breve{\imath} z \; {}^{\prime}so \cdot \breve{u} \cdot$

6 ⌣   A single curve under a written word is a reminder that it should be pronounced in ONE SYLLABLE.

     feel $\fi : \ell$ (NOT: "fee-ull" $\fi : \partial \ell$)

7 ²   After a written word indicates that there are TWO acceptable pronunciations.

     exile² ${}^{\prime}ek, sa\breve{\imath}l$ or ${}^{\prime}egza\breve{\imath}l$

     lewd² ${}^{\prime}lju : d$ or ${}^{\prime}lu : d$

8 ³   After a written word indicates that there are THREE acceptable pronunciations.

     vase³ ${}^{\prime}va : z$ or ${}^{\prime}ve \cdot \breve{\imath} \cdot z$ or ${}^{\prime}ve\breve{\imath}s$

9 =   An "equals" sign indicates HOMONYMNS; that is, words that are spelled differently but pronounced identically: dear=deer.

10 "b"   Quotation marks around a *single* printed letter indicate a letter of SPELLING in WRITTEN English and not a phonetic letter used in Spoken English: "b" as in "lamb."

11 pray   The underlining of a letter "r" in the spelling of a word indicates that in that particular word it is pronounced as a consonant sound r .

12 r   In this text the phonetic letter for the consonant r is underlined.

13 saw it   The arc over two adjacent words may be a reminder not to insert an INTRUSIVE "R" sound between them:

     I saw it. $a \breve{\imath} \; so : \breve{\imath}t^h$ (NOT: I sawr it.)

14 we act   An arc over two adjacent words may be a reminder to AVOID A GLOTTAL ATTACK when proceeding from the vowel or diphthong sound that ends the first word to that which begins the second word.

15 add up

An arc under two adjacent words may be a reminder to AVOID A GLOTTAL ATTACK when proceeding from the consonant sound that ends the first word to the vowel or diphthong sound that begins the second word.

16 far out

This is a reminder to use a linking r.

17 (wh)ch

"wh" in the spelling is circled when the corresponding sound is $\mathcal{M}$.

18 (sf)

indicates the strong form of the word: can (sf) $'k^h æn{:}$

19 (wf)

indicates the weak form of the word: can (wf) $k^h ən$

20 (n)

indicates a noun: OBject (n)

21 (v)

indicates a verb: obJECT (v)   perFECT (v)

22 (adj)

indicates an adjective: PERfect (adj)

23 (adv)

indicates an adverb: perfectly (adv)

24 OBject

Capital letters in the spelling are used to indicate the stressed syllable.

25 (American)

indicates the correct American pronunciation.

26 (British)

indicates the correct British pronunciation in Received Pronunciation (RP).

27 (England)

indicates a person or place in England, not an especially British pronunciation.

28 (German)

indicates a German word, place or person, not a pronunciation in the German language.

◆ GLOSSARY OF TERMS ◆

The technical terms in the Glossary have been defined according to the precepts of the International Phonetic Association and are acknowledged by linguists, phoneticians and speech teacher
throughout the world, although in many cases, the explanations have been simplified for a genera
audience. The Glossary also includes some terms that are not technical, but are frequently used b
actors, directors and speech and dialect coaches.

ACCENT: The way someone speaks a foreign language, a second language or any language that i
not their native tongue. For instance, a native Parisian might speak English with a French accent, an
a native of Chicago might speak French with an American accent. For a comparison, see Dialect.

AFFRICATE CONSONANT: A consonant sound comprised of a stop-plosive and a fricative conso
nant blended so closely as to seem like a single sound. The two affricate sounds of Spoken Englis
are considered members of the plosive family of sounds:

$t_ʃ$ ch**in** $dʒ$ g**in**

ALPHABET: An orderly system of written symbols or letters that corresponds to the sounds of a lan
guage. English, the Romance languages, the Germanic languages, Russian, Greek, Arabic, and He
brew are some of the languages that are written by means of an alphabet. Chinese is written withou
an alphabet, while modern Japanese employs both a set of characters and an alphabet. See Phoneti
Alphabet and Roman Alphabet.

ALVEOLAR RIDGE: The slightly convex part of the roof of the mouth that lies just behind the uppe
front teeth. It is sometimes called the bumpy spot, because of the little ridges, or bumps, that cros
its surface. It is also called the gum ridge and the teeth ridge, identified on the Consonant Chart a
Place IV.

ALVEOLAR CONSONANT: A sound made with the tip of the tongue touching the alveolar ridge
The alveolar consonant sounds of Spoken English, found on the Consonant Chart as Place IV-A, are:

t **two** d **die** n **no** l **law** $t_ʃ$ ch**in** $dʒ$ g**in**

ARTICULATORS: The parts of the body used to form each separate speech sound of a spoken lan
guage as the air passes out through the mouth or through the nose. The movable articulators are th
lips, lower jaw, tongue, and soft palate. The immovable articulators are the teeth, gum ridge, har
palate, and throat (glottis).

ASK-LIST: A compilation of words in Spoken English, such as "ask," that have three standards o
pronunciation for the "a" sound in the spelling of the word, depending on the standard of Spoke
English being used. The words on the Ask-List may be pronounced with each of the following vowe
sounds:

- ◆ The Intermediate "A" vowel sound, the Theater Standard for Good Speech a
- ◆ The Short "A," the standard for General North American speech $æ$
- ◆ The Broad "A," the standard for British Received Pronunciation (RP) $a:$

ASPIRATION: The explosion of air and ensuing puff of breath that are produced when one of th
voiceless stop-plosive consonant sounds is released. In Spoken English, the voiceless stop-plosive
are aspirated when they are followed by a vowel or diphthong sound. This is notated in the IPA by
little ^{h} at the upper right corner of the phonetic letter:

p^h **pie** t^h **two** k^h **key**

ASPIRANT: h as in "**he**" is called the aspirant consonant sound, because it is nonvibrate
breath emitted through the mouth-shape of the particular vowel sound that follows it.

BACK OF THE TONGUE: The part of the tongue that, when it is at rest, lies below the soft palate.

BACK PLACEMENT: The constricted placement of tone in which the voice seems to be trapped, or caught, in the back of the mouth or throat.

BACK VOWEL: A vowel sound made with the back of the tongue arched toward the soft palate. There are six back vowel sounds in Spoken English:

u: Wh**o** U w**ou**ld o **o**bey $ɔ$: **a**ll $ɒ$ h**o**nest $ɑ$: f**a**thers?

BILABIAL: This term refers to consonant sounds articulated with both lips. On the Consonant Chart this area is known as Place I. There are five bilabial consonant sounds in Spoken English:

p **p**ie b **b**uy m **m**e $ʍ$ **wh**eel w **w**eal

BLADE OF THE TONGUE: The extremely forward part of the top surface of the tongue that, when it is at rest, lies directly below the alveolar ridge.

BREATHED: Another term for voiceless.

BROAD TRANSCRIPTION: The accurate but not detailed phonetic transcription of the sounds of speech. Typically, Broad Transcription omits the notation of lengths of sounds; aspiration or unaspiration of the voiceless plosives; weak elements in diphthongs; and all diacritical marks. For a comparison, see Very Narrow Transcription.

BUZZES: The voiced sibilant sounds. There are three buzzes in Spoken English:

z **z**oo $ʒ$ plea**s**ure $dʒ$ **g**in

CENTERING DIPHTHONG: A diphthong sound in which the weak second element is the mid, or central, vowel sound $ə$ as in "s**ur**prise." In this textbook, the centering diphthongs are usually called the diphthong sounds of "r":

$ɪə̆$ H**ere's** $ɛə̆$ th**eir** $Uə̆$ p**oor** $ɔə̆$ **ore** $ɑə̆$ c**ar**.

CLASSIC TEXTS: A convenient catch-all term that refers to:

- ◆ Noncontemporary texts, in both prose and verse, in which the richness and eloquence of the language require verbal musicality, elegance and style in performance;
- ◆ Noncontemporary texts that do not require specific accents or dialects;
- ◆ Contemporary texts that are set in distant times and places;
- ◆ Foreign plays translated into English, but not requiring accents or dialects;
- ◆ Texts set in imaginary times and places.

Some examples of classic texts are *Oedipus Rex, The Iliad, Everyman, Hamlet, The Way of the World, Tartuffe, Life Is a Dream, The School for Scandal, Faust, Danton's Death, Hedda Gabler, The Cherry Orchard, Arms and the Man, The Causasian Chalk Circle,* and *Les Misérables.* Grouping these works together as classic texts does not imply that their diction, use of language and style of speech in performance are identical, but that this usage and style of speech might derive from the same standard of North American pronunciation, which in this textbook is called Good Speech.

Some texts that might be considered classics, but are not classic texts as defined in this book because they require specific dialects, include the poems of Robert Burns, *The Importance of Being Earnest, Major Barbara, Our Town, The Little Foxes, Carousel,* and *Death of a Salesman.*

CLOSE VOWEL: A vowel made with a relatively closed lower jaw and high arch of the tongue. An equivalent term is high vowel. There are four close vowel sounds in Spoken English:

i: L**ee** $ɪ$ w**i**ll u: wh**o** U w**ou**ld

COGNATE BLENDS: These sequences occur when one word ends with a consonant sound and the next word in the phrase begins with its cognate, its voiced or voiceless partner. In proceeding from one word to the next, the articulators do not change position, but maintain one long position. Clarity of enunciation is achieved by the change from voiced to voiceless, or voiceless to voiced, and by a fresh impulse of energy that begins the second word:

b p
Bob paid

d t
a good time

k g
look good

v f
twelve fish

$ð$ $θ$
breathe thin air

$ʒ$ $ʃ$
beige shoes

s z
this zoo

COGNATES: The pairs of consonant sounds that are made in the same place of articulation and in the same manner of articulation, with one of the pair voiced and the other voiceless. There are ten cognate pairs of consonant sounds in Spoken English:

p & b t & d k & g f & v $θ$ & $ð$

s & z $ʃ$ & $ʒ$ h & $ɦ$ $ʍ$ & w $tʃ$ & $dʒ$

CONSONANT SOUND: A sound made with the outgoing breath stopped, impeded or interrupted by the articulators in some manner. The air may be voiced or voiceless and may resonate and exit through either the mouth or the nose.

CONTINUANTS: Consonant sounds that can continue in length as long as a breath can last, since their outgoing air is interrupted, but not stopped, by a steady position of the articulators. In Spoken English, the nasal, lateral and fricative consonant sounds are all continuants.

DARK "L": The variety of the voiced lateral continuant consonant sound l that employs as its secondary articulation a gentle arching of the back of the main body of the tongue toward the soft palate, giving the l sound the resonance of a back vowel sound and a rich, dark quality. In most dialects of North American English, including Good Speech, an l sound tends to be dark:

◆ When it is followed by another consonant sound: "bulk"
◆ When it is in final position: "hell"
◆ When it is syllabic: "battle"

DENTAL CONSONANTS: The sounds made with the tip of the tongue articulating against the edge of the upper front teeth, known on the Consonant Chart as Place III. There are two dental consonant sounds in Spoken English:

$θ$ thigh $ð$ thine

DENTALIZED: This term refers to consonant sounds that are made with the tip of the tongue touching the back of the upper front teeth while the blade of the tongue touches the alveolar ridge. In Spoken English, this occurs correctly only when t , d , n , and l are followed by either $θ$ or $ð$, either within a word or in the next word of a phrase. The IPA diacritical mark for dentalization is like a little tooth placed under the phonetic letter:

$t̪$ get them $d̪$ width $n̪$ win this $l̪$ wealth

DIACRITICAL MARKS: In Narrow and Very Narrow Phonetic Transcription, this term refers to marks and signs placed in proximity to phonetic letters in order to render the actual sounds more accurately and in more detail.

DIALECT: The way in which a family, social or economic class or group of inhabitants of a particular city or region of a country speaks its native language. A native of Greenville, Mississippi, may speak English with a Delta accent. Similarly, a French person born and raised in Paris may speak French with a Parisian dialect. For a comparison, see Accent.

DIPHTHONG SOUND: A blend of two vowel sounds into a single phonetic unit. The articulators begin in the position of one vowel sound, called the first element, and move so smoothly toward the position of another vowel sound, called the second element, that it is impossible to tell where the first vowel ends and the second begins. In every diphthong sound there is movement of the articulators that can be seen, heard and felt. For a comparison, see Pure Vowel.

DIPHTHONGIZATION: A sound that occurs when the articulators move during the production of a pure vowel sound, but not so definitely or intentionally as to form one of the actual recognized diphthong sounds of the particular language. Diphthongization occurs frequently in accents and dialects of Spoken English, but is always an error in Good Speech.

EASTERN STANDARD: Another term for Good Speech.

ELEMENT: Each component vowel sound of a diphthong or a triphthong sound is called an element of that sound. In the diphthongs of Spoken English, one of the two elements (usually the second) has lesser prominence and is called the weak element.

FALLING DIPHTHONGS: This term refers to diphthong sounds in which the second vowel element is weaker than the first, producing a decrease of sonority or resonance. All the diphthong sounds used in North American speech are falling diphthongs, with the exception of the two rising diphthong sounds ĭə and ŭə , which are found only in spoken verse or in song.

FINAL POSITION: The occurrence of a given sound as the last sound of a word.

FORWARD PLACEMENT: The clear, easy placement of tone in which the sounds of the language, particularly the vowels, diphthongs and nasal consonants, are freely resonated by and through the front, or mask area, of the head. This has nothing to do with the term "head tone," which some singers use. Forward placement is essential to Good Speech for the theater.

FRICATIVE: A consonant sound produced with the breath stream obstructed in particular ways by the articulators, so that there is an audible friction of the outgoing breath. There are eleven fricative consonant sounds in Spoken English:

ɟ fish	ʋ vine	θ thigh	ð thine	ʍ so	ʑ zoo
ʃ shin	ʒ genre	r̥ red	h he	ɦ behalf	

FRONT OF THE TONGUE: The part of the tongue that, when it is at rest, lies below the hard palate.

FRONT VOWEL: A vowel sound made with the front of the tongue arched toward the hard palate. There are six front vowel sounds in Spoken English:

iː Lee	ɪ will	e let	ɛ *	æ Pat	a pass.

* In Spoken English, ɛ is used only in the diphthong sound ɛə , as in "fair."

GENERAL AMERICAN: A term used to describe that dialect of North American English most frequently found in the ordinary speech of inhabitants of the Western United States. It is acceptable to all American listeners, although they themselves may not speak that way. It does not sound like the speech of any one region of America, yet it sounds distinctly contemporary and distinctively American. A roughly equivalent term having some currency is Western Standard.

GLIDE: A consonant sound in which the articulators begin in a particular vowel shape and then swiftly move into a following sound (in Spoken English, this is always a vowel or diphthong sound). The speed and definiteness in movement of the glides qualify them to be considered consonant sounds. There are three glides in Spoken English:

ʍ wheel	w weal	j you

w and j , which are voiced and have no audible friction, are also known as semi-vowels.

GLOTTAL: A consonant sound articulated in the glottis, or throat, which is known as Place VII on the Consonant Chart. There are two glottal sounds in Spoken English:

h **h**e   *ɦ* be**h**alf

GLOTTAL ATTACK: A sudden convulsive stop and release of the breath in the glottis, or throat. It is essentially a stop-plosive, but is an undesirable one in Spoken English. The phonetic letter for this glottal stop-plosive is *ʔ* .

GLOTTALIZE: To use a glottal attack, or glottal stop, when speaking. In Spoken English, it is always incorrect to glottalize. This incorrect use is commonly found

◆ As a tense, throaty attack on words that begin with a vowel or diphthong sound:

" *ʔ* Ay, *ʔ* every *ʔ* inch *ʔ* a king." (***King Lear*** IV.vi.123)

◆ As a "hiccoughing" replacement for a consonant sound in a word or phrase:

mountain

Correct: *ˈmaʊntⁿ̈n*   Incorrect: *ˈmaʊnʔn̩*

won't you

Correct: *ˈwoʊnt̚ ju*   Incorrect: *ˈwoʊnʔju*

GLOTTIS: The space between the vocal folds, found inside the larynx, or Adam's apple. On the Consonant Chart this is known as Place VII.

GOOD SPEECH: Hard to define, but easy to recognize, Good Speech refers in this textbook to a dialect of North American English that is clearly and effortlessly articulated, easily understood in a theater, free from class and regional peculiarities, recognizably North American, and at the same time acceptable and convincing in a classic text. Roughly equivalent terms having some currency are Eastern Standard and Theater Standard.

GUM RIDGE: Another term for the alveolar ridge.

HARD PALATE: The concave dome forming the front part of the roof of the mouth. It is backed by cartilage, which accounts for its hard surface. It is also known, more colloquially, as "the place where the peanut butter sticks."

HARD "R": Another term for r-coloring, which gives the voice a hard, tense quality.

HIGH VOWEL: A vowel sound formed by a high arch of the tongue and a relatively closed lower jaw. An equivalent term is close vowel. There are four high vowel sounds in Spoken English:

i: **L**ee   *ɪ* w**i**ll   *u:* wh**o**   *ʊ* w**ou**ld

HISSES: The voiceless sibilant sounds. There are three hisses in Spoken English:

s **s**o   *ʃ* **sh**in   *t̚ʃ* **ch**in

IPA: See International Phonetic Alphabet.

IMPLOSION: Another term for nasal plosion.

INFLECTION: The change, or movement, in the pitch of the voice during the utterance of a syllable. Since inflection in Spoken English occurs on the stressed syllable of a word, it may be thought to embody the melodic action of the entire word. Inflection is just one aspect of a speaker's melody, which is called intonation. There are three basic inflections:

- ♩ Falling inflection, as when making a statement:

    Go.   (Finished thought)

- ♩ Rising inflection, as when asking a question:

    Go?   (Unfinished thought)

- ● Level inflection, as when sustaining or suspending a word:

    Go . . .   (Unfinished thought)

INITIAL POSITION: The occurrence of a given sound as the first sound of a word.

INTERMEDIATE "A": The open front vowel a , which is sometimes perceived as sounding somewhat intermediate between the Short "A" vowel sound $æ$, as in "Pat," and the Broad "A" vowel sound $a{:}$, as in "fathers." For its use as a pure vowel sound, see the Ask-List of words. The Intermediate "A" is also the first element of the diphthong sound $a{\cdot}\ddot{\imath}$, as in "my."

INTERNATIONAL PHONETIC ALPHABET (IPA): The IPA was invented by the International Phonetic Association, which was founded in 1886 by teachers and scientists who shared an interest in the science of phonetics and perceived that a phonetic alphabet would make possible the recording of any language in the world, even a language that had no written form. The IPA was first published in 1888.

The basic premise of the IPA is that there is a separate letter for each distinctive sound of the languages of the world, no matter how that sound is rendered in the writing of a language. Each sound is assigned one letter and one letter only; conversely, each letter stands for one sound only. If a person is transcribing one sound, only one letter is used. Initially, the Association used letters derived solely from the Roman alphabet, but since 1888 many nonRoman letters have been added.

INTONATION: This term refers to all aspects of the melody of a person's speaking voice. It is comprised of intonation pattern, or melody pattern (the movement in pitch from syllable to syllable), and inflection (the movement in pitch on an individual syllable).

INTONATION PATTERN: The movement in pitch of the speaking voice from syllable to syllable. It is the melodic pattern or shape of the speaker's words and phrases. It may also be called the melody pattern.

INTRUSIVE "R": A consonant $\underline{r}$ sound that is mistakenly pronounced or that intrudes in a place having no "r" in the spelling of a word. Intrusive "r" is usually introduced between two words:

the idea(r) of it   law(r) and justice

INVERSION: Another term for r-coloring, because tip-of-the-tongue placement and sound placement are tensed and inverted toward the back of the mouth.

LABIO-DENTAL: This term refers to consonant sounds made with the lower lip articulating against the upper teeth. On the Consonant Chart, this is known as Place II. In Spoken English, there are two labio-dental consonant sounds:

f fish v vine

LATERAL CONSONANT: A consonant sound that is made with the tip of the tongue touching the alveolar ridge, and the sides of the tongue released downward and in, so that the breath stream passes over the sides of the tongue. There is only one lateral consonant in Spoken English:

l law

LATERAL PLOSION: This term refers to the action that occurs when the consonant sound t or d is followed by the consonant sound l and is exploded, or released, over the sides of the tongue, the tip of the tongue remaining in contact with the alveolar ridge:

    sof*tl*y   ba*tt*le   ba*d*lands   ri*dd*le

LATERALIZATION: This term refers to the unnecessary widening and side-to-side tensing of the corners of the mouth during the production of a sound. It is to be avoided in Good Speech.

LENGTHS: The various degrees of duration of a speech sound achieved without a change in the sound's quality. The system of lengths of sounds is the basis of the rhythm of a spoken language. In the IPA

- ◆ Vowel sounds are classified as   LONG — HALF-LONG — SHORT
- ◆ Diphthongs are classified as   LONG —   and   — SHORT
- ◆ Consonants are classified as   LONG —   and   — SHORT

LINKING "R": When a word with an "r" in its spelling is followed within the same phrase by a word beginning with a vowel or diphthong sound, a linking r is the correctly realized consonant "r̲" sound that attaches to the beginning of the second word. In other words, "it's ginger ale" is pronounced as "it's jinja rail."

LIQUID "U": A popular term for the combination $ju:$, which occurs in words such as

    you=ewe   **bea*u*ty**   t*u*ne   d*u*ke   **c*u*e**   arg*ue*   m*u*se   new=knew

It is also called Long "U."

LISP: This term refers to any deviation from a correctly produced sibilant sound, especially s . Sometimes the term is used to denote an s sound that has too low a frequency; the terms "oversibilant 's'" and "sibilant 's'" are used to denote a s sound that has too high a frequency.

LONG "U": Another term for Liquid "U."

LOW VOWEL: A vowel sound made with the arch of the tongue low in the mouth and with a correspondingly open jaw position.

MEDIAL POSITION: This term refers to the occurrence of a given sound in any position in a word except first or last position.

MID VOWEL: A vowel sound made with the middle of the tongue arching toward the place where the hard and soft palates meet. There are three mid vowel sounds in Spoken English:

    $3:$ St*ir* $ə$ the s*u*rprise Λ c*u*p.

MIDDLE OF THE TONGUE: The part of the tongue that, when it is at rest, lies below the place where the hard and soft palates meet.

NASAL CONSONANT: A sound in which the breath stream is impeded or made to detour into and out through the nose. This is accomplished by relaxing and lowering the soft palate and by closing the oral passage. The development of forward placement of the nasal consonants is called nasal resonance. It is essential to Good Speech. There are only three nasal sounds in well-spoken English:

    m **me** n **no** $ŋ$ si**ng**

NASALIZATION: The production of a speech sound with the breath stream exiting through both the mouth and the nose, by the relaxation and lowering of the soft palate, and the opening of the oral passage. In correct French there are four nasalized vowel sounds. In well-spoken English, the nasalization of vowel and diphthong sounds is to be avoided.

NASAL PLOSION: The explosion, or release, of a stop-plosive through the nose, rather than through the mouth, by the sudden relaxation and lowering of the soft palate. This occurs in Spoken

English when a stop-plosive sound is followed by m or n , either within a word or in the next word of a phrase. True nasal plosion, also called implosion, occurs when the plosive and the following nasal are made in the same place of articulation:

to*p*most	su*b*marine	bea*t*nik	ma*d*ness
Sto*p* me.	Ro*b* moved.	grea*t* need	Here's ba*d* news.

NEUTRAL VOWEL: The weak second mid vowel sound ∂ , as in "th*e* su*r*prise." This sound is also called the schwa.

OFF-GLIDE: The extraneous vowel sound "uh" added to a voiced consonant sound that occurs at the end of a phrase, making a phrase such as "Let's go for a swim!" into "Let's go for a swim-uh!" Its IPA diacritical mark is a small rendering of the second mid vowel letter $^\partial$ placed at the upper right corner of a phonetic letter: m^∂ .

In Good Speech, an off-glide is always an error. Its opposite is an on-glide.

ON-GLIDE: The correct follow-through of a final voiced consonant sound at the end of a phrase and before a pause. The breath should end before the articulation ends, making a phrase such as "Let's go for a swim!" end with the consonant m without an extraneous "uh" sound, or offglide, following it.

ORAL SOUND: Any speech sound made with the soft palate in a raised position, which prevents the breath stream from exiting through the nose. In well-spoken English, all sounds are oral except nasal consonant sounds.

OPEN VOWEL: A vowel made with an easily open lower jaw and a correspondingly low arch of the tongue. There are five open vowel sounds in Spoken English:

$æ$ P*a*t a p*a*ss $\wedge$ c*u*p v h*o*nest $a{:}$ f*a*thers

PALATAL CONSONANT: A consonant sound made with the front of the tongue articulating against or toward the hard palate. On the Consonant Chart, this is known as Place V. There is only one palatal consonant sound in Spoken English:

j *y*es

PALATO-ALVEOLAR CONSONANT: A consonant made with the tip and blade of the tongue pointing toward, but not touching, the back part of the gum ridge, or alveolar ridge, while the front of the tongue arches toward the hard palate. On the Consonant Chart this is known as Place IV-B-2. There are two palato-alveolar consonant sounds in Spoken English:

$\int$ *sh*in $ʒ$ *g*enre

PHONETIC ALPHABET: An orderly system of written symbols or letters in which each symbol or letter represents one sound of the spoken language, regardless of the spelling of that sound in the written language. There are many phonetic alphabets, but the most accurate and detailed is the IPA, which is used in this textbook.

PHONETICS: The branch of language study dealing with speech sounds.

PHRASE: A rhythmic thought-group, which comprises either a complete thought or a part of a thought and which is uttered without pause from beginning to end. This differs from a breath-group, which may contain several phrases; or from a sentence, which presents a complete thought and may contain several phrases.

PLACEMENT: A broad term used in the theater and by teachers of voice, speech and dialects to describe the general areas of the head, neck or mouth from which the voice, speech or an individual speech sound seems to emanate. The two most commonly used terms are back placement, in which the voice or individual sound suffers from an excess of pharyngeal resonance and tension at the back of the tongue; and forward placement, in which the voice or individual speech sound is reso nated through a relaxed throat and back of the mouth, and seems to emanate from the front, o mask area, of the face and mouth.

PLOSIVE CONSONANT: A consonant in which the outgoing breath stream is completely stoppe by the action of the articulators. The plosive consonants, also known as stop-plosives, may be hel in check (unreleased) or exploded (released), depending on their phonetic environment and on th structure of the particular language in which they occur. There are eight plosive consonant sound in Spoken English:

p pie	t two	k key	$t\!\int$ chin
b buy	d die	g go	$d\!z$ gin

POST-ALVEOLAR CONSONANT: A consonant that is made with the tip of the tongue pointing to ward, but not touching, the extreme back of the alveolar ridge, or gum ridge. On the Consonant Char this is known as Place IV-B-3. There is only one post-alveolar consonant sound in Spoken English:

r red

POST-DENTAL CONSONANT: A consonant that is made with the tip of the tongue pointing to ward, but not touching, the front part of the alveolar ridge, or gum ridge. A swift stream of air, eithe voiced or voiceless, is sent toward the point where the upper front teeth and gums meet, and es capes between the interstices of the upper front teeth. On the Consonant Chart this is known a Place IV-B-1. There are two post-dental consonant sounds in Spoken English:

s so z zoo

PRINTED LETTERS: The IPA letters reproduced by mechanical means. The forms of the phonetic let ters used in this textbook are script letters.

PROMINENCE: This term refers to the way in which an individual speech sound or syllable stand out from neighboring sounds in a sequence. Prominence results from the sound or syllable havin different length, stress, inflection, or a combination of all three. Note the following features of prom inence in the word "window":

- The first syllable, $'w\!\imath n-$, is more prominent than the second syllable because it is th stressed syllable of the word. Its prominence can also be demonstrated by saying the wor first as a simple statement: "Window." And then as a simple question: "Window?" You ca readily hear that the main inflection or melody of thought happens on the prominent firs syllable;

- Within the first syllable $'w\!\imath n-$, the vowel sound $\imath$ is the most prominent, because i is an open sound relative to the two consonant sounds;

- Within the diphthong sound $o\breve{u}$ of the second syllable, the first vowel element is mor prominent because it is uttered with slightly more stress and length than the second vowe element. In Very Narrow Transcription of the IPA, the diacritical mark is placed over th weaker element of a diphthong to indicate that it is less prominent.

Prominence is an extrinsic feature of speech sounds, since it depends on the phonetic environmen For a comparison, see Sonority.

PURE VOWEL: A vowel sound that conforms absolutely to its definition as an open sound in whicl the articulators do not move at any point during the formation of the sound. In Good Speech, al vowel sounds should be pure; when they are not, they are said to be diphthongized.

RP: See Received Pronunciation.

R-COLORING: This term refers to the production of the vowel and diphthong sounds associated with the letter "r" in the spelling of words in Spoken English when the tip of the tongue is tensed up and over, and the body of the tongue is retracted. This gives these vowel and diphthong sounds a tense quality and back placement. This is also known as retroflexion, inversion, hard "r", and Western "R" although its frequent use is certainly not limited to the Western parts of North America. However, to think of this tongue-curling as a Western standard may help you to remember that its IPA diacritical mark looks like a little spur attached to the phonetic letter:

RECEIVED PRONUNCIATION: Popularly known as RP, or BBC English, this term refers to a standard of British pronunciation and usage that is considered by some to be the best standard of Spoken English for educated people in Southern England. Throughout the world, RP is frequently used to teach English as a second language. It differs significantly from all types of North American English, including what in this textbook is called Good Speech for classic texts.

RELEASED: This term refers to a stop-plosive consonant sound in which the air stream is swiftly exploded, or released. The term applies to both the voiced and voiceless stop-plosives, but in this textbook it is used mainly to refer to voiced stop-plosives when they are followed by a vowel or diphthong sound. The parallel term for voiceless stop-plosives is aspirated.

RESONANCE: The amplified and strengthened frequencies of the sound waves that are set in motion by the initial sound waves that are created as the breath stream passes through the vocal folds, or glottis. These modifications of the sound waves occur for each voiced speech sound (vowels, diphthongs, triphthongs, and voiced consonants) and contribute greatly to what is perceived as a speaker's vocal quality. Resonance is distinct from the pitch and volume of the voice.

When a speech sound is resonated primarily in the pharynx and the mouth, it is said to have oral resonance. When a speech sound is resonated primarily in the nose, it is said to nave nasal resonance. When a speaker's voice has a proper proportion of oral and nasal resonance, the speaker is said to have balanced resonance. For a list of the resonating chambers, or cavities, see Resonators.

RESONATORS: The chambers, or cavities, of the body that directly amplify and strengthen the frequency of the sound waves produced in the glottis. The primary resonators are the pharynx, which extends from the back of the mouth just past the soft palate to the part of the throat just above the larynx (pharyngeal resonance); the mouth (oral resonance); and the nose (nasal resonance). Other resonators may include the upper chest, or thorax; the sinuses; and to some experts, the skeletal structure of the head and upper chest.

RETROFLEXION: Another term for r-coloring, because the tip of the tongue is flexed back.

RISING DIPHTHONGS: The diphthongs in which the first vowel element is weaker than the second, producing a rise, or increase, in sonority. The two rising diphthong sounds in Spoken English are found only in certain unstressed syllables in verse texts and song lyrics:

ĭə TE-d*ious*   ŭə IN-fl*ue*nce

ROMAN ALPHABET: The alphabet of written English and other European languages and the basis for the IPA when it was first introduced in 1888. Since then many other letters have been borrowed from other alphabets for use in the IPA.

SAME-CONSONANT BLENDS: These sequences occur when one word ends with a consonant sound and the next word in the phrase begins with the same sound. In proceeding from one word to the next, the articulators do not change position, but maintain one long consonant articulation. Clarity of enunciation is achieved by a fresh impulse of energy that begins the second word:

p, p   d d   n n   v v
stop pouting   a bad day   one note   live vicariously

SCHWA: A popular term for the weak, second mid vowel sound ə , as in "th**e** su**r**prise."

SCRIPT LETTERS: The forms of the IPA letters that feature simple flowing lines and were originally assigned by the International Phonetic Association as the phonetic letters to be rendered by hand. The script letters are used in this textbook; phonetic letters produced by machine are called printed letters.

SECONDARY STRESS: A weak stress sometimes found on a syllable in a word of three or more syllables. For instance, in the word "con-ta-mi-NA-tion," the third syllable has a strong, or primary stress, while the second syllable has a weak, or secondary, stress. To show a secondary stress, the IPA adds a vertical line at the lower left corner of the phonetic letter with which the syllable begins:

$$kʰ ə n \,ˌtʰæ m ə ˈne ĭ ʃ n̩$$

Also see Stressed Syllable.

SEMI-VOWEL: A speech sound in which the articulators glide from a weaker vowel position to a stronger one, with no audible friction of the breath stream. Since the movement is swift and definite, semi-vowels are classified as consonant glides. There are two semi-vowels in Spoken English:

ʊ **w**eal   *j* **y**ou

Because it is voiceless and may contain some audible friction, *ʍ* as in "**wh**eel," is not considered a semi-vowel.

SIBILANT: A speech sound characterized by hissing or buzzing. When such a sound, particularly *s*, is excessively hissing or whistling, with a too-high frequency, it is considered "over-sibilant." The term "sibilant 's'" is a misnomer. There are six sibilant sounds in Spoken English:

Voiceless sibilants, or hisses	*s* **s**o	*ʃ* **sh**in	*tʃ* **ch**in
Voiced sibilants, or buzzes	*z* **z**oo	*ʒ* **g**en**r**e	*dʒ* **g**in

SOFT PALATE: The smooth, membranous, back part of the roof of the mouth. As an articulator, it functions as a trapdoor that separates the oral passage from the nasal passage. When the soft palate is relaxed and lowered, it allows the air stream to enter the nose, producing a nasal sound. When the soft palate is active and raised, it prevents the air stream from entering the nose, producing an oral sound. Known on the Consonant Chart as Place VI, it is also called the velum.

SONORITY: This term refers to the way in which an individual speech sound may inherently stand out acoustically in relation to other sounds uttered with the same length, stress and inflection. That *s*, as in "sin," has greater sonority or carrying power than *ʃ*, as in "shin," can be demonstrated by going into a large room or theater and having someone say the sound *s* and then the sound *ʃ* with identical force and duration. It can readily be perceived that it is much easier to hear the *s* sound than to hear *ʃ*. The same experiment can be done by comparing *ʌ* as in "c**u**p" with *ə* as in "th**e**"; the former sound is more readily heard and is more sonorous.

It is important to remember that sonority and prominence are not interchangeable terms. For example, in the word "window," the vowel sound *ɪ* in the first syllable is the more prominent of the two vowel sounds because its position in the stressed syllable of the word gives it stress and inflection. But regardless of the word or context, the diphthong sound *oʊ* has greater inherent sonority or carrying power by virtue of its relative openness. This can be demonstrated by shouting the word "Window!" over a long distance and noting that it is the second, unstressed, syllable that tends to receive both length and inflection. Another way to demonstrate the same thing is to say the simple statement, "Look out the window," noting that the first syllable has the greater stress, length and melody (the vowel *ɪ* is more prominent), and then to sing a full "Look out the window" on an improvised melody, noting that the second syllable tends to receive a long extended note because the diphthong *oʊ* is inherently more sonorous than *ɪ*.

Sonority, then, is an intrinsic feature of a speech sound and does not depend on its phonetic environment.

PELLING: This term refers only to the notation of the written language. When using the IPA to note the sounds of a language, it is incorrect to use the term phonetic spelling; the correct term is phonetic transcription. In this textbook, when a letter from the written language is referred to, quotation marks have been placed around it. For example, there is no spoken sound for the letter "b" in the spelling of the word "lamb."

PELLING PRONUNCIATION: A pronunciation that disregards the correct pronunciation of a word by misguidedly approximating the written letters of its spelling. A spelling pronunciation is usually applied out of ignorance or pedantry. For example, the area of New York City called "Greenwich Village" is incorrectly pronounced "Greenwitch Village"; the correct pronunciation is "Grennitch Village."

POKEN ENGLISH: The term used throughout this textbook to refer to the sounds of the language and to distinguish these sounds from the spelling of the written language.

TANDARD OF PRONUNCIATION: In the United States there is no single standard of pronunciation. However, the question of a standard in American speech must be addressed when considerations arise such as: What kind of pronunciation should be taught to somebody who wants to speak without a regional dialect? What speech model should be used with a foreign actor cast in a role for which the actor must sound like an American but not sound as though from a particular place? And the often-asked question: How should a performer sound when playing Antigone, Hamlet, Robespierre, or Saint Joan?

Each person who is asked these questions will undoubtedly come up with a different standard of North American speech. Setting aside standards of British English and a standard for persons or characters that are distinctly Canadian, this textbook refers to two standards: General American and Good Speech, both of which are defined in this Glossary. General American is useful to those people losing their regional American dialects, and for the foreign-born actor who must play an American. Good Speech may be used by those Americans and Canadians playing roles such as Antigone, Hamlet, Robespierre, or Saint Joan, unless a production concept requires these characters to sound as though they grew up in a specific locale.

TOP-PLOSIVE: Another term for plosive consonant.

TRESSED SYLLABLE: A syllable that features a stronger degree of force in relation to the other syllables in a word. A stressed syllable is sometimes said to have primary stress. The IPA diacritical mark for a stressed syllable is a short vertical line placed at the upper left corner of the phonetic letter that begins the stressed syllable:

$'s\Lambda b\, d\!\!\!\!\!\;\;\;_{3}ik,t^h$ SUB-ject (n) $s\partial b\, 'd\!\!\;_{3}ek,t^h$ sub-JECT (v)

TRONG FORM (sf): The pronunciation of one of a set of common words (articles, auxiliary verbs, pronouns, prepositions, and conjunctions) in a stressed, or operative, context. The Strong Form of a word is characterized by being stressed, having full articulation of its consonant sound(s), a strong open vowel, and appropriate lengthening of a sound or sounds within the word. A strong form of the verb "can" is found in the following sentence:

"Of course I can!"   can = $'k^h æ n$:

For a comparison, see Weak Form.

YLLABICATION: The division of a word into syllables. It is important to note that the precise syllabication of a given word in Written English may not coincide with the correctly uttered syllabication in Spoken English:

◆ mean-ing-ful-ly on the printed page in Written English

◆ $'mi: n\imath\eta\, f\partial\, l\imath$ or mea-ning-fu-lly as uttered in Spoken English

SYLLABIC CONSONANT: A consonant sound that, in a vowelless, unstressed syllable of a word, the most sonorous sound in the syllable, its so-called peak of prominence. The syllabic consona takes the place of a vowel or diphthong sound in the creation of a syllable. In Spoken English, thr consonant sounds may be syllabic, but only in unstressed syllables. The IPA diacritical mark for th syllabic consonant is a vertical line placed directly underneath the phonetic letter:

$m̩$ pris**m** $n̩$ butto**n** $l̩$ batt**le**

SYLLABLE: A unit of speech that contains a single peak of prominence, which in the vast majori of cases is a vowel or diphthong sound (for the exception, see Syllabic Consonant). Since vowel ar diphthong sounds have greater sonority than the consonant sounds, each vowel or diphthong soun in a word forms a peak of prominence and is thus the core of a syllable. For instance, in the wo "holiday," the vowel sounds $ɒ$ and $ə$, and the diphthong sound $eɪ̆$, are the most sonc ous sounds in the word. Each of the less-sonorous sounds clings to the vowel or diphthong that fc lows it, and together they form the acoustic unit called a syllable:

ho-li-day $ˈhɒ\,lə\,deɪ̆$

The physical action or condition that makes a syllable happen in the human vocal tract is not con pletely understood by phoneticians or scientists; therefore, no attempt is made here to offer an e planation of its physiology.

TEETH RIDGE: Another term for the alveolar ridge, or gum ridge.

THEATER STANDARD: Another term for Good Speech.

THICK "L": A consonant sound produced with extreme tension in the back muscles of the tongu causing a strangled, muffled quality of tone in the sound; or produced by such bunching and cor striction of the back of the tongue that the tongue actually touches the soft palate, or velum. This la ter action is called velarization. A thick "l" should never occur in Good Speech and should not b confused with the normal and correct darkening of an l sound that occurs:

 ◆ When it is followed by another consonant sound: bu**l**k
 ◆ When it is in final position: he**ll**
 ◆ When it is syllabic: batt**le**

TIP OF THE TONGUE: The point, or forward extremity, of the tongue. The top surface area imme diately behind the tip is called the blade.

TONE ENDINGS: This term refers to voiced consonants in final positions of words. The term i used as a reminder that these endings must receive full resonance of tone.

TONGUE-ARCH: The tongue-arch is the arc, or gentle hump of the tongue, that is created whe the tip of the tongue is relaxed behind the lower front teeth. The tongue arch is the essential articula tor, or shaper, of the vowel sounds of a language. Its primacy as the creator of the vowel sounds ca be easily demonstrated by playing ventriloquist and producing any distinct vowel sounds whil keeping the lower jaw and the lips completely relaxed and still. Any number of remarkably accurat and distinct vowel sounds can be produced simply by altering the position of the tongue-arch.

This definition does not imply that you should rely solely on the tongue-arch to create the vowe sounds. The lower jaw and the lips contribute greatly to the accuracy, full resonance and forwar placement of the vowel and diphthong sounds. It is interesting to note that the dummies of profes sional ventriloquists, who do not use the lower jaw and the lips, invariably have funny tight voices.

TRANSCRIPTION: This term refers specifically to the phonetic notation of the sounds of a lan guage. If this notation is very detailed it is called Very Narrow Transcription. If it is accurate but no detailed, it is called Broad Transcription.

TRIPHTHONG SOUND: Simply stated, a sound in which three vowel sounds are blended so close-ly that they are used and perceived as a single phonetic unit consisting of one syllable. In Spoken English, triphthongs are used only when they are needed to preserve the rhythmic line in verse or song lyrics. There are two triphthong sounds in Spoken English:

$ a \breve{\imath} \partial $ h*ire* $ a \breve{\upsilon} \partial $ fl*ower*

UNASPIRATED: This term refers to the nonrelease, or nonplosion, of the voiceless stop-plosive con-sonant sounds. In Spoken English, the voiceless stop-plosive sounds are stopped when they are fol-lowed by another consonant sound either within a word or in the next word of a phrase. Stopped or held voiced consonants are termed unreleased. The IPA diacritical mark for an unaspirated conso-nant sound is a vertical line placed at the lower right corner of the phonetic letter:

$ p_, $ a*p*t $ t_, $ hi*t*s $ k_, $ *d*ay

$ p_, $ sa*p* flows $ t_, $ ge*t* down $ k_, $ loo*k* good

In some languages, notably French, the term unaspirated may refer to the absence of a puff of breath when a voiceless stop-plosive is followed by a vowel sound.

UNRELEASED: The term used to define the lack of a plosive when one of the voiced stop-plosive sounds is followed by another consonant sound, either within a word or in the next word of a phrase. The parallel term for voiceless consonants is unaspirated.

UNSTRESSED SYLLABLE: A weak syllable that has little or no force of utterance within a word or sentence. Most syllables are unstressed and receive no marking or notation in phonetic transcription.

UNVOICED: Another term for voiceless.

UVULA: The little piece of flesh that hangs down at the back of the roof of the mouth and is the tip of the soft palate. In old cartoons, it is the thing in the back of the mouth that shakes like the clapper of a bell when a character yells.

VANISH: A term that refers to the decrease in prominence of the weak second element of a falling diphthong sound. The element is said to vanish, because in many instances of Spoken English the articulators move toward the position of the second element but do not actually reach it.

VELAR: The term used to describe the sound that is formed with the back of the tongue articulating against the soft palate, or velum. On the Consonant Chart, this area is known as Place VI. There are three velar consonant sounds in Spoken English:

$ k $ *k*ey $ g $ *g*o $ \eta $ si*ng*

VELARIZATION: The production of a speech sound with the back of the tongue tensed and bunched up so that it touches the soft palate, or velum. In well-spoken English, the velarization of a sound is to be avoided.

VELUM: Another name for the soft palate.

VERY NARROW TRANSCRIPTION: The accurate and detailed phonetic transcription of the sounds of speech. Typically, Very Narrow Transcription employs many diacritical marks and signs to notate such details of pronunciation as the lengths of sounds, aspirated and unaspirated voiceless stop-plosives, weak elements of diphthongs, and tongue modifiers.

VIBRATED: Another term for voiced.

VOCAL CORDS: Another term for vocal folds.

VOCAL FOLDS: The two curtains of membranes situated at the top of the larynx. They open and close. When the the folds are closed, the breath passing through them results in vibrations that con-stitute voice. The folds are also known as vocal cords.

VOICED: This term refers to the sounds produced with vibration of the vocal folds. In Spoken English, all the vowel and diphthong sounds are voiced. There are sixteen voiced consonant sounds Spoken English:

b buy   *d* die   *g* go   *m* me   *n* no   *ŋ* sing

l law   *v* vine   *ð* thine   *z* zoo   *ʒ* genre   *r* red

ɦ behalf   *w* weal   *j* you   *dʒ* gin

VOICELESS: This term refers to the sounds produced without vibration of the vocal folds. Many the consonant sounds in Spoken English are voiceless. Other terms for this sound are whispered and breathed. There are ten voiceless consonant sounds in Spoken English:

p pie   *t* two   *k* key   *f* fish   *θ* thigh   *s* so

ʃ shin   *h* he   *ʍ* wheel   *tʃ* chin

VOWEL SOUND: A speech sound in which the breath stream is open, or uninterrupted and unimpeded by the articulators. For each vowel sound, the oral passage takes one particular shape, and no movement or change in the articulators occurs while that sound is being produced. For this reason, vowel sounds are called pure sounds. In Spoken English, all vowel sounds are voiced. In Good Speech, they are oral sounds, made with a raised soft palate.

WEAK ELEMENT: The vowel element with less prominence or sonority in a diphthong sound. In the falling diphthong *ıə* , the second vowel element *ə* is the weak element. In the rising diphthong *ıə* , the first vowel element *ı* is the weak element.

WEAK FORM (wf): A particular pronunciation of one of a set of certain common words (articles, auxiliary verbs, pronouns, prepositions, and conjunctions) when that word is unimportant or not operative in a given context. A Weak Form of a word is typically unstressed, lacks one or more consonant sounds found in its strong form, has a weak vowel sound, and is quickly uttered:

You can say that again!   can = *kʰən*

WESTERN "R": Another term for r-coloring.

WHISPERED: Another term for voiceless.

◆ SUGGESTIONS FOR FURTHER STUDY ◆

UDIO AND VIDEO TAPES

inner, Edith. *Good Speech for the American Actor.* New York: Drama Book Publishers, 1980. (Audio.)

:inner, Edith. *The Seven Points for Good Speech in Classic Plays.* Mill Valley, Ca.: Performance Skills, 1983. (Audio and video available from Performance Skills, P.O. Box 1436, Mill Valley, CA 94941.)

e Voice Foundation. (Audio and video relating to the care of the voice available from The Voice Foundation, 40 W. 57th St., New York, NY 10019.)

ITERPRETATION AND TEXT

arton, John. *Playing Shakespeare.* Portsmouth, New Hampshire: Heineman, 1984.

erry, Cicely. *The Actor and The Text.* New York: Applause Theatre Books, 1992.

enedetti, Robert L. *The Actor at Work.* Englewood Cliffs, NJ: Prentice-Hall, Inc., 1986.

ark, S.H.. *Interpretation of the Printed Page.* Chicago: Row, Peterson and Company, 1915.*

oft, Kenneth. *A Practice Book on English Stress and Intonation.* Washington, DC: Washington Publications, 1961.*

mar, Nedra Newkirk. *How To Speak the Written Word.* Old Tappan, NJ: Fleming H. Revell Company, 1967.*

e, Charlotte I., and Timothy Gura. *Oral Interpretation.* 7th ed. Boston: Houghton Mifflin Company, 1986.

cLean, Margaret Prendergast. *Oral Interpretation of the Forms of Literature.* New York: E.P. Dutton and Co., 1936.*

ims, John Frederick. *Western Wind: An Introduction to Poetry.* New York: McGraw-Hill, 1982.

nions, C.T. *A Shakespeare Glossary.* New York: Oxford University Press, 1986.

xford English Dictionary. New York: Oxford University Press, 1989.

hmidt, Alexander. *Shakespeare Lexicon and Quotation Dictionary.* 2 Vols. New York: Dover Publications, Inc., 1971.

anislavski, Constantin. *Building A Character.* New York: Routledge, Chapman and Hall, 1989.

IONETICS

ercrombie, David. *Elements of General Phonetics.* Edinburgh: Edinburgh University Press, 1967.*

imson, A.C. *An Introduction to the Pronunciation of English.* New York: Routledge, Chapman and Hall, 1989.

nes, Daniel. *An Outline of English Phonetics.* Cambridge, England: W. Heffer and Sons Ltd., 1972.

nes, Daniel. *The Pronunciation of English.* 4th ed. New York: Cambridge University Press, 1956.

RONOUNCING DICTIONARIES

nder, James F. *NBC Handbook of Pronunciation.* New York: Harper and Row, 1984.*

ster, Charles. *There Is No Zoo in Zoology.* New York: Macmillan Publishing Company, 1988.

nes, Daniel. *Everyman's English Pronouncing Dictionary.* Rev. ed. London: J.M. Dent and Sons Ltd., 1981.

nyon, John S. and Thomas A. Knott. *A Pronouncing Dictionary of American English.* Springfield, Massachusetts: Merriam-Webster Inc., 1953.

keritz, Helge. *Shakespeare's Names: A Pronouncing Dictionary.* Ann Arbor, Michigan: Out-of-Print-Books on Demand, University Microfilms International, 1979.

EECH

anser, Ruth B., and Leonard Finlan. *The Speaking Voice.* New York: Longsman, Green and Company, 1950.*

cLean, Margaret Prendergast. *Good American Speech.* New York: E.P. Dutton and Co., 1954.*

)ICE PRODUCTION

rry, Cicely. *Voice and the Actor.* New York: Macmillan Publishing Company, 1973.

klater, Kristin. *Freeing the Natural Voice.* New York: Drama Book Publishers, 1976.

rner, Clifford J. *Voice and Speech in the Theatre.* London: Sir Isaac Pitman and Sons Ltd., 1972.

brary only, out of print.

defined, 386
ḏ as in "width," 213, 267-268, 316
ḻ as in "wealth," 252, 268, 316
n̪ as in "tenth," 238, 267, 316
t̪ as in "get them," 213, 268, 316
Diacritical Marks
  defined, 386
  list of, 380-383
Diagrams
  articulators, 11
  gum ridge, 292
Dialect
  defined, 386
Diction
  practice material for, 321-332
  warm-up exercises for, 30-35
Dictionaries, Pronouncing, 376-379
Diphthong Sounds
  centering, 169-182
  defined, 385
  examples, 6, 11, 143, 168
  falling, 144-182, 387
  information about, 140-142
  long, 143-167
  of "r," 169-184
  rising, 189-190
  short, 144-182
Dots Used To Indicate Lengths of Sounds, 18
Duration
  as in "die," 202-213
  dentalized as in "width," 213, 267-268, 316
  as in "dream," 212, 295-296
  as in "judge"; "gin," 223-227

E

pronounced iː as in "Edith"; "Lee," 58-60
pronounced e as in "let," 68-72
pronounced ə as in "the," 92-99
pronounced ɛ̆ə̆ as in "their," 171-173
Editor, 3
  as in "let," 68-72
  as in "pay," 144-148
  the pure vowel sound, 57
  as in "their," 171-173
  as in "the," 92-99
  as in "stir," 89-91
  as in "surprise," 92-100

F

pronounced f as in "fish," 256-263
Falling Diphthongs
  defined, 387
  practice material for, 144-184
Final Consonants, Voiced
  See Tone Endings
Final Position, 387
Forward Placement
  defined, 387
  necessary for articulation, 29
  practice material for, 30-35
French, 5
Fricative Consonants
  defined, 387

examples, 14, 253
information about, 254-255
practice material for, 256-302
Frictionless, 304
Front of Tongue, 387
Front Vowel Sounds
  chart, 11
  defined, 387
  diagram, 57
  practice material for, 58-87
f as in "fish," 256-263

G

"g" pronounced g as in "go," 214-220
  pronounced ʒ as in "genre," 289-291
  pronounced dʒ as in "gin," 223-227
General American, 387
Glides
  defined, 387
  examples, 14, 303
  practice material for, 305-312
Glottal Attack
  defined, 388
  elimination of, 54-56
Glottal Fricative Consonants, 301-302
Glottalization, 388
Glottalized Consonants
  defined, 388
  practice for elimination of, 329-332
Glottal Stop
  See Glottal Attack
Glottis
  defined, 388
Good Speech, 388
g as in "go," 220

H

"h" pronounced h as in "he," 301-302
  pronounced ɦ as in "behalf," 301-302
Half-Long, 18-19
Hard Palate
  defined, 388
  diagram, 4
Hard R's
  See R-Coloring
High Vowels, 388
Hisses
  defined, 388
  example of, 388
  practice material for, 223-227, 271-291
h as in "he," 301-302
ɦ as in "behind," 301-302
hw as in "wheel," 305-307

I

"i" pronounced ɪ as in "will," 61-67
  pronounced aːɪ as in "I"; "my," 149, 153
  pronounced aɪə as in "hire," 186-188
  pronounced j as in "William," 308, 311
IPA
  See International Phonetic Alphabet
Implosion
  defined, 388

Single-handedly, Edith Skinner has changed the course of American theater history. Her life's work was devoted to developing a unified standard of speech for American actors. Her teaching is ationally recognized in professional theater, film and television circles as THE most clear, precise, ficient, and comprehensive standard for acquiring effective and expressive speech in this country.

William Ball

The first time I saw Edith was at her office at Carnegie Tech. She was unbelievably chic and vely and said in dulcet tones, after my first utterance, "New Jersey!" She was wonderfully ipportive and kind to me over long years and came to see everything — always interested. And she nequivocally taught me to hear.

Sada Thompson

In 1950, Edith Warman Skinner began to teach me why I was born with a tongue, teeth, lips, alates, and a diaphragm. Edith's and my artistic collaboration and ever-deepening friendship ntinued for nearly forty years, during which she taught me why I was born with an imagination nd a talent as well as with a soul and a spirit. As a teacher and coach she was a strict scientist. As a oman she was an inspiring, seductive and hilariously original personality. The techniques she udied, evolved, taught, and persistently developed are forever a liberation of the creative process, s well as a definitive instrument of human communication.

Ellis Rabb

Speak with Distinction is THE serious book for the THE serious actor.

Henry Hewes

Edith has been the single most important influence on speech for the stage in America. It's a joy have her back among us.

Martin L. Platt, Founding Artistic Director
Alabama Shakespeare Festival

An extraordinary achievement! A celebration of Edith's lifelong devotion to the beauty of the oken word.

Samuel "Biff" Liff
William Morris Agency

Edith Skinner's *Speak with Distinction* remains at the heart of serious training for actors in assic plays. Timothy Monich and Lilene Mansell are uniquely qualified to update Edith's work. hose of us who train actors for professional careers are beholden to them for making this essential ok widely available.

Sanford Robbins, Director
Professional Theatre Training Program
University of Delaware

Edith Skinner's influence on the American theater was profound. Throughout decades of hanging fashions in training and performance, her straightforward, commonsensical, effective, and ficient methods of speech training and text study have prepared American actors for the classic age. Her book *Speak with Distinction* is now available again in a new and updated edition, vised by two of the outstanding teachers she trained. The book should be required reading in ery American theater school: it is a splendid achievement.

David Hammond, Artistic Director
PlayMakers Repertory Company

Speech is our highest evolutionary tool. And it is the actor who makes the highest use of it. This ok is truly a gift.

Zelda Fichandler

All the information one could need about the practice of English speech, with an excellent phonetic analysis, an exceptional glossary and good practical application for the actor and public speaker. A vital book for the teacher of voice and speech, and a fascinating read for anyone who love language. Decidedly still setting the standards of speech for all speakers of the English language.

Julia Wilson-Dickson,
Lecturer in Voice and Speech, London

At last it is here, and my congratulations to the authors of the revised edition of *Speak with Distinction*! It is a clear, concise and practical update of the original — a fitting tribute to the principles of articulated speech for classic texts introduced by Edith Skinner at this University over fifty years ago and still used as the core of our actor training.

Bob Parks
Carnegie Mellon University

This book addresses a growing need among American actors to develop a taste for language. I should be subtitled "The pleasure of speaking eloquently." Bravo!

Michael Howard

This new edition of *Speak with Distinction* is a well-organized, easy-to-understand wealth of information and a practical exercise manual — indispensable to students, teachers and professiona actors. Lilene Mansell and Timothy Monich understand the work and methods of Edith Skinner and by transmitting them in such a clear manner, have rendered an invaluable service to the international English-speaking theater community.   Tom Peacocke, Department of Drama
University of Alberta, Canada

Edith Warman Skinner instructed and inspired several generations of American actors, especia in her classes at Carnegie Mellon University and at the Drama Division of The Juilliard School. He devotion to good American stage speech was unending, as those fortunate enough to have known her or to have been her students will attest, and her devotion as matched only by her stylish elegance and her personal warmth. Her principles and methods, as embodied in her newly-revised textbook, should continue to instruct and inspire all actors who aim for the highest standards of theater speech.   Robert Neff Williams
Drama Division, The Juilliard School

Working with the Edith Skinner method has been an invaluable asset to my work. With a good ear and this method, the battle for correct speaking in your acting is definitely won.

Raul Julia

Edith Skinner's importance in the development of speech training for the American actor canno be over-estimated. Her workbook is a valuable guide to those standards she treasured and taught.

Hugh Whitfield, Director
American Academy of Dramatic Arts

The inspiration of Edith Skinner and the training and guidance of Timothy Monich have afforde me a wide variety of opportunities in my acting career.

Kelly McGillis

Speak with Distinction is THE practical text for the beginning actor and seasoned professional alike. It is a gold mine.   Stuart Howard